ACCOLADES FOR DAVID VON DREHLE'S *TRIANGLE*

New York Times Extended List Best Seller
New York Times Book Review Notable Book
Washington Post Book World Rave of the Year
New York Public Library Book of the Year
New York Society Library Book of the Year
Fresh Air Critic's Top Book of 2003
Hadassah Top Ten Jewish Best Seller
ALA Notable Book of the Year
Winner of the 2004 Christopher Award
Winner of the 2004 Sidney Hillman Foundation Award
Amazon Top 50 Book of the Year
San Jose Mercury News Best Book
Rocky Mountain News Best Book
Providence Journal Critic's Choice

Praise for *Triangle:*

"There are many reasons to praise Von Drehle's accomplishment. Von Drehle is interested in far more than the tragic events of a single afternoon . . . [he] has clearly immersed himself in the spirit and energy of a time long ago: the grimy, industrializing, electrifying years when colorful machine politicians battled socialists, suffragists and upright progressive reformers for the soul of an increasingly immigrant city. . . . Von Drehle has written a piece of popular history that reads like a novel and is rich in characterization and thoughtful analysis. It is a great introduction to the drama that was early-twentieth-century New York."
—Annelise Orleck, *Chicago Tribune*

"Von Drehle re-creates this period with complete mastery. . . . Besides bringing many of these characters to life, Von Drehle shows how pivotal the fire proved to be in the history of labor unions and in the rise of urban liberalism."   —John C. Ensslin, *Rocky Mountain News*

"In a gripping, mind-numbing description of the horrific event—the conditions leading up to it, what resulted from it—*Washington Post* writer David Von Drehle describes the 'crucial moment in a potent chain of events, a chain that ultimately forced fundamental reforms from the political machinery of New York and, after New York, the whole nation.'"   —*Hadassah* magazine

"Superb social history . . . Chapters on the fire are so spellbinding that readers will need air at the end. Von Drehle painstakingly imagines the lives, motives and overseas passage of two teenagers who came to work at Triangle and died in the fire—Rosie Freedman of Poland and Michela Marciano of Italy."   —Lyn Millner, *USA Today*

"Behind the fire lay the extraordinary history of sweatshop labor and the fledgling beginnings of union organizing. The heart of Von Drehle's book is its detailed, nuanced, mesmerizing description of the fire. The descriptions [of the trapped workers], woven into the cogent analysis, . . . leave a reader staring into space."
—Vivian Gornick, *Los Angeles Times Book Review*

"Von Drehle ably describes the growth of the garment industry, the lives of its immigrant workforce, the politics of early-twentieth-century New York, and the 1909 strike. But he truly excels in telling the harrowing story of the fire itself."   —Joshua Freeman, *The Washington Post*

"Von Drehle's account of the Tammany transformation is a real contribution to a much neglected chapter of American history. The author shows how the activist workers in the garment sweatshops of Manhattan were as crucial to the progress of the period as the intellectuals who moved into Federal offices in Washington, D.C."
—Gus Tyler, *The New Leader*

"An amazing, long-forgotten tale. A riveting history written with flair and precision."   —Bob Woodward

"Terrific and troubling . . . Von Drehle demonstrates convincingly how the Triangle case produced major pieces of workplace safety legislation. . . . Meticulous research furnishes *Triangle* with the necessary historical authority."   —Daniel Dyer, *The Plain Dealer* (Cleveland)

"Von Drehle attaches a name and where possible a story to every one of the Triangle Shirtwaist factory's victims. The biographical summaries provide the occasion for a reimagination of everyday life in the immigrants' Lower East Side tenements."
—Laurence Wieder, *The Weekly Standard*

"Like the Titanic disaster that took place a year later, the Triangle fire contains all the melodrama needed to make a blockbuster Hollywood weepy. So it's part of the triumph of Von Drehle's book that while paying homage to the dead and the terror of their last moments . . . he also successfully urges us to look beyond the fire, which lasted a scant half-hour, to the larger political and social world the Triangle workers inhabited. . . . Gripping narrative history."
—Maureen Corrigan on *Fresh Air*

"Von Drehle has reconstructed with unprecedented care one of the formative events of twentieth-century America. He has managed to convert dry research into human drama by making us see how much burned in those flames."
—Samuel Kauffman Anderson, *The Christian Science Monitor*

"For more than thirty years, historians thought the transcripts lost, but in what is an extraordinary feat of investigative journalism, Von Drehle found them through a "cryptic endnote" in a biographical dictionary entry for Max D. Steuer, the defense attorney in the case."
—Isabel Vincent, *National Post*

TRIANGLE

Also from the same author

Among the Lowest of the Dead: Inside Death Row

David Von Drehle

TRIANGLE

THE FIRE THAT CHANGED AMERICA

Grove Press
New York

for Karen

Copyright © 2003 by David Von Drehle

Published simultaneously in Canada
Printed in the United States of America

Library of Congress Cataloging-in-Publication Data
Von Drehle, David.
Triangle : the fire that changed America / by David Von Drehle. —1st ed.
p. cm.
Includes bibliographical references and index.
ISBN 978-0-8021-4151-4 (pbk.)
1. Triangle Shirtwaist Company—Fire, 1911. 2. Fires—New York (State)—New York—History—20th century. 3. New York (N.Y.)—History—1898–1951. 4. Clothing Factories—New York (State)—New York—Safety measures—History—20th century. 5. Labor laws and legislation—New York (State)—New York—History—20th century.
6. New York (N.Y.)—Biography. I. Title.
F128.5.V688 2003
974.7'1—dc21   2003041835

Grove Press
an imprint of Grove/Atlantic, Inc.
154 West 14th Street
New York, NY 10011

Distributed by Publishers Group West

www.groveatlantic.com

13 14 15 16   13 12 11 10

CONTENTS

The "Triangle" company . . . With blood this name will be written in the history of the American workers' movement, and with feeling will this history recall the names of the strikers of this shop—of the crusaders.

Jewish Daily Forward
January 10, 1910

PROLOGUE:
MISERY LANE

Manhattan's Charities Pier was known as Misery Lane because that was where the bodies were put whenever disaster struck. On March 26, 1911, the makeshift morgue at the end of the pier was filled with the remains of more than a hundred young women and two dozen young men, victims of a catastrophic fire in a high-rise garment factory. Some of the bodies—the ones that plunged from windows and down the elevator shaft—were readily identifiable. The ones that remained in the burning loft, trapped by flames and a locked door, were not.

One hundred thousand people lined up outside the morgue that day. Gum-chewing boys and their giggling girlfriends waited alongside stunned or sobbing relatives of the dead. The line stretched down the pier, into the street, around the corner, and out of sight. A policeman at the door to Misery Lane estimated that six thousand people per hour walked past the rows of coffins. Finally, late in the afternoon, some twenty-four hours after the fire broke out, an angry police official ordered his men to purge the queue of ghouls and thrill seekers. "What do they think this is," he grumbled, "the Eden Musee?" That was the city's most popular silent movie house.

Dominic Leone was one of the legitimate searchers. The previous morning, two of his cousins, Annie Colletti and Nicolina Nicolosci, and his fourteen-year-old niece, Kate Leone, strolled an easy mile on a brisk spring morning from their East Side neighborhood to their jobs at New York's largest blouse factory. Later that day, at closing time, a small fire erupted in a bin of scraps. Within minutes, bells and sirens could be heard throughout downtown Manhattan as fire horses charged into the streets with their engines rattling behind them. A plume of smoke rose from the midst of a forest of ten- and twelve-story towers near Washington Square. Onlookers by the hundreds hurried toward the action, and the fastest among them arrived in time to see tangles of bodies, some trailing flames, tumbling from the ninth-floor windows of the Triangle Waist Company.

The entire blaze, from spark to embers, lasted half an hour. But the damage done in this brief, terrible span was plain on Misery Lane. Dominic Leone found Nicolina fairly quickly; her broken body was only slightly burned. The other two—cousin Annie and young Kate—were not so easy to identify. He stood over one narrow pine box for a long time, but no matter how long he stared, the contents did not really look human. The shape was familiar, propped up like a charred princess reclining on a pile of pillows. She could, conceivably, have been either Annie or Kate—or neither one. Everything recognizable was burned away. The ferocity of the fire was hard to fathom.

All around Leone, bewildered, grieving people stared and murmured over other boxes—hundreds of people studying scores of boxes. They strained to recall a nondescript ring or a heat-damaged comb that might seal an identification. Survivors turned worn shoes over in their hands, hoping for a glimmer of recognition: if they could say *This is her shoe*, then they could say *So this is her body*. But there were no such clues in the box at Dominic Leone's feet.

Finally, his aunt, Rose Colletti, standing beside him, decided that yes, this was Annie. Leone tried again to match the picture of her in his mind with the poor dead girl in the coffin, but he couldn't. Yet he did not seriously protest when morgue workers closed the box, labeled it with Annie's name, and prepared the paperwork to transfer the remains to a mortuary.

At home that night, Leone and his Aunt Rose continued to talk about the body in the coffin. After a while, Rose Colletti's confidence began to fade. The next morning, she returned to the morgue and announced that she had changed her mind. The corpse was not that of her daughter. So the coffin was recalled from the mortuary, restored to the dwindling line of unidentified victims, and reopened.

The Triangle fire of March 25, 1911, was for ninety years the deadliest workplace disaster in New York history—and the most important. Its significance was not simply the number dead. The 146 deaths at the Triangle Waist Company were sensational, but they were not unusual. Death was an almost routine workplace hazard in those days. By one estimate, one hundred or more Americans died on the job every day in the booming industrial years around 1911. Mines collapsed on them, ships sank under them, pots of molten steel spilled over their heads, locomotives smashed into them, exposed machinery grabbed them by the arm or leg or hair and pulled them in. Just four months before the fire at the Triangle, an almost identical fire in a Newark garment factory trapped and killed twenty-five young women, and experts predicted that it was only a matter of time before a worse calamity struck in Manhattan. Yet workplace safety was scarcely regulated, and workers' compensation was considered newfangled or even socialist.

Disaster followed disaster, but little changed. Then came the Triangle fire. It was different because it was more than just a horrific half hour; it was the crucial moment in a potent chain of events—a chain that ultimately forced fundamental reforms from the political machinery of New York, and, after New York, the whole nation. Around the turn of the twentieth century, America experienced a huge immigration, an almost unprecedented transfer of labor power and brain power from abroad (especially from Europe) to the United States. The arrivals were met in the cities by contempt and exploitation—but also by a rising spirit of progressivism. In late 1909 and early 1910, new blood and new ideas coalesced in the Manhattan garment district, as immigrant workers and wealthy progressives combined to lead a strike by women's waist makers that shocked and thrilled the city. This uprising was a trumpet blast signaling the future: a future of women's rights and labor power and the urban liberalism that would define mid-century civic life.

A few factory owners resisted that strike despite incredible pressure to give in. These holdouts were led by two of the most prominent manufacturers, immigrants themselves: Max Blanck and Isaac Harris. Blanck and Harris refused to recognize the garment workers' union; instead, they hired strikebreakers, commissioned thugs to beat up strike leaders, and pressured police to arrest young workers on the picket line. This stubborn reaction earned them a footnote in American labor history—until, a year after the strike, their names became far more notorious.

As Dominic Leone wandered through Misery Lane, Isaac Harris brooded in his luxurious town house on the Upper West Side, nursing a badly cut hand. He had injured it the afternoon before by punching out a skylight. Harris had been in his office, negotiating with a salesman for some supplies, when the factory fire alarm began ringing. As Harris rushed into the corridor, Max Blanck appeared, looking befuddled. Blanck had been preparing to take two of his daughters shopping in his limousine. Instead, they ran for their lives. With Harris leading the way, Blanck, the girls, and more than fifty employees skirted flames to reach the roof of their burning building. The villains of the waist makers' strike and the owners of the doomed Triangle Waist Company were the same two men.

The day after the botched identification of the woman in the coffin, Dominic Leone returned to Misery Lane. Again, he accompanied his Aunt Rose up and down the rows of boxes until they found a body they could claim as Annie's. That left only Kate still missing. After much reflection, and with growing desperation, Leone decided that a lock of hair in one of the boxes was enough to make an identification.

But who was the girl he had studied so long the day before?

An older man named Isaac Hine stopped that day by the same box, and stood, and stared, remembering Rosie Freedman, his niece. She was an industrious young woman, and a brave one. As a girl of fourteen, after surviving a murderous anti-Jewish riot in her hometown, Rosie traveled alone from Russian-occupied Poland to live with her uncle and his wife in their small apartment near the Triangle factory. Her timing could hardly have been worse. Soon after she arrived, the American economy collapsed, and after the depression came the strike. Still, every payday, she had sent a portion of her earnings to the family she left behind. Things were just starting to look up in spring of 1911, when Rosie Freedman headed off to work one Saturday morning and never returned.

Isaac Hine lingered a long time over the box. Finally he said: that's her. Again, the coroner's men closed the lid.

This book is one more attempt to open up the horror of the Triangle fire, to gaze intently and unflinchingly at it, and to settle on the facts and their meaning. For although Isaac Hine received a small stipend to place a marker on Rosie Freedman's grave, she is more to us than a name on a stone over a featureless form. She stands, with all the young women she represents, at the center of one of the great and tragic stories of American history. The story begins with a strike . . .

1

SPIRIT OF THE AGE

B urglary was the usual occupation of Lawrence Ferrone, also known as Charles Rose. He had twice done time for that offense in New York state prisons. But Charley Rose was not a finicky man. He worked where there was money to be made. On September 10, 1909, a Friday evening, Rose was employed on a mission that would make many men squeamish. He had been hired to beat up a young woman. Her offense: leading a strike at a blouse-making factory off Fifth Avenue, just north of Washington Square in Manhattan.

He spotted his mark as she left the picket line. Clara Lemlich was small, no more than five feet tall, but solidly built. She looked like a teenager, with her soft round face and blazing eyes, but in fact Lemlich was in her early twenties. She had curly hair that she wore pulled tight in the back and sharply parted on the right, in the rather masculine style that was popular among the fiery women and girls of the socialist movement. Some of Clara's comrades—Pauline Newman and Fania Cohn, for example, tireless labor organizers in the blouse and the underwear factories, respectively—wore their hair trimmed so short and plain that they could almost pass for yeshiva boys. These young women often wore neckties with their white blouses, as if to underline the fact that they were operating in a man's world. Men had the vote; men owned the shops and hired the sometimes leering, pinching foremen; men ran the unions and the political parties. At night school, in the English classes designed for immigrants like Clara Lemlich, male students learned to translate such sentences as "I read the book," while female students translated, "I wash the dishes." Clara and her sisters wanted to change that. They wanted to change almost everything.

Lemlich was headed downtown, toward the crowded, teeming immigrant precincts of the Lower East Side, but it is not likely that she was headed home. Her destination was probably the union hall, or a Marxist theory class, or the library. She was a model of a new sort of woman, hungry for opportunity and education and even equality; willing to fight the battles and pay the price to achieve it. As Charley Rose fell into step behind her—this small young woman hurrying along, dressed in masculine style after a day on a picket line—the strong arm perhaps rationalized that her radical behavior, her attempts to bend the existing shape and order of the world, her unwillingness to do what had always been done, was precisely the reason why she should be beaten.

Lemlich worked as a draper at Louis Leiserson's waist factory— women's blouses were known as "shirtwaists" in those days, or simply as "waists." Draping was a highly skilled job, almost like sculpting. Clara could translate the ideas of a blouse designer into actual garments by cutting and molding pieces on a tailor's dummy. In a sense, her work and her activism were the same: both involved taking ideas and making them tangible. And the work paid well, by factory standards, but pay alone did not satisfy Clara. She found the routine humiliations of factory life almost unbearable. Workers in the waist factories, she once said, were trailed to the bathroom and hustled back to work; they were constantly shortchanged on their pay and mocked when they complained; the owners shaved minutes off each end of the lunch hour and even "fixed" the time clocks to stretch the workday. "The hissing of the machines, the yelling of the foreman, made life unbearable," Lemlich later recalled. And at the end of each day, the factory workers had to line up at a single unlocked exit to be "searched like thieves," just to prevent pilferage of a blouse or a bit of lace.

With a handful of other young women, Clara Lemlich joined the International Ladies' Garment Workers' Union (ILGWU) in 1906. She and some of her fellow workers formed Local 25 to serve the mostly female waist makers and dressmakers; by the end of that year, they had signed up thirty-five or forty members—roughly one in a thousand eligible workers. And yet this small start represented a brazen stride by women into union business. The men who ran the ILGWU, which was young and struggling itself, composed mainly of male cloak makers, did little to support Local 25. Most men saw women as unreliable soldiers in the labor movement, willing to work for lower wages and destined to leave the shops as soon as they found husbands. Some men even "viewed women as competitors, and often plotted to drive them from the industry," according to historian Carolyn Daniel McCreesh. This left the women of Local 25 to make their own way, with encouragement from a group of well-to-do activists called the Women's Trade Union League.

The Leiserson's strike was Lemlich's third in as many years. Using her gifts with a needle as an entrée, Lemlich "zigzagg[ed] between small shops, stirring up trouble," as biographer Annelise Orleck put it. She was "an organizer and an agitator, first, last and always." In 1907, Lemlich led a ten-week wildcat strike at Weisen & Goldstein's waist shop, protesting the company's relentless insistence on ever-faster production. She led a walkout at the Gotham waist factory in 1908, complaining that the owners were firing better-paid men and replacing them with lower-paid women. The Louis Leiserson shop was next. Did Leiserson know what he was getting when the little draper presented herself at his factory and asked, in Yiddish, for a job? Leiserson was widely known around lower Manhattan as a socialist himself, so perhaps he was complacent about agitators. More likely, he had no idea what was in store when he hired Clara Lemlich, beyond the appealing talents of a first-rate seamstress. The waist industry was booming in New York: there were more than five hundred blouse factories in the city, employing upward of forty thousand workers. It was all but impossible to keep track of one waist maker in the tidal wave of new immigrants washing into the shops.

A socialist daily newspaper, the *New York Call*, was a mouthpiece for the garment workers and their fledgling unions. According to the *Call*, late in the summer of 1909 Louis Leiserson, self-styled friend of the workers, reneged on a promise to hire only union members at his modern factory on West Seventeenth Street. Like many garment makers, Leiserson shared the Eastern European roots of much of his workforce and, like them, he started out as an overworked, underpaid greenhorn fresh off the boat. But apparently he had concluded that his promise was too expensive to keep. Leiserson secretly opened a second shop staffed with nonunion workers, and when the unionists at the first shop—mostly men—found out about this, they called a clandestine strike meeting. Clara Lemlich attended, and demanded the floor. A men's-only strike was doomed to fail, she insisted. A walkout must include the female workers. "Ah—then I had fire in my mouth!" Lemlich remembered years later. She moved people by sheer passion. "What did I know about trade unionism? Audacity—that was all I had. Audacity!"

She was born with it, in 1886 (some accounts say 1888), in the Ukrainian trading town of Gorodok. Clara's father was a deeply religious man, one of about three thousand Jews in the town of ten thousand. He spent long days in prayer and studying the Torah, reading and pondering and disputing the mysteries of sacred scripture. He expected his sons to do the same with their lives. It was the job of his wife and daughters to do the worldly work that made such devotion possible. Clara's mother ran a tiny grocery store, and Clara and her sisters were expected to help.

A memoirist once described life in a similar Russian *shtetl*. It "was in essence a small Jewish universe, revolving around the Jewish calendar," he wrote, a place where a wedding celebration might go on for a week and where the Sabbath was inviolate. Twice a week, however, Clara went with her mother to the *yarid*, or marketplace, and there her life intersected, at least briefly, with the Russian Orthodox Christians who alone were allowed to own and farm the land.

Lemlich's childhood corresponded with a period of enormous upheaval for Eastern European Jews, a time, as Gerald Sorin has written, "of great turmoil, but, also, [of] effervescence." The traditions of *shtetl* life eroded under a wave of youthful radicalism, which erupted in response to the traumatic decline of the Russian monarchy. It was a very hard time for Russian Jews, a time of forced poverty and violent oppression, but it was also an environment where a girl could assert herself. Clara Lemlich was not content simply to work while her brothers studied and prayed. She hungered for an education. Realizing that she would have to pay for it herself, Lemlich learned to sew buttonholes and to write letters for illiterate neighbors whose children had immigrated to America. With the money she earned, she bought novels by Turgenev, Tolstoy, and Gorky, among others. But Clara's father hated Russians and their anti-Semitic czars so deeply that he forbade the Russian language in his home. One day, he discovered a few of the girl's books hidden under a pan in the kitchen, and he flung them into the fire.

Clara secretly bought more books.

In 1903, Lemlich and her family joined the flood of roughly two million Eastern European Jewish immigrants that entered the United States between 1881 and the end of World War I. This was one of the largest, and most influential, migrations in history—roughly a third of the Jewish population in the East left their homes for a new life, and most of them found it in America. What was distinctive about the emigration was that an entire culture pulled up stakes and moved. It was not just the poor, or the young and footloose, or the politically vanquished that left. Faced with ever more crushing oppression and escalating anti-Jewish violence, the professional classes, stripped of their positions, had reason to leave. So did parents eager to save their sons from mandatory service in the czar's army; so did the idealists frustrated by backsliding conditions, as did the *luftmenschen*, the unskilled poor who had no clear way of supporting themselves in a harsh land. Although most of the arrivals in America were met by severe poverty, they kept coming. If their numbers were averaged, they arrived at the rate of almost two hundred per day, every day, for thirty years. They made a life and built a world with their own newspapers, theaters, restaurants—and radical politics.

* * *

She would not be able to run very fast in her long skirt, and was no match for a gangster. But to be on the safe side Charley Rose had recruited some help. William Lustig fell in alongside the burglar as they started down the street after Clara Lemlich. Lustig was best known as a prizefighter in the bare-knuckle bouts held in Bowery back rooms. Several other men tagged along, lesser figures from the New York underworld. In their derby hats and dark suits, they moved quickly along the sidewalk, past horse-drawn trucks creaking down the crowded avenue. With each step they narrowed the distance.

The policemen patrolling the picket line watched the gangsters set off, but did nothing to stop them. The cops weren't surprised to see notorious hoodlums moonlighting as strikebreakers. Busting up strikes was a lucrative sideline for downtown gangsters. So-called detective agencies were constantly looking for strikebreaking contracts from worried bosses in shops where there was unrest. One typical firm, the Greater New York Detective Agency, sent letters to the leading shirtwaist factory owners in the summer of 1909, promising to "furnish trained detectives to guard life and property, and, if necessary, furnish help of all kinds, both male and female, for all trades." In other words, this single company would—for a price—provide sewing machine operators *and* the brawny bodyguards needed to escort them into the factory. "Help of all kinds" might also describe the professional gangsters occasionally dispatched to beat some docility into strike leaders.

The gang's footfalls sounded quickly on the pavement behind Clara Lemlich. When she stopped and turned, she recognized the men instantly from the picket line. The beating was quick and savage. Lemlich was left bleeding on the sidewalk, gasping for breath, her ribs broken.

Charley Rose had done his job, and no doubt he collected his pay. But Lemlich returned to the strike a martyr and a catalyst. Within days after the beating, she could be found on street corners around the garment district, brandishing her bruises and stirring up her comrades. Everywhere she went, she preached strike, strike, strike—not just for Leiserson's but for the whole shirtwaist industry.

*   *   *

This violent convergence of the hired hoodlums and the indomitable Clara Lemlich was the clashing of the old against the new. From the summer of 1909 to the end of 1911, New York waist makers—young immigrants, mostly women—achieved something profound. They were a catalyst for the forces of change: the drive for women's rights (and other civil rights), the rise of unions, and the use of activist government to address social problems. One man who grew up on New York's Lower East Side in the 1880s remembered his mother's desperation the day his father died. There were no government programs to help her, no pension or Social Security. Yet she knew that if she couldn't support her children they would be taken away from her to be raised in an orphanage. So she went directly from the funeral to an umbrella factory to beg for a job. Eighteen thousand immigrants per month poured into New York City alone—and there were no public agencies to help them.

The young immigrants in the garment factories, alight with the spirit of progress, impatient with the weight of tradition, hungry for improvement in a new land and a new century, organized themselves to demand a more fair and humane society.

What begins with Clara Lemlich's beating leads to the ravenous flames inside the Triangle Waist Company, which trapped and killed some of the hardiest strikers from the uprising Lemlich worked to inspire. Together, the strikes and the fire helped to transform the political machinery of New York City—the most powerful machine in America, Tammany Hall.

Late summer in those days was almost unbearable for the poor in New York. "It sizzles in the neighborhood of Hester Street on a sultry day," a magazine writer summed up simply. Swampy and feverish, the heat soaked into the stone and iron of the city by day and leaked out again by night, so that it was never gone but was just ebbing and surging like a simmering tide. Heat amplified the smells, the overripe scent of sweaty humans lacking adequate plumbing, the sickly sweet pungency of baking garbage, the sour-earth odor of wet manure from the countless horses pulling the wagons of the city's insatiable commerce.

So many people in so little space: eight hundred per acre in some city blocks. Flies were fat and brazen and everywhere, because in summer the windows and doors had to be open all the time in hopes that a breeze might find its way down the river and through the crowded streets and among the close-packed tenements and across the back of one's neck. Along with the flies came the noise of steel wagon wheels on paving stones, the wails of babies, peddlers bellowing, the roar of elevated trains, hollering children, and the scritch-scratch and tinkle of windup phonographs.

Late summer was a season of dust and grime. Half the metropolis, it seemed, was under construction, a new tower of ten or more stories topping out every five days, competing skyscrapers racing toward the clouds, a third and then a fourth bridge stretching across the East River (where a generation earlier there had been none). The hot, damp air was full of dirt, cement powder, sawdust, and exhaust from the steam shovels.

Inside a sweltering, poorly ventilated, three-room apartment, the whole thing no more than four hundred square feet, the air never seemed to stir. It was so stifling inside the tenements that in late summer people slept on the rooftops, on the fire escapes, on concrete stoops, or in the parks. Yet the air did move. The mothers, the sisters, the wives could read the evidence written in gray on the family linens. A white tablecloth—an heirloom or a wedding present from an earlier life across the ocean—would turn dingy within a day or two beside an open window.

Then there was nothing to do but scrounge a penny from the purse and put it in the gas meter on the kitchen wall. Enough gas would flow to heat water for the laundry. Out came the washboard and up went the sleeves. Late summer was the season of exhausted women with sweat running in streams down their necks and noses, dripping from tendrils of upswept hair, women bent over steaming tubs of water to scrub the grime from the tablecloths, and from the dirty white workshirts of their husbands and sons and brothers, and from their own white aprons and their light cotton shirtwaists. Beside them, inches away, fires roared in coal stoves to heat the irons and warm the starch. Scrub. Rinse. Scrub again. Then the bluing solution, the starch, the isometric muscle strain of wringing the laundry dry. After the hot irons, a day or two later, the grime was back.

Newspapers and magazines frequently published wrenching portraits of the squalor and filth of tenement life. William Dean Howells sounded a fairly typical note in his description of a tenement basement: "My companion struck a match and held it to the cavernous mouth of an inner cellar half as large as the room we were in, where it winked and paled so soon that I had only a glimpse of the bed, with the rounded heap of bedding on it; but out of this hole, as if she had been a rat, scared from it by the light, a young girl came, rubbing her eyes and vaguely smiling, and vanished upstairs somewhere." In 1909, there were more than one hundred thousand tenement buildings in New York City. About a third of them had no lights in the hallways, so that when a resident visited the common toilet at night it was like walking lampless in a mine. Nearly two hundred thousand rooms had no windows at all, not even to adjoining rooms. A quarter of the families on the Lower East Side lived five or more to a room. They slept on pallets, on chairs, and on doors removed from their hinges. They slept in shifts. Some, especially the women who worked all day and took home piecework from the factories at night, seemed never to sleep at all.

Somehow they kept their dignity even when they had little else, even in the most brutalizing days of summer. Howells noticed this. "They had so much courage as enabled them to keep themselves noticeably clean in an environment where I am afraid their betters would scarcely have had the heart to wash their faces and comb their hair." A morning glory climbing a trellis outside a third-floor window; tiny rooms painted with a stencil to resemble fancy wallpaper; a starched white tablecloth as crisp and smooth as paper—with signs like these, the poor of New York asserted their humanity.

There were larger signs, too. The summer of 1909 was a season of strikes in New York's garment district. In August, more than fifteen hundred tailors walked off the job. Then there was a brief strike by the men who ran the buttonhole machines. This activity wasn't unusual in itself. Garment strikes had long been a regular feature of a hectic, rapidly growing industry. They were generally brief wildcat affairs, single-shop walkouts designed to grab an owner's attention long enough to squeeze a raise out of him. But the garment industry had become quite large and had begun to mature, having doubled in size over the previous decade. By 1909 more people worked in the factories of Manhattan than in all the mills and plants of Massachusetts, and by far the largest number of them were making clothes.

After the latest in a string of economic depressions, business was once again brisk, but factory owners were slow to raise pay and improve conditions. Young workers earning "training wages" made as little as three dollars per week, barely enough to cover room and board. Even the most highly paid workers, who earned twenty dollars per week or more, had seen their wages decline with the depression. All of them had to tolerate a highly seasonal business with long idle periods of no pay at all.

This was the climate in which Clara Lemlich was operating, buoyed by the Women's Trade Union League. It says something about the era that the league was founded by a man, William English Walling, the son of a Kentucky millionaire. As a volunteer social worker in the New York slums, Walling had noticed the legions of women going to work in factories, and heard the general contempt for them among the men who ran the unions. Inspired by the labor socialists of England, Walling created the WTUL in 1903 "to assist in the organization of women wage workers into trade unions." A subcurrent of sexual concern also energized the league: members worried that young women of the New York slums were being forced into prostitution to support themselves and their families. This problem of "white slavery" was a frequent theme of sensational congressional hearings, sermons, and investigative journalism. Higher wages, the WTUL reckoned, would solve the problem, and the way to get higher wages was to build strong unions.

Walling quickly passed the leadership of the WTUL to women. Pioneering reformers, such as Jane Addams of Hull House and Lillian

Wald of the Henry Street Settlement, served as early officers, and a young New York society woman named Eleanor Roosevelt—a niece of the president of the United States—was a member. Still, the early years were frustrating ones for the WTUL. It is a truism of politics that people rarely agitate when conditions are at their worst, and the depression of 1907 left many workers struggling simply to survive. With the revival of the economy a year or so later, however, the WTUL began to find its way, led by a pair of wealthy sisters, Mary Dreier in New York and Margaret Dreier Robins in Chicago. Through the sweltering summer of 1909, WTUL members could be found two or three days each week on the streets of New York's garment district, unfurling their banners outside factories at closing time.

In July, some two hundred workers walked out of Rosen Bros., one of the largest waist manufacturers in the city, demanding a 20 percent pay hike. Management refused to negotiate, instead hiring strikebreakers to attack the picket line. When the strikers fought back, the Tammany police force intervened on the side of the owners. This was Tammany's custom. Strikers, after all, had no money, no "sugar," to pass around the station house. They added nothing to the stream of graft that powered the political machine. This time, however, nightsticks and jail time did not have the desired effect. The Rosen Bros. strikers held their ground, and after nearly a month, with the busy season pressing down on anxious owners, the workers got their raise.

News of this success spread quickly through the garment district. In August, nearly seven thousand neckwear workers—mostly teenaged girls—walked out of some two hundred shops. Their monthlong strike was a desperate, heroic effort. Many of the neckwear girls toiled in tiny sweatshops crammed into tenements, making neckties and scarves for puny wages. Among their simple demands was an end to work in bedrooms and cellars. Because they were so poorly paid, the strikers had no savings to sustain them, yet they refused to give in, and eventually forced some concessions. The *Call*, the socialist newspaper, hailed the neckwear strike as a model of what might be possible everywhere. "Disgusted with the misconduct of many a strike, disappointed by defeat after defeat . . . not a few Socialists have lost faith in unionism," the *Call* noted. "A visit to the striking neckwear workers will make these misguided ones see the labor movement in a new light."

With the WTUL's support, Local 25 invited waist workers to a rally at which Frank Morrison, secretary of the muscular American Federation of Labor, urged them to build up their union. The turnout was surprising: more than two thousand workers showed up. New York garment workers were famous in the labor movement as dedicated strikers but indifferent unionists, keen on action but hard to keep organized. Some labor leaders wondered whether there would ever be a viable, enduring union in the garment industry. Local 25's paid membership numbered only in the low hundreds, and its strike fund was nearly penniless. But by then Clara Lemlich had galvanized the Leiserson's strike, and she could be found on a different street corner each day, proud of her welts and scrapes, belting out exhortations despite her aching ribs.

Two weeks after the beating of Clara Lemlich, in the last days of September, New York City staged one of the grandest extravaganzas the world had ever seen—parades, light shows, fireworks, concerts, lectures, and exhibitions. The festival honored Henry Hudson, the first European to sail New York's waters, and Robert Fulton, the steamship pioneer. Exploration and invention were the two faces on the coin of progress, and progress was the spirit of the age. Visitors came from around the globe: women in huge hats and perfect posture, men in stiff collars and slim-legged trousers. An armada was assembled from the world's navies. Giant balloons rose overhead. Wilbur Wright and Glenn Curtiss made the first airplane flights in New York City skies.

One million people lined the Hudson River, from the Battery to Riverside Park, for the opening of the Hudson-Fulton celebration. They crammed themselves into every available space, jamming the piers, climbing trees, leaning from windows so that "not an inch of standing room was open," according to the *New York Times*. Street vendors sold popcorn and sarsaparilla and ice cream served in that recent invention, a crunchy, edible cone. Boys hawked newspapers—New York boasted more than a dozen dailies in English and others in Yiddish, German, Italian, Chinese. A debate was raging on the front pages: Who was first to the North Pole? Was it Frederick Cook, who was holed up at his home in Brooklyn, refusing to offer his proof? Or was it Robert Peary, whose battered ship *Roosevelt*, fresh from the Arctic, was on its way to New York to join the festival fleet? Beside the news stories, advertisements extolled a luxurious array of products, from silk gowns to hand-pumped vacuum cleaners, from Persian rugs to player pianos, written in prose meant to capture the moment. "Progress is the life of age; betterment the foundation of success," declared an ad in the *Times*. "The conception and evolution of the Sterling Playerpiano . . . is the result of untiring effort and scientific endeavor."

Up the Hudson River came the armada, a parade of ships forty miles long. Gunboats representing Britain, France, Germany, Italy, and a dozen other nations fired booming salutes, and no one imagined that in a few years they would be shooting at each other. On Seventy-second Street, an estimated ten thousand automobiles crept along toward the river in what was probably the world's largest traffic jam to date. "A casual glance at the license placards displayed by the automobiles showed that they had come from every state within a radius of 100 miles," a reporter wrote—a lot of hard driving in a nation with fewer than a thousand miles of paved roads. Civic leaders looked forward to the day when every street would be filled with cars. The automobile was so quiet, with its rubber tires, and its emissions seemed so benign when compared with heaps of green dung in the streets.

When night fell, even more spectators filled the streets and rooftops and riverfronts for the grandest display of electric lights the world had ever witnessed. For the first time, Manhattan and its nearest neighbors were lit up from end to end—a man-made starburst spanning nearly twenty miles. Searchlights raked the sky. The city's bridges sparkled as if riveted with diamonds. Fifth Avenue became a "city of light," a "screen of brilliance," from the dark blanket of Central Park to the arch in Washington Square. Bulbs highlighted the cornices and columns and carvings of the sumptuous, soaring new hotels near the park—the Plaza, the Netherland, the St. Regis, the Savoy. The commercial towers of Manhattan were "marked out in points of fire," from the gold-domed headquarters of Joseph Pulitzer's *New York World* downtown—the tallest building on earth when it opened in 1890, more than three hundred feet high—to the new record holder, just completed: the Metropolitan Life tower on Madison Square, a full seven hundred feet tall. Fifty stories! The clean, classical lines of the skyscraper were transformed that night into "a pencil of light" topped by "a fairy palace, substantial as a sunset cloud" in which the tower clocks seemed to glow. Hundreds of thousands looked on that scene—people who, as children, had strained their eyes to read by the light of a wick soaked in whale oil. Progress wasn't a theory—it was everywhere they turned. It was a "spectacle [that] will not soon be surpassed in this world," the *Times* predicted. Then the fireworks began.

Afterward, revelers streamed through the city, the normal Saturday night crowd swelled by half a million out-of-towners. They headed to Broadway and to the restaurants that stayed open all night: Martin's, the Marlborough, Maxim's, Murray's, the Knickerbocker, Shanley's, the Cadillac, and the Madrid. Waiters set up extra tables in every niche and kept them full until nearly dawn.

For those who found Broadway too tame, there were big horse-drawn wagons destined for downtown, the "Chinatown rubberneck wagons." Barkers touted the amazing sights to be seen: mysterious pigtailed gentlemen from the East, opium dens, and all manner of depravity, not to mention the Brooklyn Bridge. "Every wagon was filled as soon as it drew up to the curb." The wagons passed the Bowery on the way downtown; it was the most notorious street in America, packed with sensations. Police had done a sort of census there a few years earlier and determined that only fourteen of nearly a hundred establishments could be called "respectable." Farther south, the rubberneck wagons passed prostitutes beckoning from cellar doors and drunks sleeping on sidewalks, while the drivers described in harrowing detail the latest craze among dope fiends—cocaine. Within a few blocks was a neighborhood famous for some of the toughest criminal

hangouts in the world, some of them already Gotham legend: Gallus
Mag's saloon on Water Street, for example. Mag was a formidable
woman who kept a jar behind the counter full of ears she had bitten
off troublemakers. And Sportsman's Hall, where the main sport was
rat fighting. A champion dog called Jack once killed a hundred rats in
the Sportsman's ring in less than seven minutes. When Jack died, he
was stuffed and put on display. The truly rough stuff at Sportsman's
Hall, however, involved seeing how many rats a *man* could kill with his
bare hands and teeth.

Progress had its own political movement: progressivism, a gospel of
the new and improved. Progressives supported the vote for women,
protection for consumers and workers, trade unionism. More than any
platform, though, progressivism was a mind-set. It was pragmatic and
scientific. Progressives took the tools of engineers and turned them
to the new fields of social work and socially conscious politics. It made
no sense to them that there should be millions of poor people groping through dark and stifling tenements in a city of fifty-story fairy
palaces and scientifically evolved player pianos.

Just a glance around the city revealed plenty of things to be fixed:
filthy housing, unsafe workplaces, garbage in the streets, orphans running wild, widespread vice and corruption. But the progressives did
not deal in simple glances. Impelled by the belief that truth drives
out error, they dedicated themselves to documenting, firsthand and
in great detail, precisely what was wrong. Bright young people from
America's leading colleges flocked to settlement houses, such as Hull
House in Chicago and Manhattan's University Settlement and Henry
Street Settlement, to live and work with the poor. Their firsthand
reports, full of tables and charts and verbatim testimony, explained
what it was like to work in a factory, how many tenement workshops
were in a particular neighborhood, how much money a family could
earn by picking the meat from nuts by gaslight, and why New York's
slums were so prone to fire. Their findings appeared not only in specialized journals like *Survey*, but in major magazines like the muckraking monthly *McClure's*.

In 1909, the progressive movement was building to a peak. A progressive governor, Charles Evans Hughes, served in Albany, pushing insurance reforms, backing an early version of workers' compensation (struck down by the courts), and crusading against drinking and gambling. A progressive president, Theodore Roosevelt, had just completed nearly two full terms in which he challenged monopolies, championed food and drug safety, promoted conservation—even sided with labor in a coal strike and dined with a black man at the White House. Roosevelt was scarcely fifty, and few people believed that his political career was over. At the time of the great festival, the young ex-president was on safari in Africa, and the newspapers competed desperately for pictures of him, gun in hand, peering at a freshly killed zebra or jaguar or rhino. With his high boots and astounding certitude, Roosevelt represented so much about the nation: its youth, audacity, appetite, even arrogance. He was the embodiment of pure possibility.

Tammany Hall, the political machine that had dominated New York for half a century, represented precisely the opposite. Many Tammany leaders expressed nothing but scorn for the progressives. "A reformer can't last in politics," said George Washington Plunkitt, the longtime leader of the West Side. Big Tim Sullivan, boss of downtown, agreed: "Reform? There ain't nothin' to it." Rarely did the reformers accomplish anything, Tammany argued, beyond cutting patronage jobs and closing neighborhood saloons. But Tammany also feared them. The progressives wanted a civil service system, in which municipal jobs and promotions were given without regard for politics. This was a bullet aimed directly at the heart of the machine. Plunkitt called civil service "the curse of the nation." "How," he once wondered, "are we goin' to provide for the thousands of men who worked for the Tammany ticket?" As journalist William Allen White observed, "Tammany preaches contentment." The machine protected the established order—which was, after all, quite good to Tammany.

The Hall was as much a part of New York history as Henry Hudson and the Brooklyn Bridge. It was founded in revolutionary days for philosophical reasons: to oppose elitism and resist British sympathizers. The strange name (officially the Society of St. Tammany) derived from a Delaware Indian chief, Tamamend, and this Indian motif was carried out in the Hall's fraternal lodge–style symbolism—members were called "braves," district leaders were "sachems," the headquarters was known as "the Wigwam." Tammany might have evolved into a debating club or fraternity and faded quietly from history. But the clash of elitism versus populism turned out to be one of the formative struggles of American politics, and Tammany instead grew into a purely political organization, the Democratic party in New York—and from there into a mighty machine.

As rigidly ordered as any army, Tammany Hall was based on a network of errand boys and block captains—the infantry. Ward heelers and district leaders were the colonels and brigadiers. The boss was the commanding general. Like any army, Tammany placed a high value on loyalty and discipline. Politics, Tammany style, was less a matter of ideas than of hard work and attention to mundane details—what one Tammany boss called "thorough political organization and all-the-year-around work." Take one East Side district, for example. There, the machine was so efficient that by 3 P.M. on election day, the leader knew the names of every voter who had not yet cast a ballot, and he controlled enough foot soldiers to send each slacker a personal reminder. Picture scores of workers knocking urgently on hundreds of doors in an era before household telephones. Tammany politics were practical politics, and the most practical question of all was: Who had the votes? A man who could reliably deliver even a few votes mattered more to the Hall than a whole faculty of theorists. To succeed in Tammany, "get a followin' if it's only one man," counseled Plunkitt, the machine's most quotable sage. "Go to the district leader and say . . . 'I've got one man who'll follow me through thick and thin.'" And build from there.

Although Tammany soldiers were known to pay up to two dollars per vote in a tight election, in most cases the Hall paid off with jobs and charity rather than cash. Young men who wanted to become Tammany braves would hang out in saloons or clubhouses favored by the district leaders and wait to be given "a contract." This was an errand that required quick attention. A fellow might "take a contract" to visit a landlord and reassure the man that Tammany would cover an unemployed voter's back rent. He might take a contract to alert the madam of a nearby brothel to an upcoming police raid. He might take a contract to hurry over to night court and tell the Tammany magistrate to turn some prisoner loose. And on his way back, he might stop by a funeral home to cover the expenses for a bereaved widow. District leaders welcomed news of constituents in need, and were never happier than when they could be of service. That was how they became district leaders. Plunkitt told of a man whose contract involved waiting at the marriage bureau. Every time a couple came in for a marriage license, he was to alert the district leader, so that the leader—and not some more alert rival—could be the first to deliver a wedding gift. Tammany asked only for votes in return.

Tammany's little kindnesses solved no social problems, but they did help people through difficult times. Tammany was there with coal in a blizzard, with shelter after a fire. As a result, the machine built up tremendous loyalty among the poor immigrants and children of immigrants who tripled the population of New York between the Civil War and the turn of the century. In summer, Tammany leaders sponsored free boat rides upriver and wagon trains to Westchester for tens of thousands of working people. When the crowds arrived in the countryside, they found long tables piled with food, gambling games for the parents, heaps of toys for the children, lakes of lemonade and beer. At the end of the day there were fireworks. These summer outings were so nice that hardly anyone asked why Tammany didn't build more parks for picnics back home in Manhattan. In winter, the leaders gave away holiday turkeys, coupons for free shoes and socks, and mountains of Christmas trinkets.

All this was easily financed, as long as Tammany men were elected to office. For the machine was also a model of efficiency in squeezing private profits from the public purse. Tammany skimmed kickbacks from government contracts, favored its own companies with lucrative city concessions, deployed the police to shake down gamblers and prostitutes. The Hall collected bribes in exchange for licenses, extorted protection money from small businesses, and bloated the city payroll with patronage jobs. Once Tammany men had the jobs, the machine raised government salaries. This pleased everyone who had a patronage job, and everyone who hoped to get one. Then the Hall demanded a cut of the extra money.

Tammany reached a grim perfection under "Squire" Richard Croker, who presided over the garish corruption of the 1890s. While scattering crumbs and lip service in the hungry slums, Croker gave the moneyed interests of the city the conservative government they desired. "Richard Croker was the anti-liberal patriarch of New York's working class," a Tammany historian wrote, "a hero to the mob and an invaluable ally to the aristocracy." Downtown, in the most populous working-class precincts, Big Tim Sullivan and his extended family exercised such complete control that in one late-nineteenth-century election the Democrats outvoted Republicans 388 to 4 in a particular precinct. Afterward, Big Tim told Croker that it was "one more [Republican] vote than I expected there—but I'll find the feller." Sullivan's operation grossed an estimated three million dollars per year from gambling and prostitution graft (roughly fifty million per year in current dollars).

The key to the corruption was a lawless police force. Anyone who wanted a position, from patrolman to precinct captain, had to pay for it. There was a sliding scale of prices, ranging from three hundred dollars for a beat cop's job to as much as fifteen thousand dollars for a captaincy in a lucrative part of town. (At the time, a thousand dollars was a decent annual wage.) The tribute was paid willingly, because it could be earned back many times over through cuts of the graft from the city's gambling houses, brothels, saloons, drug dens, bail bondsmen, and so forth.

Croker's reign came to an end when a crusading minister named Charles Parkhurst began exposing some of Tammany's worst excesses in a series of scandalous sermons. New York's upstate Republican leader, Boss Thomas Platt—seeing a chance to crush the rival machine—ordered an investigation by the state legislature. The resulting scandals put a reformer in the mayor's office in 1901. The Squire fled into exile in England. Cushioned by the millions he had skimmed, Croker lived in a castle and raised racehorses.

* * *

There was no picketing at Leiserson's on Tuesday, September 28, the fourth day of the great festival. Fifth Avenue and every street around it was blocked for the biggest parade in New York's history. (Everything that week was the biggest, grandest, most spectacular, never equaled . . .) A reported two million spectators lined six miles of city avenues. Buildings were festooned with bunting and there was a lusty feeling in the air. Near the Flatiron Building a group of young men sat on the awning of a cigar store. An attractive young woman walked by, and they invited her up. This would have been hard to imagine a few years earlier: an unmarried woman climbing a ladder in public. But now nearly half of all single women in New York worked for wages, supporting themselves and often their families. They could be found, unchaperoned, on the beach at Coney Island, or in the racy "dance academies" doing the latest steps from Vernon and Irene Castle. The young woman started gamely up the ladder. All eyes followed her. When a gust of wind whipped her skirt up almost to her knees, the crowd roared its approval.

Teams of matched horses pulled fifty-two elaborate floats, each one illustrating an important phase or moment in New York history. Column after column of marchers represented the city's national societies, each with its own brass band: Norwegians, Germans, Poles, Hungarians, Italians, French, and Irish. "The colored societies, though not largely represented, attracted a good deal of attention," the *Times* observed.

Word spread down the long parade route: *Charlie Murphy is marching!* This was truly news. Charles F. Murphy was rarely seen but often talked about. He was the Grand Sachem of Tammany Hall, Squire Croker's successor as boss of the city. People craned for a look as the Tammany banner passed. First they saw a long column of men with their faces painted red—the Tammany "braves." They were supposed to be Indians, but most of them were easily recognizable by a familiar blond mustache or shock of red hair. In a city of more than four and a half million, these men—the nuts and bolts and gears and cogs of the city's political machine—were minor celebrities. Behind the braves came the sachems, wearing silk top hats rather than face paint, for they were men of distinction, some of the most famous individuals in the city: Tom Foley of the Second District, a rotund saloon keeper whose battle with Paddy Divver for the leadership—among the bloodiest elections in city history—was still fresh in many minds. Thomas MacManus of the Fifteenth, known to everyone simply as "The" (as though there could be no MacManus but he). "Battery Dan" Finn, the jolly judge who ran the First. And the baron among barons, Big Tim Sullivan of the Sixth, the beloved, clear-eyed "feller" who stood squarely at the intersection of New York politics and vice, directing traffic and collecting tolls.

Murphy turned out to be a solidly built man with rimless eyeglasses and brush-cut hair. Though he had run the Hall for more than seven years, "it was the first time that many in the crowd had ever seen Mr. Murphy on parade," the *Times* observed. The crowd eyed him carefully. So this was the man all the newspapers hated. The citizens sized up the boss and apparently many liked what they saw, because as he marched past the crowd burst into song. *Oh! You! Charlie Murphy!* The ditty followed him southward down the island. The boss was plainly pleased by this reception. Elite opinions did not worry him much. "It is the fate of political leaders to be reviled," Murphy once said, in a rare burst of oratory. "If one is too thin-skinned to stand it, he should never take the job." But the mood of ordinary voters was the most important variable in his life, especially with an election fast approaching. Amid one of the largest gatherings of ordinary people in the history of New York City, they were cheering and singing his name.

Someone called out: "Tell us yer man for next mayor!" Murphy just smiled.

At age fifty-one, Charles Francis Murphy stood, as much as any man, precisely poised between past and future, one foot in the stifling tenements and the other in the electrified skyscrapers. Born to poor Irish immigrants in 1858, Murphy was classic Tammany material. He grew up in a crowded neighborhood full of Irish and German families, where many of the fathers earned their meager livings at the looming power plant that gave the Gas House District its name. Murphy left school when he was fourteen to work in a wire factory. Later he caulked seams of wooden ships at an East River boatyard. He experienced enough of hard labor to know that he didn't want a lifetime's worth. And so— probably after saving up a bribe for Tammany—Murphy landed a job driving a horse-drawn bus for the crosstown Blue Line.

He lived frugally, carrying his lunch with him in a tin pail, and saved enough money to open a saloon on the corner of Nineteenth Street and Avenue A, known as Charlie's Place. New York in those days had a lot of bars where a man could, in an evening, be poisoned by wood alcohol, serviced by a child prostitute, and beaten to death for the change from his dollar. Charlie's Place was not like that. Murphy did not tolerate gambling, prostitution, or fighting on the premises. A friend once said, "I would have just as soon thought of telling an off-color story to a lady as I would to Murphy." He served his customers a schooner of beer and a bowl of soup for a nickel. Only men were allowed.

Upstairs was the headquarters of the Sylvan Club, a social society founded and led by Murphy. Sylvans were popular young men around the Gas House District, fine athletes and fierce Democrats. Sylvan baseball teams, with Murphy at catcher, were perennial champions. Sylvan rowers were smooth with an oar. In 1880, as the presidential election was heating up, Republican leader Barney Biglin challenged the Sylvans to a boat race. On the appointed day, a huge crowd lined the bank of the East River for thirty blocks above One Hundredth Street. Biglin and his three brothers crewed the Republican boat. The Sylvan crew was led by a sturdy shipyard worker known as Tecumseh. Just before the race was to start, however, Tecumseh got violently ill. Rumors of poison swept through the crowd and fistfights broke out. The scene was on the verge of a riot.

Without saying much, Murphy climbed into the empty seat. The future boss set the cadence and kept it steady as the Democrats went stroke for stroke with the Biglin brothers. Then Murphy poured it on, and the Sylvan boat surged to victory. That night, a happy crowd marched through the shadowy, lamplit streets of the Gas House District, cheering, singing Tammany anthems—and carrying Charlie Murphy on their shoulders.

He was a model barkeep, all ears, and over his bars (eventually he owned four) Murphy met a lot of people. In time, by listening, he came to see how the voters of the Gas House District could be organized and motivated. He performed countless favors, won thousands of friends, and eventually became district leader. Murphy liked to conduct the political business of the neighborhood while leaning against a lamppost on Twentieth Street. Anyone who needed a son out of jail, or a job, or relief from a hassling policeman knew that Mr. Murphy would hear pleas in the flickering glow of the gaslight.

He was a rare man: keen, cunning, patient. When he died in 1924 after almost a quarter-century as boss, Franklin D. Roosevelt pronounced him a "genius." He was "the most perceptive and intelligent leader" in Tammany's history, according to one chronicler of the Hall, "with an unsurpassed feel for power and its uses, a superb instinct for timing, and a remarkable ability to cut through surface personalities and judge the prospects and motives of the men beneath. As a political chess player, he never met his match." When he successfully maneuvered himself onto Squire Croker's empty throne, Murphy began to realize—slowly, gradually—that progress was inevitable, and that Tammany must be part of it. "He fully understands," one observer said, "that a political organization cannot survive and grow broader on patronage alone, without political ideas and virtue."

But how much change was required? What kind? When? Those were more complicated questions. Murphy began with internal change, in hopes of quieting the critics of Tammany corruption. According to George Washington Plunkitt, there were two kinds of graft in Tammany's world: "dishonest graft" and "honest graft." Dishonest graft was "robbin' the city treasury or levyin' blackmail on disorderly houses, or workin' in with the gamblers and lawbreakers," he explained. "Honest graft," on the other hand, involved the use of inside information and government contracts to enrich Tammany investors. "Supposin' it's a new bridge they're going to build," Plunkitt said. "I get tipped off and I buy as much property as I can that has to be taken for approaches. I sell at my own price later on and drop some more money in the bank."

As district leader, and later as boss, Murphy apparently took his share of "honest" graft. In 1897, Squire Croker appointed him dock commissioner, a lucrative position in which Murphy "set up a system of dock leasing which would later be of great profit to Tammany politicians," according to Murphy's biographer, Nancy Joan Weiss. He set up his brother and two associates in the New York Contracting and Trucking Company, which grew rich on no-bid government jobs. Over the years, Murphy's foes tried without success to prove that he secretly collected money from this company. But just because they couldn't prove it did not mean it wasn't true. Somehow, Murphy became a wealthy man, despite the fact that he quit his last paying job at the age of forty-three. He maintained an estate on Long Island, built a private golf course, and vacationed at exclusive resorts.

But Murphy believed that Tammany had to shake free of "dishonest" corruption. When he took control of the Gas House District, "practitioners of 'skin games' and corrupt police captains fell by the wayside." Later, as Grand Sachem, he ousted several corrupt district leaders. Yet he moved cautiously. It wasn't always clear, in fact, whether Murphy was simply consolidating the dirty business in Big Tim Sullivan's powerful hands downtown. Sullivan, after all, was the only man in Tammany strong enough to challenge him.

Murphy's external problems were more difficult. After the turn of the century, Tammany was in danger of losing its base among the city's poor immigrants. The downtown of Murphy's youth had been Irish and German and a smattering of "other." However, the old immigrants began moving up and out, and the New Immigrants, as they came to be known, moved in. These were predominantly Eastern European Jews and, in even greater numbers, Italians.

Of the two groups, Tammany was most interested in the Eastern Europeans. The Italians were, for many years, a transient community, disproportionately male—legions of young men, mostly from the rural south, trying to earn enough money in America to return home and buy a piece of land. Relatively few of them had long-term aspirations in America; therefore, they had little interest in American politics. "It

is hard to understand the merriment" of New York's Italian neighborhoods, one writer declared, "after a walk down from Mott Street, past
rickety tenements, dingy hallways, and dark cellars. . . . Perhaps it is
because many of them knew worse alleys in sunny Italy and hope to
go back to them some day." Italian laborers dug tunnels for the sub-
ways, lugged iron for the skyscrapers, hammered spikes for the rail-
ways. But they rarely voted: their voter registration numbers were the
lowest of any ethnic group in New York. Until they voted, they would
count little in Charles Murphy's calculus.

On the other hand, political activity in the Jewish community—
from Republicanism to socialism to anarchism—was growing more
intense every year. Some Tammany leaders recognized this early, and
tried to win over the New Immigrants through the kind of personal
gestures Tammany understood best. John Ahearn of the Fourth District appointed his first Jewish lieutenant as early as the 1890s, and
was "as popular with one race as with the other," according to Plunkitt.
"He eats corned beef and kosher meat with equal nonchalance, and
it's all the same to him whether he takes off his hat in the church or
pulls it down over his ears in the synagogue." Big Tim Sullivan went
to the rescue of a Jewish enclave being harassed by Irish hoodlums; he
even seized the gang's clubhouse and turned it over for use as a synagogue. With Murphy's approval, a few Jewish names had begun appearing on neighborhood ballots. On a less lofty plane, Sullivan welcomed
a generation of Jewish mobsters—most notably Arnold Rothstein, the
eventual fixer of the 1919 World Series—into the gambling rackets.

But it wasn't working. Murphy nearly lost the mayor's office in his
very first municipal election, a fate that surely would have ended his
career. In 1905, William Randolph Hearst, flamboyant publisher of the
New York American, announced his intention to become mayor. Hearst
was the spoiled, willful, creative only child of a struck-it-rich California
gold miner. Somewhere along the way he developed a keen sense for
working-class attitudes and tastes. Hearst's genius for publicity was
unsurpassed, and his ambition unbounded. He wanted to be president.

The path to the White House was obvious. Two of the three most
recent presidents—Grover Cleveland and Theodore Roosevelt—had

made their careers by opposing corruption in New York. So Hearst, too, wrapped himself in the mantle of reform. He promised to take over the private utilities—the gas, streetcar, and other companies—that he said were gouging New York customers at Tammany's behest. "Municipal ownership," as he called his program, was a huge hit in the downtown slums. "An immense new multitude of voters has come into [the city] from all parts of the earth," the *Times* said in an editorial. "It is a wonderful field for the Socialistic propaganda, and socialism has a great army of devotees here. They are for the most part Hearst men."

The 1905 contest was one of the closest and most controversial elections in New York City history. Thanks to his strength among Jewish immigrants, Hearst actually drew more downtown votes than the Hall's incumbent mayor, George B. McClellan Jr. Citywide, McClellan led Hearst by fewer than four thousand votes out of 650,000. The publisher demanded a recount, while the city buzzed with stories that Sullivan's gangster friends had gone to extraordinary lengths to intimidate Hearst voters, and that Tammany "repeaters" had set new records for multiple voting. There were even reports of entire ballot boxes from Hearst strongholds thrown unopened into the East River. Never had the machine's hold on the working class been shown to be so tenuous. According to one analysis, the only poor wards in the entire city where Tammany managed to beat Hearst were Murphy's own Gas House District and the three downtown districts controlled by the Sullivan clan.

East Side radicalism had only grown more intense since then. When Theodore Roosevelt ran for president in 1904, the Lower East Side voted heavily for him, hailing the progressive Republican as "the worker's liberator." Four years later, after a devastating depression, the slums turned to socialist presidential candidate Eugene V. Debs. The coffee shops of the Lower East Side were filled each night with radicals debating various obscurities of Marx. For most people, the preferred agenda was a sort of *kibbutz* socialism, heavy on ideas of community and justice; it was more an attitude than an ideology. Lower East Side socialism favored the worker over the boss and the group over the individual. Its binding institutions were a Yiddish newspaper called the *Jewish Daily*

Forward, a fraternal society called the Workmen's Circle, and a confederation of unions called the United Hebrew Trades. All were highly critical of unfettered capitalism. At the same time, as the cultural historian Irving Howe explained, they were completely committed to the United States. The *Forward*, in particular, was the greenhorn's guide to fitting in and becoming American.

In 1909, Hearst once again ran for mayor. The mood of the downtown immigrants must have been a constant worry for Charles Murphy as he went about his daily routine—which was both numbingly regular and richly exotic. Every morning, the boss rose at nine and dressed in his banker's outfit, neatly knotting whatever tie his wife had chosen for that day. He liked to walk to his office at the Wigwam on Fourteenth Street, feeling the blood pounding lightly in his aging athlete's fattened body, enjoying the jostle and shout of the citizens whose strings he pulled—and who pulled his. Murphy would work for an hour or two at his rolltop desk, meeting job seekers and businessmen and minor party figures. At noon, he traveled uptown in a horse-drawn cab to Fifth Avenue and Forty-fifth Street, to the world-famous Delmonico's restaurant. There, Murphy held court in a private sanctum on the second floor. Room No. 4—the Scarlet Room—featured a long mahogany table with legs carved into tiger paws, in honor of the Tammany mascot. The walls were hung with red fabric and the floors were thick with red carpets. The chairs were red plush and the buffets were red mahogany.

In this "room of mystery," as some enemies liked to call it, Murphy conducted his most important business—convening executive councils, debriefing confidants, and hearing the petitions of lawyers, politicians, and millionaires. "A card identifying each visitor and explaining his mission would pass from outside doorman, to inside elevator boy, to liveried attendants standing watch at the door of the second-floor anteroom," according to Weiss. Eventually, each calling card reached "Smiling Phil" Donahue, Murphy's gatekeeper. "If Murphy chose to see the petitioner, the massive paneled door would swing open just enough to admit the man in question, while still obstructing the view of those waiting in the outer chamber."

The visitor stepped into the dim and bloodred room. Inside, like a king on his throne, sat the Chief (as he liked to be called; he also liked "Commissioner," and would tolerate a simple "Mr. Murphy"). The setting could not have been more intimidating. But for a man of his power, Murphy was seemingly without ego. He was a listener and a watcher, and his taciturnity was legend—the press called him "Silent Charlie." "Most of the troubles of the world could be avoided if men opened their minds instead of their mouths," he once told a protégé. He preferred asking questions to delivering pronouncements. If he spoke at all, it was in short sentences often separated by pauses lasting a minute or more. But when he spoke, his word was law. Murphy's silences always gave the impression that he knew more than he was saying; silence also saved him from making promises. This was important to Murphy, because any promises he made, he kept.

Most of the visitors to the Scarlet Room were men of stature. Now and then, however, someone quite ordinary would send up a calling card and—to the amazement of fancier men cooling their heels—be ushered immediately into the sanctum. Shopkeepers, schoolteachers, factory foremen: these men were scouts in Murphy's personal army, his eyes and ears on New York, his double check on the information flowing through official Tammany channels. Whenever he met a trustworthy observer, Murphy kept him close forever. This network of watchers brought the boss gossip and data of every imaginable kind. In the late summer and early fall of 1909, Murphy's scouts were surely telling him about the confrontations stirred up by Clara Lemlich and the other *farbrente maydlakh*—the fiery girls—in the garment district.

New York City was theater-mad in those days when movies were still new and short and silent, and radio was but a dream. On September 17, 1909, Israel Zangwill's new play, *The Melting Pot*, opened on Second Avenue, the Yiddish Broadway, after a long tryout on the road. It was an immediate smash. The play managed to capture, in an up-to-the-minute way, the tensions at the heart of the immigrant experience: old versus new, tradition versus experiment, certain loss versus prospective gain. The title quickly entered common conversation, and from there moved into routine speech as a metaphor for the crucible in which America blended its newcomers. The cheapest tickets were within reach of all but the lowest-paid shop girls; conversation about the latest popular play was as common in the factories of 1909 as movie chatter is today.

The garment workers who managed to get seats to *The Melting Pot* found themselves face-to-face with their own lives. As the set darkened at the end of the third act, the upraised torch of the Statue of Liberty appeared glowing in the background, and the main character, a Russian immigrant, asked: "What is the glory of Rome and Jerusalem where all nations and races come to worship and look back, compared with the glory of America, where all races and nations come to labor and look forward?"

2

THE TRIANGLE

One day in 1908—it was payday, so it must have been a Saturday afternoon—at the Triangle Waist Co., a worker named Jacob Kline studied his envelope. As he did, his anger began to swell. Kline headed a crew of several sewing machine operators and contracted with the factory on behalf of all of them. Given the sum in the envelope, he calculated that he would have almost nothing left for himself after paying his workers. Normally a soft-spoken man, Kline screwed up his nerve and caught the attention of Samuel Bernstein, the factory manager and a relative of the bosses. Loudly enough that the nearby workers could hear him, Kline announced that he was "sick of the slave driving" at the Triangle. He demanded more money.

The foreman applied the firm's usual solution. He ordered Kline to finish sewing the blouse on his table and get out. Supremely confident, as befit his station, Bernstein turned and walked away. But a second contractor, Morris Elfuzin, raised his voice to echo Kline's complaint. Bernstein wheeled and ordered him out, too. Yet the angry workers made no move to leave.

Bernstein hurried through a door in the corner of the factory and returned moments later from the floor below. With him was Morris

Goldfarb, a burly, powerful man unafraid of violence. In quiet times, Goldfarb was a cutter, one of the highly skilled garment workers who slashed stacks of cloth into many hundreds of identical pieces, using a single set of patterns and a razor-sharp, thin-bladed knife. In tense times, like this one, Goldfarb was the factory's muscle.

Jake Kline knew what it meant when the muscle arrived. Still, he refused to leave. He was yelling now; the whole factory floor could hear him. Samuel Bernstein grabbed the little man and dragged him toward the door, slapping him as they went. Goldfarb hauled Elfuzin behind them.

"With his shirt torn and his glasses broken, Jake managed to twist free and shouted into the shop," wrote author Leon Stein, "'Will you stay at your machines and see a fellow worker treated this way?'" The other operators barely paused to think about it. Almost as one, they rose and followed the men out the door.

The walkout fizzled. Come Monday morning, everyone was back at their machines—including Kline, who would one day pay the ultimate cost for his labor at the Triangle. But the unhappiness did not end there. A year later, in autumn of 1909, amid storms of unrest in other New York garment factories and after Clara Lemlich and her comrades at Leiserson's had been picketing for more than a month, a strike finally came to the Triangle.

A strike fixes a simple template over the often complicated structure of life, dividing the world sharply into workers and bosses. Choosing sides—labor's side or the side of the bosses—was a familiar part of Lower East Side existence. And if Clara Lemlich was the idealized worker, indomitable in her struggle, then the role of boss was equally well filled by Max Blanck and Isaac Harris, owners of the Triangle. They were rich men, and when they glanced into the faces of their workers they saw, with rare exceptions, anonymous cogs in a profit machine. Max Blanck was a well-fed, moon-faced man with a big Daddy Warbucks head and beefy hands. He rode around in a chauffeur-driven car. Isaac Harris was smaller, sharper, with rodentlike features and piercing eyes. They lived in splendor near the Hudson River in neighboring town houses. Isaac Harris's place on West One Hundred

First Street easily housed his wife, two children—and four servants: a governess, a maid, a cook, and a laundress. Around the corner on West End Avenue lived Max and Bertha Blanck, with their six children. A bigger family required more help: Blanck's live-in staff numbered five, including a nurse for the baby.

They were the Shirtwaist Kings. On any given day during busy seasons, Blanck and Harris presided over five hundred or more employees at their flagship factory, the Triangle Waist Company. It was the largest blouse-making operation in New York, according to the state labor department. The Triangle's shipping plant bundled, boxed, and dispersed two thousand garments per day, sometimes more, a million dollars' worth of waists per year. Women across the country—in cities, in towns, and on farms, at school, at work, and in church—wore blouses made in factories owned by Max Blanck and Isaac Harris. Their salesmen were on the road four or five months each year, visiting department stores and women's shops in every major city and many minor ones. Besides the Triangle, Blanck and Harris owned a number of other factories— the Imperial Waist Company, Diamond Waist Company, and International Waist Company, to name just three—in New York, New Jersey, and Pennsylvania. Blanck was a partner with his brothers in yet more shirtwaist factories.

They worked long hours. Some of these hours were spent meeting with major customers and suppliers in their tenth-floor offices near Washington Square, sunny offices with big, arched windows. But often Blanck and Harris could be found striding through the Triangle factory, watching to see that the cutters were conserving cloth, that the machine operators had a steady supply of pieces to work on, that the stitches were even and the buttons were snug, that the finished blouses were consistently sized. Even their veteran employees, many of whom were relatives of the owners, greeted them formally: "Good afternoon, Mr. Blanck," or "Please look here, Mr. Harris." But most of the workers only stole glances as the bosses passed. It would not have occurred to the young women at the machines to address such Olympian figures. Likewise, it never occurred to Blanck or Harris that they might pause from their rounds to talk to their workers. People came and went from the Triangle assembly line, here one day, gone the next. Though they shared the same space, and toiled in the same enterprise, it was as if the bosses and the workers lived in entirely distinct worlds.

And yet, only a few years, a few strokes of fortune, maybe a little more drive or a few less scruples, separated Blanck and Harris from the ranks of the workers. Like Lemlich and Kline and Elfuzin, both men were born in Russia: Harris in 1865 and Blanck in 1868 or 1869. In their twenties, when Lemlich was but a child, the two men entered the stream of oppressed Jews leaving Eastern Europe for the United States. It is not known whether they had been acquainted in the old country. Perhaps they were *landsmen,* from the same city or *shtetl,* but there were tens of thousands of young Eastern Europeans arriving every month in the United States in those days, so chances are they were strangers from the Old World destined to meet in the New. By the early 1890s, both men had settled in New York City. It was a hard time to begin, one of the hardest. As difficult as life was for immigrants in 1909, it had been even more wretched seventeen years earlier. A severe depression devastated the economy in 1892. Wages collapsed. Armies of workers lost their jobs. For the first time, the United Hebrew Charities opened soup kitchens on the Lower East Side to feed legions of destitute families.

In those grim years, Blanck and Harris entered the garment business, like roughly half of all Jewish immigrant workers in that period. They started just in time to experience the very worst the industry had to offer—the infamous sweatshop years. Today, the word "sweatshop" describes any crowded factory full of poorly paid workers. But in the late 1800s, the meaning was more specific, and more dismal. Sweatshops were generally dim and claustrophobic tenement rooms where independent contractors "sweated" greenhorns—that is, the newest immigrants—by working them more and more hours for less and less pay. The sweatshops represented a nadir of the Industrial Revolution, a dark age of chaos between the eruption of manufacturing and the arrival of various forces—such as labor unions, more efficient management, government regulation, and improved technology—to impose a new order.

The growth of the garment industry had been sudden and wild, like an economic tornado. A century earlier, in 1791, Alexander Hamilton had estimated that two-thirds or even four-fifths of all clothing in America was homemade, and that ratio was little changed over the next fifty years. Then, in the mid-1840s, came the development of the lock-stitch sewing machine, and the ratio was soon reversed. The Civil War put hundreds of thousands of Union soldiers in mass-produced uniforms cut to standardized sizes. When these troops mustered out of the army, they went home familiar with the quality and convenience of manufactured clothing. Merchants made it easy for them to continue buying off the rack: city dwellers had their choice of ever-larger department stores, while mail-order catalogs took retail to the farmhouse.

The next breakthrough came in the 1870s, with the invention of the "cutter's knife." Using this instrument, a strong, skilled man could cut the pieces for dozens, or even hundreds, of identical garments in just a few strokes—the number depended only on the thickness of the fabric. The industry's capacity to produce clothes quickly and cheaply rose exponentially.

Europe provided the last crucial ingredient of the garment industry: cheap and abundant labor. The Jews of Hungary and greater Russia (including what is now Poland) fit easily into the shops. Under the czars, Jews were strictly limited in the occupations they could pursue. One approved business was refurbishing and altering secondhand clothes; as a result, a large proportion of Russian Jews were skilled with needle and thread. When these tailors and their families began fleeing Eastern Europe in large numbers in the early 1880s, they formed a ready and inexpensive supply of garment workers. Unskilled workers followed their kin and neighbors into the garment shops, sometimes paying for the privilege of a slavelike apprenticeship. By the turn of the century, more New York immigrants worked in clothing factories than in any other business, and the industry was doubling in size every decade.

Countless greenhorns arrived in Manhattan clutching a scrap of paper bearing a simple name or address—their link to a job in the needle trades. Often they had a relative who had opened a shop and needed workers. Maybe they had a friend whose boss was always looking for new help. The link might be nothing more than a *landsman* who already worked in the garment shops. Greenhorns with no connections would find their way to the *Chazir Mark* on Hester Street, an odiferous cacophony of barter, haggling, and invective whose name translated ironically as "Pig Market." (The only thing one *couldn't* find there, supposedly, was pork.) Among the fishmongers and the wig merchants, the peddlers, pickpockets, and shills, garment contractors trolled for workers. Their appetite was insatiable.

The new immigrants were generally poor but frequently entrepreneurial. If they lacked the capital to build large workshops, they could cram small teams of laborers into their tenements and put them to work assembling garments for the big manufacturers. Soon, enough of these independent contractors were working in the tenements that large apparel makers realized they could farm out nearly all their work. By the end of the nineteenth century, relatively little of the sewing on mass-produced clothing was actually done by the "manufacturer." Instead, the label in a cloak or suit or dress meant only that the pieces had been cut from that company's pattern, and the finished garment inspected before sale. Between cutting and inspection, the garments traveled from sweatshop to sweatshop. Boys scarcely ten years old, bent double under huge bundles of fabric, were a common sight on the Lower East Side. They toted bundles from the manufacturer to some cramped little shop to be basted together, then to another contractor's squalid room to be stitched, then on to another shop to be lined or decorated—and then back to the manufacturer. In other cases, all the work would be done in a single four-hundred-square-foot apartment. This was a cut-rate and cutthroat business; the man with the lowest costs and the highest volume was the only one sure to survive. Labor historian John R. Commons concluded that the contracting system was to blame for the squalid conditions in the industry. "The contractor in the clothing trade is largely responsible for the primitive modes of production," he wrote, "for the foot-power sewing machines; for the shops in the alleys, in the attics, on top floors, above stables, and in some cases, in the homes of the people."

By 1893, of roughly one hundred cloak manufacturers in Manhattan, only about half a dozen assembled their own garments, according to an estimate by the New York bureau of labor. The rest were assembled in sweatshops. Manufacturers loved this system because it saved them the trouble of dealing with workers. Contractors accepted the system because it was an accessible half step up in the world—Commons estimated that a man could set himself up as a contractor with as little as fifty dollars in capital. Workers had no choice but to endure the system because there was always fresh blood at the Pig Market.

When a greenhorn left the market with her new boss, she was likely to end up in a "shop" that was no more than a tiny room or two—maybe just a hallway—in an East Side tenement, into which eight or ten or a dozen or more workers were crowded hip to elbow. If the weather was fair, the shop might spill onto the fire escape or relocate to the roof. Inside, the air was fetid and the light was bad. Union leader Bernard Weinstein described one such shop of the 1890s: "The boss of the shop lived there with his entire family. The front room and kitchen were used as workrooms. The whole family would sleep in one dark bedroom. The sewing machines for the operators were near the windows of the front room. The basters would sit on stools near the walls, and in the center of the room, amid the dirt and dust, were heaped great piles of materials. On top of the sofas several finishers would be working," he said, while older workers would "keep the irons hot and press the finished [garments] on special boards."

According to one survey in the 1890s, the average workweek in these shops was eighty-four hours—twelve hours every day of the week. During a busy season, it was not unusual to find workers on stools or broken chairs, bent over their sewing or hot irons, from 5 A.M. to 9 P.M., a hundred or more hours per week. Indeed, it was said that during the busy seasons the grinding hum of sewing machines never entirely ceased on the Lower East Side, day or night.

But the essence of the sweatshop was not just the squalor or even the long hours. It was the practice of "sweating" workers—that is, squeezing out more work for less pay. The depression of the early 1890s provoked an epidemic of sweating, as the growing army of contractors competed for too little work. Manufacturers drove down the price they paid per bundle. Contractors wrung the losses from their workers.

A laborer might agree to stitch linings into suit jackets for five cents per dozen, and work sixteen hours a day stitching a lining every five or six minutes—nearly a dozen per hour. At the end of a hundred-hour week in the dark, crowded, stinking shop she would think she had earned five dollars for her backbreaking, eye-ruining work. But then the worker would find that the contractor had decided to charge her for the thread and the needles she used. She would discover that she was required to pay a steep weekly installment for the decrepit sewing machine she was pumping with her feet. She might be told that the first ten or twenty or fifty dozen linings had been unpaid "training." There was little point in protesting the fees and withholdings. If she walked out, she would be paid nothing, and the next shop was likely to be just as bad. All the worker could do was try to sew faster and hope the rate per dozen would not be cut in half without warning.

The sweatshops broke the spirit of many women and men, and drove countless workers into early graves. Tuberculosis spread so easily among the exhausted laborers in the cramped, poorly ventilated shops that it was known as "the tailors' disease" or "the Jewish disease." Many who survived were radicalized; they helped build the labor unions and newspapers and study groups that spread socialism through the Lower East Side. Some, like Max Blanck and Isaac Harris—and like Clara Lemlich's boss Louis Leiserson—became shop owners themselves. And such men moved the garment industry into a new era of large factories and electric machines, a much better era for workers, in many ways, than the sweatshop era. Men like Blanck and Harris, having survived the worst, grew blind to the ways in which the garment shops continued, even in this new era, to be mean places to toil. Over the years, they lost any spirit of fellowship they might once have felt with their workers.

When Max Blanck was about twenty-five, a young man in a new country, struggling through a dire depression, he married another Russian, a teenager named Bertha. Other men might delay taking on responsibility in such a difficult time, but Blanck enjoyed betting on himself. He was a shrewd man with a passion for risk. About the same time, he set up shop as a garment contractor. He started small, a few bundles, but by 1895 was doing well enough that his brother Isaac joined him in New York. Isaac Blanck lived with Max and Bertha in a tenement apartment on East Eighth Street in Manhattan, and ran a sewing machine in his brother's shop. Other brothers, Harry and Louis, would eventually follow. In 1898, Max's oldest child, Henrietta, was born.

Blanck's eventual partner, Isaac Harris, was slightly older and notably more conservative. He was also more skilled with needle and thread; Harris may have apprenticed as a tailor in Russia. His family life is more obscure than Blanck's because census records from 1900 and 1910 are difficult to reconcile. One way to interpret them would suggest that Harris had a wife and three small children at the turn of the century, and that he left them to start a new family with a young woman named Bella, who happened to be the cousin of Max Blanck's wife. Bella Harris and Bertha Blanck shared a set of grandparents. In this scenario, it might be that his love for Bella brought Isaac Harris into partnership with Max Blanck, or that the business partnership came first, and led Harris into contact with Bella. All this happened around the same time, roughly the turn of the century; Harris entered Blanck's business and joined his family. The partners lived two blocks apart in 1900, with Harris occupying a small apartment on East Tenth Street.

This mingling of business and family was typical of the New York garment industry, like so many businesses built by immigrants. A young worker would arrive in America and, with luck and labor, eke out the beginnings of a small enterprise—making blouses, say. Brothers and sisters and cousins and nieces would follow. As the business accumulated capital, the entrepreneur might use it to set up an uncle or an old neighbor from back home in the button business or the lace trade, and these became his suppliers. And if the blouse maker's son married the lace maker's daughter, all the better.

Once Blanck and Harris became in-laws and got to know each other well, they must have realized that between them they had all the skills and most of the personality traits necessary to succeed in business. Blanck was a large man, in size and in personality, bluff, blustery, and daring, a salesman and deal maker. In their partnership, Blanck handled the money. Harris was smaller, both literally and figuratively (although the day would come when he would show that he had a superior streak of courage). He had dark hair and dark eyes, and a face that could look timid at one moment and crafty the next. He knew the myriad details involved in making clothes, from the fold and fall of the fabric, to the precise height of a proper cutting table, to the maximum workable density of sewing machines in a given space. "I laid out the factory and I put in the machines and everything that was done about putting up the factory was done by me," Harris once explained.

Together, their talents situated them perfectly to capitalize on an extraordinary fashion sensation of the 1890s—the shirtwaist, or woman's blouse. It was one of America's first truly class-shattering fashions. The waist-and-skirt combination both symbolized and enabled a wave of women's liberation. As a symbol, the outfit was a perfect repudiation of corsets and bustles and hoops—all the ludicrous contraptions that literally imprisoned women in their own clothes. On a practical level, the simple shirtwaist (in fact, many of them were elaborately beautiful and very costly) was acceptable garb for nearly every activity, from the factory to the temperance hall, from the athletic field to the suffrage rally. The fact that women needed such practical clothes was a mark of the seismic change that industry and urbanization were bringing to their lives. The phrase "industrial revolution" tends to evoke big-shouldered, classically masculine images of steel mills and oil derricks and steam engines. In fact many of the tasks that were centralized and mechanized in America's factories and mills were traditionally the work of women, once done at home: the sewing, the spinning, the making of sweets and pickles and soap. Legions of women followed this work out of the kitchen and into the shop—and from there moved into jobs as clerks and bookkeepers and even factory foremen—until there were more than five million women in the workforce by 1910, when the entire U.S. population was only ninety million. Nearly a third of all factory workers in the state of New York at that time were women. And the majority of them dressed in a shirtwaist and a skirt. Women had become "as active as men," according to fashion historian Caroline Rennolds Milbank. "The outfit of a plain dark skirt (light in summer), a belt, and a crisp white blouse was suitable for working women and college students, for street wear and lunching in a restaurant, and also for golf, tennis, boating, and other summer sports."

It was a fashion statement that truly stated something. Take, for example, the length of the skirts: They did not go all the way to the floor, as skirts had done in the previous generation. These skirts ended just above the ankle, to accommodate women who were bustling about the cities, through mud puddles and over dirty sidewalks and into crowded factories. But like blue jeans—a similarly empowering and enduring fashion—the waist-and-skirt combination could be sexy as well as practical. Charles Dana Gibson thought so, anyway, and what Gibson thought was all that mattered on the subject of feminine beauty. Gibson was a magazine illustrator, said to be the most highly paid artist in the world, and his signature creation was an archetype of young womanhood known as the "Gibson Girl."

She evoked the era. The Gibson Girl was fresh-faced and pure, overtly intelligent, pert-nosed, large-eyed, full-lipped; narrow at the waist and slender through the hips (though curvy); her hair and chin were always up to display a throat like a pedestal. She was "the Helen of Troy and Cleopatra of her day," in the words of writer Sinclair Lewis, but Gibson's biographer adds that "for all her queenly airs and graces, [she] was a truly democratic figure." Another writer, Robert Bridges, stressed the force and competence of Gibson's beauties. "Under her coat she had a pair of shoulders able to drive an oar or put a hunter to a fence. Healthy, brave, independent, well bred, a flash of mischief lurked in the corners of her intelligent eyes. She was the ideal girl whom many expected to find some day in flesh and blood."

From her birth in 1890 to the arrival of the First World War, the Gibson Girl reigned, "the most famous art creation of this century, or any century," according to the *New York Times*. (The artist also created a counterpart, the Gibson man, whose clean countenance spelled the death of a million mustaches.) Gibson Girls did not wear only waists and skirts; they could also be found in ball gowns and one-piece dresses. But the shirtwaist was a Gibson favorite, and if he liked it, then everyone liked it.

Max Blanck and Isaac Harris began their partnership in the shirt-waist trade with a little shop on Wooster Street a few blocks from their homes. In August 1900, they dubbed their enterprise the Triangle Waist Company. Now in their thirties, the partners were driven by an ambition born in oppression and distilled by economic hardship. They knew the waist craze was a rare opportunity and they were determined to seize it. They began shopping for more space.

They found their perfect location a year later. In the 1902 city directory for Manhattan, Triangle's address was listed as 27 Washington Place, and a second shop, Harris & Blank [*sic*], was next door at 29 Washington Place. In reality, both addresses took customers to the same doorway, half a block east of Washington Square, in an impressively utilitarian new ten-story skyscraper built by, and named for, the developer Joseph Asch. Harris and Blanck had taken a lease on the ninth floor, a little more than nine thousand square feet of usable space—thirty times the size of a typical tenement workshop. Large windows on the eastern and southern exposures pulled in plenty of sunlight. The height from floor to ceiling was nearly twelve feet. High above the crowded streets they designed a modern factory, worlds removed from the sweatshop hovels of their recent past.

With this move into a brand-new skyscraper, the partners helped remake the industry. Certainly it had been *possible* to make blouses in tenement sweatshops. But the coming of the steel-framed high-rise suddenly and completely changed the economics of New York manufacturing. For decades in Manhattan, a simple, relentless calculus defined the shape of the society: ever more people and ever more commerce crammed into a fixed amount of real estate. The "loft" skyscrapers, however, added a new dimension to the island's geometry. Large empty rooms rose one above another, eight, ten, twelve, even twenty stories high. The Asch Building alone—a completely typical, nondescript building—created more than ninety thousand square feet of usable space on ten floors, into which entrepreneurs could stack half a dozen decent-sized factories. And the Asch Building was just one among hundreds of similar towers: Between 1901 and 1911 an average of three new loft buildings were finished every two weeks in Manhattan—nearly eight hundred new skyscrapers in a decade.

Some writers have suggested that the most important advantage of the loft factories, compared to the tenement sweatshops, was the high ceilings. In theory, this allowed employers to pack more workers into the shop while still providing 250 cubic feet of air per person, the legal minimum. But in reality, no one—contractors or city authorities—paid meaningful attention to laws against crowding. The true advantage of the lofts was much simpler: large, open rooms made it possible to attach long rows of sewing machines to a single electric motor by means of a drive shaft and flywheels. This was a huge improvement over the sweatshop, with its pedal-powered machines. For a small cost in electricity, a modern factory owner could make large gains in speed and worker productivity. The lofts also gathered the entire operation—cutting, sewing, examining, and shipping—under one roof, creating significant savings in time and transportation costs.

Blanck and Harris mastered this new urban factory economy, and it made them rich. Between 1902 and 1909, the Triangle expanded twice, first adding the floor below the original factory, then taking the floor above it, too. The rise of Blanck and Harris coincided precisely with the maturing of the garment industry. Between the time they entered the business and their arrival at the top, the amount spent each year by Americans on ready-to-wear clothing roughly tripled, to $1.3 billion (equal to about $23 billion today). This could never have happened without modern factories.

* * *

The new factories had two drawbacks, one for the workers and one
for the owners. A decade into the new century, half the workers in
Manhattan toiled on the seventh floor or above—which was at least
one floor higher than the city fire department could easily reach. "A
fire in the daytime would be accompanied by a terrible loss of life,"
Chief Edward Croker predicted. Few, if any, factory owners gave this
problem much thought.

They worried a lot about the second drawback: As owners of modern factories, they were no longer insulated from labor strife and
strong unions. Dispersed in handfuls across the tenements of lower
Manhattan, sweatshop workers were extremely hard to organize.
Wildcat strikes were easily defeated, because a contractor could simply shutter his shop and move to a new building overnight. Fresh
labor was as near as the Pig Market. Chances were that the con-
tactor's former workers would never even find him. In the loft factories, in contrast, scores—even hundreds—of workers gathered each
day in the same place. The workers could discuss grievances during
their lunch breaks or pass word of secret union meetings. Owners of
large factories were highly vulnerable to strikes; they had significant
investments sunk into equipment, leases, and materials. They needed
to keep the line running to pay their bills, which meant settling
strikes or breaking them quickly. The bigger the factory, the more
vulnerable the owners felt.

Despite the failure of the wildcat strike at the Triangle in 1908,
when Jake Kline and Morris Elfuzin were thrown out of the shop and
the rest of the workers followed, Blanck and Harris worried constantly
about the labor unrest of 1909. They had adopted a variety of tactics
to thwart the radicals. One was the "inside contractor" system: management gave space on the assembly line to a contractor who, in turn,
hired machine operators to fill the chairs. Blanck and Harris paid a
lump sum to this contractor based on the number of waists his team
completed, and the contractor then decided how much to pay each
worker. This was an effort to preserve the veil between owners and
workers by bringing the old system of contractors into the modern

factories. But as the altercation with Kline clearly showed, once they were inside the shop the contractors often identified more with labor than with management.

The owners also established an in-house union, called the Triangle Employees Benevolent Association. It was a sham: its officers were all relatives of Blanck and Harris. Their hope was that the new association might divert some of the idealism and solidarity they noticed bubbling among rank-and-file workers. Lastly, if they found a rabble-rouser on the payroll, they fired him or her.

None of it worked.

In late September 1909, with the valiant young neckwear workers picketing shops throughout the garment district and Clara Lemlich delivering her white-hot speeches on street corners—with the night sky aglow from the light of a million bulbs and the streets dense with crowds celebrating the march of progress—word went whispering through the Triangle factory of a secret organizational meeting at Clinton Hall on the Lower East Side. About 150 Triangle employees— one in three nonmanagement workers—attended the meeting, where they heard from leaders of Local 25 and the Women's Trade Union League. Blanck and Harris caught wind of the gathering and sent spies. The next day, the owners stalked onto the factory floor and interrupted work for an unusual announcement. As a surprised silence fell over the room, the bosses gave a pitch for their in-house union. Then they dropped the boom: employees found to be organizing a competing union would be fired.

The uncertainty lasted only a day. Buoyed by the spirit moving through the garment industry, the Triangle unionists refused to repent. The next morning, Blanck and Harris delivered on their threat. When Triangle workers arrived at the Asch Building for work, they found the factory shuttered. Meanwhile, the bosses placed advertisements seeking new employees in several of the morning papers.

Locked out, the Triangle workers decided to strike.

On October 4, 1909, shortly after dawn, a dozen or so young women were picketing outside the Triangle, at the corner of Washington Place and Greene Street, when a garish battalion of Bowery prostitutes came marching up the street, followed by a group of replacement workers. Here was a new variation on the theme of violent strikebreaking. Evidently Max Blanck—the audacity and the shadiness of the gambit were pure Blanck—had decided that female strikebreakers would be preferable to men, and that streetwalkers would be best of all. They were tough, for one thing, and their arrival was a way of saying that the strikers were no better than whores themselves. As the "scab" workers neared the Greene Street factory entrance, women on the picket line began pleading with them to join the strike. That was when the prostitutes attacked.

There was kicking, punching, and tearing of hair; clawing and poking and jabbing with hat pins. For a few minutes, a flock of pimps stood watching, keeping tabs on their own labor force with obvious amusement. But they could not resist joining in. The fight became a rout.

By and by, police arrived from the nearby Mercer Street station—the city's infamous "penitentiary precinct." Brandishing batons, they rounded up the bloodied strikers while the Bowery gang strolled away. A Triangle worker named Ida Janowitz demanded to know why she was being arrested. "Shut up," she was told, or she would get a clubbing. Anna Held arrived for picket duty as her comrades were being hauled in. When she asked what was happening, she was arrested, too.

Clearly, Tammany Hall's one-two punch—the police and the gangsters—remained squarely on the side of the owners. After October 4, in fact, police actually increased pressure on the Triangle strikers, sending plainclothes detectives to monitor the factory entrances as a favor to Blanck and Harris. The *New York Call* reported frequent clashes on the Triangle picket line and catalogued the arrests of Triangle workers. One was Beryl "Ben" Sklaver, a twenty-three-year-old bachelor who sent money home to Russia to support his elderly mother. Like Kline and Elfuzin, Sklaver was an independent contractor who clearly sided with the workers. Early in October, he was on the picket line at closing time. Out of the Greene Street exit came a phalanx of men, breaking a path through the strikers for the replacement workers close behind them. When Sklaver pleaded with the workers to join the strike, one of the escorts seized him and began beating him. Police officers on the scene quickly intervened—to arrest the bleeding young man.

Sklaver was trucked across Washington Square to the Jefferson Market magistrate's court, a fanciful redbrick castle filled each night with the petty criminals and ne'er-do-wells of Greenwich Village and surrounding precincts. When his case was finally called, Sklaver tried to explain that he had done nothing wrong, but the magistrate wasn't interested. He levied a two-dollar fine and moved on.

A week later, hired thugs went after Joe Zeinfield, chairman of the Triangle strike committee. In a replay of the attack on Clara Lemlich, downtown gang leader Johnny Spanish took a couple of his men—including the veteran East Side brutalizer Nathan Kaplan, known to his friends as "Jack the Ripper"—in search of Zeinfield, a young sewing machine operator. They found him at the corner of Clinton and Broome streets on his way to a nearby union hall. Zeinfield was making the rounds in search of donations to support the Triangle strike. When the hoodlums were done with him, Zeinfield was moaning in the gutter, his scalp torn, his face like hamburger. He required more than thirty stitches.

Two strikers noticed Johnny Spanish standing in an Asch Building doorway the next day and pointed him out to Officer Joseph D. Cantilion from the Mercer Street station. Instead of arresting the leader of the downtown assault, Cantilion merely walked over to the notorious gangster, whispered a few words in his ear, and watched as Johnny Spanish sauntered away.

It was significant that Johnny Spanish had to go looking for Joe Zeinfield. The strike chairman was not to be found on the picket line. Union leaders had come to the conclusion that picketing should be done by young women; the public was likely to find their suffering far more compelling and sympathetic than labor agitation by young men. The police from Mercer Street played directly into the union's strategy by arresting scores of female strikers each week and hauling them to the Jefferson Market court.

The challenge for the strikers was to get New York to pay attention to the mistreatment of poor immigrants. About a month into the violence on the Triangle line, the Women's Trade Union League hit on the idea of seeding well-to-do progressives among the strikers on the picket line. One day in early November, Marjory Johnson, a WTUL volunteer, was doing picket duty outside the Triangle near dusk. A police officer tried to shoo her away, but Johnson persisted. Exasperated, the policeman arrested her, and as he marched her across Greenwich Village toward the courthouse, the officer asked: "What do you educated women trouble yourselves with this affair for anyway?"

"If some people were better educated, they would understand," Johnson answered.

They continued walking, side by side, as the officer pondered her words. Finally, he said, "You mean that I am *not* an educated policeman?"

"Well . . ." Johnson replied. The word hung between them. When they reached Jefferson Market, the officer added a charge of insulting a policeman.

Another day, Helen Marot, a WTUL executive, showed up to observe the picket line. A policeman growled at her: "You uptown scum! Keep out of this, or you'll find yourself in jail."

The key confrontation, however, came when WTUL president Mary Dreier visited the Triangle picket line at quitting time on November 4, 1909. As the factory emptied onto Greene Street, one of the firm's managers overheard Dreier talking to a "scab," presumably urging the worker to join the union cause. "You are a dirty liar!" the manager shouted. "You are a dirty liar!"

Officer Cantilion, the man who had tipped off Johnny Spanish, was once again on duty at the scene. Dreier turned to him and demanded: "You heard the language that man addressed to me? Am I not entitled to your protection?"

"How do I know that you are *not* a dirty liar?" Cantilion replied. And then he arrested Dreier for threatening to assault a worker.

The arrest of Mary Dreier was front-page news in the mainstream papers: Pulitzer's *World*, Sulzberger's *Times*, Hearst's *American*, and others. Her arrest came just two days after the November elections, and found Charles F. Murphy, the Tammany boss, still reeling from defeat. A progressive surge had routed Tammany at the polls. The Hall lost every important municipal office below the mayor's, and Murphy had managed to hold on to the top job only by endorsing an irascible and independent Brooklyn judge, William Gaynor. The mayor-elect immediately let the press know that he would do his own hiring and firing without regard for Tammany patronage. Even worse, perhaps, was that the key office of district attorney, always a potential danger to Tammany, went to an ambitious young Republican reformer named Charles S. Whitman.

Now, as Murphy perused his newspapers, he must have noticed that progressive women were being dragged to jail by Tammany cops. This was precisely the wrong image to project. Somehow, word was passed to lay off, and for a time police activity against the strikers dropped sharply.

Meanwhile, momentum built toward a general strike. Local 25 called a strike meeting in late October, but quickly canceled it. The union was still nearly broke and woefully unprepared. The strikers at Leiserson's and the Triangle pressed on, and Lemlich continued to urge other shops to join them.

As for the bosses: Max Blanck and Isaac Harris, the Shirtwaist Kings, took the lead in preparing their fellow owners for a general strike. Blanck welcomed a reporter from the pro-management *Times* into the Triangle factory to prove that strikers could not halt a healthy production line. "Nearly every machine was being operated," the reporter observed. Blanck promised forcefully that he would never accept the shirtwaist union, which he derided as "three or four East Side gentlemen" who wanted to "[step] in and tell us how to run our business."

Blanck and Harris echoed this public call to arms with a private letter to their fellow waist manufacturers. "Gentlemen," they wrote, "you are aware of the agitation that is now going on in our shops; our satisfied workers are being molested and interfered with, and the so-called union is now preparing to call a general strike. In order to prevent this irresponsible union in gaining the upper hand . . . let us know as soon as you possibly can if you would be willing to form and join an EMPLOYERS MUTUAL PROTECTION ASSOCIATION."

As November ebbed, then, a full-scale confrontation was inevitable, grand and awful, between the defining forces of downtown New York: the workers and the bosses.

3

UPRISING

Clara Lemlich's moment finally arrived, nearly three months after she and her comrades walked out of Louis Leiserson's shop—and ten weeks after her terrible beating. On November 22, 1909, following a month of postponements to build up its membership and its treasury, Local 25 at last convened a meeting to discuss a general strike. Thousands of workers were packed alongside Lemlich into the Great Hall at Cooper Union, a low-slung, windowless auditorium in the cellar of a brownstone behemoth four blocks east of the Triangle Waist Company. In this same room, some of the nation's most portentous issues had been discussed and debated by some of its most important figures. But there had never been a bigger throng here, not even for the speech that launched Abraham Lincoln to the presidency in 1860. Every seat was taken; people jammed the aisles and stood shoulder to shoulder along the walls. More than a hundred men and women were shoehorned onto the little stage, leaving only a tiny gap for the podium. Overflow crowds filled several nearby meeting halls.

After two hours of speeches, however, the excitement was fading. Lemlich could feel the people around her growing restless. Speaker after speaker—the gifted socialist lawyer Meyer London, for example, and Mary Dreier of the WTUL, and Abraham Cahan, editor of the *Forward*—squeezed from their seats on the stage to stand at the podium and urge the workers to fight . . . but maybe not right now. A general strike was the ultimate test of strength for a union, and who could say with certainty that Local 25 was strong enough? The speakers counseled caution and deliberation.

Samuel Gompers was the star attraction. A round man with a fiery speaking style, Gompers had been head of the American Federation of Labor since its creation in 1886 and was by far the most powerful union leader in the country. Born in London in 1850, he moved to New York at age thirteen and quickly established himself as an especially able labor organizer in the cigar factories where he worked. He was practical above all else, relentlessly focused on the bread-and-butter issues of better wages and shorter hours. Gompers scorned the socialism that motivated much of his audience that night; he once described it as "mere dreaming . . . [of] a new society constructed from rainbow materials."

"We recognize the poverty, we know the sweatshop, we can play every string of the harp, and touch the tenderest chords of human sympathy," Gompers once declared. "But while we recognize the evil and would apply the remedy, our Socialist friends would look forward to the promised land, and wait for 'the sweet by-and-by.' Their statements as to economic ills are right; their conclusions and their philosophy are all askew."

Many labor leaders believed that Local 25 could not win—or even survive—a general strike, and Gompers probably shared that view. A supremely practical man, he knew that "the history of labor is littered with the skeletons of organizations done to death because of hasty strikes gone into for the best of reasons but unprepared." And so, after a thunderous ovation from the waist workers, Gompers, too, counseled caution—tempered by a rousing defense of the waist makers' cause. "I have never declared a strike in all my life," he said. "I have done my share to prevent strikes." On the other hand, "there comes a time when *not* to strike is but to rivet the chains of slavery upon our wrists. . . . I say, friends, *do not enter too hastily*. But when you can't get the

manufacturers to give you what you want, *then* strike! And when you
strike, then let the manufacturers know that you are on strike!"

At that, the audience roared. Surely this was such a time.

But then—nothing happened. Instead of a vote at the conclusion
of Gompers's speech, Lemlich was distressed to hear moderator Benjamin Feigenbaum begin yet another introduction. She felt her pale
complexion flush with a rising panic. This entire meeting, she feared,
was just "talk—talk that meant nothing." Everyone on the Lower East
Side knew Feigenbaum, and talk was what he was known for. Socialist, atheist, freelance pundit, the folksy Feigenbaum happily spoke,
at length, on virtually any subject at any forum anywhere in the neighborhood. Older men loved him, for he represented a style and attitude familiar to them from an earlier life. But the new generation had
less patience for him. Lemlich realized that Feigenbaum was intro-
ducing Jacob Panken, a favorite stem-winder among New York socialists. Panken was sure to give a rousing speech, but most of the workers
had probably heard it before.

She could imagine the crowd beginning to drift away now that
Gompers was finished speaking. The moment was passing. Suddenly,
Lemlich was on her feet, shouting over the applause for Panken, shouldering her way down the aisle. "I want to say a few words!" she called
in Yiddish. She explained afterward: "I knew that we must declare a
strike or perhaps the chance would not come again."

Feigenbaum and Panken were together at the podium, one going
and one coming; they stared at the small young woman with the gleam-
ing eyes and pulled-back hair. The moderator no doubt knew Lemlich,
the most famous striker on the East Side, and if he knew Lemlich then
he realized that it would be pointless to resist her. As voices around
the hall shouted, "Get up on the platform!" Feigenbaum gave an apolo-
getic glance toward Panken, and then offered Lemlich the podium.

One authority, historian John F. McClymer, has suggested that,
given Lemlich's prominence in the union, her dramatic speech must
have been scripted beforehand. But in interviews later that night, she
insisted that she acted on the spur of the moment, and her brief
speech certainly struck the audience as spontaneous. "I have listened

to all the speakers," she said. "I have no further patience for talk, as I am one of those who feels and suffers from the things pictured. I move that we go on a general strike."

Pandemonium ensued. The cheering, the stamping, the waving of hats and handkerchiefs went on for five minutes. When Feigenbaum finally quieted the room, he called for a second to Lemlich's motion. The audience erupted again. Feigenbaum gestured once more for quiet. According to the *Forward,* he gravely warned the workers to think carefully about what they were doing. Those afraid to suffer, "that have fear for hunger and cold, should not be ashamed" to vote against the strike, he said. Those who voted in favor, on the other hand, were sealing a pact to "struggle until the end." Feigenbaum melodramatically raised his right hand. "Do you mean faith?" he cried. "Will you take the old Jewish oath?" Thousands of hands went up and the audience recited in unison: "If I turn traitor to the cause I now pledge, may this hand wither from the arm I now raise."

A committee of fifteen women (with a young man appointed to lead them) was quickly dispatched to the overflow meeting halls with news of the vote. Everywhere they went the strike was approved unanimously.

But the next morning, when a sixteen-year-old sewing machine operator named Rose Perr sat down in her row at the Bijou Waist Company, she had no idea what would happen. "I did not know how many workers in my shop had taken that oath at that meeting," she later recounted. "We all sat at the machines with our hats and coats beside us, ready to leave. . . . And there was whispering and talking softly all around the room among the machines: 'Shall we wait like this?' 'There is a general strike.' 'Who will get up first?' 'It would be better to be the last to get up, and then the company might remember it of you afterward and do well for you.' But I told them, 'What difference does it make which one is first and which one is last?'"

They whispered like that for two hours. Finally, Perr stood up. "And at just the same minute all—we all got up together, in one second . . . and all walked out together. And already out on the sidewalk in front the policemen stood with the clubs. One of them said, 'If you don't behave, you'll get this on your head.' And he shook his club at me."

Similar scenes played out all over the garment district. The *Call* estimated that fifteen thousand waist makers walked out on the first day of the strike. But once they were on the sidewalk, the strikers had no idea what to do. Like the proverbial congregation that prays for rain but neglects umbrellas, the union had called a strike but hadn't made any plans for a massive walkout. Organizers had expected, at most, five thousand strikers.

At Perr's factory there was an American-born seamstress who knew how to use a telephone. As the other workers crowded around her, she called the Women's Trade Union League. The volunteer who answered the phone directed the strikers to a nearby meeting hall. As more and more shops struck, leaders of Local 25 and the WTUL frantically rented more and more meeting rooms—concert halls, Masonic halls, lecture halls, and theaters. "After we were there," Perr recalled, "we wrote out on paper what terms we wanted: not any night work, except as it would be arranged for in some special need . . . and shorter hours, and to have wages arranged by a committee . . . and to have better treatment from the bosses."

This exercise was probably designed simply to fill time while strike leaders rushed to prepare plans for the next day's picketing. In fact, the union had already published its demands: a 20 percent pay raise, a fifty-two-hour workweek and recognition of the union as the bargaining agent for all waist workers—the so-called closed shop. The leaders also wanted a more rational way of dealing with the seasonal nature of the garment business. In busy seasons, they wanted clear rules and extra pay for overtime; in slack seasons, they wanted advance notice given when shops would have no work to do, so that workers could plan their time off. (Many writers would later assert that workplace safety was a major issue in the strike, but that does not seem to be the case. Even the socialist *Call*, which covered the strike in detail from the union perspective, did not mention safety as a reason for the uprising.)

Near the end of the day, WTUL members fanned out to fourteen packed halls to deliver lectures on proper picketing. The WTUL had already shown its knack for public relations during the strikes at Leiserson's and the Triangle. The group's advice remained constant: It was essential, they believed, to run orderly picket lines made up entirely of polite young women. This was the key to winning over the public.

As the WTUL leaders lectured the strikers, their instructions were simultaneously translated into Yiddish. Elizabeth Dutcher, a WTUL executive, put it plainly on the opening day: "The strikebreakers are all Italians and the strikers Jewesses." As much as this fact worried the union, it intrigued the bosses, and they did everything they could over the coming days and weeks to divide workers along ethnic lines. At the Triangle and other shops, for example, Italian priests from conservative Catholic parishes were invited into the factories to explain the workers' obligation to be obedient. Dutcher worried that when the picket lines formed at 7:45 the next morning, factory owners would find a way to incite "race warfare."

"In general, Italian girls and women took jobs after the head of their family had decided on the matter. . . . [T]hey had no chance of independent economic decision and were at a disadvantage to the Jewish female breadwinner who, as a rule, made these decisions by herself," one historian explained. The role of women was different in the two cultures. Both gave authority to the father or oldest brother, but in traditional Jewish homes men were encouraged to shun the workplace in favor of religious study and prayer; the role of women was to make this possible. This ideal was only rarely achieved in poor Jewish families, Gerald Sorin has noted. "Jewish women, however, did indeed play an extraordinarily time-consuming and essential role in providing for their families." As a result, many Jewish women and girls arrived in America accustomed to making their own economic way.

But there were other reasons—at least as important—for the different attitudes of the two main cultures in the shirtwaist workforce. The religious oppression and political ferment of Russia had made firebrands out of many thousands of immigrant Jews; they were, in a sense, political refugees. Early arrivals from Eastern Europe had quickly established in New York a thriving world of newspapers, lectures, and *landsmanschaften*—mutual aid societies organized by hometown—that all preached the importance of unionism and worker solidarity. By contrast, most Italians immigrated for strictly economic reasons. The south of their country, stripped of lumber and poorly irrigated, had become an ecological disaster area; drought and disease ravaged their lives. They came to America to make money—not to make a new social order. Mary Dreier of the WTUL believed that Italian garment workers, "heavily shackled by old customs and traditions," were "very much afraid of trade unions."

Picketing began the morning of November 24, with the first of two daily shifts. From 7:45 A.M. to "9 or 9:30 in the morning," according to Dutcher, the strikers would march as the shops opened. Then they would regroup at 5:15 P.M. for another hour of picketing at closing time. Rose Perr arrived for morning picket duty to find that "our factory had begun work with a few Italian strikebreakers." But Dutcher's feared race war did not develop. In fact, Salvatore Ninfo, the leading Italian official in the union, asserted that at least a thousand Italians were part of the picket lines. WTUL volunteers began making plans to visit the homes of more than twelve hundred additional Italian workers to promote the goals of the strike. (Ultimately, Italians made up somewhere between 6 percent and 10 percent of the shirtwaist strikers, by most estimates. American-born workers constituted a similar portion. Eastern European Jews, who were two-thirds of the shirtwaist labor force, made up three-quarters or more of the strikers.)

Euphoria swept the East Side on that second full day of the strike. An estimated five thousand additional workers joined the walkout, bringing the total number of strikers to at least twenty thousand. After morning picket duty, swarms of workers and sympathizers marched through downtown streets, chanting and singing, flowing from union hall to union hall and exploding with applause as word spread of shop owners already caving in. Clara Lemlich, founder and spark of Local 25, walked the circuit, too, delivering a short, ripping speech at each of the meeting halls. "We know that if we stick together—and we are going to stick—we will win!" she declared. A union official hailed "the strongest spirit of solidarity among [strikers] that I have ever seen."

Even more important, perhaps, was the decision by the cutters' union to honor the strike. Cutters—invariably men—were the best-paid workers in any garment shop; unlike machine operators, they were very difficult to replace. Their skill with the knife, whisking pieces from piles of fabric with a minimum of waste, made them almost irreplaceable. Garment factories would be hard-pressed to continue without them.

Roughly five hundred shops were hit by the waist makers' strike. More than seventy owners—roughly one in seven—surrendered in the first forty-eight hours. They were all smaller shops, less able to endure a long stoppage. Their workers returned immediately, having won a pay raise, a fifty-two hour week, and a pledge to run a union-only factory.

Max Blanck and Isaac Harris were horrified by the scale of the strike and by the swift capitulation of so many owners. Nothing like it had ever happened before. For the first time, manufacturers suspected that the union was *under*estimating the strength of the workers. Factory owner David Hurwitz fearfully reckoned that forty thousand workers, not twenty thousand, had joined the uprising. "For once, the strike leaders have not exaggerated," he told the *New York Times*. "It is the most astonishing strike I ever knew."

Something had to be done to stop the rout. Twenty leading factory owners, including Blanck and Harris, convened an emergency meeting at the Broadway Central Hotel for the purpose of stiffening the spines of their fellow manufacturers. They agreed on several points: the strike must be resisted; the stampede to settle must end; the union must be crushed. At this closed-door gathering, the bosses agreed to the Triangle owners' proposal that they form a manufacturers association. "The action of some of the smaller firms in settling with the union hastened the movement to form an association," an attorney for the owners said after the session. Not one member of the new group had granted a single union demand, the lawyer added—nor would they.

The Triangle owners had a galvanizing effect on their colleagues, because they were living proof that it was possible to endure the strike. After all, roughly half their workforce had already been picketing for nearly two months, yet Blanck and Harris had kept the factory going (although at reduced capacity). The Triangle owners fought every way they could think of. They waged physical war, sending Nathan Kaplan to beat up Joe Zeinfield. They waged political war, making allies of the police. And they waged psychological war, dreaming up enticements to keep as many workers as possible on the job.

Even many years later, some Triangle sewing machine operators remembered when there was dancing in the shop. Every day at lunchtime during the strike, Blanck and Harris invited the eighth-floor workers up to the ninth floor where, in a small open space, Blanck installed a crank-operated phonograph. The workers peeled oranges and ate rolls and sipped tea between dances to the music of the Victrola. Once a week, the owners gave prizes to the best dancers.

At the same time, Blanck and Harris were scheming to open a new shop in the outlying town of Yonkers, beyond the reach of the union. They planned to advertise in the conservative Yiddish *Morgen Journal* for workers willing to move to the suburbs.

The emergency session was a success, and the next day a much larger group of factory owners was summoned to the elegant Hoffman House hotel. There, about a hundred firms signed a "no surrender" declaration. The stampede to settle was quelled and a policy of muscular resistance—the chosen strategy of Blanck and Harris—became the official position of the newborn Allied Waist and Dress Manufacturers Association.

Inevitably, perhaps, once management hardened its position, violence returned to the picket lines. At the J. M. Cohen & Co. factory, just down the street from the Triangle, strikers and scabs waged a bloody fight. Dozens of reserve officers charged in from the Mercer Street station, clubs flying. Evidently the police were no longer on a leash.

Outside the Bijou factory one day, Rose Perr and her comrades watched incredulously as replacement workers came and went from the curb in *automobiles*. The novelty, the luxury, were almost unimaginable. After several days of watching such scenes, Perr turned to a friend, Annie Albert, and announced that she was going to talk to the strikebreakers. She intended to "ask them why they work, and tell them we are not going to harm them at all." But as Perr and her friend moved forward, a tall man escorting the strikebreakers punched Albert in the chest. She sank to the ground, gasping for breath. Perr yelled for a policeman. When he arrived, the officer immediately arrested both strikers.

Rose Perr and Annie Albert were taken, like hundreds of strikers before them, to the Jefferson Market magistrate's court and locked into a cell. After a little wait, they received a visit from Violet Pike of the WTUL. She was a recent graduate of Vassar College, one of the "Seven Sisters"—the women's answer to the all-male Ivy League. Pike was a familiar face at the magistrate's court, keeping an eye on the proceedings and paying strikers' fines with WTUL money. On other days she did other tasks, even toting sandwich boards up and down city blocks, advertising the grievances of the workers. "Dainty little Violet," one comrade remembered her, "her hands deep in her pockets, her beaver hat a bit to the side and an angelic smile on her red lips."

Pike had come to reassure arrested strikers and to post their bail. Rose Perr and her friend were released pending trial. Their fates would depend on which judge heard their cases. There were friendly magistrates at Jefferson Market who generally could be counted on to uphold the right of strikers to picket peaceably. But others on the bench took a dim view of the workers. (One in particular, Magistrate Willard Olmsted, considered strikes an offense against God.) The antistrike magistrates were losing their patience. Day after day and night after night, strikers were hauled before them; guilt was determined; fines were imposed—and then rich women from the WTUL stepped forward with the money. Magistrate Joseph Corrigan announced that he was going to start sending strikers to the workhouse, and other judges quickly followed his lead.

When she appeared for trial, Rose Perr drew a hostile magistrate, Robert Cornell. She looked ridiculous in the same dock where drunks and rowdies and thieves routinely were tried. Perr was a wisp of a girl, with a high, gentle, and childlike voice; and she wore her smooth, dark hair in braids. People generally guessed her to be ten or twelve years old—no one thought she looked sixteen. But Cornell quickly found Perr and Albert guilty of assaulting the man who punched Albert in the chest. "It would be perfectly futile for me to fine them," Cornell explained peevishly. "Some charitable women would pay their fines . . . I am going to commit them to the workhouse." This experience, he said, would give the strikers "an opportunity of thinking over what they have done."

Violet Pike was in the gallery. Aghast, she stood up and called out: "Cannot this sentence be mollified?"

It could not.

Rose Perr and her friend spent the night in the Tombs, New York City's aptly named downtown jail, where they shivered on bare iron beds as addicts and prostitutes in nearby cells "laughed and screamed and said terrible words." When morning came, they were taken by boat to Blackwell's Island (now Roosevelt Island) to serve five days at hard labor. Nineteen other strikers joined them in the days that followed, all sentenced by the angry magistrates.

As each one arrived, she was stripped of her clothes and dressed in heavy woolen stripes. Even the smallest uniform was far too big for Rose Perr—the sleeves drooped over her hands, the skirt dragged on the ground. To get any work done she had to roll and fold and safety-pin. The other inmates mocked her: "Look! Look at the little kid!" At first the strikers were assigned to scrub floors, but Perr couldn't get the hang of it and Albert was so inept that she managed to soak herself. Prison matrons moved them to the sewing room. Rose Perr was a stoic. She decided, for example, that the constant cold and damp were, on balance, good—because they kept the stench under control. "I think if it were any warmer, you would almost faint," she said.

She befriended other strikers as they arrived and slowly the five days passed. At last the boat came to take her back to Manhattan. Something amazing had happened while she was gone. The shirtwaist uprising had swelled to an epic—"the Lexington and Bunker Hill of woman's revolution for her rights," in the words of the city's biggest newspaper, Pulitzer's *World*. Perr and her fellow workhouse inmates returned to applause and parades. They were, after all, the bravest of the "brave girl strikers," Gotham's biggest sensation.

Being a sensation was Alva Smith Vanderbilt Belmont's special talent. She painted her life in bold strokes: marrying millionaires, matching her teenaged daughter to an English duke, throwing society's most lavish parties, storming the closed doors of men's clubs in the name of women's rights. Born on a slaveholding plantation in Mobile, Alabama, she was, by her fortieth birthday, queen of New York society. Marble House, her "cottage" in Newport, Rhode Island, was the center of summertime high society. The lavish home was a birthday present from her first husband, shipping plutocrat William K. Vanderbilt. Its Corinthian columns were massively scaled to evoke the Temple of the Sun at Baalbek. Even the driveway was white marble. The mansion and its furnishings cost nine million dollars—the equivalent of more than 150 million dollars today. "Extravagance and ostentation marked every social gathering" at Marble House, the *New York Times* observed, and "the jewels worn at balls were valued in the millions of dollars."

It was there, in 1895, that Alva staged the most gilded ball of the Gilded Age, to mark the engagement of her daughter Consuelo, then seventeen, to the Duke of Marlborough. The marriage was entirely Alva's idea. Consuelo loved a boy in New York, but her mother wanted a duke in the family. She threatened to kill herself if Consuelo resisted. When the match was made, Marlborough received a dowry of two million dollars, without which he risked losing his vast and beautiful Oxfordshire estate, Blenheim Palace. Alva's coup inspired a fad among wealthy American families. Rich American parents with suitable daughters rooted through Europe in search of eligible nobles with dwindling bank accounts. Charles Dana Gibson, for one, was appalled, and he launched a campaign against the practice in his cartoons.

By then, Alva had divorced Vanderbilt in favor of banker Oliver Hazard Perry Belmont, and was said to have quieted down a bit. But when O.H.P.—as the newspapers invariably called him—died a dozen years later, Alva was finally free to assert herself completely.

With her great wealth and greater will, she took over the women's suffrage movement, spoke of the coming "war of the sexes," and advised her feminist sisters to "pray to God; She will help you." Scarcely a week went by without headlines reporting Belmont's latest rally or pronouncement or excursion to crash a stag gathering.

In the autumn of 1909 Alva, then fifty-six, began to hear from various rich and progressive friends—members and supporters of the pro-suffrage WTUL—about the outrageous treatment of the shirtwaist strikers. Such things would not happen if women had the vote, Belmont mused. Then came the general strike, one of the largest political actions ever undertaken by New York women. Belmont swiftly concluded that her cause and theirs must be united.

Up and down Fifth Avenue, Madison Avenue, and Park Avenue, from Gramercy Park to Murray Hill, word of the strike passed through the neurons of New York progressive society from woman to woman. One messenger was Rose Pastor Stokes, wife of an heir to a great mining and railroad fortune. Rose Stokes was an ideal conduit between the salons and the strikers, because she had lived in both worlds. She, too, had been a poor Russian immigrant; the factory in which she began work at age thirteen made cigars, not blouses. Rolling cigars was so tedious that Rose began composing poems in her head, which she then wrote down and sent to Jewish papers in New York. This led to a job as a journalist with the *Jewish Daily News*, which in turn led to an interview with the rich, handsome socialist James Graham Phelps Stokes. He had recently given up his Madison Avenue mansion to live at the University Settlement on the Lower East Side, where he could attack the problems of the poor directly. Newspapers could not resist the story of this blueblood of the slums, with the generous heart and regal profile of a Renaissance saint. After Rose's interview, the heir and the factory girl fell in love; their wedding was hailed as the Cinderella story of the decade.

The Stokeses backed the strike from the start, appearing at crowded meeting halls to cheer on the workers. They distributed thousands of ribbons embossed with a slogan Rose had coined: "Starve to win, or you'll starve anyhow." Like Alva Belmont, Rose Stokes was an ardent suffragist. "It is far more important for women to have a share in the making of the laws . . . than even the winning of this strike," she declared at a union hall on Second Street. Rose drew her rich sister-in-law, Helen Stokes—among many others—into the ranks of strike supporters.

Other society women learned of the uprising from friends or daughters at the top women's colleges, such as Vassar, Bryn Mawr, Wellesley, Smith, and Barnard. Young leaders in the WTUL, like Violet Pike, Elizabeth Dutcher, and Elsie Cole, were recent graduates, and they spread their enthusiasm to their friends who were still in school.

In the beginning, the downtown radicals—Clara Lemlich and her comrades—didn't recognize or understand the unique effect the shirtwaist strike was having on the upper class. Of course they knew that the WTUL had rich women in it. But the newcomers, like Alva Belmont, were a different matter. Some union leaders began to grow uncomfortable when Belmont sent pro-suffrage buttons to distribute at the union halls. Suffrage was not high on the list of socialist priorities; the issue of votes for women was seen as a distraction from the class struggle.

Belmont took no notice of any complaints, however, and seized the chance to turn the labor uprising into a broader feminist revolt. On November 30, 1909, a week into the strike, and just hours after staging a triumphant appearance at Cooper Union by the legendary English suffrage leader Emmeline Pankhurst, Belmont announced that she would host a "monster meeting"—the largest in New York labor history—to support the shirtwaist strikers. Supremely confident, she rented the massive Hippodrome amphitheater for the afternoon of December 6. It was typical Alva Belmont: assembling two huge rallies in a single week. She was a human steamroller.

The sidewalks were jammed an hour before the doors opened. Policemen turned hundreds of people away. The seven thousand who got inside the Hippodrome ranged from strikers to bishops to Maori suffragettes. They heard Rose Pastor Stokes quote Marx: "Workers, unite! You have nothing to lose but your chains—and you have the world to gain." They heard suffrage leader Anna Shaw link low pay for women to the scourge of prostitution: "We are not in factories and sweatshops to escape the duty of mothers and the joy of home life. We do not take half the pay that men do because we like money any the less. . . . We must live. How shall we live—in the factory or on the street?" They heard heated condemnations of police unfairness and brutality, and were shocked by the story of Yetta Ruth, a seventeen-year-old strike leader from Beekman & Hayes, a waist house near Leiserson's. Arrested at the insistence of her boss, Ruth was taken to the Twentieth Street police station, where she endured taunts and teasing from the officers and other "insinuations" that "a girl is ashamed to talk about." All the powerful themes of the strike—sex, socialism, votes, and justice—were on display. Between speeches, Belmont had arranged for music from a military band.

The Hippodrome meeting caught the attention of the major newspapers, and the shirtwaist strike hit the front pages for the first time since Mary Dreier's arrest a month earlier. It would remain there for weeks to come. The Hippodrome rally was the lead story in the *Times:* THRONG CHEERS ON THE GIRL STRIKERS. This headline could not have escaped the eye of Charles Murphy the next morning. Suffragists and socialists, seven thousand strong! The story beneath the headline noted that John Howard Melish, rector of Brooklyn's Holy Trinity Church, had addressed the crowd. "There are two great spirits abroad in the land today," he preached. "One is the spirit of self-help; the other is the spirit of cooperation." Neither was necessarily a good thing for Tammany.

Alva Belmont had invited nearly the entire city administration to her meeting, but the lame-duck members of the Tammany government all skipped the event—a fact that the progressive organizers noted from the stage. Reverend Melish charged that "Mayor McClellan . . . wasn't interested in the welfare of 40,000 striking girls." The *Times* printed an entire paragraph listing missing city officials. The corporation counsel, police commissioner, and superintendent of schools had all declined to sit in Belmont's personal box. Tammany was in danger of finding itself on the wrong side of something very big.

On the other hand, there was, for Murphy, a heartening note of division, published in the best possible place for such a note. "The strikers listened eagerly, gravely, but without enthusiasm to the speakers who advocated equal suffrage as the key to the labor puzzle, and in the end rejected the proposition," according to the *World*. Joseph Pulitzer's lively newspaper, though liberal, never veered far from the beliefs and tastes of the mainstream public. The paper quoted an unnamed waist maker saying: "We want something now, not next summer. . . . The right of men to vote does not prevent strikes, does not affect them, so would *we* be improved by the ballot?" It was a first small crack in the façade of sisterhood.

The uprising in the garment district was an unprecedented coalition, and a genuine threat to the familiar order. This sudden flowering of support from progressive women allowed the strikers to resist the extraordinary pressures that began to build against them. Led by Blanck and Harris, the manufacturers had dramatically slowed the rate of settlements with their declaration of no surrender. They now felt so confident about the future that in mid-December they flatly rejected the union's offer to negotiate. From their Hoffman House headquarters, the owners predicted that it was only a matter of time before the strike "goes to pieces."

Police continued to arrest picketers, and magistrates continued to dispatch them to the workhouse. Some frustrated strikers began carrying rotten eggs to fling at strikebreakers and police. "You girls are getting to be a nuisance and a menace to the community," one judge scolded a group of strikers charged with egging Detective Kemp from the Union Market station.

Worst of all, the strike fund—after an initial infusion of money from supportive unions across the country—was nearly depleted and the meager savings of the workers had dried up. "With the beginning of the fourth week of the fight the strikers enter upon the hardest struggle," the *Times* reported. "They are coming to see that they are facing something terribly real and terribly hard." Though the shirtwaist workers possessed amazing spirit and endurance, it is doubtful that they could have lasted much longer without progressive money.

At just this low point, however, a woman whose name was almost a synonym for money joined the cause: Anne Morgan, daughter of the most powerful capitalist in the world.

Her father, J. Pierpont Morgan, controlled the steel industry. He directed railroads and financed oil companies. In those days, before the creation of the Federal Reserve, Morgan was America's dominant financial institution all by himself. His word ruled Wall Street; two years earlier, he had personally prevented a stock market collapse by organizing, and underwriting, a huge purchase of shares. As the shirt-waist strike raged in the garment district, J. P. Morgan was busy waging a lightning campaign to take over the American banking industry. GREATEST FINANCIAL POWER EVER CONCENTRATED IN ANY SET OF PRIVATE INDIVIDUALS IN THE WORLD, read a typical headline. An editorial cartoon, published as the strike was raging, expressed the general view of the situation. Astronomer Percival Lowell had recently announced the discovery of civilization on Mars. The cartoonist imagined Earth as the Martians would see it. The globe bore the universally recognized mustache and monstrous pocked nose of J. P. Morgan.

Anne, at thirty-six, was his youngest child. As a girl she was an avid athlete, "irresistibly funny" and unpredictable, according to her siblings. As an adult, she became her father's frequent traveling companion, crisscrossing the world with him—all to prevent the newspapers from noticing that there was a third member of the traveling party: Morgan's mistress. Anne lived a comfortable, perpetually single life at the Morgan palace on Madison Avenue, enjoying a lavish allowance of twenty thousand dollars per year.

Around age thirty, with two wealthy friends, Anne decided that New York women should have a private club to rival the all-male Metropolitan and Union clubs. They quickly signed up 550 women from the cream of society, bought a large lot near the Morgan mansion, and commissioned the glamorous architect Stanford White to build a clubhouse complete with swimming pool and squash courts. The women dubbed their haven the Colony Club. While working on this project, Anne Morgan befriended the club's interior decorator, a young and likable social climber named Elsie de Wolfe. De Wolfe was the companion of literary agent Elizabeth Marbury, a memorable personality who represented such controversial writers as George Bernard Shaw and Oscar Wilde. The willowy de Wolfe and the masculine Marbury made an unusual couple, cutting a wide path through Manhattan society. Gossips called them "the Bachelors." They knew all the interesting people and they always made a splash—suggesting, perhaps, that America was not as prudish or as sexually ignorant in those days as some might imagine. "They are grand and universal," Henry Adams wrote of the pair. On another occasion, after a dinner party in Paris, Adams reported that Marbury and de Wolfe were "the only men of the lot."

Anne Morgan was enchanted by the two of them—especially by Marbury, with whom she fell in love. Elizabeth Marbury was seventeen years older than Anne, and "bore distinct physical and managerial resemblances" to her father, according to Jean Strouse, biographer of J. P. Morgan. Their love affair allowed the younger woman to blossom. "Anne began to escape from the strictures of Madison Avenue spinsterhood to a brilliant international demimonde of aesthetic appreciation, social activism, and female independence."

When Anne Morgan learned the details of the shirtwaist strike, she was moved. "We can't live our lives without doing something to help them," she explained to the *Times.* "Of course, the consumer must be protected," she hastened to add, but "fifty-two hours a week seems little enough to ask."

Morgan and Marbury invited a group of strikers and strike leaders to lunch at the Colony Club on December 15. One hundred fifty club members attended the event in the gymnasium. For the workers, it likely was their first experience with a salad fork and linen napkins, in the company of women who "could write their fortunes in seven figures," as the *World* put it. "In halting and broken English," the strikers "unfolded the tale of their grievances.

"'My employer,' said one small Italian who scarcely looked the sixteen years she claimed, 'got the priest to come around and tell the Italian girls that if we went out on strike with the Jewish girls we would all go to hell—excuse the language.'"

Another young woman, a Jewish immigrant, said: "I have a sick mother and two little sisters to support. I get three dollars and a half a week."

Another said she worked at the Triangle Waist Company. "When a girl comes five minutes too late she is compelled to go home. She may live outside the city. It does not matter. She must go home and loses a day." The worker continued, detailing the long hours of the busiest times of year. "We work eight days in the week," she said. "This may seem strange to you . . . but we work from seven in the morning until very late at night, and sometimes we work a week and a half in one week."

When Clara Lemlich rose to speak, she took the opportunity to defend herself against a recent allegation by the manufacturers. They had called her a liar after discovering a newspaper story that quoted Lemlich as saying that she earned a scant three dollars a week. In fact, Leiserson paid her five times that amount. Lemlich assured the clubwomen that the reporter misunderstood her. She had been describing the worst conditions, not her own situation. And those conditions were not exaggerated, she insisted. "You can go to see for yourselves," she said, directing the clubwomen to a particularly bad shop on Wooster Street.

The Colony members were impressed. Mrs. Archibald Alexander rose to ask Mary Dreier what the strikers needed most.

"Money to fight with," Dreier answered briskly.

"I hope I may have the honor of beginning the collection," Mrs. Alexander responded. Elsie de Wolfe and another club member offered their hats. In a matter of minutes, about $1,300 was raised—roughly $20,000 in current terms. Anne Morgan's own contributions, beyond the Colony Club collection, were widely rumored to be much larger. One newspaper asserted that she always received a huge Christmas check from her father, and this year had given all of it to the strike fund. Elizabeth Marbury, meanwhile, prevailed on her connections in the theater world to raise money. At her behest, the Shubert family, owners of numerous Broadway venues, pledged the profits from a week's run at one house. (Alva Belmont was also busily raising money, including a one-thousand-dollar check from Mrs. Collis Huntington, wife of the railroad magnate. The wife of tin czar Warner Leeds gave one hundred dollars. The daughter of real estate giant J. J. Astor gave fifty dollars. Lists of donors appeared in many leading papers.)

The owners were plainly worried by the entry of Morgan's daughter. They didn't have a brush to tar her with. She didn't grab headlines like Alva Belmont, nor was she a socialist like Rose Pastor Stokes. And they couldn't divorce the name Morgan from notions of sound business and the profit motive. So they decided to try to win her over. From the Hoffman House, the manufacturers association circulated an open letter inviting Morgan and Marbury to tour their shops and see conditions firsthand. The women declined.

The alliance of progressive women and radical workers had now reached its peak. Society women lent their automobiles and chauffeurs (Anne Morgan rented seven taxicabs) to stage a motor parade down Fifth Avenue and around the garment district. Rose Perr and several other strikers fresh from the workhouse smiled and waved as they passed their cheering comrades. They wore big bronze medals awarded by the WTUL in recognition of "hardship . . . endured in a righteous cause." Sympathizers waved flags and handkerchiefs. Other sacrifices were also honored. Near the head of the parade, in a snazzy maroon car, drove Inez Milholland, a dazzling young Vassar graduate with a lovely singing voice. Milholland represented scores of college women who had traveled from the Seven Sisters to join the strikers. Some of the students even lived with shirtwaist workers, experiencing firsthand the exotic life of the Lower East Side. "The college girls have made a great hit," the *American* reported. "They can be seen almost every night at the Grand Street restaurants, drinking Russian tea and eating noodle soup prepared in the real Russian way." Alongside Milholland sat Fannie Horowitz, a trailblazing woman lawyer who worked night after night in the magistrate's court to free arrested strikers.

Other students back on campus organized a boycott of nonunion waists. When plans were hatched to start a cooperative factory staffed by strikers, women at Wellesley pledged to buy the first thousand blouses. Pro-strike sentiment spread up and down the East Coast, carried by WTUL volunteers who traveled relentlessly to address crowds in churches, union halls, and college lecture rooms. Even Helen Taft, daughter of President William Howard Taft, attended a meeting to support the uprising.

Strike leaders did not reach out only to the rich, however. They also tried to cross racial lines. Elizabeth Dutcher of the WTUL took two waist workers with her to Brooklyn to address a meeting of blacks at the A. M. E. Zion Church. Black workers were being recruited as strikebreakers, and Dutcher appealed for help in resisting this effort. During a question-and-answer period after the speeches, the audience complained about racist attitudes in the labor movement—even inside Local 25. Dutcher agreed, and the point was included in a resolution passed that evening. "Resolved, that the colored citizens of Brooklyn, in mass meeting assembled, protest and urge the women of color to refrain from acting in the capacity of strikebreakers," the proclamation began. "We further urge . . . that organized labor exercise a proper consideration of the claims and demands of the men and women of color who desire to enter the various trades." Such efforts received no attention in the mainstream press, however, and little notice on the Lower East Side.

On December 19, 1909, Alva Belmont and Anne Morgan were named to head a strike committee to challenge police behavior and recruit volunteer pickets. Despite the bad publicity over the arrests of WTUL leaders a month earlier, Tammany police had reverted to form, openly siding with management against the strikers. In fact, a study by the Hearst paper, the *American*, showed that the female shirtwaist strikers were receiving harsher treatment from the police and courts than male taxi drivers had during their big strike of 1908. Salting the picket lines with rich young women would, it was hoped, inspire more caution from the police, who could never be sure when they might arrest someone whose name would make headlines.

The new committee also hoped to cow the magistrates. With that goal, Belmont spent the night of December 19 at the Jefferson Market courthouse. As ever, she cut quite a figure. Hour after hour, Belmont sat straight as a statue at the end of the first row of hard wooden seats. She wore a large black hat with a geyser of feathers rising from it, and scrutinized the proceedings through an upraised lorgnette.

A long line of petty criminals passed by the bar of justice. There was a young woman who had been offered a dollar by a policeman. When she accepted it, he arrested her for soliciting. Two black defendants faced charges of loitering—one was heavily bandaged, having been clubbed by the arresting officer. An elderly woman was hauled in for sleeping on the street. Finally, at 11 P.M., Belmont saw her first strikers, seven young women charged with shouting "scab" at strikebreakers outside the E. H. Jackson & Co. factory on Fifth Avenue. One was fined $10 and the rest were discharged. Belmont wondered aloud what "scab" might possibly mean.

Four more hours dragged by. Belmont's lawyer, exhausted, received her permission to leave. But the grande dame's posture never drooped. Finally, at 3 A.M., four more strikers were hauled in. They did not have money for their bail.

Belmont stood and announced: "I can give my house, No. 477 Madison Avenue, as surety for these poor girls." The magistrate looked at her wearily. "The bail is $100 for each of the girls—$400 in all," he said.

"I haven't so much money with me, sir," Belmont said, "and my lawyer carried away the deeds to my property that I brought along."

By rote, the judge inquired whether Alva Belmont owned property, above and beyond her debts, worth at least twice as much as the bail: $800. Her house, she answered, "is valued at $400,000, and I think there may be a $100,000 mortgage on it, which I raised to help the cause of the shirtwaist workers and the women's suffrage movement."

This scene was splashed all over the newspapers: a Manhattan mansion pledged to cover bail for a group of immigrants in night court. As Alva Belmont left Jefferson Market, "the street lamps were beginning to grow pale in the gray dawn," the *American* recounted. Belmont's chauffeur awaited her patiently as she stopped to address a reporter. "There will be a different order of things when we have women judges on the bench," she declared. "Let me assure you, too, that the time is not far away when we *will* have women judges."

The papers tried to put these events in context, but could find none. "For almost the first time women of widely different social ranks have joined forces in a common cause which, though directly for the betterment of one element, is for the ultimate political advancement of all," the *World* editorialized. "The support given to the waist-makers by women of prominence is unprecedented." Other newspapers came to the same conclusion: a new alignment, a shifting of the political plates, was under way in New York.

Perhaps the momentum of the strike was shifting, too. In Philadelphia, fifteen thousand waist makers walked off the job after learning that work was being shifted out of New York and into their shops. On Washington Place, fifty replacement workers walked out of the Triangle factory to join the strike. For the first time in three months of unrest, Blanck and Harris had to shut down, albeit briefly.

But just as the alliance seemed strongest, it was already falling apart, poisoned by resentment, envy, and ideology. Radicals among the strike supporters resented the arrival of the rich ladies. They rightly felt that Alva Belmont and Anne Morgan had done nothing previously to build unions or defend workers. Yet, because of their great wealth, they got all the attention. Theresa Serber Malkiel certainly felt this way. She was quite well off herself; her husband was a well-known lawyer and real estate developer. Like Belmont, Malkiel worked for women's suffrage, but her crucial commitment was to socialism. An early immigrant from Russia, she had worked alongside many of the key figures in New York's socialist leadership: Abraham Cahan of the *Forward*, Bernard Weinstein of the United Hebrew Trades, attorneys Morris Hillquit and Meyer London, and so on. Always gently but skillfully, she tried to make room for more women in what was often an oppressively male movement. She was a charter member of the Socialist Women's Committee and, with her husband, a founder and key financial backer of the perpetually struggling *Call*. She was also active in the Women's Trade Union League. Clara Lemlich was her protégée, according to historian Annelise Orleck.

Early in the uprising, Malkiel organized a march of ten thousand shirtwaist strikers on City Hall. There, a small delegation met with lame-duck Mayor McClellan, and presented a petition asking him to investigate police brutality. A Triangle striker named Lena Barsky was part of the delegation; two days later, she was arrested after a confrontation on the picket line.

Malkiel was appalled by the Colony Club luncheon; to her, it reeked of hypocrisy and bathos. Her reaction was reflected in the *Call*. "A remarkable meeting, one that was as peculiar as it was interesting, and as unique as it was pathetic," the paper declared. The "bejeweled, befurred, belaced and begowned audience" stood in contrast to the "ten wage slaves, some of them mere children" who told their stories. "Seldom, if ever, have [rich women] listened with such interest to the tales of the war between capital and labor, to the incidents of pain, of misery, of grief in the great struggle between the classes." The *Call* scoffed at the donations collected in Elsie de Wolfe's hat—"less than a quarter per striker." (In fact, the Colony Club members contributed about twenty-five times as much as the executive committee of the Socialist Party.) It is not clear whether Malkiel wrote the *Call* story. In general, her pieces carried bylines. But the assessment was identical to the one Malkiel later expressed in her novel, *Diary of a Shirtwaist Striker*.

After the luncheon, a note of disdain for the wealthy progressives became a standard element of radical press coverage. Of the parade in the donated automobiles, the *Call* commented: "It was amusing to see rich women carrying cards on which was proclaimed the need for organization for labor and which demanded shorter hours and increased pay."

Malkiel believed that the high profile of the super-rich was actually having a *negative* effect on the strike. On December 28, she joined other members of the Socialist Women's Committee in an appeal for strike fund donations, saying: "A belief is prevalent that because certain women of wealth have allied themselves with the cause of the strikers there is plenty of help for the girls. Such is not the case, however, as many of the girls have not yet received any strike benefits and are in great need of food and money to pay their room rent." Inside the WTUL, a number of key figures increasingly agreed with Malkiel, including Leonora O'Reilly, the group's finest orator, and Rose Schneiderman, its best organizer.

Whose strike was it, anyway? Did it belong to the genteel humanitarians? To the suffragists? To Karl Marx? To feminism? Just when the uprising of the waist makers seemed strongest, this question fractured the coalition. Petty tensions—over such trivial matters as who would be first to welcome the workhouse prisoners back to Manhattan—festered into outright enmity, as the various factions and parties began to focus intently on their differences. The breakup began in the last, frozen days of December.

Christmas Day 1909 dawned to a blizzard, the worst snowstorm to hit New York in twenty years. The city was muffled and snarled. After the snow came bitter, relentless cold, driven through the narrow streets by knifing winds. Garbagemen and vagrants were pressed into service as day laborers to shovel the streets by hand. Drifts piled so high that under one, in Brooklyn, a man's frozen body went undiscovered for more than a week. He had died while trying to reach the corner bar for a pail of beer.

In the cozy fastness of the Hoffman House, the key factory owners—Harris and Blanck and the others—brooded over the accumulated effects of three weeks of favorable publicity for the strikers. Even the *New York Times,* a reliable friend of management in nearly every circumstance, had run an editorial justifying the uprising. Every day, another handful of manufacturers settled with the union, like deserters slipping away from an encircled army. Most of the small shops, and many of the midsized factories, had given up, leaving only the largest firms as holdouts. Most of the original strikers were back at work, victorious.

The owners had to do something to shake things up. Their next move, whether consciously or not, was perfectly calibrated to split the opposing forces. The manufacturers association offered to submit the strike to an arbitration panel—and the manufacturers strongly hinted that they would agree to higher pay and shorter hours. At the same time, though, they refused to discuss one point: the status of Local 25. Strike leaders wanted the factories to hire only union members while the manufacturers fiercely resisted the "closed shop." But they did offer to stop punishing union members and to begin treating union and nonunion workers equally in hiring and pay decisions.

This proposal was announced just as the strikers were enjoying another wave of good press. At Jefferson Market, the magistrates announced that they would send no more picketers to the workhouse. A chastened Robert Cornell, whose sentencing of "little Rose Perr" had scandalized progressive society, wrote in the *American* that "the harm done to respectable girls by throwing them into close contact with vicious women on Blackwell's Island has convinced me I should do everything to prevent them being sent there." (He added defensively: "Society women who have hysterically taken up sides with the strikers are to blame for the prolongation of the strike." Eventually, Cornell quietly resumed imposing workhouse sentences.)

A special "strike extra" of the *Call,* meanwhile, sold tens of thousands of copies. Strikers in thin coats and old shoes endured icy temperatures and slicing winds to hawk the papers throughout Manhattan and Brooklyn. The purpose of the project—organized by Elizabeth Dutcher and Elsie Cole, both of the WTUL—was partly to raise money for the strike fund. But Dutcher said it was also designed to show the public "how intelligent, well-dressed and refined" the strikers were. Several bold young women endured jeers from Wall Street bankers and strode into 23 Wall Street, the fortress of J. P. Morgan, the very citadel of capitalism, bearing copies of the socialist sheet and wearing crisp white sashes across their chests. They didn't meet the titan, but they got as far as Morgan's clerk, who handed over a dollar bill for the nickel newspaper. This extravagance was outdone by an unnamed gent outside the Astor Hotel on Broadway, who paid ten dollars for his copy. "What nice, pretty girls," exclaimed the *World.*

So it was understandable that the members of Local 25's executive board were feeling almost invulnerable when they received the mediation proposal from the manufacturers. The union flatly rejected the offer and refused to discuss anything less than full union recognition and the closed shop. It might be said that this was awfully bold for a union that began the year with fewer paid members than there were shirtwaist factories. The closed shop provision, if achieved, would give Local 25 a membership of forty thousand. But this was what the rank-and-file wanted. At a series of mass meetings, thousands of strikers voted unanimously to insist on the closed shop. For the idealistic waist makers, the goals of worker solidarity and a union with genuine power had come to matter more than a simple raise and shorter hours.

This refusal to negotiate, however, persuaded many progressive sympathizers of the strike—apparently for the first time—that their radical allies were *too* radical. Although closed shops would become standard in many fields as labor gained power toward mid-century, at the time the idea was widely felt to be extreme. The *Times* immediately denounced the union for trying to "take away the right of working from all but their own members. . . . If the demand is granted the shops would be closed to all but unionists. All others might starve for all the strikers care." A committee from the upper-crust Manhattan Congregational Church, appointed to investigate the strike on behalf of progressive pastor Henry A. Stimson, concluded that the waist workers had gotten nearly everything they wanted and that their remaining demands were unreasonable.

For several days Anne Morgan and others pushed ahead, dispatching emissaries back and forth between the union hall and the Hoffman House, hopeful that the breakdown was simply a matter of semantics. Perhaps the owners could agree to "recognize" the union without agreeing to the closed shop. But the talks went nowhere—and so it was that the night on which the strike reached its glittering climax was also the night it fell apart.

Carnegie Hall was full from stage to rafters on Sunday, January 2, 1910. Labor had never enjoyed such a night. Hundreds of strikers sat on the same stage where, on another night, the New York Philharmonic had performed a Mahler symphony under the baton of the composer.

Twenty strikers, across the front row, wore sashes labeled "Workhouse Prisoner," while the others wore sashes that said "Arrested." Banners hanging from the private boxes announced some of the sponsoring organizations, from the Women's Trade Union League to Alva Belmont's Political Equity League to New York's Liberal Club. The audience applauded as Theresa Malkiel unfurled the Socialist Women's Committee banner, neatly stitched in red. Only one city magistrate had agreed to attend—the ambitious young socialite Frederick Kernochan. So loathed were the judges that when members of the Typographical Union were offered the empty box that had been reserved for magistrates, the typesetters refused to occupy it. The crowd saw what was happening, and cheered.

The trouble began with the speakers. Attorney Morris Hillquit, one of the two or three most important socialists in the city, drew an explosion of applause even before he began. His fiery message justified the excitement. In powerful terms, Hillquit insisted on the importance of a closed shop—"the crux, the very heart" of the uprising of the shirtwaist workers. Only through the union, he declared, did labor have any power—it was "the last barrier between [the owners'] greed and the workers," and if the union were weakened, "the same old conditions of virtual servitude would be restored in the shop." Hillquit deployed many of the favorite ideas and terms of the left, placing the strike in a larger context of class struggle. The owners, he declared, were wielding "the mailed fist of the exploiter." The courts were "nothing but personal prejudice, personal vindictiveness, personal partisanship." He received another wild ovation when he reached his ringing finale: "Be of good cheer, sisters, you are not alone in the struggle. Your fight is our fight, your cause is good, your fight is brave, your victory will be glorious!"

Hillquit was followed by the noted lawyer Martin W. Littleton, who was taken aback by the intensity of Hillquit's message, especially the attack on the courts. In almost an academic tone, Littleton argued that the magistrates indeed were acting illegally to disrupt legal picketing. He ventured the novel notion that the strikers might even want to sue the judges. But these problems were the errors of individual men,

Littleton declared. "Injustice to the working class is not inherent in the laws and legal procedure of the land," he said, according to a summary in the *Call*. Littleton's speech defending American justice "was coldly received." Leonora O'Reilly of the WTUL spoke next, and she "administered a gentle rebuke" to the lawyer, the *Call* reported, "for some of his views unacceptable to trade unionists."

O'Reilly declared that six weeks of the shirtwaist strike had done more to unite New Yorkers than years of preaching in churches and schools. That was true, but not for much longer. Many of the people who left Carnegie Hall that frigid night headed for homes below Fourteenth Street, and they went away inspired by Hillquit and grumbling about Littleton. But some of the audience returned to nearby mansions, shocked by the extreme—even revolutionary—tone of Hillquit's speech, and by O'Reilly's defense of it.

The next day, Anne Morgan issued a statement criticizing Hillquit and O'Reilly for preaching "fanatical doctrines of socialism." And though she said that she continued to support the strikers, she receded from the action, taking much of the mainstream press interest with her. O'Reilly responded scathingly: "Perhaps if Miss Morgan had ever been face to face with hunger or eviction for the sake of principle . . . she would understand the way those strikers felt." This dispute nearly split the WTUL board. At least one board member, Eva McDonald Valesh, shared Morgan's distress, and began promoting the idea of using Morgan's money to form a competing shirtwaist union. Valesh was not a society woman; she was the American Federation of Labor's representative to the WTUL. Many on the Lower East Side assumed—with good reason—that her views were actually those of her boss, Samuel Gompers, who saw no place for socialism in the American labor movement. (He was lukewarm, at best, on the idea of women and new immigrants in the movement.) For the bread-and-butter Gompers, the ideological stance of the shirtwaist union must have been annoying.

A DISGRACEFUL SPECTACLE, shouted the headline on an editorial in the *Call* when the bile finally spilled into the open. In a wide column running the length of the page, the paper denounced Morgan, Valesh,

Gompers, and factions of the WTUL. "Will these 'society' ladies succeed in their . . . noble effort to obtain control of the organizations of their wage-slaves? With the aid of Samuel Gompers and his understrappers it is possible that they will succeed—for a time. . . . The efforts of the exploiters will prove to have been made in vain. But what a despicable role Samuel Gompers is playing in seconding those efforts!"

It's impossible to say how many of these details penetrated the Scarlet Room at Delmonico's. But around this time Charles Murphy surely realized that an unprecedented alliance for change—centered in the very heart of Tammany's power, downtown Manhattan—had shattered as quickly as it had come together. Though the strike continued through January, it no longer threatened Murphy's world. He could continue to approach change at his own pace. The uprising once hailed as another Lexington or Bunker Hill had deteriorated into a tangle of resentments.

However, Murphy had seen what was possible.

Whose strike was it?

Ultimately, the strike belonged to the waist makers and to their crowded little world on the East Side (and, to a lesser extent, to their counterparts in Philadelphia). The last few thousand strikers from the large, unyielding firms stayed in the streets for six long weeks after the heady days of late December. Their resistance took on a more homely quality compared with the benefit concerts and mass rallies and motor parades. Four young strikers paid twenty-five dollars in fines with twenty-five hundred pennies. New heroes were discovered right in the neighborhood: Kalman Rosenbluth, for example, "the labor bailer." He was an East Side landlord and a regular at the Jefferson Market court, where he quietly guaranteed bonds for scores of arrested picketers.

The idealistic stand of the shirtwaist strikers attracted new celebrity support from the far left. At a rally in Philadelphia, a thousand strikers heard from William "Big Bill" Haywood, the notorious leader of the Western miners' union, an advocate of violence to overthrow the capitalist order. "I tell you girls," Haywood said, "that the Western miners are hearty admirers of your courage and fighting qualities. And I assure you that if any of you want to get married, all you will have to do is insert an ad in the *Miners' Magazine*." After the laughter faded, Big Bill turned serious. "For every girl that is slugged in this strike a cop ought to be sent to the hospital."

The Lower East Side busied itself with small but fervent fund-raising events: benefit plays at the theater of Yiddish matinee idol Boris Tomashevsky, silent movies at Jacob's Moving Picture Theater, performances at the Third Street Vaudeville House, and a constant whirl of balls and teas and dances and recitals. Waist workers whose shops had already settled collected dimes for their still-striking colleagues. The United Hebrew Trades called on all Jewish workers to donate a half-day's wages to the cause. The East Siders could not write checks for hundreds or even thousands of dollars the way Anne Morgan and her friends could do, but they kept the uprising alive with hard-earned coins. Though strikers received only the barest benefits—no more than two dollars per week—the cost of the uprising still severely taxed the community. Yet the effort never flagged. Quite the opposite: the number and variety of events supporting the strikers seemed to grow with each passing week.

And some wealthy supporters remained faithful. Alva Belmont called, unsuccessfully, for a sympathy strike of all women in all lines of work. Enthusiasm for the uprising remained high on college campuses. Inez Milholland—daughter of the progressive millionaire John Milholland, who built a network of pneumatic tubes under Manhattan to speed messages among key businesses—was arrested one frozen January evening on the Triangle picket line. Capt. Dominic Henry of the Mercer Street station had gone to the corner of Washington Place and Greene Street to urge the pickets to go home. But as he stood debating with Milholland, a group of strikers surrounded him and playfully pulled his coat up over his head. The hapless Capt. Henry hauled Milholland to Jefferson Market and was rewarded with one last flurry of criticism in the popular press.

* * *

Max Blanck and Isaac Harris never backed down. They were relent-lessly aggressive against the pickets, spending an unknowable, but substantial, amount on hired muscle from Max Schlansky's private detective agency. But the slow season was ending. Shirtwaist shops would soon be drowning in work, and they needed every experienced hand they could find. Union leaders, too, had grown tired of the waist makers' strike and were turning their attention to an even bigger walk-out planned for the cloak-making industry. Both sides had strong incentives to close the books on the "Uprising of the Twenty Thou-sand," as the strike came to be called.

Leaders of Local 25 essentially accepted the deal they had refused in late December. Most of the remaining shops—including Leiserson's, Bijou (Rose Perr's factory), and, finally, the Triangle—took back their strikers at higher wages and shorter hours. They "recognized" the union, but only in the sense that they no longer prohibited membership. Strike supporters tried to present the result as a victory. On February 8, 1910, the *Call*'s lead headline announced: TRIANGLE CO. YIELDS AFTER BIT-TER FIGHT. A week later, Local 25 published a long list of settled shops, including the Triangle Waist Company. This was the union's story, half true at best. There was no doubt about the "bitter fight," but Blanck and Harris had successfully resisted the closed shop.

Few on the Lower East Side believed that these most notorious of owners had yielded. Instead, this factory above all others, above even Leiserson's, represented violent resistance to the uprising. "The 'Tri-angle' company," the *Forward* prophesied. "With blood this name will be written in the history of the American workers' movement, and with feeling will this history recall the names of the strikers of this shop—of the crusaders." Blood, then, was already the Triangle's legacy, even before history paid another visit, one year, one month, and seventeen days later.

4

THE GOLDEN LAND

Saturday, March 25, 1911:

Sometime after 8 A.M. they began converging near the corner of Washington Place and Greene Street, just east of Washington Square: some five hundred workers, mostly young women—teenagers—but also some older women and young men. They streamed from cramped tenements into clotted streets; they wound through the jostling, thrilling crowds past the peddlers lugging their junk, the horses double-parked in their traces, the fire escapes crowded with boxes and bedding and children; past the Irish cop, the Italian barbershop, the kosher butcher, the Chinese laundry; past the gray acres of laundry flapping in the dirty air; past the Catholic church and the storefront synagogue; past the billboards painted on the sides of buildings (*Uneeda Biscuit 5 cents*); past newsboys hawking papers, and men with huge biceps shoveling coal into cellars; past the wagons delivering barrels of beer to Bowery saloons; past the marquees touting vaudeville and Yiddish melodrama and moving pictures—to arrive here. Here at the freight entrance of the Asch Building, where they waited for the elevators to hoist them skyward to the Triangle Waist Company.

Workers weren't welcome aboard the passenger elevators. Those were for management and customers. Those were for Max Blanck, who pulled up that morning in his chauffeur-driven automobile from his brand-new house in suburban Brooklyn near Prospect Park. The passenger elevator was waiting for him, and the operator, wearing a neatly knotted tie, Joe Zito or Gaspar Mortillalo, levered the doors shut and launched the car smoothly to the top floor.

The Triangle workers depended on two freight elevators to take them upstairs, so there was a line along the sidewalk waiting to get in. Sam Lehrer was there that morning, with his exuberant light-colored curls, and Gussie Bierman, matronly in her pince-nez, and slender Yetta Goldstein, and formidable Sarah Weintraub, known to her friends as Sally. Jennie Rosenberg's look suggested she knew something funny. Jennie Stern, who had a direct and sultry gaze, and Ben Sklaver, the contractor who had been beaten on this same sidewalk during the early days of the uprising, were there. So were plump Tessie Weisner and Pauline Levine with her worldly, skeptical look. Rebecca Feibisch was the one with the faraway eyes, a slim, haunted beauty with dark hair worn casually piled on her head, an oval face, a full-lipped mouth, and a long, Gibson-girl neck. All of them went into the factory that morning, but none of them made it out. All their families had left was just a photograph.

In the city's shock and horror at what befell these workers and many others, no one paused to piece together their stories. Newspapers reported the names of the dead but scarcely anything else about them. Others on the sidewalk that morning resurrect fleetingly in the report of a union relief committee. To justify its distribution of donated funds, the committee sketched a few bare fragments from the lives of some of the fire victims, using only initials and ages for identification. Matching these wisps of information with the rosters of the dead, it is possible to glimpse the character and the promise of those young people, and to see how much was riding with them as they traveled up to the factory floors.

Anna Cohen was twenty-five—old for a Triangle seamstress—and the main support for her younger sisters. Her brother, though he had a good job, refused to help them. She lived in Brooklyn, not far from Dinah Greenberg, who was eighteen. Greenberg shared an apartment with her brother and his wife. Together, they sent enough money home to Russia to support the rest of their "very needy" family. But things weren't going well for the brother and he had begun talking about going back, and leaving her alone. Ida Pearl, eighteen, lived on the East Side with her brother, who earned barely enough to support himself. It was up to her to earn the money for monthly stipends to keep the rest of the family going in Russia.

Esther Harris was twenty-one, chief breadwinner for her family in Brooklyn. Her father was a failure as a peddler, but the family made do because Harris was one of the best-paid craftswomen at the Triangle, probably a draper or a sample maker. She earned an impressive twenty-two dollars per week, and had arranged for her mother and sister to be hired as trainees. Life was harder for Rose Manofsky, twenty-two, whose father, a tailor, was bent with rheumatism and "hardly a proper guardian" for her fourteen-year-old sister. Two wives had left him. Only Rose remained, caring for his failing shop on the Upper East Side and the tiny apartment behind it, and paying the bills with her earnings from the Triangle. Sadie Nussbaum, eighteen, dreamed of being a schoolteacher, but had to quit high school and work in a factory to help support her family.

And there were even more difficult lives. Becky Reivers, eighteen, a recent orphan, had journeyed from Russia the previous winter with her sister, who was four years younger. They were all that was left of their family; how their parents died is unknown. As a new hire, Becky earned just seven dollars per week, scarcely enough to support herself, let alone the two of them. They boarded in a cheap apartment on the Lower East Side. Becky still owed money on their steamship tickets.

In such a group, there would be nothing unusual about a young woman who, at eighteen, had already survived a murderous riot, traveled to America alone, mastered an occupation, and begun supporting the other eight members of her family back home. Such a person was almost typical.

R.F., 18 years old, dead, union member, boarded with uncle, sent
regular remittances to father and mother in Byalestock, Grodner Gub,
Russia. . . . Father earned a little money through teaching Hebrew, has
seven children ranging in age from 22 years old to seven, none of whom
earn much. R. sent 30 roubles a month in support to the family . . .
　　　　　　　　　　—from the relief committee report

Rosie Freedman was born in the spring of 1892 in the city of Bialystok, in the Grodno province of Russian-occupied Poland. Hers was a world half old and half new. Her father, like Clara Lemlich's, was a deeply religious man. He would have been found daily in one of Bialystok's numerous synagogues. His meager earnings came from the lessons he gave in Hebrew to neighborhood boys.

Bialystok was a thriving mill town in which 80 percent of the textile factories, 299 out of 372, were Jewish-owned, and 60 percent of the textile workers were Jews. Jews also worked as tailors, cobblers, wagon makers, cattle traders, blacksmiths, midwives, and butchers. But in the decade before Rosie's birth, generations of discrimination and humiliation of the Russian Jews had deepened into outright oppression. On March 13, 1881, Russian revolutionaries detonated a bomb that killed Czar Alexander II. This was a doubly devastating blow to the empire's roughly five million Jews. While the Russian monarchy had never been progressive, Alexander II was less crudely anti-Semitic than his predecessors were. The Jews not only lost a mild czar; they were also blamed for the attack. During the months after the assassination, Russian mobs burned Jewish homes, murdered residents, and looted businesses in more than thirty cities and towns. Some of these pogroms appeared to be sponsored by the police; in any event, the police did little to stop them. Not until late summer did government troops move to end the outbreak. For the next three years, the pogroms flared anew each spring, at Easter, when local priests reminded their flocks that the Jews killed Christ (just as they had killed the czar) and rumors circulated afresh that the matzo of Passover was seasoned with the blood of slain Christian children.

Along with the pogroms came severe restrictions on Jewish liberties. Access to higher education and professional jobs was cut off. The Russian heartland—including the capital, St. Petersburg, and the largest city, Moscow—was closed to Jews. Some were driven from the cities in chains. Approximately one million people were forced to move into the so-called Pale of Settlement, a stretch of land from Odessa in the south to the Baltic Sea in the north—386,000 square miles of land now in Poland, Lithuania, Belarus, and Moldova. Within the Pale, half a million Jewish peasants were forced off their land and into the already crowded cities and *shtetls*.

The first wave of emigration began immediately after the death of the czar and lasted about ten years, until a severe depression in the United States briefly slowed the flow. In New York City alone, this decade brought some two hundred thousand Eastern Europeans, including Max Blanck and Isaac Harris. Rosie Freedman's hometown of Bialystok saw at least a thousand residents uproot and depart in that first decade—headed for South America, Canada, and, especially, the United States: the *goldene medina*, as they said in Yiddish, the Golden Land.

And yet it was not easy to give up everything—even when "everything" was so harshly circumscribed. Most people tried to make a go of life in the Pale. In fact, Rosie's youth, around the turn of the century, was a politically and intellectually vibrant time in Bialystok and throughout the region, a period of "ferment and enlightenment . . . an upsurge of the Jewish masses to social awareness, revolt and self-education," according to Irving Howe. Despite the intense pressures of life under the czars—or perhaps because of those pressures—utopianism flourished. Thousands of young people joined the Bund, a socialist revolutionary movement. Others became anarchists. Others joined the fledgling Zionist movement. Bialystok, with its large numbers of textile workers, became a center of the labor movement. And the ferment was not only political; it was also religious and cultural. The faith of the fathers, practiced with intensity and discipline for generations, began to lose its grip. Orthodoxy struggled against a new era entranced by "freethinkers." One boy of the period later recalled that while the grandmothers of his town wore traditional wigs, their daughters and granddaughters no longer did: "The generation gap . . . was growing."

And so Rosie Freedman's childhood was shaped by tradition and also by upheaval, in a community threatened by the larger world. After her tenth birthday, those threats became terribly real, as the Pale was swept by a wave of violence far worse than the pogroms of the early 1880s.

By 1903 Russia's monarchy was decrepit, its peasantry destitute, its radicals inflamed. In the face of this crisis, the governing aristocracy stupidly chose to entrench. This besieged upper class saw radicalism as the root, not the product, of everything wrong with the empire. And the age-old anti-Semitism of Europe made it easy for them to blame radicalism on the Jews. "There is no revolutionary movement in Russia, there are only Jews, who are the true enemies of government," the Russian interior minister said. It was true that most Jews understandably wanted change, but they would have been happy with reforms well short of revolution. A leading historian of the period estimates that no more than one hundred thousand Jews were actually active in revolutionary groups—only about 2 percent or 3 percent of the Jewish population. However, the dangerously incompetent Czar Nicholas II encouraged his ministers to foment bigotry rather than to modernize government. As part of this effort, Russian leaders supported a sensational and reactionary anti-Semitic newspaper called *Bessarabets* in the southern Pale city of Kishinev.

Bessarabets was the only daily newspaper in the province of Bessarabia, so its influence in the region was enormous. Editor P. A. Kruschevan, who was also the provincial tax collector, poured out the most hateful fancies in its pages: no Christian child anywhere in Russia died, it seemed, without *Bessarabets* inventing a blood-eating Jewish murderer. "Death to the Jews!" was a typical headline.

During Passover 1903, a Christian girl employed by a Jewish family in Kishinev committed suicide. Kruschevan fed rumors that the death was a ritual murder to get blood for the matzo. At the same time, another (apparently unfounded) rumor spread among peasants in Bessarabia that the czar had personally ordered a pogrom in Kishinev. In this context, Easter Sunday arrived.

In the predawn gloom of the lamplit local churches, Christians heard the customary accounts of the supposed guilt of the Jews for the crucifixion of Jesus. They emerged from the services in a bloodlust. A mob of perhaps two thousand people began rioting through the Jewish precinct of the city; by some accounts, the number grew to nearly twenty thousand rioters before the pogrom was over. At least forty-five people were murdered. Some of them had nails driven into their skulls. Others were disemboweled, beheaded, crucified. Children were killed alongside their parents. A baby was used to break windows. Block after block of houses and shops was burned. For nearly two days, the police stood by. Along with the dead there were uncounted hundreds wounded and fifteen hundred buildings destroyed.

Kishinev shocked the Jews of Russia—and decent people around the world. One hundred fifty thousand New Yorkers marched up Fifth Avenue in protest. (The czar, however, sent an admiring letter to editor Kruschevan.) But it was only the beginning of a reign of terror. Later in 1903, the city of Gomel endured a pogrom as bloody as the Kishinev disaster—though in Gomel, the Jewish population staged a stirring self-defense. Smaller pogroms devastated villages throughout the Pale. After the czar's brief, disastrous war against Japan in 1904, blame for that defeat, too, fell on the Jews, and the pogroms intensified.

The failed war also galvanized the revolutionaries of Russia, who organized a powerful series of strikes across the country, eventually paralyzing most major cities. The strikers forced Czar Nicholas to negotiate, and reluctantly he agreed to create a parliament and to begin granting civil rights—even to Jews. This "October Manifesto" of 1905 provoked the most violent reaction of all by the Russian monarchists, who now drenched the Pale in blood. In November 1905 alone, there were more than six hundred pogroms—twenty per day—including a ghastly rampage through Odessa that left eight hundred people dead and five thousand wounded. Then the violence reached Bialystok.

* * *

It began on June 14, 1906. Rosie Freedman was fourteen years old.
As Christians marched through the center of the city in the annual
Corpus Christi parade, a bomb went off, killing a priest named Federov.
From a window overlooking the parade route, men fired revolvers.
Soldiers returned fire. Almost instantly, word ran through the crowd
that the attack was the work of "Jewish anarchists," but there was at
least as much reason to suspect the reactionary group known as the
Black Hundreds. This shadowy czarist movement was violent, con-
spiratorial, and above all anti-Semitic; its motto was "*Bei Zhidov!*"—
"Beat the Jews!" Rumors of a coming pogrom had been circulating
for more than a week in Bialystok. Proclamations issued from a government printing office had been distributed around town, calling for
the "extermination of the Jews." Afterward many concluded that the
bomb and the gunfire had been a ruse to incite the mob.

"After the bomb outrage the Christians attacked and began to mas-
sacre the Jews," the *New York Times* reported on Friday, June 15, 1906.
From the center of the city, a crowd of Jewish men, women, and children ran toward the railway station, apparently hoping to find soldiers
to protect them or to escape by train. The mob followed, and quickly
overran the station. "Three Jews were thrown from second-story windows of the station building."

Just then, a train full of passengers, some of them Jewish, pulled
into the yard. Men rampaged into the cars and dragged the Jews out,
"and many of them were murdered," the *Times* reported. From the station, the mob moved back into the city, to the main thoroughfares of
Jewish commerce—Alexandrov Street and Suraz Street—where the
rioters pulled owners from their stores and savagely beat them. As the
merchants lay wounded and dying, the mob pillaged the shops, taking
what they wanted, dumping the rest in the gutters, smashing the fixtures. Then came the fires.

As dusk approached, hundreds if not thousands of Jews fled into the
surrounding forests, "with mobs in pursuit." The violence in Bialystok
continued for three days while troops quartered in the city did nothing
to stop it. Indeed, many soldiers joined the pogrom, and in one case

troops opened fire on a group of Jews fleeing from the rioters. When the madness and blazes finally burned themselves out, two hundred people had been killed and seven hundred wounded in a city of fewer than ninety thousand. Bialystok was one of the most violent and destructive of all pogroms—worse even than the notorious Kishinev. The community of Rosie Freedman's childhood was decimated.

The pogroms of 1903–06 damaged even the resilient hopes of the Russian Jews. A historian of these atrocities, Shlomo Lambroza, summarized the destruction wrought in the years immediately after the October Manifesto: "The Jewish community was in shambles; over 3,100 Jews lost their lives, at least one-fourth of whom were women; the number of children left totally orphaned is estimated at 1,500; about 800 children lost one parent. In all, it was reported that 2,000 Jews were seriously injured, and more than 15,000 wounded. . . .

"The greatest destroyer of property was fire," Lambroza observed. "Many reports and letters described entire towns being destroyed by fire."

Rosie's uncle, Isaac Hine, had left for America in 1902, and his wife Bella joined him two years later. After the pogrom, the Freedman family decided to send Rosie—then nearly fifteen years old—to live with her aunt and uncle in New York. She joined the greatest surge of immigrants the United States had ever seen—one million arrivals in 1907. On some days, the new immigration center at Ellis Island processed as many as five thousand people.

If she followed the most common route, Rosie traveled with other emigrants westward across Poland, crossed illegally into Germany, and made her way to a seaport—Hamburg or Bremen, via Berlin. Another well-trodden path would have taken her southwest past Krakow, into the Austro-Hungarian empire and on to the port of Trieste on the Adriatic Sea. The men who arranged such trips charged fifty dollars or more, including the cost of passage on a steamer: close to half a year's wages for her entire family.

Rosie Freedman then descended into the bowels of a steamship for the Atlantic crossing, a week or more of pitching and rolling among vomiting strangers in cramped and dismal quarters, where the noise of the ship's screw was a perpetual groan. "Crowds everywhere, ill-smelling bunks, uninviting washrooms—this is steerage," one veteran wrote. "The odors of scattered orange peelings, tobacco, garlic, and disinfectants meeting but not blending. No lounge or chairs for comfort, and a continual babel of tongues. . . . The food, which is miserable, is dealt out of huge kettles into the dinner pails provided by the steamship company. When it is distributed, the stronger push and crowd. . . . On many ships, even drinking water is grudgingly given."

If she traveled on a modern ship, Rosie shared a room with eight or ten other women. On an older ship, she would have found herself thrown together with scores of people of all ages and both sexes, a fearful girl in a ship's belly crowded with men. A female investigator told a U.S. Senate committee in 1909 about the discomfort and menace that haunted a woman in steerage. "I lived in disorder and in surroundings that offended every sense," she said of her twelve-day voyage. "The vile language of the men, the screams of the women defending themselves, the crying of children, wretched because of their surroundings, irritated beyond endurance. . . . Everything was dirty, sticky, and disagreeable to the touch. Every impression was offensive." Crew members were especially outrageous, she reported, groping and grabbing young women whenever they passed, and loitering before breakfast to leer at the women trying to wash in cold seawater.

But there were other Russians to talk and sing with, and Rosie had access to the bracing air by climbing slippery, narrow stairs to the lowest deck. No doubt she passed some time trying to learn a few words of English to prepare for her coming ordeal with the immigration officials.

Although there is no perfect match for her name and age in the records of arriving passengers at the port of New York, a Rosa Friedmann, of about the right age, landed on February 23, 1907, aboard the steamer *Francesca* of the Austro-American Line. At Ellis Island, an immigrant's first experience of the Golden Land was noisy and intimidating. The vast redbrick arrivals hall was full of tired and bewildered people feeling lost and rubbery-legged as they tried to take in the long lines, the hurry-up-and-wait, the mixed air of hope and longing and fear. Immigrants were steered and herded this way and that through chutes formed of metal railings. Rosie had probably been warned along the way to fear the eye test at Ellis Island most of all—signs of infection meant instant deportation. So with every itch and blink she grew more anxious as she shuffled slowly toward the brief but crucial medical examination. A cough, which could signal tuberculosis, was often enough to get an immigrant pulled from the line and sent into quarantine in the island's dreary hospital.

As the line inched forward, the men and boys were separated from the women and girls. The doctors poked and prodded midsections, listened for the telltale rattle of the lungs and, most humiliating, peered at private parts for signs of venereal disease. And then, the immigrants were branded as if they were cattle, with chalk right on their clothing: *H* on the jacket lapel for heart disease, *SC* for lice or other scalp problems, *X* for insanity or dim-wittedness. Then into another room, another line, leading, eventually, to an impatient inspector.

Do you have any money?
Where will you live?
Are you an anarchist?
Do you have a job waiting?

An intrepid youth might think: Ah! I'll lie—I'll tell them I have a job waiting. Surely that was the right answer. But volunteers from the Hebrew Immigrant Aid Society worked around the clock at Ellis Island to help Eastern European Jews through the ordeal. HIAS counselors previewed the questions and gave advice on how best to answer them, so Rosie knew that the question about a job was a trick. People who claimed to have jobs waiting for them were immediately suspected of being illegal contract workers.

The barrage of questions was so brusque and hurried that it was easy to become confused. Stories are legion of immigrants having their names and ages forever altered by the careless mistake of a harried, half-listening inspector. Even the littlest children, barely two years old, were interrogated to determine if they were deaf or mute.

An immigrant who passed through Ellis Island in fewer than twenty-four hours was considered lucky. For many, the process took days—or, in the case of quarantined travelers, weeks. When it was finally over, someone like Rosie Freedman was hustled to the ferry for a short ride to the Battery, under the looming shadow of the Statue of Liberty. Pimps and sharpers and cons awaited the fresh crop of greenhorns when they landed. Rosie would have made a fine catch for a "white slaver" in the crowd, a seemingly friendly lady or gentleman who would offer to show her the way to her uncle's apartment—except that when they arrived where they were going, there would not be any uncle, just an ordeal of forced prostitution. A writer to the *Forward*'s popular advice column, the "Bintel Brief," described what happened to her under similar circumstances. A woman posing as a matchmaker "handed me over to bandits, and when I wanted to run away from them they locked me in a room without windows and beat me savagely. Time passed and I got used to the horrible life. . . . They used to send me out on the streets, but life had become meaningless for me anyway, and nothing mattered any more." When she became sick, the slavers dumped her at a public hospital.

At the ferry slip Rosie made it safely through the crowd and into the narrow streets that ran among the tall buildings, buildings that, as she traced them upward with her eye, rose eight, nine, ten, even fifty stories high.

She made her way to the tenement building at 77 East Fourth Street, just off the Bowery, where her aunt and uncle lived. The block between the Bowery and Second Avenue was lined with nearly identical six-story apartment houses, each twenty-five feet wide, broken up by a couple of Chinese laundries, a bakery, a small bowling alley, and the little Heiss beer brewery. Directly across the street from No. 77 was the Manhattan Lyceum, a complex of meeting rooms and a theater, where lectures and concerts and political gatherings were scheduled nearly every night of the week. In Rosie's new neighborhood alone lived more people than in all of Bialystok. At home, the streets were wide and fairly quiet; here, the streets were tight, paved, unnerving torrents of traffic.

But her culture shock was eased by much that was familiar. Rosie's new universe was, one resident later recalled, "a completely Jewish world. . . . The only Gentiles we knew were the janitor . . . the barber around the corner, and the policeman on the beat." The language of the street was her own tongue, Yiddish, expressive and slangy, full of color and emotion. The foods on the peddlers' carts and in the delicatessens were her own foods: meat stews, smoked and pickled fish, potato pancakes. South of her new home, near the foot of the Williamsburg Bridge, was a bustling community of her *landsmen*, fellow emigrants from Bialystok. In the former Willett Street Methodist Church was the grand, new Bialystoker Synagogue, a large, dark fieldstone edifice, where richly colored light poured through the stained-glass windows beneath a lofty ceiling. A single generation after those first thousand Bialystokers fled the Pale, they and those who followed had managed to put down impressive roots.

As she explored the city sidewalks, Rosie quickly learned to pick the veterans of four or five years in America from the mass of her fellow greenhorns. The veterans were the close-cropped and clean-shaven young men who rolled their eyes at the older generation in hats, beards, and even caftans disputing outside the countless storefront synagogues. The veterans were the young women boarding trains to Coney Island to sunbathe and flirt. The veterans were the rising shopkeepers who not only had their own businesses but also kept them open on the Sabbath. They were the ones with enough English to read Hearst's gaudy and thrilling *New York American* for its tales of lurid crimes and shenanigans among the elite. They were the flashy-dressed gangsters, the Arnold Rothsteins and the Beansy Rosenthals, who watched the way Tammany Hall had organized the city and learned carefully the lessons. Most of all, they were the ones unseen, because immigrants with experience typically graduated from the Lower East Side—to Brooklyn, to the Upper East and Upper West sides, to Harlem.

Yet, no matter how quickly the earlier immigrants moved on, there was never enough room for the arrivals. Families doubled up, took in relatives, and let space to boarders. There was no privacy in the tenements, and the buildings were almost never quiet, not just because of the crowding but because many tenements included at least one, and often several, workshops. Many mothers toiled long into the night, sewing buttons, linings, and cuffs on clothing; fashioning corset covers and tassels for dance cards; rolling cigarettes; tatting lace; stringing beads for moccasins and handbags; sorting human hair for wigs; picking the meat from tens of thousands of nuts; stitching collars; assembling brushes; making doll clothes. Children worked alongside their mothers. An investigation in 1911 found children as young as three picking nuts in tenement kitchens, and as young as four making brushes.

The building at 77 East Fourth Street was an example of a notorious and ubiquitous style of New York tenement, the so-called dumbbell design. In 1878, a trade magazine for engineers staged a competition to design the best tenement—in terms of "safety" and profitability—for New York's typical twenty-five by one hundred–foot lot. James E. Ware's winning concept covered virtually the entire lot, with small front windows opening on the street and rear windows opening in a tiny, enclosed yard. Each floor was sectioned into four apartments, two in the front of the building and two in the back. The largest rooms, the family rooms, had the outside windows, front and rear. A small airshaft was cut into the center of the building on each side—this narrowing at the middle gave the dumbbell its name. The smallest rooms, barely large enough for a bed, had windows opening into these shafts. Between the family rooms and the bedrooms were the kitchens, which had no direct ventilation. All four apartments opened from a narrow central stairway; on the landings were two toilets to serve everyone on the floor. This basic dumbbell design was extremely popular among developers, who threw up thousands of them during the following twenty years. A law passed in 1901 required more ventilation and a toilet in every apartment, but by then the East Side was fully built up with "old law" tenements.

Rosie Freedman's building was six stories high, a popular height for tenement apartments. More than six meant paying for the installation of an elevator; fewer than six seemed like a lost opportunity. When the census taker arrived at the building in the spring of 1910, he found seventeen households totaling eighty-two residents, all Russians and Hungarians. With an average of fourteen people per floor, it was a comparatively roomy place. Crowded buildings of the same size held twice as many people, 150 or more residents on six floors. The density of certain East Side neighborhoods reached a thousand residents per acre.

In many tenements, the airshafts were used as garbage chutes, leaving residents no choice but to nail half their windows shut to keep out the stench. But no matter how well tenements were cared for, the sheer crowding and density made them grim to behold. The reformer Jacob Riis concluded that the dumbbell apartment building was "the one hopeless form of tenement construction. It cannot be well ventilated, it cannot be well lighted; it is not safe in case of fire."

Arthur E. McFarlane was a young progressive writer and social worker living in a downtown settlement house. His experience of the East Side persuaded him to make a special study of arson and fire prevention because, as he put it, New York tenements were "the most dangerous human habitations in the world." McFarlane documented the curse of tenement fires. There were hundreds each year. The flames generally took hold in cellar wood bins and coal bins. They went up the stairway and through the airshafts, blocking escape. The only other way out was the fire escape—but on the East Side, those fire escapes that existed were generally boarded over to make play rooms and storage space.

In 1910, Rosie Freedman's tiny apartment was home to four other adults. Her uncle was a presser in a garment factory and her aunt kept house. They had two boarders: a greenhorn named Sam Grossberg, who worked making wigs, and Jacob Goldstein, a sewing machine operator in a skirt factory, who had arrived in America as a four-year-old boy. Both men were in their early twenties, a few years older than

Rosie, and single. This fact surely made the cramped conditions even more difficult. Assuming that her aunt and uncle shared the bedroom and the boarders bunked in the family room, Rosie would have slept, like many immigrant teenagers, on the kitchen table or on a pallet on the kitchen floor.

The sexual tensions of such living arrangements were a staple of Yiddish literature and drama. Letters to the "Bintel Brief" often recounted stories of wives and daughters seduced by their male boarders. "Neighbors began to whisper that my wife was carrying on an affair with this boarder," one man wrote. "She swore to me that it was a lie . . . but people did not stop talking, and as time went on I saw that my wife was a common liar and that it was all true."

At eighteen, Rosie Freedman was managing to put aside thirty rubles a month to send to Bialystok—about fifteen dollars, probably a week's pay during the busy seasons. Room and board was approximately that much again. She had to stretch her money to cover the long weeks of the year when the Triangle factory was idle and she earned nothing at all. Ultimately, she had, after subtracting rent and food and the money to Russia, no more than two dollars per week. Because she lived within walking distance of the factory, she saved a dime a day in trolley fares. Triangle workers who lived farther away had to weigh whether to pay the fares or walk to work in cheap shoes that wore out quickly, shoes that could easily cost fifty cents per week to replace. Two new skirts and a new jacket each year chewed up one-fourth of Freedman's disposable income, but she was lucky in that she could make her own waists. She lived near the center of the budding Yiddish Broadway, but a play at Boris Tomashevsky's theater, or David Kessler's, or the new Loew's cost thirty-five cents. The flickering motion pictures around the corner on Second Avenue lasted only a few minutes, but cost a nickel or a dime. Dances were generally a quarter.

The East Side of 1911 was unlike the urban ghettos of contemporary America in one crucial respect: There was always plenty to do. Rosie had no reason to spend more than the eating and sleeping hours in her apartment. Though she was strapped for money, she would not have felt constricted: the city was full of young people just like her. Two blocks away was the Cooper Union, with its constant programs of working-class edification. She had the Lyceum across the street and Beethoven Hall around the corner for concerts.

In the heart of the Lower East Side, not far from the Bialystoker Synagogue, was the Educational Alliance, a large orange brick building in the Greco-Romanesque style popular at the time. "A curious mixture of night school, settlement house, day-care center, gymnasium, and public forum," as Irving Howe put it, the Alliance was a gift from New York's highly assimilated German-Jewish citizens to their coarse greenhorn coreligionists. Having arrived two or three generations earlier, German Jews now owned banks, investment houses, department stores, and newspapers. They were embarrassed by the Eastern Europeans who seemed to call attention to themselves in every way, with their guttural speech, dramatic gestures, and traditional dress. So, in 1893, the Germans established the Educational Alliance to Americanize the newcomers. By the time of Rosie Freedman's arrival, the Alliance "bristled with activity," according to Howe. "There were morning classes for children needing preparation to enter public school; night classes for adults struggling with English; daytime classes for waiters, watchmen, and bakers who worked at night; classes in Yiddish and Hebrew; classes in cooking and sewing; classes in Greek and Roman history . . . classes in music and art . . . low-cost lessons in violin, piano, and mandolin . . . birthday celebrations of great figures ranging from Aristotle to Longfellow . . . a Legal Aid Bureau to aid deserted wives; endless theatrical performances . . ."

But the Alliance was primarily for boys and young men. If Rosie managed to take a course or two, it was only after a long day at work. It was her lot in life to work—even as young men her age were encouraged to finish high school and even to enter City College, the Harvard of immigrant Jews.

This dual standard for boys and girls created a tension widely felt by East Side women. "I ask you," one wrote to the "Bintel Brief," "whether a married woman has the right to go to school two nights a

week." Female immigrants lived in a world passionate for advancement, for education, for ideas, and for improvement. But they also
suffered under the limitations of the time and the place. Rosie
Freedman's New York years were a period of rebellions and self-asser-
tion against this ingrained sexism, as the Uprising of the Twenty
Thousand vividly demonstrated. And so, though she had no hope of a
high school education, Rosie likely attended some of the lectures that
were a constant feature of the East Side, and afterward joined others
from the audience at one of the countless cafés where politics and literature were endlessly discussed.

On oppressive summer days when there was no work at the factory,
Rosie walked over to the river in search of a breeze. Public piers along
the water were equipped with benches where she could sit and watch
the spectacle of New York promenade past. As the sun dropped, a brass
band started playing at the end of the pier, Strauss waltzes and show
tunes and Sousa marches. A few bold boys leaped naked into the filthy
water and splashed around until a policeman came near. "Cheese it,
cops!" the ringleader would cry, and they would heave themselves out,
scoop up their clothes, and go dashing down the pier dripping and
laughing.

On days off—Sunday in the busy seasons, and nearly every day in
the slack times—the young people of the East Side flocked to the
dance halls. Everyone in those days was crazy for dancing. One of the
biggest shows on Broadway in the winter and spring of 1911 was a
musical comedy called *Madame Sherry*, set in a dance academy run by
a disciple of the scandalous and exotic modern dancer Isadora Duncan.
Night after night inside the American Musical Theater, sold-out
houses marveled at the footwork of the cast—especially in the show-
stopping "Apache Rag" sequence—and came away humming the
show's hit song, a lilting little polka devoted to the expressive power
of dance:

> *Ev'ry little movement has a meaning all its own.*
> *Ev'ry thought and feeling by some posture can be shown.*
> *And ev'ry love thought that comes a-stealing o'er your being,*

Must be revealing all its sweetness
In some appealing little gesture all its own.

Nowhere was the dance fad more intense than in Rosie's neighbor-hood. "Some of those east siders certainly can dance," the *World* re-ported as part of an investigation into the dance hall phenomenon. "The ease, the grace, the dash of their style would shame many of the most fashionable dancers of Fifth Avenue. It is their sole pleasure and amusement, and often every evening of the week is devoted to it." The reformer Lillian Wald fretted about the sensuality of the dance halls: "An entirely innocent and natural desire for recreation afforded continual opportunity for the overstimulation of the senses and for dangerous exploitation."

Recreation of any kind, however, was an adjunct to Rosie's life. The center, the part that consumed most of her waking hours, was past the Bowery and beyond the elevated tracks. When she crossed Broad-way, to her right she could see the graceful Gothic spire of Grace Episcopal Church standing sentinel on downtown. From there it was two short blocks to Washington Place and Greene Street, where she waited among her colleagues to be lifted up to the ninth floor.

It was midday now. Saturday was the short day of the week—9 A.M. to 4:45 P.M., with forty-five minutes for lunch. Seven hours, which, when added to five nine-hour days, made fifty-two hours per week. Saturday was also payday. A generation earlier in the garment district, Saturday was known primarily as the Sabbath, but that was not mod-ern life. No more than a handful of the Triangle's Jewish workers missed a day's pay to observe the Sabbath.

Those faces seen earlier on Greene Street were now visible over the sewing machines stretching in rows south to north across the ninth floor—278 machines in all, some Singers, some Willcox and Gibbs. The machines were installed on each side of eight long tables. The opera-tors sat facing each other, with a trough between them for finished work. There were eighteen machines on Table One, thirty-four on Table Two, forty on Table Three, thirty-six on Table Four, forty on

Table Five, thirty-eight on Table Six, thirty-four on Table Seven, and thirty-eight on Table Eight. The space between the tables ranged from about five feet to seven feet. Isaac Harris personally designed this irregular layout, to accommodate structural pillars positioned through the loft.

To run their machines, the operators pressed a floor pedal that drew power from a drive shaft running beneath each table. Despite the appearance of so many nearly identical machines, the work was minutely differentiated. In a shirtwaist factory, there were body makers who spent their days stitching only the torsos of blouses. There were sleeve makers, and sleeve setters, who attached the sleeves to the bodies, and cuff setters, who added the cuffs. There were yoke setters and collar makers and tuckers. There were closers, hemmers, joiners, finishers, and pressers. There were buttonhole makers and button sewers. This particular season, lacy and embroidered waists were fashionable, so there were lace runners and embroidery trimmers. Each of these jobs fit somewhere on a subtle ladder of skills—from the lowly trainee clipping stray threads to the gifted sample maker crafting the garments that salesmen showed to department store buyers. Each job paid accordingly.

The busy season was about six weeks old and nearing its end. It had not been a great success. Fashion editors in Paris and New York had recently renewed their campaign to replace the waist with the one-piece dress; to be on the safe side, the Triangle began making dresses. Keeping the shirtwaist fresh and popular had become a constant battle. The decorated waists of 1911 were teasingly sheer, made of a light cotton fabric known as "lawn," from the French word *lingerie.* One recent season the dominant feature of shirtwaists had been the overlarge "mutton-leg" sleeve. Another year it was the elaborately pleated, draped, and tucked "pigeon-front." Another year the style had been decidedly plain and masculine.

Each season began for the Triangle when Isaac Harris designed or adapted a handful of waists to constitute the new product line. The range of possibilities was always large—waists in New York shops ranged from simple garments selling for less than a dollar to hand-embroidered silk blouses at more than a hundred dollars. The Triangle specialized in moderately priced garments that retailed for three dollars or so.

Like many ready-to-wear designers, Harris was more copyist than creator. His talent lay in discerning how to make a desirable blouse in the quickest and least wasteful way. Sewing the initial waists required great skill, but the best seamstresses never lost sight of the need to come up with an efficient, easily replicated design. When Harris's design was finally rendered as an actual garment, the finished waist was carefully snipped apart and the pieces were used to trace patterns on thin paper. The design was adjusted to create patterns for larger and smaller sizes. The patterns were then copied, and each set of patterns was edged in metal for durability.

Once the patterns were finished, everything fell to the cutters. They were confident, swaggering men, the divas of the garment district. They hung their coats on pegs beside their big custom-built tables on the eighth floor. When the cutters arrived at work, on each table lay stretched more than a hundred layers of lawn, separated by sheets of tissue paper. The tables had been prepared at the end of the previous day by their assistants. (Each cutter had multiple assistants.) Patterns dangled from wires over the tables. The cutters took down pattern pieces and fiddled with them like a puzzle until all the pieces fit into the smallest possible stretch of fabric. A wasted inch multiplied by a hundred layers was almost three wasted yards of fabric, and three wasted yards for every hundred waists added up to 360 wasted yards of fabric per week. The cutter's art—of placing the patterns with maximum efficiency and whisking their distinctive knives like industrial cavaliers—was the bedrock of the garment industry. As a result, cutters were well paid and well treated.

Like most factories, the Triangle Waist Company had a no-smoking policy—it was posted on every floor of the workshop in English, Italian, and Yiddish. But the cutters behaved as if they were exempt, and no one called them on it. Cutters smoked in the stairways and even on the shop floor, hunching over to take a drag and exhaling through the lapels of their jackets. The butts sometimes went into the bins under the cutting tables, which were piled with scraps of highly flammable lawn and tissue paper. Even the most efficient cutters produced hundreds of pounds of scraps each week.

About 60 percent of the Triangle workers, along with management and, of course, the owners, were Eastern European Jews. Most of the rest came from Italy, part of a migration even larger than the Jewish exodus. A few who made this trip were skilled tradesmen or political refugees from the north of Italy. But most, by far, were penniless peasants from the rural south. Italian immigration to the United States in the thirty years before 1911 averaged 1.2 million people per decade; of these, five-sixths were unskilled rural laborers.

They were fleeing an environmental disaster. The end of feudalism and of the Papal States in the nineteenth century put millions of acres of Italian land in private hands. Nearly every new owner made the same decision: to cut down the trees, hoping to sell the lumber and expand the fields. The result was massive soil erosion along the hillsides of once beautiful Southern provinces like Calabria, Basilicata, Apulia, and Campania. Topsoil washed into the rivers, ruining the farm economy. When the silted rivers flooded in the wet winter months, they created low stagnant pools and swamps, which in turn bred mosquitoes, which produced epidemics of malaria. Without trees to hold the topsoil, what had been a tenuously balanced ecology became a strange and deadly combination of tropical disease and desertlike aridity. Conditions were worst on the island of Sicily, where "within sight of the blue sea the grass . . . is a lifeless brown and the road a powder of white. . . . In many regions it is necessary to go long distances to procure drinking water," as one early writer on Italian immigration explained.

The resulting migration, according to an early expert, Robert F. Foerster, "has been well-nigh expulsion; it has been exodus, in the sense of depopulation." Between 1900 and 1910 more than two million Italians entered the United States. And even though roughly eight hundred thousand returned to Italy in the same period, by the end of the decade there were more Italians living in the state of New York than there had been in the entire country ten years earlier.

This migration began as a movement of men. Husbands or sons of southern Italian families set out for America, sometimes as virtually indentured workers under the notorious *padrone* system. There was nothing for them in Italy, but there was work, and plenty of it, in the United States. Over time, most of the Italians brought their families. Many wives and daughters entered the garment factories. Michela Marciano was one.

M.M., 20 years old, married four months, union member, earned $12.00 a week, lived with husband, J.C., and supported same . . . Also sent money to old parents, A.M. and T.S. at Striano, Italy. M. helped brother through art school. . . . [H]aving ascertained, with the help of the Italian Consul, that M. had really been sending remittances to needy parents in Italy, sent $200.00, through Italian consul, to aforesaid A.M. and T.S.

—from the relief committee report

She came from Striano, a tiny village about six miles east of Mount Vesuvius. On the other side of the volcano, about twenty miles as the birds flew, was Naples. Striano lay among rolling hills, a small cluster of houses around a small square, where the well was. The Vesuvius region had been spared much of the damage of Italy's deforestation, and life in Striano was bucolic and changeless. Rain came regularly off the Bay of Naples, forming thunderclouds over the steel-gray pyramid of the volcano, to fall gently on the farmlands of the western Campania. Long lines of white grapes corrugated the countryside, ribbing the hills like sweaters, and in the autumn these were pressed and fermented into a wine called Lachryma Christi—"tears of Christ." The calendar of saints' days gave an order to the slow passage of time. This was a place and a culture in which people could grow up without ever visiting even nearby villages. The people of Striano had little reason to join the emigrant tide—until 1906.

In May 1905, an American scientist named Frank Perret, living on Vesuvius, was watching the mountain near sunset. Suddenly he saw "a cloud of white vapor . . . shoot horizontally from the side of the cone," he wrote. "In a few moments there appeared through the vapors the red glow of lava, which later, as the cloud lifted, was seen to be descending the cone in a brilliant stream of fire." Over the next eleven months, the residents of the region witnessed various spittings and gurglings from the volcano—but nothing more than they had become accustomed to, off and on, over the centuries. Of course they knew the harrowing story of Pompeii, the ancient town literally entombed by Vesuvius in 79 A.D. But nothing comparable had happened in hundreds of years, and so they thought they knew the limits of the menace.

Then, on April 5, 1906, a horrible, dazzling eruption began. A river of lava poured from Vesuvius and ran swiftly south to bury the village of Bosco Trecase. Farther up the mountain, boulders weighing a ton or more were thrown into the sky like spitwads. "The inhabitants of the villages in the vicinity of Mount Vesuvius are in a condition of panic," the *Times* reported. "Many homes have been abandoned for the open air, although there has been a thick fog all day and the atmosphere has been dense with volcanic ashes and the fumes of subterranean fires."

Michela Marciano was a teenager, and likely she had heard stories of a ferocious eruption forty years earlier, when Striano went nearly unscathed thanks to favorable winds. Now she and the other villagers packed into church to pray for another deliverance. As they beseeched the Virgin Mary, the earth shook under them and the mountain resounded with deep, terrifying explosions. For a day, their prayers seemed to be answered. Once again, the wind took the ashes away from Michela's village and toward Naples, where residents charged through the streets crying: "The Madonna has forsaken us! The end of the world has come!"

The very air was tingly with electrical charges and snapped blindingly with lightning, while the underground artillery continued firing. Large, red-hot stones blown three thousand feet into the air returned to smash the railroad tracks along the flank of the mountain. As the people of Striano watched helplessly, the wind swung around and sent the ash plume toward them.

In San Giuseppe Vesuviano, four miles from Striano, falling embers seeded the town with fire. Ashes began to pile up, until the load was

so heavy on the rooftops that building after building collapsed. The
residents fled to church, where nearly fifty people were killed when
the roof fell in. Thirty-seven more died, in that single town, in the
debris of their houses. This was, the *Times* pronounced, the worst eruption of Vesuvius in nearly two thousand years.

For a week, ashes fell across a wedge of countryside centered over
Striano. Villages closer to the cone got the worst of it. In the immediate vicinity of San Giuseppe, some two hundred people ultimately
perished. By the fourth day of the eruption, the death toll for the region was estimated at five hundred and climbing. But things were
scarcely better in Striano, and Michela, with her aging parents, probably joined the ragged, dust-covered multitude slogging toward Naples
for relief. One hundred fifty thousand people trudged through drifts
of ash up to their knees, in places up to their chests. The whole world
was gray—until the rain came, and then it became "an immense lake
of chocolate colored mud," the *Times* correspondent wrote. "Crowds
of women thereupon attacked the churches, pulled down the doors
and took possession of the pictures and statues of the saints, which
they carried about as a protection against death."

VESUVIUS DISTRICT IS A VAST DESERT, the *Times* headline declared
after a week of disaster. "One cannot exaggerate the suffering inflicted,"
the paper's correspondent cabled. Finally, the ash in the air lightened
to a scrim, and the damage could be surveyed. Two of the largest villages upwind from Striano—Ottaviano and San Giuseppe—had been
left "indescribably wretched." The city of Cabonara di Nola, a bit to the
north of Striano and equidistant from the crater, had "suffered severely."
Striano was too small to merit its own report, but everything Michela
had known—the clustered houses, the surrounding fields and vineyards,
the church, the olive and orange trees—everything was shrouded, buried, and gray. Someday the ash would become richly fertile soil, but that
day must have seemed impossibly far off to a teenaged girl.

Meanwhile, the volcano continued to rumble. As late as May 30—
just two weeks before the pogrom in Bialystok—the pimple-dome in
the Vesuvius crater collapsed, sending smoke hundreds of feet into
the air and briefly blocking the sun.

*   *   *

After the eruption, Michela "Mechi" Marciano left her parents amid the sulfurous ash and sailed by herself, perhaps from Naples, to New York City. Her passage in steerage was much like the trip taken by Rosie Freedman. She, too, entered the factories and began sending money home to her parents. Late in 1910, Michela married a young man with whom she set up house at 272 Bleecker Street.

Like Rosie Freedman, Michela found much that was familiar in her new life. Bleecker Street was the core of Italian Greenwich Village. Her parish, which met in an old African-American Baptist church, was dedicated to Our Lady of Pompeii. She could find good bread, oil, and cheese in the neighborhood shops.

Every morning, she had an easy walk through the narrow Village streets, across Sixth Avenue just below the Jefferson Market court, and into Washington Square. She passed the upthrust campanile of the orange brick Judson Memorial Church, and the fresh white arch dedicated to George Washington. Old men played bocci and, as she neared the Triangle factory, there was a statue of Garibaldi, Italy's pivotal modern leader.

If it was hard for Rosie Freedman and her Jewish counterparts to get an education, for Michela and the other Italian women it was almost impossible. "The [Italian] immigrant does not ask that his wife be his mental companion, or that she know much of the outside world," wrote Philip Rose, author of *The Italians in America*. "She, and perhaps he, marry young, her family duties are numerous, and, not infrequently, she dies, worn out by work or child-bearing, just when the older children need her guidance most. . . . She certainly is not [her children's] intellectual companion and commonly she is illiterate . . ."

As the number of young Italian immigrant women expanded after the turn of the century, some of them went to night school, where they learned to read and to speak some English. Once they were married—and certainly once children arrived—they experienced intense pressure to return to the traditional patterns of womanhood. An Italian woman was supposed to defer to her husband and even to her brothers, and to indulge the old superstitions—especially concerning the awesome powers of the Evil Eye.

Michela apparently tested these boundaries. What little is knowable about her home life does not appear entirely conventional. She worked while her husband remained at home. She brought in the money. She even joined the union. These choices placed her over a sewing machine on the ninth floor of the Triangle, as the sun angled slowly down the Washington Place windows.

One Triangle employee remembered, years later, how much "fun" it was to work in the Asch Building shop. Pauline Pepe told an interviewer, "My mother didn't want me to go to work. But my friend says, 'Come on, we have a good time.' All young girls was there— and girls to be married, engaged and everything. So I thought I'd take a chance." Pepe remembered walking through Greenwich Village along West Fourth Street, talking and laughing with coworkers who were, like her, young Italian immigrants. "We used to have a lot of fun," she repeated.

Many of the available jobs in those days were physically exhausting or numbingly tedious. Thousands of women in American cities worked in commercial laundries, cleaning restaurant linens, hospital bedding, and the clothing of the well-to-do. There were long hours in hot, wet basement rooms, shaking, pounding, mangling, folding, pressing with heavy irons. A team of investigators, progressive social scientists, spent much of 1909 working in a series of such places and determined that "this, then, is the situation in general for women workers in the commercial laundries. With respect to sanitation, the heat is excessive . . . Many of the rooms are full of steam. Some of the laundries have insanitary toilet- and cloak-rooms. . . . A twelve- to fourteen-hour working day is not infrequent. In a few places . . . the working day runs up on occasions to seventeen hours. Almost all the laundry work is done standing. Wages for the majority of the workers are low."

They continued: "With respect to the danger of injury, in a large proportion of places there is unguarded or inadequately guarded machinery." A veteran washerwoman was likely to have at least a few crushed or missing fingers.

Sewing, by contrast, was fairly safe, it seemed, and it was work a person could do sitting down. Many women, especially in the busy holiday season, found employment in the bustling department stores, where they were forbidden to sit when customers were on the premises. During the Christmas rush, a store clerk could easily spend more than fourteen hours a day on her feet, from 8 A.M. to almost midnight, with only forty-five minutes for lunch and half an hour at suppertime (and no overtime pay). Because clerks were notoriously low paid, many of them had no choice but to hike to and from work in worn shoes. At mealtime, these women were known to forgo eating in favor of soaking their feet. The only strains in a garment factory were on the eyes and concentration.

Another common employment for women was housework. With immigration so common, the price of labor was fairly cheap, and even middle-class families could afford household help. But many working women looked down on domestic labor, or preferred the wider social milieu of a factory full of people their own age. At a shop like the Triangle, there was always plenty of company. All sorts of working women sewed, from poor immigrant girls to young wives to single daughters of the middle class to widows.

More than a thousand blouses had taken shape in the seven working hours of March 25, one stitch at a time. The freshly cut pieces went in bales to the foremen, who distributed them to the wicker baskets on the floor by each operator's feet. Runners and foremen scurried back and forth, up and down the stairs, hunting for the pieces they needed to keep each part of the assembly line busy. The operators fed the pieces through their humming, stuttering machines, and no matter how quickly the foremen cleared away the finished work, the tables always seemed to be heaped with garments. Piece by piece the blouses emerged, with each completed step of the process noted in a bookkeeper's ledger.

Near closing time, the scene inside the Triangle was just short of frenzy. It was the time of day when a sleeve-setting foreman would discover that he had three dozen bodices and only three dozen sleeves, and go dashing off in search of three dozen more; when shipping clerks would rush onto the floor to badger the foremen for another five dozen to complete a rush order. Everyone was hurrying to squeeze a few more garments through the assembly line. It was the time of day when garments began to pile up at the balky buttonhole machine, which was always breaking down, and on the examining tables in the back corner of the ninth floor, next to the windows that looked into a gloomy airshaft. There, eagle-eyed women appraised the work, occasionally pulling a measuring tape tight to assure that the sizes were precisely right.

A little after 4:30 P.M., Mary Laventhal, the pretty and popular ninth-floor bookkeeper, slipped down to the eighth floor for a bundle of cuffs so that a few more waists could be finished before closing time. She spoke briefly to a young admirer, and then headed back up the stairs. She and foreman Anna Gullo distributed the weekly pay envelopes. A moment before the closing bell, operators began moving from their seats, hoping to beat the crowd. Then, at 4:45, Gullo rang the bell, and the power cut off abruptly, silencing the machines. The sound of wooden chairs on the wooden floor was a symphony of creaks and squeaks.

The machines stopped with half-finished work piled around the shop—in the wicker workbaskets, in the troughs, on the examining tables—and finished bundles uncollected by the shipping clerks. It would all keep until Monday.

Workers began making their way up the aisles between the sewing machine tables. Then, talking and laughing, they made for the dressing rooms along the west wall of the factory. It was spring and many of them had new clothes, new hats, new fiancés. They were headed home for dinner, or to a dance, or to a picture show. Years later, a worker recalled that Rose Glantz struck up the popular tune:

Ev'ry little movement has a meaning all its own . . .

Several of her seatmates chimed in.

Ev'ry thought and feeling by some posture can be shown . . .

Someone noticed a muffled noise, much like screaming.

And outside the windows: smoke.

Then . . . *fire.*

5

INFERNO

D inah Lipschitz had a head for numbers. Morning to evening, six
days a week, from her little desk in the back corner of the factory, she tracked every cog of the machine like a human computer.
When sewing machine operators finished stitching a bundle of sleeves,
bodices, cuffs, or buttonholes, the pile went to Dinah's station. She
counted the work quickly, calibrated the pay rate, multiplied the factors, and tallied the credits in her ledger. It was an exceptionally large
volume of data to keep track of: There were about 150 operators on
the eighth floor, assembling pieces for ten thousand to twelve thousand shirtwaists per week. But she did not make many mistakes. Now,
however, right at closing time on March 25, Dinah Lipschitz experienced a data malfunction. A new employee, two days on the job, stood
before her eager to be paid—and Dinah did not know what her base
rate should be.

So she called out to the factory manager, Samuel Bernstein, who also
happened to be her cousin. Management of the Triangle was a family
affair. Samuel Bernstein was the brother of Max Blanck's wife, Bertha—
and thus a cousin of Bella Harris, Isaac's wife. Bernstein was one of the
earliest employees of the Triangle factory, dating back to the days when

the shop was still on Wooster Street. For many years he managed the entire factory, until it became too large for one man. Today he ran the eighth and ninth floors—the production plant—while Louis Alter, an older cousin, supervised the pressing, packing, and shipping departments on the tenth. Alter's daughter, Mary, typed the bills and helped out with the switchboard. Bernstein's brother and his elderly uncle operated sewing machines on the ninth floor.

Samuel Bernstein sized up the new worker and "made a price" for her, as he liked to say: fourteen dollars for a week's work. (This was Bernstein's recollection. The rate seems exaggerated, but it's possible that the worker had experience from another shop.) "She was perfectly satisfied," the manager later said. "And then when she walked away . . . I heard a cry."

Isaac Harris's sister, Eva, was running toward him shouting, "Fire! There is a fire, Mr. Bernstein!" This was not the first time he had heard those words at the Triangle. He could remember at least three small fires during working hours—always doused quickly, using the red fire pails stationed around the factory and kept full of water. But when Bernstein spun toward Eva Harris, he saw something much worse than on the previous occasions. At the cutting table closest to the Greene Street windows, in the northeastern corner of the shop, there was "a big blaze and some smoke."

The Asch Building occupied the northwest corner of Washington Place and Greene Street, but there was no entrance where the two streets met. Instead, the building thrust itself at the intersection like the prow of an ocean liner. The two entrances were halfway along each block. Ninety feet west of the corner on Washington Place, toward Washington Square, was the formal entrance. This door led to a stairway and two small passenger elevators. And there was a service entrance about ninety feet north of the corner on Greene Street, with another stairway and two larger freight elevators. A person entering the Triangle factory floor from the Washington Place side could look diagonally across the big square room and see the Greene Street exit at the opposite corner. Two long lines of windows marched from the doorways to meet in the third corner, overlooking the intersection. In the fourth corner, the rear corner of the room, a few windows looked into a grim little areaway—basically a large airshaft—where city officials in 1900 had allowed developer Joseph J. Asch to hang a little fire escape in place of the required third stairway when he erected the building.

The eighth floor was basically open space, apart from an enclosed dressing room and toilets along the western wall. There were seven long wooden cutting tables, each forty inches high, with boards surrounding the legs of each table to create a large bin underneath. Between the top of the bin and the surface of the table was about ten inches of open space. This design innovation, boxing off the space under the tables, allowed the cutters to sweep their scraps directly into a container that was always handy, no matter where they might be working around the tables. Five of these cutting tables ran parallel to Greene Street, filling about half the room. Two more cutting tables, somewhat shorter, ran along the north side of the eighth floor, in front of the windows leading to the fire escape. Dinah Lipschitz had her desk between those tables and the dressing room on the western wall. The remaining space on the floor was filled by rows of sewing machines running from south to north, connected to a power plant under the Washington Place windows.

Rank upon rank of parallel tables—half of them cutting tables, half sewing machine tables—filled a large open space between two widely separated exits. Way in the gloomy back, two more tables ran perpendicular to the rest and obstructed the path to a little fire escape.

The cutting table closest to the Greene Street windows belonged to Isidore Abramowitz. At closing time, his assistants had just finished stretching 120 layers of lawn and tissue paper across the tabletop in preparation for Monday morning. Beneath the table, in the wooden bin, were several hundred pounds of scraps, the leftovers from thousands and thousands of waists that had been cut since the last time the bins had been emptied. Dangling from a wire over the table were tissue-paper patterns, edged in steel. Fabric, paper, wooden tables: The steel trim was the only thing in the vicinity that was not highly flammable.

Abramowitz was taking his coat and hat from a nearby peg when he noticed the fire in his scrap bin. Perhaps the cutter had been sneaking a smoke while his assistants prepared the table. Or maybe it was another cutter—they were a close-knit group and liked to stand around talking together. Or maybe it was a cutter's assistant. At any rate, the fire marshal would later conclude that someone tossed a match or cigarette butt into Abramowitz's scrap bin before it was completely extinguished.

Cotton is even more flammable than paper, explosively so. Those airy scraps of sheer fabric and tissue paper, loosely heaped and full of oxygen, amounted to a virtual firebomb. Just above the peg where Abramowitz kept his coat was a ledge with three red fire pails on it. The cutter grabbed one and dumped it on the little flame, but this did no good. The fire grew geometrically in the space of a few seconds. Other cutters grabbed pails and splashed in vain. And now Samuel Bernstein, the manager, came hurrying across the room, calling out for still more pails of water.

As Bernstein ran, he passed a crowd of workers lined up at a thin wooden partition that screened the Greene Street exit from the main factory floor. The partition was designed in such a way that only one employee could pass through at a time. Workers were required to show their handbags to a night watchman as they left. This was to prevent theft of lace or fabric or waists.

Just beyond the partition, a young freight elevator operator named Frank was sitting with his doors open, waiting for his first load of off-duty workers. When he heard Bernstein's cry, he sprang from the elevator, dunked a fire pail into a water tank near the factory entrance, pushed his way inside the room, and handed the pail to Bernstein. In that moment, the fire seemed to leap. Bernstein sensed that the March wind, blustering down Greene Street, up the elevator shaft and through the open doors, was driving and feeding the blaze.

About 180 people had worked that day on the eighth floor, mostly sewing machine operators, but also cutters and supervisors and machinists. The rushing, the shouting, and the leaping flames sent panic ripping through them. Those clustered at the Greene Street partition stampeded into the small opening, pushing and shouting and wrestling toward the stairway. Behind them, others in the factory saw this pileup and ran toward the opposite corner of the room, where they bottle-necked at the Washington Place elevators and at the door to the Washington Place stairs. Still others began rushing toward the fire escape outside the rear windows, swarming over and around the cutting tables that stood in their way. The first ones to reach the windows flung them open and crawled onto the narrow balcony.

Amid the screams and the rushing, Dinah Lipschitz worked feverishly to alert the executives upstairs on the tenth floor. She thought first of a new contraption on her desk called a telautograph, a very early and failed cousin of the fax machine. The device linked two pens standing over two pads of paper. When the operator moved one pen, electrical impulses caused the other pen to duplicate the movements. So a message scrawled on one pad would appear, simultaneously, on the other. But the device required rigging the wires one way to send a message and another to receive one. Nobody in the factory was adept at using the machine. Why Lipschitz preferred it to the telephone, which was also sitting right there, is a mystery. But she did. She pressed a button that sounded a buzzer upstairs, signaling that a telautograph message was on its way. Then, using the pen on her desk, she scrawled "FIRE!"

Two floors up, Mary Alter was busy typing bills. She was also minding the switchboard for Edna Barry, the regular Triangle telephone operator, who was out sick. Alter heard the telautograph signal and watched the pen on her end. But the pen never budged. Alter thought nothing of it; she simply assumed that workers downstairs were playing with the gizmo as they passed the bookkeeper's desk—common enough around closing time. She went back to her typing.

For two endless minutes or more, Lipschitz waited desperately for a response to her message. Finally, she gave up and grabbed the phone. It rang immediately at the tenth-floor switchboard.

Mary Alter went right on typing. She was determined to finish the bill she was working on; she kept the totals in her head and did not want to lose her place. By the time Alter finally answered, Lipschitz was frantic, and for a moment Alter could not imagine what she was trying to say. Dinah was screaming. Everyone was screaming. Then she picked out the word "fire!"

Mary Alter remained on the line just long enough for Lipschitz to tell her to alert Max Blanck. Then she dropped the telephone. Two floors down, Lipschitz was left hanging—she couldn't be certain that the alarm had registered. Far more importantly, she couldn't warn the ninth floor. The way the Triangle's phone system was rigged, all calls had to go through the switchboard. A message from eight to nine had to be connected by the switchboard operator on the tenth floor—and she had simply vanished.

Down from the tenth floor and into the burning room came a young shipping clerk named Louis Senderman, struggling against the mass of workers swarming through the Greene Street door. "Louis!" Samuel Bernstein shouted when he saw him, "get me the hose as quick as you can!" In each stairwell, on each floor, there was a fire hose neatly folded into an iron bracket at about eye level, with a valve beside it to activate the flow of water from a tank on the roof. Senderman worked his way back to the Greene Street stairs. A cutter named Joe Levitz went with him. As Levitz dragged the hose to Bernstein, Senderman turned the valve.

Nothing happened.

"Is it open wide?" the manager shouted. Senderman tried again. "But it didn't work," Bernstein recalled later. "No pressure, no water." He struggled with the nozzle. "I turn it one way and then the other and . . . it don't work."

Another young man, a new buttonhole machinist named Meyer Utal, ran for the hose on the ninth floor. He pulled it down to Bernstein, but the result was the same. "Where is the water? Where is the water?" the manager cried as he worked the nozzle.

"There is no pressure, nothing coming," Utal yelled back.

From the bin under the first table, flames licked up to feed on the many layers of flimsy cotton and tissue paper stretched across the surface. Bernstein grabbed more pails and climbed onto the next table, hoping to get a better angle to drown the flames. He was a small, stocky man, capable on a normal day of both tyranny and tenderness in the space of a few steps across the factory floor. But now, his colleagues saw, he did not lack courage. Yet his efforts were hopeless. "The fire was running away from me," he realized.

"The line of hanging patterns began to burn," cutter Max Rothen later told author Leon Stein. "They began to fall on the layers of thin goods underneath them. Every time another piece dropped, light scraps of burning fabric began to fly around the room. They came down on the other tables and they fell on the machines. Then the line broke and the whole string of burning patterns fell down."

Bernstein felt Meyer Utal tugging at his hand. He turned to look, and saw that "the boy was burning," the manager later said. "He ran away from me. . . . That boy was lost in the fire." Better than anyone else in the room, Bernstein now realized the astounding velocity with which the fire was growing. The bins under the remaining cutting tables each represented a new firebomb. Burning wisps of cotton and tissue paper swirled around the room, riding the fluky, churning winds that gusted from various directions: up through the elevator shafts, in through the windows, and pulsing from the convection of the flames themselves. Wherever these wispy torches touched down, they seeded fire. Fire floated into the half-full wicker baskets along the aisles. Fire floated onto the bales of half-finished blouses. Fire floated into the troughs, littered with lawn, which ran down the centers of the sewing tables. Fire floated into the coats hanging on pegs, and onto the bolts of cloth and rolls of paper. Samuel Bernstein scanned the room, sized up the evacuation, and concluded that the eighth-floor workers had only moments remaining in which to escape.

And yet, to his amazement, some of them were still moving toward the dressing room for their coats and hats. It's spring, he thought, and they've got new clothes. Bernstein jumped down from the second cutting table and began herding the workers past the flank of the fire through the Greene Street door. "For God's sake, get out of here as quick as you can!" he roared. The manager knew how to give a forceful order. He grabbed and pulled and shoved the employees. "One of the girls I slapped in the face; she was fainting and I got her out." Another seamstress pleaded for the pocketbook she had left by her machine. Bernstein insisted she keep moving. "I just drove them out," he said.

Across the room, Bernstein could see a stymied scrum piled up at the Washington Place stairway door. He also glimpsed Louis Brown rushing over from the men's room, where he had been washing his hands. Brown was the machinist in charge of the Triangle's sewing plant. He began looking around wildly for a pail of water to throw, but Bernstein told him it was too late. "Try to get the girls out as quick as you can!" Brown remembered saying as he pointed toward the Washington Place stairs.

Louis Brown yanked and pulled and bulled his way through the crowd piled up at the door. The problem was obvious: stairway doors in the Asch Building were designed to swing inward, because the stairway landings were too narrow to accommodate outward-swinging doors. But the workers were jammed so tightly against this one, and thronged so thickly against one another, that the door couldn't possibly open. "You couldn't get it no tighter," Brown recounted. Compounding the crisis, it was possible that the door was actually locked. Brown wouldn't know for sure until he managed to reach it.

Ida Cohen, a sewing machine operator, was right up against the door. "All the girls was falling on me and they squeezed me to the door," she remembered. It was made of wood, with a top panel of wired glass. Cohen's face was being pressed against the glass, tighter and tighter, until she imagined that the churning mass behind her would shove her right through. "Please girls, let me open the door!" she gasped once, twice, three times. She prepared for the awful feeling of glass slicing into her face. "And then Mr. Brown came there and pushed the girls away on one side."

By brute force, Brown cleared a bit of space. He fumbled with a key in the lock, and somehow managed to open the door. Scores of terrified young people flooded down the stairs.

The room was darkening with smoke and the heat was rising quickly. Choking, Samuel Bernstein made his way back to the bookkeeper's desk, where Dinah Lipschitz was still shouting into the phone, sobbing, desperate to reach the ninth floor. "I can't get anyone!" she cried. Bernstein ordered his cousin to run. Then, frantically, he gave a last look around the loft. As far as he could see, he was the last one left on the floor.

Then he thought of his relatives, thirteen feet above him, up on the ninth. "For God's sake," he cried, "these people don't know. How can we make them know?" Nearly blind and gasping, Bernstein made his way through the Greene Street exit just before the flames enclosed him.

He headed up the stairs.

The day had turned out to be quite lovely and springlike. Hundreds of New Yorkers were enjoying the late afternoon in the simple symmetry of Washington Square, with its curving walks and its canopy of budding trees. This attractive little park, once a pauper's graveyard, was cheerful with the stewpot mélange of humanity that has long made New York so attractive to some people and so unnerving to others. Children from the tenements south of the square ran and laughed and chattered in a half-dozen languages. Greenwich Village intellectuals strolled past benches where round Italian grandmas sat with their groceries. Well-bred Yankees walked briskly to tea at the elegant town houses still clinging to the edges of the square. Students from New York University hailed their friends alongside the pickpockets at rest. The city had so little pleasant open space and so many people. Everyone shared. They had no choice.

Among those meandering through the square was an off-duty reporter named William Gunn Shepherd. He had a good name for a war correspondent, and soon enough he would be one. But today he was just a general-assignments man for Roy Howard's scrappy little United Press news agency. About 4:45 P.M., Shepherd was nearing the eastern edge of Washington Square and the biggest story of his life. He had just passed the Garibaldi statue and was looking directly down

Washington Place. The Asch Building was plainly visible halfway along the block. "A puff of smoke issuing from the factory building caught my eye," Shepherd was to write.

Even closer to the scene, a laborer named Dominick Cardiane had paused near the Greene Street entrance of the Asch Building and lowered his wheelbarrow to rest for a moment. High above, he heard the sound of a window bursting—a little explosion, a "poof" more than a smashing sound. Glass rained onto the street, spooking a horse parked nearby. The animal reared, shrieked, and bolted down the cobblestones, dragging its driverless wagon. Smoke poured from the broken window. Seeing this, another bystander, John Mooney, ran to the nearby fire alarm box, No. 289, and pulled it. Seconds later, his signal was answered by the keening of fire whistles and clanging of bells as engines rolled into the streets from stations in every direction.

Shepherd hurried toward the action. At the edge of the square he was passed by another galloping horse, a feisty beast named Yale, urged on by mounted policeman James Meehan. Outside the Washington Place entrance, Meehan reined his mount hard, jumped down, and dashed into the marble lobby. He took the narrow stairs two at a time. Above the fifth floor, the policeman met a swarm of frightened workers making their way down the tight, faintly lighted helix. On he went, pressing himself against the wall—the stairs were but thirty-three inches wide. Between seven and eight he found Eva Harris, the owner's sister, slumped in a faint and blocking the way. People were screaming and clambering over her. Meehan hauled Harris to her feet, steadied her nerves, and got the stream moving again in a more orderly frenzy.

Down below, bystanders—from the square, from nearby shops and restaurants and streets—quickly filled the sidewalks. They craned their necks to study the cloud slowly forming over the skyscraper. It looked to Shepherd like "a mushroom of smoke." They saw fire in the windows of the eighth floor as the first horse-drawn engines arrived. Next, the bystanders saw something large and dark fall from one of the windows. "Someone's in there, all right," said a voice in the crowd. "He's trying to save his best cloth." When the next bundle began falling, the onlookers realized that it was a human being.

Shepherd knew he would need a telephone. He began writing his story in his head. But he kept his eyes trained on the upper floors, observing, examining, focusing on the details. He noticed the sign affixed to the prow of the building at the level of the eighth floor: TRIANGLE WAIST COMPANY, it declared, along with the company's logo, a triangle inside a circle. Shepherd also listened. "I learned a new sound," he wrote afterward, "a more horrible sound than description can picture. It was the thud of a speeding, living body on a stone sidewalk."

Officer Meehan reached the blazing loft on the eighth floor. The flames were just eight feet from the door. A scant five minutes, maybe six, after blinking to life under Isidore Abramowitz's cutting table, the fire had consumed most of the room—more than nine thousand square feet. For the first two or three of those minutes, half the life of the blaze, the fire had been small enough for Samuel Bernstein to consider fighting it by hand. The transformation was stupefying—this was a firestorm.

The sheer speed of it must be kept in mind. All the crucial things that happened inside the factory that awful afternoon—the heroics, the terror, the tragedy, the strokes of fortune both saving and deadly—transpired in a handful of minutes and in the presence of a hideously voracious fire.

At the Washington Place doorway, Officer Meehan met Louis Brown, the machinist who had started the workers down the stairs. Meehan did not immediately see anyone else in the loft. But then he noticed, through the dark, grimy smoke, two women in the windows overlooking Washington Place. They were gasping for air and screaming for help. Meehan thought they were preparing to jump. He sprang forward and grabbed one, pulling her back into the shop. Brown grabbed the other. In that instant, the fire surged closer, and they all turned to flee.

For some reason, though, Brown paused another moment at the window—perhaps he wanted to suck in a lungful of air. The machinist saw hundreds of people on the street below, waving and shouting:

"Don't jump! Help is coming!" Then he pulled his head back in, just as a new wave of smoke closed around him. Suddenly, Brown could see nothing. But he knew in which direction safety lay, so he dropped to his hands and knees and groped his way through the door.

Stumbling down the stairs, Brown caught up to Meehan outside the sixth-floor loft. On the other side of a locked door they could hear screaming and pounding. Inside, for all they knew, was more flame. The policeman turned his back to the door and wedged his feet against the lowest step of the stairs, then drove with his legs, straining with all he had, until the doorframe splintered and the lock gave way. There were no flames inside, only "frightened women. They were screaming and clawing," Meehan told Leon Stein years later.

The women told the policeman they had come down the fire escape. After crawling over the cutting tables and through the rear windows on the eighth floor, they found themselves in an L-shaped airshaft enclosed on all sides by the three buildings that occupied that city block. Their route down the fire escape had been terrifying. Each balcony was scarcely wide enough for one person to walk along it. The sloping ladders connecting the balconies were even worse: less than eighteen inches wide. If, somehow, the workers managed to race down a hundred feet to the bottom of the escape, they would find that it ended futilely over a basement skylight. There was no way to get from the bottom of the fire escape to the safety of the street. In short, the escape was pathetically inadequate in an emergency involving hundreds of workers on multiple floors; it could accommodate only a handful of people at a time—and even then, it was not much good.

The first workers onto this sorry apparatus had picked their way down two floors as, behind them, their colleagues wailed and shoved and bumped and stumbled. The escape grew more crowded with each moment. At the sixth floor, the head of the line wisely decided that an overcrowded fire escape, high above an enclosed pit that was filling with fire and smoke, was a very bad place to be. So she pulled open the sixth-floor shutters and broke a window. Inside, she found another garment factory, safely below the fire, closed for the day and empty. She led the way back into the building and ran to the Washington Place door. It was locked. This must have seemed unbelievably cruel: they had fled the fire and dared the fire escape but still they were trapped by this horrible inch of locked wood. Some of them ran to the Greene Street side, only to find that door locked, too. Some went to the windows and looked down, wondering whether they would have to jump. All of them feared that the fire would soon find them. Then Officer Meehan burst in and guided them the rest of the way down. By the time the group reached the bottom, more policemen were on the scene, and these officers refused to let them leave the lobby. It was too dangerous outside, the policemen explained: too many bodies in the air.

After Mary Alter dropped the phone on the tenth floor and started away from the switchboard—leaving Dinah Lipschitz unable to alert the ninth floor—she immediately encountered a bookkeeper named Levine. She told him to telephone the fire department, and he darted into one of the executive offices. According to fire department dispatch logs, he got through between 4:45 and 4:46 P.M., about half a minute after the alarm was sounded from Box 289 down on the street. At almost exactly the same time, someone downstairs pulled the factory alarm for the first time and bells began jangling on all three floors. Mary Alter, meanwhile, resumed her search for Max Blanck or Isaac Harris. She did not have to go far; she met the owners just outside their offices.

The precise layout of the tenth floor is impossible to ascertain from available records. But a rough sketch goes like this: Visitors stepped from the Washington Place passenger elevators into a small reception area. The first person they met was Edna Barry at her switchboard. Beyond her desk, down a small corridor, the owners had large offices with big, arched windows overlooking Washington Place. Past their offices was a showroom, where department store buyers could examine the Triangle's latest styles. This was where the company's salesmen loitered when they weren't pounding the pavement or riding the rails.

Along the Greene Street windows was the pressing department. Rows of ironing boards stood amid a jungle of flexible tubes, which connected the heavy irons to a supply of pressurized gas that they burned for heat. After finished waists were examined for flaws or dirt on the ninth floor, they were hauled up to the pressing department. From there, they went to the packing department in the rear of the tenth floor, back by the fire escape. The last stop on the Triangle line was the shipping department, which occupied the center of the tenth floor. Eyewitness accounts suggest that the office space and the showroom, enclosed by partitions, occupied fairly little of the tenth-floor loft, while the pressing, packing, and shipping space was sufficiently open to allow clear views through most of the loft.

Isaac Harris had been at his desk, ordering some embroidery from Louis Silk, a salesman for the firm of Knauer & Tynberg, when he heard a commotion. He stepped from his office and stood at the edge of the shop floor briefly mystified, trying to figure out the significance of the clanging bells, the running employees, the shouts, and the escalating anxiety. Max Blanck was standing nearby with two of his daughters: Henrietta, who was now twelve, and five-year-old Mildred. The girls had come to the office that afternoon with their governess, because Daddy had promised to take them shopping after work.

"Everyone hollered 'fire!'" Harris later recalled.

Like Samuel Bernstein two floors below, Isaac Harris was not unfamiliar with this situation. A year or two earlier, he had been patrolling the factory and spotted a fire starting in one of the wicker baskets that operators kept at their feet to hold unfinished work. Coolly, Harris snatched up the burning basket and carried it to a relatively uncrowded section of the room, calling for fire pails as he went. After the fire was doused, the owner dug through the soggy mess and pulled out a cigar butt. He immediately fired the operator.

This was different. As Harris scanned the loft, trying to understand what was happening, he saw—clear across the room, beyond the packing department, through the windows that looked into the airshaft—*flames*. He could not tell where they were coming from, but obviously something very bad was happening.

Estimates of the number of people working on the tenth floor that day range from forty to seventy. The higher number is probably closer to the truth. They now crowded into the vestibule near the receptionist's desk, where the Washington Place elevators ran. Workers rang for the elevator repeatedly; when a car finally arrived, Harris filled it with women, mostly pressers, and told the operator to come back right away. The car sank slowly without stopping, past the ninth floor, all the way to the ground, then rose again directly to the executive floor. Again, Harris loaded the car. In the wild push to get aboard, little Mildred Blanck was swept into the elevator. Her father saw the terrified look on the girl's face, grabbed her wrist, and heaved her out just before the doors slammed shut.

While the car was gone the second time, Harris heard a new and even more urgent cry of "fire!" He left the vestibule and reentered the loft to find that the flames had come through the rear windows, igniting the crates, boxes, and finished waists heaped around the packing department. "Girls," he shouted to the workers nearby, "let us go up on the roof! Get on the roof!"

Still, he seemed to hesitate a moment. A group of pressers cried out to him, "Mr. Harris, save us!" The owner experienced a surge of courage—much like the day when he snatched up the flaming wicker basket. In the next minutes, a significant distinction was revealed between the longtime partners, Max Blanck and Isaac Harris. Harris—whose memory of these events was generally corroborated—got hold of himself and moved decisively to help save his tenth-floor employees. Harris turned to Emile Teschner, a traveling salesman for the Triangle, who had stopped by the shop during a sojourn in Manhattan to pick up some new samples before returning to the road. "Let us go this way if we can, Mr. Teschner," Harris called, as he led a sizable group past the blaze in the packing area toward the Greene Street door.

Blanck, on the other hand, was nearly paralyzed by fear and indecision. The chief shipping clerk, Eddie Markowitz, came up the Greene Street stairs from the ninth floor, having rushed down moments earlier to warn the workers. He found Blanck with his little girl in one arm, holding his older daughter by the hand. The owner was "standing there with a look of terror on his face," Markowitz remembered.

The clerk had returned to the tenth floor to rescue his order book, "because that was very valuable to the firm." But when he saw Blanck, Markowitz decided the boss's life was even more valuable. He dropped the order book, took Mildred from Blanck's arms, and pulled the big man by the coat. "Come on along," Markowitz coaxed. "Come ahead." They, too, moved toward the stairs.

The Asch Building's two stairways were almost identical, but not entirely. The Greene Street stairs were designed for heavier use, lighted by windows looking into the rear enclosure. They started in the basement and ran all the way to the roof. The stairs on the Washington Place side, by contrast, were built with no illumination at all, save for one dirty skylight; only recently had light fixtures been installed. These stairs ended at the tenth floor. Fortunately for the tenth-floor workers, Isaac Harris, Eddie Markowitz, and a number of others clearly knew which stairway offered hope. They led the way directly into the smoke, toward the fire, to reach the Greene Street exit. It was tentative going, because everyone was frightened and disoriented. Smoke burned their eyes and obscured even the flames themselves. There was a danger of walking right into the blaze. Breathing was more difficult with each step, given the toxic gases and the hyperventilating terror. Harris urged his workers forward: "Go, one of you, two of you!" Still they hung back. "If you can't all go," he cried, "better one of you get out!"

Then Samuel Bernstein arrived, bursting through the Greene Street door at the crucial moment. The factory manager had tried to offer help on nine, but the fire got there first, boiling up through the airshaft. He was driven back from the door. So he continued up. When he got to the tenth floor and saw Harris and Blanck, the bosses seemed aimless and impotent, moving this way and that, dithering. In contrast, Bernstein had become, in a matter of minutes, a sort of Dante who, alone among them, had seen and comprehended the inferno. Bernstein knew exactly what conditions existed below, how dire the situation was, how few their choices, how short their time.

"The only way for you to get out is the roof!" he commanded. "There is no other way." Bernstein galvanized the escape. One by one, the trapped employees steeled themselves, wrapping their faces and hair in their shawls or coats or in stray fabric that they found lying around the shop. Then they dashed into the smoke and up the stairs. At least most of them did. Louis Silk, the embroidery salesman un-lucky enough to be calling on his best customer that afternoon, stood on a table in the middle of the loft, in the shipping department, vainly trying to smash the sturdy skylight—an effort that Harris had already pronounced "ridiculous." Nearby, Lucy Wesselofsky, the young foreman of the pressers, was sprawled on the floor, having fainted. Bernstein ordered Silk down from the table and hauled Wesselofsky up from the floor. He prodded the salesman and slapped the presser. Then Bernstein took Wesselofsky in his arms and carried her to the roof. Adrenaline was roaring through the little man. "I felt as strong as a bull at that time," Bernstein remembered.

The passage to the roof was hellish. Flames in the enclosed airshaft had shattered the windows in the Greene Street stairwell. "The fire was . . . blowing right into the window," Isaac Harris recalled. "Right in the face." To reach open air, survivors had to skirt the growing fire on the tenth floor, start up the stairs through the flames licking, pok-ing, and leaping in the stairway windows, and continue climbing even as their clothing and hair began to burn. Workers reached the roof gasping, coughing, and tearing at their coats and hats and scarves.

Then, when they had stopped smoldering, the escapees looked up to see a terribly dispiriting sight.

To the south and the east, there was fresh air, a wide vista—and a 130-foot drop to the pavement. To the north and west two adjoining buildings represented safety and life and future. But both were signifi-cantly taller than the Asch Building. These two safe havens loomed like contemptuous battleships beside a leaky little lifeboat.

Firefighter Daniel Donahue was the chief dispatcher that afternoon. When Box 289 was pulled at 4:45 P.M., he noted that the signal was answered by firehouses throughout the neighborhood. He also noted the barrage of phone calls and the repeated pulls at the factory's pri-vate alarms that erupted twenty or thirty seconds later. Although there was another fire already burning in the neighborhood, there was plenty of equipment to respond to the Asch Building. New York City was famous for having the newest and best fire-fighting gear in the world. At least eight wagons answered immediately, beginning with Engine Co. 72, which came charging down Broadway just ninety seconds after the first alarm.

As 72's wagon swung west onto Washington Place, firefighter Oliver Mahoney saw flames from the Asch Building reaching out of "all the windows on the eighth floor." He also saw streams of frightened young people fleeing from the building. When the horses slowed, Mahoney jumped from the wagon along with three other Irish firefighters—Bernard McKenny, John McNulty, and Thomas Foley. They shouldered a length of hose and began fighting their way through the survivors and into the lobby. "The people was running out the door—panic-stricken people I presume," Mahoney remembered. "I couldn't get in the door in the first place." When he did manage to squirm inside, Mahoney found that "the hallway inside the doorway was crowded with these people. . . . As I got in, the elevator opened up and another crowd of people came from the elevator. They blocked the way a little while again." Finally the firefighters were able to reach the stairs.

Meanwhile, two other men from Engine 72 stretched a hose to connect the nearest hydrant to a standpipe running upward through the building alongside the Washington Place stairway. There was a standpipe in each stairway, fed by a water tank on the roof. But the city water supply from the hydrant was vastly superior. New York had recently begun installing a system of shutoff valves that allowed water engineers to concentrate pressure quickly under fire hydrants in a particular area. The Triangle's neighborhood was one of the earliest high-pressure zones. At the first alarm, engineers in the district pumping station began diverting more water pressure to hydrants near the fire.

Oliver Mahoney's team reached the seventh floor. There, they disconnected the house fire hose, still nestled in its iron bracket, and tightened their own hose on the standpipe connection. Down below, the standpipe had been connected to a fire hydrant. The fire cast a ghastly dancing light in the smoke and gloom of the darkened stairway. The firefighters pushed on.

At the eighth floor, they found "all one mass of flame and nothing else there but one mass of flame," Mahoney recalled. The door to the loft was burned away, but the fire was not in the vestibule or the stairs. This gave the firefighters a little room to take their stand. They opened the nozzle and blasted.

By then Battalion Chief Edward Worth had reached the scene after a two-minute trip up Mercer Street from his station house. It was 4:47 P.M., and the chief saw from the ground exactly what Mahoney was encountering far above the street: "The fire had entire possession of the eighth floor." Worth thought he also saw fire in the western part of the ninth-floor loft—the area farthest from Greene Street—but he did not perceive fire on the tenth floor. As the ranking fireman on the scene, Worth decided in an instant to issue a second alarm from Box 289, which could be done only with a special key carried by officers. The key was turned at 4:48 P.M.

As this was happening, Engine Co. 18 rolled into Waverly Place from Greenwich Village to the west, with Captain Howard Ruch in command. He ordered his men to run a hose from the hydrant at the corner of Waverly and Greene—half a block north of the Asch Building—to the Greene Street standpipe, the one by the service entrance. As his team executed the order, Captain Ruch studied the scene. On the Greene Street side of the building, fire was burning in the eighth-floor window trim and sashes. Flames rising from those windows were being sucked into the ninth floor, and from there the fire lapped up into the top-floor windows. The captain saw workers filling the windows of the ninth floor, screaming for help. One particular cry stood out in his memory: "I heard the shriek, and saw the people start to jump. And I ran to the apparatus and ordered the life net to the street."

No one could recall a person ever being saved by a net after falling nine stories. But what else was there to do? After calling for a team of his men to set up the net, Ruch turned and led another squad up the Greene Street stairs. At the sixth floor, they hooked into the standpipe. Nearing the eighth, they noticed the slate treads of the stairway were cracking from the heat in the underlying iron framework. Fire in the eighth-floor vestibule was so intense that Ruch and his men could not even stand up to face it. For a moment the captain considered his options. They could keep going, up one more floor, to try to rescue the people he had seen trapped in the windows—but if they did, they risked being cut off themselves by the insatiable blaze. "We had to extinguish the fire on the eighth floor" first, Ruch decided, so he and his men sprawled on the hot floor and opened the nozzle.

Two minutes, perhaps three, had passed since Samuel Bernstein steered Dinah Lipschitz through this door and then headed up the stairs. In that time the blaze had become "a mass of traveling fire along the floors," and most of the thin partition screening the Greene Street entrance had been consumed. The smoke and fire were so thick that the firefighters could not even see the team from Engine 72 pouring water through the opposite entrance, less than 140 feet away.

Frank Sommer, law professor and former sheriff of Essex County, New Jersey, was lecturing that afternoon to fifty law students at New York University. He cut a handsome figure, tall and red-haired, and his students enjoyed his genial nature. Sommer's class met on the tenth floor of the American Book Building, a block-long giant facing Washington Square, bordered by Waverly Street to the north and Washington Place to the south. This was the Asch Building's western neighbor.

As Sommer spoke, the sound of fire engines came into the room, faintly at first, but louder and louder, until they were converging from every direction *right there*. The professor stopped, excused himself, and hustled into the nearest room with a window. This window looked into the ugly airspace formed where the Asch Building met its neighbors, the space in which the fire escape dangled.

A few months earlier, just after the big fire in a Newark garment factory, one of Sommer's colleagues, Professor Francis Aymar, had written to the city's building department to report crowded and dangerous conditions in the Triangle Waist Company, which he had seen through these same windows. Aymar got back a polite letter vaguely promising an investigation. Now Sommer saw that his colleague's worries were justified. Flames shot up the airspace from two floors below. He heard the "ear-piercing shrieks as the girls in the factory appeared at the windows."

Sommer ran back into his classroom and ordered his students to the roof. When they got there, they found, as if by providence, two ladders that had been left by painters the previous day. The American Book Building topped out fifteen feet higher than the Asch Building. From that vantage point, Sommer's students could see below, through veils of smoke, a growing number of shaken, smoldering women and men wandering and shouting on the neighboring roof. It was a good thing that the cornice of the Asch Building rose three feet above the slag rooftop; otherwise, some of the survivors might have stumbled right over the edge. Sommer and his students lowered the first ladder to the skylight over the Washington Place stairs. Then they ran the second ladder from the skylight to the Asch roof. Several students climbed down and began helping Triangle workers up the ladders. In the next few minutes, surrounded by flames and squinting through smoke, these students saved scores of people.

One of the rescuers, Charles Kramer, found an unconscious woman sprawled at the top of the Greene Street stairs. Her clothing was smoldering, riddled with tiny embers; he extinguished them with his hands. Then Kramer dragged her across the roof, only to realize that he had no good way to get her up the ladders. So he hauled her up by her hair.

The students had not yet reached the Asch Building when Isaac Harris escaped up the Greene Street stairs. Instead, the boss was met by the implacable fact that the nearest rooftop—the one just to the north—was thirteen feet higher than the place he was standing. Harris hesitated a moment, then threw himself at the wall. Somehow—"I don't know how exactly"—he and another man were able to scale the adjacent building. First they climbed to the top of the elevator machinery, and from there they hauled themselves to the top of the stairwell. They pulled themselves up from there by clutching a wire attached to the bricks. When they reached the taller building, the two men tried the rooftop door. It was locked. So Harris smashed a skylight with his hand, cutting himself badly, and began yelling for help.

A custodian heard them and rushed up with a stepladder, which the men then lowered to the castaways stranded on the Asch Building. The ladder was only about six feet tall, but with Samuel Bernstein and Louis Senderman pushing from below, and Harris pulling from above, a number of Triangle workers were able to escape by this route.

Louis Silk, the embroidery salesman, was lifted up from this ladder. A moment later, Max Blanck's small daughter Mildred came up. Silk offered to carry the girl to safety. She was crying and trembling so pitifully that Silk couldn't bear to take her in the elevator. He carried her down eleven flights of stairs to the street.

Emile Teschner, the traveling salesman, also escaped up the Greene Street stairs. Senderman noticed Teschner on the smoke-shrouded roof, "shivering like a fish," "crying like a baby," and ready to jump over the side. The clerk grabbed the salesman and dragged him to the ladder. Teschner was a very big man, perhaps 250 pounds. Boosting him to the next roof required an almost superhuman effort. Even the unflappable Bernstein had to admit later that "we had some trouble with him."

Now Bernstein looked around.

He saw flames to the west, roaring and spitting in the L-shaped airshaft, which was functioning as a perfect chimney, drawing the fire up and up, from eight to nine, from nine to ten, from ten to the roof. Fire in the airshaft had burst the rear windows of the American Book Building, and was threatening the NYU law library. Faculty members organized a group of students in an urgent mission to evacuate the books, armload by armload.

Bernstein saw flames to the east also, lapping over the cornice of the Asch Building, boiling up from the Greene Street windows. He saw smoke pouring through the skylight in the center of the building—the one Louis Silk had tried to smash minutes earlier. Soon the flames would be roaring up there as well.

But the Triangle manager did not see anyone to boost him from the ladder to the adjacent roof. "Nobody was there to push me up any more," he remembered. "So I ran all the way over to the Washington place side," where he found the law students and their ladder relay.

As few as twelve minutes—and as many as fifteen—had passed since Samuel Bernstein made a price for a new employee and heard Eva Harris crying, "Fire!" In that brief span he had saved many lives with no apparent concern for his own. He had also lost the factory that had always filled him with pride. The Triangle was "the most perfect" shirtwaist factory he knew. "I never seen one like it [in all the] New York factories I was in," he said later. At other factories, the cutting tables were just boards on sawhorses and the scraps were flung into boxes on the floor. But it was precisely the Triangle's innovation—converting the very tables themselves into giant bins by boarding up the space beneath them—that had made this blaze so explosive. Once the fire was born in a cozy nest of some three hundred pounds of tinder, there was no way to slow it, much less to stop it. Bernstein's decision to fight the fire for three or four precious minutes, minutes that could have been spent spreading the alarm and rescuing workers, was disastrously wrong, no matter how brave.

At the top of the ladder, Bernstein learned for the first time just how wrong things had gone. He paused a moment and looked down into Washington Place, and as he did he saw "five or six girls falling from the windows." They seemed to start out just a few feet below him, barely out of reach, but then they dropped into space and got smaller and smaller until the world, for them, came to a sudden end.

6

THREE MINUTES

There was never a day when every seat was full, the Triangle owners later explained. They could not say precisely how many people came to work on March 25. The factory was too large for that—among hundreds of employees, some were sure to be missing on account of quitting, or falling ill, or staying up too late the night before. Certainly the Triangle was not entirely full on the Sabbath. A certain number of workers still kept the old traditions, even though it cost them a day's pay.

So the exact number of employees on the ninth floor that day is unknowable. There were 278 sewing machines on the ninth-floor assembly line. There were also examiners and foremen and bookkeepers. But how many chairs were filled? How many others were in the loft? History can only guess. Roughly 250 is a fair estimate. Most were women; about three dozen were men. At the sewing machines, they hunched over their work side by side and head to head, like Oliver Twist and his fellow foundlings at their gruel.

With such a crowd, there was always a lot of angling and jockeying for a head start on quitting time to beat the long line that formed quickly at the Greene Street door. Yetta Lubitz was in just her seventh week at the Triangle, but at twenty-four she was a seasoned survivor of the workplace, and a master of the quick getaway. On this particular afternoon, after receiving her pay envelope, Lubitz slipped out of her seat, which was almost precisely in the center of the room, and sidled up the long row of chairs to the main aisle. Then she darted into one of two adjacent dressing rooms—cloak closets, really, separated from the factory floor by thin partitions.

Lubitz was coming back out of the dressing room with her coat and hat as most of the workers were rising from their seats. She vaguely noticed that the others weren't heading for the dressing rooms, however. "I saw a crowd of girls run right toward the Greene Street door," she said later. That was the door she normally used, but now it was crammed with people struggling to get out.

For a moment, this strange behavior failed to sink in. Lubitz continued to follow her routine, taking her time card from her purse and walking toward the nearest time clock, one of two on the floor, to punch out. Finally, she understood: "I heard . . . a cry of 'fire!'"

The warning and the blaze reached the ninth floor at nearly the same moment. One floor below, flames had spread to the two cutting tables near the airshaft in the rear corner of the factory, where they were driven and fed by a steady rush of wind making its way from street level through the elevator shafts. These rear tables were the entire width of the room away from the fire's starting point. But the blaze was carried across the room in light, swirling embers that fell amid perfect conditions for a fire. Very quickly, this wing of the fire was extremely intense. It burst the rear windows and entered the airshaft. The shaft worked like a flue, sucking the fire upward—which is why a scant moment after Lubitz heard the word "fire!" she saw the blaze through the airshaft windows.

"A girl, an examiner, came right over to me and she ran to the fire escape," Lubitz recounted. "I followed her and I ran to the fire escape, too. And then a whole crowd of girls came over right to us—so many girls. They ran to the window, to the fire escape, but I got scared: all the floors were with flames."

Lubitz looked to her right and saw that the Greene Street door was still jammed. She didn't know where to turn. Then she noticed "a young, dark fellow," another operator whom she recognized, though she didn't know his name. He headed to the door of the Washington Place stairway, across the room. She followed. At the door, the young man grabbed the knob, twisted it, pulled it, pushed it—in vain. "Oh," he cried, "the door is locked! The door is locked!"

A wave of smoke filled the room, and Lubitz retreated with a crowd of workers into a dressing room. When the smoke briefly lifted, they ran out again. Now the windows were gaping. "I don't know whether anybody broke out the windows or the flames broke out the windows," she said. Either way, fire began lapping in from every direction, bringing the eighth-floor embers into the wicker workbaskets beneath the ninth-floor machines. "And when the flames came in we ran again in the dressing room and we started—we were crying and waiting. . . . I was waiting until the dressing room will get burned," Lubitz remembered. "I was crying terribly, I was screaming."

"Oh, keep quiet!" someone snapped.

It was the same young, dark fellow. "What is the use of crying?" he demanded. Lubitz was ashamed of herself. She stopped screaming for a moment—but then she thought, "Well, my life is lost anyway." What possible meaning could shame or pride still have? "I started to scream again."

All this had taken perhaps four minutes. In that time, the fire had climbed through the rear windows onto the ninth-floor examining tables—which were covered with shirtwaists and dresses—and now it was advancing across the loft. The dressing room walls began to smolder. Time was dwindling. Yetta Lubitz saw a rush of workers, and once again she followed the crowd, heading back toward her original destination, the Greene Street door. Though Lubitz did not know it, Eddie Markowitz, the chief shipping clerk, had just come down from the tenth floor and shouted for the trapped workers to come to the roof. "All of a sudden I see that the girls all started to run to the Greene Street door, and I started to run, too," Lubitz said.

The most athletic seamstresses were jumping from table to table, so that they would not have to pass as close to the fire pushing toward them from the airshaft. But Lubitz was not agile enough. She could not keep up with them. After two tables she hopped down and started dodging up the aisle between the sewing tables, sidestepping burning workbaskets and trying not to trip on the tangled wooden chairs. She could see the red flames ahead. Fortunately, she had her long coat on.

Lubitz covered her face with the skirt of the coat and ran for it. From the corner of her eye she noticed a heavyset Italian woman collapsed across a machine table, gasping for breath. She reached the Greene Street door a moment after the crowd passed through it. But where had they gone? Because she had not heard the shipping clerk call them to the roof, she assumed that the others had fled downstairs.

"When I opened the door I didn't think to go up to the roof," she said, "but I thought to go down—and downstairs the stairs were full of flame." This was the fully raging inferno on the eighth floor that would, in a few more seconds, force experienced firefighters to their bellies. "I got scared," Lubitz said, "and I shut the door again." This, she decided, must be the end. There was no way out. In a minute or two she would be dead.

Then, like an angel coming out of the smoke, her friend Annie Gordon reached the door, along with several other women. "Come to the roof!" Gordon cried. They opened the door and ran up, past the now-empty tenth floor, past the flames leaping and licking into the stairway window, and burst into the cool air of the roof. Their clothes and hair were smoldering when they made it. Students from the adjacent law school smothered the embers and helped them to the ladders leading to safety.

Yetta Lubitz had a good memory of her movements, but she was not very precise on the subject of time. A minute, she believed, was made up of "sixty moments," and her moments apparently were very brief indeed, because she estimated that she spent some twenty minutes trying to escape from the ninth floor. In reality, the whole terrible experience—from the first alarm to the time she set foot on the American Book Building roof—lasted no more than five or six minutes.

This was all the time there was. Behind her on the ninth floor, her colleagues were beginning to jump.

The layout of the ninth floor was simpler than that of the eighth. Eight rows of sewing machines ran south to north, parallel to the Greene Street windows. Seven of the rows were roughly equal in length, about seventy-five feet. The last table, the one farthest from Greene Street, was about half as long as the others. Every row went right up to the Washington Place windows, where the electrical power plant connected to the driveshafts. In all, the footprint of the sewing machines was roughly seventy-five feet square. This left about twenty feet of space along the western and northern walls—but because space was money, it did not remain empty.

When Max Blanck and Isaac Harris originally occupied the ninth floor in 1901, they filled the loft with cutting tables and sewing machines and—according to one early Triangle employee—a big box in which to hide child workers when inspectors stopped by from the labor department. They did not provide much in the way of washrooms, coat closets, dressing rooms, or toilets. During the strike of the shirtwaist workers, though, union members barraged city authorities with complaints about the Triangle. Eventually an inspector was dispatched, and he ordered the owners to install adequate rest rooms and other amenities. During a slow season in 1910, the ninth floor was emptied while the improvements were made. Landlord Asch took this opportunity to give his star tenants new floorboards as well. Out went the old, scarred, and oil-soaked boards. When the work was finished, dressing rooms, washstands, and expanded toilet facilities filled most of the space at the western end of the factory.

In the rear of the room, in front of the airshaft windows, stood four long examining tables arranged in an L-shape. The arrangement of the tables matched the shape of the shaft. There was a small space between the examining tables and the Greene Street door. This was where bookkeeper Mary Laventhal had her desk, and behind that was the distribution desk, where work was handed out.

The whole room was filled with row after row of tables noisy with humming machines and muttering workers, separated by narrow aisles. At one end of the room were thin doors leading to cloakrooms and rest rooms. Along the perimeter, there were stations heaped with blouses and parts of blouses being handed out, turned in, counted, examined, and stacked. And always people bustling here and there.

Ethel Monick, sixteen, was a "floor girl," which meant that she scurried around the factory transporting garments in various stages of completion from one work station to the next. Monick had been employed at the Triangle for about three months. Her primary post was at the distribution desk, just inside the Greene Street door. The job didn't pay much, but it was ideal for getting a jump on quitting time. A time clock sat right next to her desk, so she could easily see when the closing bell was about to ring. And because she was always dashing off here or there in pursuit of shirtwaist parts, no one noticed if she slipped away from her post a minute or two early.

So, like Yetta Lubitz, Ethel Monick already had her coat and hat on when foreman Anna Gullo rang the bell at 4:45 P.M., but she was not fast enough. There was already a line at the Greene Street exit of workers waiting to have their handbags searched.

Three things happened at once: the bell rang, Monick noticed smoke rising near the radiator beside her desk, and people began shouting and rushing past her to the door. The shouting resolved itself into a simple: *Fire!* Just that quickly, though, the escape routes were jammed. Monick saw the Greene Street door crowded with "quick girls," and she thought: "I can't get out of there." On the other side of her desk, women were stampeding over the examining tables to reach the fire escape—"and the fire escape was very small; two people could not go down [abreast]." So—again like Yetta Lubitz—Monick set off across the room toward the Washington Place door.

She hurried past the examining tables, past the dressing rooms, and reached the exit just as an elevator door was closing. Many of the workers who failed to squeeze into the car rushed off in search of another way out, leaving Monick nearly alone by the stairway door. "I tried the door and I could not open it, so I thought I was not strong enough," she recalled. "So I hollered, 'girls, here is a door!' And they all rushed over." They elbowed her aside.

Being pushed aside saved her life, because the next thing she knew, the second elevator came up, and Monick was standing right there. She "rushed right into it." So many people shoved in behind her that she was pressed face first against the back of the car. She couldn't move. But she survived.

Such tiny strokes of fortune decided, repeatedly and remorselessly, who would live and who would die. Consider Max Hochfield, a sixteen-year-old greenhorn who had recently joined his older sister and their parents in New York. Years later, Max told his story to author Leon Stein. He said his mother wanted him to be a plumber—a man's job, she felt—but his father thought sewing machine operators had excellent jobs. Max's sister Esther had worked for three years at the Triangle and she had done just fine. So, about three weeks before the fire, Esther got a job at the factory for Max.

Esther was in love and newly engaged. A few days before the fire, the family had stayed up nearly all night celebrating her betrothal. Come morning, neither Esther nor Max felt well enough to go to work. When they returned to the Triangle the next day, they discovered that their eighth-floor sewing machines had been reassigned and they were given seats on nine. Max was just lucky enough to have been given a seat near the Greene Street exit, and just lucky enough to have no friends at work to slow his departure. At quitting time, the boy grabbed his coat from a handy peg and darted through the door. He was at the eighth floor before he even realized there was a fire. A bit farther down, it dawned on him that Esther was surely still inside. By then it was too late to go back up.

Esther, by contrast, was unlucky enough to have friends and a fiancé who was planning to meet her at the factory door and take her out for the evening. She didn't dash out with her brother. She went to the dressing room to talk and laugh and make herself look nice.

* * *

Panic.

"Yes, screaming and crying and shouting," said Mary Bucelli, an operator with two years' experience at the Triangle. Everything blurred as she ran through the loft looking for a way out. The smoke thickened and parted at the whim of the crosswinds. The rumble of the flames was the bass and screaming was the treble. It was hard, afterward, for Bucelli to describe what she had done or where she went. "I can't tell you because I gave so many pushes and kicks. I gave and received. I was throwing them down wherever I met them," Bucelli said of her coworkers, "no matter whether they were in front or the back. I was throwing them down. I was only looking for my own life. . . .

"At a moment like that, there is a big confusion and you must understand that you cannot see anything," she explained. "You see a multitude of things, but you can't distinguish anything. With the confusion and the fright that you take, you can't distinguish anything."

Lena Yaller remembered thinking that the fire alarm was a joke— and then seeing flames through the Greene Street windows. Within a minute or two, "I seen the examining tables were all burning." She fled into a dressing room and had to fight her way back out through a throng of women seemingly paralyzed by terror. Their wails were dizzying: "I could not make out what they did say, simply. It was so many languages. . . . They all spoke in another language. The smoke and all. And some were screaming about their children."

It became hotter and darker. "I felt like fainting and I couldn't see anymore," said Mary Bucelli. She stumbled on a gap in the fire on the examining tables and made it through the window to the fire escape. Pushing, pulling, and shoving, she started down the narrow iron catwalk. Just behind her was Abe Gordon, a savvy young man who started at the Triangle as a button puncher but soon had his eye on the machinists who kept the sewing plant going. He coveted their jobs. So he saved twelve dollars from his pay—an enormous amount, more than a week's wages for a buttonholer—to buy a watch fob for the head machinist. It worked: Gordon was given the job of belt boy, the first step toward his goal. The belt boy kept the sewing machines connected to the flywheels that regulated their power. Whenever a belt broke and a machine went dead, it was Gordon's job to squirm under the table— without disturbing the other operators—and replace the belt.

As soon as he stepped onto the fire escape, Abe Gordon could tell that it was a very dangerous place to be, overcrowded, flimsy, and awfully close to the flames. So when he managed to get as far as the open window on the sixth floor, he slipped back into the building. "I still had one foot on the fire escape when I heard a loud noise," he told Leon Stein years later. And then, "The people were falling all around me, screaming all around me. The fire escape was collapsing."

The Asch Building fire escape was badly conceived, badly designed, and badly installed. The problems began with the gooseneck ladder leading from the tenth-floor balcony up to the roof. It was long, skinny, and high enough to make even a lumberjack nervous. At the other end, far below, was the contraption's pathetic dead end above a basement skylight—a situation so obviously flawed that city officials had spotted it on the original architect's plans. The architect promised to come up with a better landing, but never did, and the city failed to follow up. Between the perilous summit and the useless base was a series of narrow balconies connected by even narrower steps. Most menacing of all, as it turned out, were the steel shutters that covered the windows leading onto the fire escape. These shutters opened *outward*. Unless they were carefully folded back and hooked to the exterior wall, they tended to flop open and block the escape.

That was what happened an instant or two after Abe Gordon passed the eighth floor on his way down to the sixth. A shutter swung across the balcony like a car door opening in the path of traffic. Worse, the iron bar that was intended to attach the shutter safely to the wall instead slipped between the slats of the balcony floor. It got stuck. The shutter became a locked steel door. The fire escape was essentially sealed. Under leisurely conditions, with plenty of time and breathing room, someone could easily have pried the bar loose, folded the shutter, and hooked it neatly to the wall. But there was no time or space. More and more terrified workers squeezed through the ninth-floor windows and onto the balcony. Their bodies piled up behind the jammed shutter and crowded the sloping ladder between the eighth and ninth floors. Some of the workers at the rear of the pileup turned and headed toward the roof. But the tenth-floor shutters had also flopped open, obscuring the perilous gooseneck ladder. All human progress stalled in both directions, up and down; only the fire continued to make headway. The flames, roaring in the rear of the airshaft, closed in on the fire escape. The stranded workers began to smolder. In a matter of moments, they would be roasted alive.

This was when the flimsy fire escape groaned, twisted, and dumped its load of humans into the dark, smoky pit. Some victims smashed through the skylight and into the cellar. Others were impaled on the spiked iron fence that bisected the bottom of the shaft. Some came down burning and, when they landed, set off fires in the Asch Building basement. "It looked to me like a big pile of rubbish coming out of the windows," said the owner of a hat factory in the adjacent building. He had seen it all through his own airshaft windows; perhaps worse, he had *heard* everything. "I hope I never hear anything like it again."

When Chief Edward Worth arrived on the scene at 4:47 P.M., two minutes after the alarm, he saw fire everywhere on the eighth floor. He also saw "indications on the west wall on the ninth floor [that] looked to me like fire." This was the blaze involving the examining tables in the westward rear of the loft. Worst of all, he saw that the ninth-floor windows along Washington Place were "full of people." Worth ordered Engine Co. 13 to train its hose on the cornice of the building and spray an inch-and-a-half stream of water back and forth. "The water was driven out at one hundred and twenty-five pounds pressure," Worth later testified, which was enough to deliver a gentle rainfall ten stories up. The idea was "to cool [them] off," the chief later explained, "to prevent the people . . . from jumping. It swept the cornice from one end of the building to the other for about, possibly, two minutes." Worth wanted to reassure the terrified people— although he already realized that he could do very little for them.

Then a man in one of the windows closest to Washington Square launched himself toward the ground. Said Chief Worth: "When he jumped, it appeared to encourage everybody else."

The time was 4:50 P.M. Inside, Yetta Lubitz was making her risky dash toward the Greene Street door. Just below, firefighters were reaching the eighth floor and opening their hoses on an all-consuming fire. In the airshaft, the fire escape was hanging useless, twisted and silent. The Washington Place door remained closed. Samuel Levine, the last person to make it *down* the Greene Street stairs, lay badly burned on the third-floor landing after tumbling down a flight of stairs.

The options for survival were nearly gone. By the eleventh minute of the fire—the sixth minute of the nightmare on the ninth floor—only two escape routes remained, and they, too, would be gone in thirty or sixty or ninety seconds more. To survive at this point required decisiveness, a sudden burst of action, and good luck, which was a vanishing commodity.

One way out was the Washington Place elevators. Joseph Zito and Gaspar Mortillalo, the elevator operators, were sitting in their cars waiting for the Triangle closing time when suddenly their bells began ringing wildly. As they started up, they could hear muffled shouts. Then they heard glass breaking in the elevator doors and, after that, the shouts became perfectly clear: *"Fire!"* In the aftermath, there would be much confusion about which floors the elevators visited and when, but they probably went first to the eighth floor, saved a load of grateful survivors, then headed up to the executive floor. Zito estimated that he made two trips to the tenth floor—but when he got there the second time, everyone was gone. The rest of their work was on nine.

The ninth-floor loft was dotted with scattered fire when they stopped there the first time, probably around 4:46 or 4:47 P.M. Yet the brave drivers returned two more times, perhaps three, pushing their cars past the inferno on eight, where the flames were so close they could almost touch them. Each elevator was built to hold about a dozen people. On their final runs, the cars carried at least twice that number. Between them, Zito and Mortillalo probably rescued 150 people or more—approximately half the total number of survivors.

"When I first opened the elevator door on the ninth floor all I could see was a crowd of girls and men with great flames and smoke right behind them," Zito said. "When I came to the floor the [last] time, the girls were standing on the window sills with the fire all around them."

The other escape route remaining at 4:50 P.M. was the Greene Street stairway to the roof, a path quickly being closed off by converging lines of fire. To escape this way, a worker had to steel herself and run through a wall of flame.

Anyone who failed to choose—and choose quickly—was doomed. Ida Nelson, Katie Weiner, and Fannie Lansner paint the grim picture. Nelson was standing by her chair, which was near the end of the first row of machines by the Greene Street windows, putting on her hat, when she heard the alert at 4:45 P.M. She did not take the threat very seriously at first, merely picked up her pace a bit as she moved along the aisle. She found herself beside Lansner, who was both her friend and her foreman. It was fun to have such an important chum: sometimes Lansner let Nelson ride with her in the Washington Place elevator, which was only for management, not for workers. Once they got clear of the aisle, the two women rushed toward the dressing room to get their coats, but they were swept up in a tide of people headed for the Washington Place door. They both tried to open it, Nelson recalled, but it was locked.

They noticed Katie Weiner beside them. For about five months, the gregarious Weiner had been cutting lace at a little table on the ninth floor. She had beaten the bell to the dressing room that day and was "standing there talking to some of the girls while putting on [her] hat and coat." That's when she heard the first screams. Weiner looked frantically around for her sister Rose—and for a way out. She saw that the Greene Street passage was full of smoke. So she went to the Washington Place elevator, but couldn't squeeze into the car. She started back across the room.

"I was choking with smoke. I couldn't stand it no more," Katie

Weiner remembered. "I went to the windows and put my face out to get some air, and I called down. I said, 'fire!' . . . and people were looking up." Other workers, also desperate for air, were pushing her from behind, forcing her through the open window. She realized she was about to fall. So Weiner squirmed free and ran to the Washington Place door. There she met Nelson and Lansner.

For a brief moment, the three of them stood by the closed door. Time was nearly gone, and they had to decide. Ida Nelson made the first choice, which was to follow a small crowd headed for the Greene Street door. Some of them were calling out: "To the roof!" As Nelson started across the room, she urged Fannie Lansner to join her. "But she didn't care to go."

Near the bookkeeper's desk, beside the Greene Street exit, were piles of fabric—"plain white goods." Women were wrapping themselves in the lawn for some protection against the flames before setting off up the stairs. They emerged on the roof frantically tearing the burning cloth from their arms and faces. Nelson covered herself in the thin cotton and "went out through the roof." Her hands were burned in her mad dash up the fiery stairs.

Katie Weiner and Fannie Lansner stayed behind by the locked door. "Suddenly, I seen the Washington Place elevator come up, and all the girls that were at that door all went towards the elevator," Weiner remembered. "And I went also there." It was Joseph Zito's car. She tried to push her way in, but once more failed to make it.

Survival had become a question of will and hunger. Joseph Brenman was also there when the elevator came up for the last time. He was an inside contractor, employing his two sisters; he worked alongside the younger girl, Sarah—Surka in Yiddish—at the third table from the Greene Street windows. (His sister Rosie worked across the room.) When the first alarm was heard, Brenman could already see flames. His immediate reaction was to run—in fact, he made it through the Greene Street door. Then he stopped: "I remembered my sister." Because he was a contractor, Brenman had the authority to dismiss his sisters a minute or two early. He had seen Sarah start off toward the dressing room. Brotherly love took him back into the loft.

"Sarah! Where is Sarah? *Surka!*" Brenman cried as he crossed the room, looking frantically into the faces that he met. He saw people standing on a burning examining table, pushing toward the fire escape. He found a crowd at the Washington Place door—but no Surka. "The smoke and flames came from different sides," he remembered. And people "began to go out the windows." When he saw this, Brenman abandoned his search and surrendered to a blind, brutal instinct for life. "I heard the elevator coming up. . . . I pushed myself into the crowd and into the car. . . . I pushed through by force." He recalled having little trouble shouldering through the throng. "They were girls who felt faint," he said, "and they couldn't withstand my force."

Zito's elevator started down. Katie Weiner knew it would not be back. "The flames were too strong," she said. Almost without thinking, she grabbed the cable that ran through the elevator car. (The operators gave the cable a strong tug to get started upward, and a sharp yank to head down.) The falling car pulled her in; she landed on the heads of women so tightly packed they could not lift their arms to hold or help her. Her feet dangled through the door, banging violently on every landing. Weiner's face was buried in the mass of flesh and clothing; she was gasping for breath and trying to scream. "Girls, my feet are being crushed!"

Ida Nelson survived by running to the roof. Katie Weiner survived by diving into a sinking elevator car.

Having made neither choice, Fannie Lansner was doomed.

Another trio:

Two Kates—Rabinowitz and Alterman—were getting their coats and hats from the dressing room with a third friend, Margaret Schwartz. They heard the cry of "fire!" First they tried to scramble over the machines to the familiar Greene Street exit, but that way was too crowded, so they reversed field and headed to the Washington Place door, the locked door. The critical last minute soon arrived. As the flames converged, Rabinowitz saw her colleagues start to jump from the windows. "I reminded myself I was on the ninth floor," she said. Jumping meant death. She forced her way onto the last elevator.

Kate Alterman chose the fiery race to the roof. She pulled her coat up around her face and moved toward the blaze. As she hurried, stumbling, across the room, she saw people catching fire around her. She looked down to find that her pocketbook was burning in her hands. Passing the examining tables, Alterman grabbed a few unburned garments and tried to cover her head. The flames were closing across the doorway, and someone grabbed Alterman's dress to hold her back. "I kicked her with my foot and I don't know what became of her."

Margaret Schwartz did not make it out. The last Alterman saw of her, she was screaming, "My God, I am lost!" as her hair caught fire.

People survived thanks to a short head start, or a seat assignment near an exit, or by following the right mad rush in one direction or another—or by ignoring the wrong rush. They survived by acting a bit more quickly, or boldly, or brutally. But the truth is that most people working on the ninth floor that day did not survive at all.

It was 4:51 or 4:52 P.M. Now there were no good choices left. Sarah Cammerstein watched the elevator falling into the long, dark shaft and "made the decision of my life. I threw my coat down onto the roof of the elevator and jumped for it." She was knocked unconscious but survived. Behind her was Celia Walker, twenty, an examiner and "a real Yankee," who spoke with an authentic New York accent after fifteen years in America. She gripped the sides of the elevator opening as the workers behind her pressed forward. "I could feel them pushing more and more," she told Leon Stein. "I knew that in a few seconds I would be pushed into the shaft. I had to make a quick decision. I jumped for the center cable. I began to slide down." The friction burned through her clothes; fortunately, she was holding a muff and this saved the flesh of her hands. "I remember passing the floor numbers up to five—then something falling hitting me." Sarah Friedman slid down a cable on the side of the shaft, badly tearing her hands. May Levantini jumped when the elevator was a couple of floors below her. She blacked out. When she came to a moment later, she was face up on top of the car and she could see, far above her, the burning lofts. She watched as a worker lost her grip on the elevator doorway and plunged into the shaft. Levantini tried to squeeze her body to the wall.

Then more came down, pushed or jumping.

Joseph Zito, the heroic elevator man, described that moment:
"The screams from above were getting worse. I looked up and saw
the whole shaft getting red with fire. . . . It was horrible. They kept
coming down from the flaming floors above. Some of their clothing
was burning as they fell. I could see streaks of fire coming down like
flaming rockets."

At first, they went to the windows for relief from the smoke—"a
great volume of smoke . . . blinding, choking smoke," as Chief Worth
described it. Also, they went to reconnect themselves to the world:
to see with their own eyes that help was coming, that their plight
was known, that this sudden and profound shock to their lives was
reverberating. That they mattered. "In America," one of them remembered her mother saying, "they don't let you burn." From the
windows they called out again and again to the people below: "Call
the firemen!" and "Save us!" and "Get a ladder!" and even "Fire!"—
though everyone could see what the problem was. Smoke boiled up
into a mushroom cloud over the building, and flames flickered in
the windows, but still they cried "fire!" because what else was there
to say? The view from the windows was a vicious, almost mocking,
juxtaposition of life and death, of the temperate and the hellish.
Behind the workers in the windows were screams of terror and the
rising growl of more and larger flames. As they stood on the sills,
fire licked up beneath their feet. Through the shimmering, distort-
ing heat waves they saw fear and trembling on the faraway faces of
the strangers on the sidewalk. All the little mouths down there were
perfect tiny Os, masks of round-mouthed dread, because they were
all yelling "NO!" as in *No, don't jump!* Their tiny hands were up, as if
a gesture could hold the doomed workers forever in the mouth of a
furnace.

Fireman Jacob Woll Jr. and his colleagues looked almost like play-
things as they cranked the gears to raise the ladder on Hook and
Ladder No. 20. The ladder rose steadily toward the trapped workers,
closer, closer, like a saving hand stretching upward—then stopped,

inexplicably, some thirty feet below them. They waited for it to start up again, but no, that was as high as the ladder could go. The tallest ladder in New York was not tall enough.

Such were the useless and desolating things they saw.

And yet, if those souls in the Washington Place windows looked up or right or left they could see the cool, clear air beyond the furnace; the gray-brown tracery of bare trees quilting Washington Square (faintly washed with the first whisper of new green); the faraway towers of the newspaper buildings on Park Row, where the telephones had begun jangling with reports of their peril; the birds startling from nearby eaves and wheeling through the sky; the elegant campanile of the church on the square, and the pleasing aesthetic echoes of it in the two orange brick loft buildings that faced the Asch Building. New York was a place and 1911 was a time in which even the designers of mere factory buildings cared enough to emulate beauty. Even the coldly functional Asch Building, one of the least decorated in the neighborhood, featured miniature terra-cotta columns, fluted in the classical style, as dividers between the upper-floor windows. Workers were clinging to these decorations now.

This, then, was their universe: panic and fire behind them, horror and helplessness on the faces far, far below—and something cool, something beautiful, *just out of reach* beyond the heat waves and the blinding smoke.

The first man stepped off about 4:50 P.M. Like the survivors who lived by making a hard choice at the right moment, he died by making a hard choice in a terribly wrong moment. He chose to die by falling rather than by burning. Most of the people in that room—having seen the pogroms of Russia or the tenement fires of New York—had a clear idea what the flames would do to them. Jumping had the advantage of leaving their bodies identifiable. Perhaps there was also an element of self-determination in the decision, a desire to assert a last grim sliver of control. The man could not possibly have expected to survive the fall. The drop was just over one hundred feet to solid pavement and it looked, from up there, every inch of that.

Among the survivors were some that considered the choice to jump far braver than their own decisions, for they had stood at the windows and looked down and realized how much resolve it would take to step off. Anna Gullo, for example: after the twenty-year-old foreman rang the quitting bell, she dashed to the Washington Place door and tried in vain to open it. After waiting briefly, she lost faith that the elevators would return. "I thought it was no hopes for me to be saved," she remembered. "I went to the fourth window of Washington Place. I broke the window and I threw a pail of water." Of course it did no good. Then "I done the sign of the Cross [and] I thought I would jump out of the window. But I couldn't—I had no courage to do it."

When the first jumper lurched into thin air, Chief Worth ordered his firemen to open a net to catch the others. Captain Ruch delivered the same order at virtually the same moment around the corner on Greene Street. "Hook and Ladder 20 took a life net from the side of the truck, went into the sidewalk with it and caught one girl," Worth remembered. "She was tipped out onto the sidewalk. . . . I lifted her up when they tipped it, and I said, 'Now, go right across the street.' She walked ten feet, but it was like an automatic motion. Probably six feet—and dropped."

Freda Velakowsky landed in a net and was rushed to New York Hospital, where she briefly regained consciousness several hours later. According to the occasionally fanciful *New York World*, she spoke to the doctors, saying: "I paused a moment on the ledge of the window, and the street below, with its hundreds of people, seemed to swirl . . . I grew dizzy, and had a sensation of falling, falling, oh, ever so long. Then everything was dark." Hours later she died.

Chief Worth thought the nets would work. But their effect surely was to encourage more jumpers, some of whom conceivably still had time to race to the roof. But it is hard to fault the chief for trying *something*.

So many people launched themselves that two nets weren't enough. An ambulance driver ran his vehicle up on the sidewalk, hoping that jumpers might land on the roof of the ambulance and thus break their falls. Deliverymen pulled a tarpaulin from a wagon and stretched it taut—but the first body to hit the tarp tore it from their hands. Bodies fell with such force that at least one crashed through the glass bricks of a basement skylight set in the sidewalk. "The first ten shocked me," wrote reporter William Gunn Shepherd. But when he looked up and realized there were scores of young women in the same windows, he braced himself for what was coming.

Shepherd noticed the grace with which the early jumpers came down. "One girl," he wrote, "tried to keep her body upright. Until the very instant she touched the sidewalk, she was trying to balance herself." He noticed that the people in the windows watched every fall, all the way down. He noticed that when two young women jumped together, they tore the life net like "a dog jumping through a paper hoop," and that before the firemen could move the ruined device "another girl's body flashed into it."

"When they came down one at a time we could have helped," Chief Worth insisted against all evidence. "When they came down entwined with one another, it was impossible." By 4:53 P.M. the nets were abandoned.

At that point—thirteen minutes after the fire began and eight minutes after the quitting bell rang on the ninth floor—eighty or ninety workers remained trapped in the loft, and nothing could save them. Zito's elevator was stuck at the bottom of its shaft under the weight of many bodies. Mortillalo's car could not rise because its rails were warping in the heat. Fire from the airshaft and the Greene Street windows had converged at the rear of the shop, closing off the Greene Street door. Fire was burning in the dressing rooms, where women huddled pitifully behind the thin wooden walls. It was driving relentlessly across the room, led by skipping little flare-ups in the wicker baskets, from machine table to machine table, and its destiny was manifest: to swallow the whole room and everything in it.

A young woman stood in a window as flames flickered around her. She flung her hat grandly into the air. Then she opened her purse and threw all the money down. Then she jumped.

Two young women wrestled at another window; one was trying to keep the other from jumping. She failed and her friend went down. The one remaining, Sally Weintraub, steadied herself against the building, raised her hands, and began gesturing. To those watching from far below, she appeared to be delivering a speech to the nearby, beautiful air. She finished speaking, and followed her friend.

Shepherd saw a young man wearing a hat appear in a Washington Place window. The man helped a young woman step onto the windowsill, then held her away from the building—like a dancer, perhaps. Or, as Shepherd put it, like a man helping a woman into a streetcar. He let go.

"He held out a second girl in the same way and then let her drop," Shepherd wrote. "Then he held out a third girl. They didn't resist." The fourth one was apparently his sweetheart. Amazed, the bystanders saw them embrace and kiss. "Then he held her out into space and dropped her. But, quick as a flash, he was on the windowsill himself. His coat flattened upward; the air filled his trouser legs; I could see that he wore tan shoes and hose. His hat remained on his head."

The reporter later walked up to the body. "I saw his face before they covered it," he wrote. "You could see in it that he was a real man. He had done his best."

The last one out of the Washington Place windows was a woman who flung herself at the fire department ladder three stories below, hoping to catch it—an impossible attempt. Then Shepherd heard fresh screams from the witnesses on Greene Street, so he hurried around the corner in time to watch the final scene.

It was now about 4:55 P.M., fifteen minutes after the birth of the fire, ten minutes into its assault on the ninth floor. The two teams of firefighters battling the blaze on eight had begun to make slow progress, half step by half step, into the loft; they were within four or five minutes of having the eighth floor under control. But it was too late.

Above them, on nine, the fire had spread from the rear examining tables, through the dressing rooms to the Washington Place door, where a crowd of victims still tugged, pushed, pounded, and clawed.

They kept trying the door until the very last moment, but apparently they turned away from it as they died, because their bodies were found in a heap ten or twelve feet into the loft. The fire blocked, suffocated, and burned a second cluster of victims by the Greene Street exit—workers who had waited too long to make the dash toward the roof.

Burning vigorously along the wooden machine tables, devouring the wooden chairs, marching in ragged formation across the room, the flames drove the last forty victims toward the Greene Street windows. The blaze pressed them back and back and back, into the burning window frames. These victims did not choose to jump. They avoided every variety of death until there was nowhere else to go. They retreated from the flames as a matter of reflex and instinct; they tried to stay in the loft even as they began to burn. Finally, the impulse to retreat overwhelmed everything else and they tumbled through the windows in horrible heaps.

Shepherd watched it happen. As ghastly as the vision on Washington Place had been, he wrote, it "was not so terrible as what followed. Girls were burning to death before our eyes. There were jams in the windows. No one was lucky enough to be able to jump, it seemed. But one by one the jams broke. Down came bodies in a shower, burning, smoking, lighted bodies, with the disheveled hair of the girls trailing upward. . . . There were thirty-three in that shower."

The last body fell at about 4:57 P.M. Her dress snagged on a steel hook at the sixth floor, probably part of the sign hanging just under the Triangle Waist Company's logo. "Meyers Crown & Wallach 'High Standard' Clothing," it said. For a moment, she hung there grotesquely until her clothing burned and tore away and she dropped to the sidewalk.

Three minutes: If the workers on the ninth floor had been warned of the fire at 4:42 P.M. instead of 4:45, every one of them might have been saved. With a three-minute head start on the flames, chances are good they could have gotten the Washington Place door open—remember Officer Meehan's success in breaking down the sixth-floor door. They would have discovered the path to the roof before the insufficient final seconds. On the eighth floor, about seven minutes (from 4:40 to

4:47 P.M.) were needed to evacuate two hundred people. If the warning had reached the ninth floor at 4:42 P.M., there would have been about nine minutes before the last exits closed off at approximately 4:51 or 4:52 P.M. That might have been enough time to evacuate 250 workers.

This is speculation, but not idle speculation. It points to the bafflingly irresponsible attitude the Triangle owners had toward fire. Many other New York factory owners had similar attitudes, but that doesn't make them any less baffling.

By 1911, fire-safe factories had been a reality for more than a generation; in fact, the science of factory fire prevention was older than that. In 1835, a Rhode Island cotton mill owner, Zachariah Allen, became indignant when he discovered that fire insurance companies would charge the same rates to insure his mill, which was state-of-the-art for safety, as they charged to insure firetraps. "A cotton mill is a cotton mill," he was told. "We average them all together." Allen hatched the idea of a "factory mutual system," in which safe mills would band together to insure themselves. This was a revolutionary twist on the economics of insurance. Traditional insurance companies had little incentive to reduce the risk of fire too steeply—because if people grew less conscious of fire danger, they might buy less insurance. A front-page story about a costly, deadly fire was great advertising. Instead, the strategy of the insurers was to spread the risk widely, and to charge sufficiently high rates to make a profit despite the occasional large claim.

Allen's mutual system reversed the incentives. Because the members paid the cost of every fire, safer factories meant lower premiums and more money in their pockets. The impact of this innovation was gradual, but extraordinary. Given cotton's explosive nature, the mills had been extremely high risks from their inception, and deadly mill fires were commonplace. By the 1880s, however, the standard New England cotton mill was equipped with automatic sprinklers, firewalls, and fireproof doors (to restrict fires to one section of the factory and create safe zones for employees to run to). Death by fire was no longer a serious risk of mill life. Other safety measures were developed elsewhere. In Philadelphia, for example, by 1911, enclosed fireproof stairways were taking the place of exposed iron fire escapes in commercial buildings.

All these innovations—firewalls, fire doors, fire stairs, and, most of all, automatic sprinklers—were available, in theory, to Manhattan factory owners. But it was virtually impossible to find such features anywhere in the city. A study quickly done after the 1910 Newark High Street fire found just one garment factory equipped with sprinklers, out of more than a thousand shops surveyed.

City officials explained that loft buildings were originally built for storage and were not intended to be used as factories. So why require firewalls or doors? But the lack of fire safety in Manhattan was also a problem of power. Power over the insurance industry in New York City belonged to the politically connected insurance brokers, who made their money not by reducing risk but by selling more and larger policies. Since brokers collected a percentage of every sale, they fared better when premiums were high. Safer buildings meant lower rates and smaller commissions. The brokers protected the insurers by dividing the riskiest policies into small shares, so that no one company bore the brunt. Insurers that refused to accept a share of high-risk policies were shunned by brokers when they placed their low-risk, high-profit policies.

Blanck and Harris were perfect examples of this skewed system. Few factory owners paid higher rates than they did, and as a result, they commanded the loyalty of the most powerful brokerage in town. The Triangle owners were so-called rotten risks, in insurance parlance, because they kept having fires—and not just little ones that they put out by hand. They were "repeaters," having collected on several substantial claims. And yet they had little difficulty buying all the insurance they wanted.

A little after 5 A.M., on April 5, 1902—not long after Max Blanck and Isaac Harris opened their big, modern factory—the New York City fire department answered a call at the ninth floor of the Asch Building. They arrived too late to save the contents of the Triangle Waist Company. Fortunately, no one had been at work so early in the day. And the Triangle partners had adequate insurance.

Half a year later, on November 1, 1902, firefighters found themselves back at the same address, at the same early hour, with the same result. Blanck and Harris collected about thirty-two thousand dollars in damages from the two fires—roughly half a million dollars in current terms. Interestingly, both fires occurred around the end of the twice-a-year busy seasons, which was always a risky time for the owners of garment factories. Unless they precisely estimated their markets, garment makers might well reach the end of the season burdened with excess inventory and with dwindling hopes of unloading it.

Unsold inventory is the bane of any business, and a frequent cause of death for fledgling enterprises. In 1901, Blanck and Harris had moved out of their little Wooster Street shop and into the pricier new Asch Building loft. No doubt a year later they were still enduring some lean and critical months as they tried to grow into their new capacity. They traded unsold waists and excess lawn for insurance checks not once, but twice in a single crucial year. The right fire at the right time was good for business.

They had another fire in 1907, at the Diamond Waist Company, which they had created in a nearby Mercer Street loft. Once again, the flames came in the predawn hours of an April day. Once again, insurance paid. And three Aprils later, yet another fire—again at Diamond. This one, too, was after hours, and reimbursed by the insurance companies.

If the shirtwaist kings occasionally arranged to have their premises torched, they were hardly alone. In a series of articles published by *Collier's* magazine in 1913, Arthur McFarlane profiled New York's large and prosperous commercial arson industry, which he blamed for the fact that New York City "has more fires annually than all the capitals of Europe." McFarlane took particular note of the way the whimsies of fashion editors corresponded to the combustibility of Manhattan garment factories. One year, the Paris salons frowned on hats with feathers. "Within a month . . . three feather factories burned in New York," McFarlane noted, and within two years the last remaining feather companies could no longer buy insurance no matter how high the brokers' commissions. In 1910, Paris decreed that women's dresses should be plain. Soon there were weekly fires in New York's braid and embroidery factories.

The following year, Paris turned a very cold eye on the venerable shirtwaist. "By the end of 1911," McFarlane wrote, "one small insurance company had paid losses on ten shirtwaist factories. It had had losses on only six during the preceding *three years*." One large insurer, he reported, began canceling shirtwaist factory policies right and left, cutting its exposure by 40 percent—and still the number of claims doubled. A leading industry journal, *The Insurance Monitor,* concluded that the epidemic of shirtwaist fires in 1911 was "fairly saturated with moral hazard." That is to say, it smelled extremely fishy.

Arthur McFarlane did not accuse the Triangle owners of arson in the March 25, 1911, disaster. (Indeed, he was careful to acknowledge that fire marshals had not charged arson in any of the partners' factory fires.) They had, after all, an excellent alibi: What men would arrange to burn their factory when they were still in it, as well as their sisters, cousins, precious daughters? But there was no denying the strange relationship that Blanck and Harris had with fire. They seemed to view it as another manageable aspect of their business, avoidable by day and welcome by night; more complicated than the height of a cutting table, perhaps—but no more roguish than the Bowery gangsters and prostitutes they hired to harass their strikers.

Thus, they prepared for blazes not with safety measures—as someone with a healthy *fear* of fire would do—but by buying ever-larger fire insurance policies. By March 25, 1911, the partners were paying extremely high rates to carry insurance far in excess of the total value of the Triangle's contents. They carried about two hundred thousand dollars in coverage on the factory, which was estimated to be eighty thousand dollars more than the factory was worth (about $1.4 million of excess insurance in current terms). This was at a time when the costs of the previous year's strike, and the ongoing Parisian anti-shirtwaist crusade, had endangered the Triangle's credit rating. How could it possibly make good business sense to carry so much excess insurance?

Here's a possibility: If the owners were planning, in the last days of the season, to consolidate all their excess inventory, from all their factories, at the Triangle, and if they were pretty sure they were going to experience a fire in the night that would destroy all those shirtwaists and all that lawn, then it would be very smart indeed to have extra insurance, and well worth the premiums.

This cool, commercial view of fire as something to be managed, not feared, might explain the fatal decisions the owners made. They could not put sprinklers in their factory if they thought they might need to burn it sometime. And they might think that instituting fire drills, in a world where few factories had them, would make them look suspiciously conscious of the issue.

It could have been otherwise. When Blanck and Harris applied to increase their fire insurance coverage in 1909, the insurance companies insisted that the Triangle factory be inspected. Fire prevention expert Peter J. McKeon of Columbia University was hired to do the job. Apparently, McKeon did not object to the layout or cleanliness of the factory. But he did notice that the doors on the Washington Place side were "usually kept locked" to restrict unauthorized comings and goings by the workers. This apparently was a particular obsession of Max Blanck's; many workers remembered how he would test the locks and check the doors every time he passed.

These locked doors only added to McKeon's main worry that the fundamental danger at the Triangle Waist Company was the sheer number of people working so far aboveground. He tried to impress on the partners the life-and-death importance of a quick, orderly, rehearsed evacuation if fire swept the factory. McKeon recommended another expert, H. F. J. Porter, to organize fire drills for the company, and on June 19, 1909, Porter wrote to the owners offering his services. He never heard back.

Years later, as a man in his sixties, Max Hochfield told Leon Stein—in one of a number of interviews that Stein conducted with survivors—that March 25, 1911, was the first time he had seen a fire in America. The Triangle workers, he said, were, like him, totally unprepared. They "were foreigners," he said. "They weren't trained." A fire drill would have given them what they needed, which seems like very little but in fact was everything for 146 of them. It would have given them three minutes.

* * *

Captain Howard Ruch and his men got the blaze under control on the eighth floor at about 5 P.M., just ten minutes after they first opened the nozzle. They went directly up the Greene Street stairs to the ninth floor. Ruch said the conditions they found there were basically the same as he had found on eight—"a mass of traveling fire"—except that the ninth-floor blaze was "in a more uneven condition. . . . There appeared to be some kind of machinery stretched along in rows, and there seemed to be the sort of remnants of a board partition next to the doorway." The firefighters needed only a few minutes to knock down the blaze and start into the death loft. Behind the rush of water they moved step by step all the way to the Washington Place windows and back again. Then the captain took a bucket and began dousing the window trim. In this way, he "tramp[ed] more or less about [the] loft."

The room was full of charred and smoldering wood, in which the blackened flywheels of the sewing machines rested neat and even, like a convoy of threshing machines working a hideous field. There were also "furrows [that] appeared to be the remains of burned material, either linen or muslin—fabric, light fabric," Ruch recalled. Near the doorway was a large can of some liquid; the firefighters could hear it boiling. It turned out to be machine oil.

The first bodies Ruch encountered had fallen only "an inch or two inches" inside the Greene Street partition. They had probably been the last to attempt to race through the fire to the roof, and had not made it. The captain found other bodies under the windows; some did not look like anything recognizable. While dousing some flames near the prow of the building, where Greene Street and Washington Place came together, Ruch "stepped on something that was soft, in my hurry and my anxiety to finish up my work. And I looked down and my attention was called to a body by that means. . . . When I looked at that one I saw three or four that I had not noticed previous."

Firefighter Felix Reinhardt was part of a team attacking the blaze from the Washington Place side. "The heat was so intense we had to fight our way with quite some difficulty up from the eighth floor to the ninth floor," he recalled. The upper loft was "one roaring mass of flame." When the three-man team reached the landing on nine, they saw that most of the stairway door was burned away—but what was left made it clear that the door had been firmly shut. "The side jamb of the door remained, as well as small pieces . . . of the lower panels. . . . Flames were shooting through the door." Reinhart's team blasted the fire with water from the hydrant, and pressed forward, kicking down the fragments of the door as they went. When they had pushed the flames back to what had been the cloakroom, they saw a heap of bodies "a short distance from the door," the nearest being "perhaps nine or ten feet" (others estimated twelve to fifteen feet) into the loft, near the tiled remains of the washrooms.

By 5:15 P.M.—a little more than half an hour after it had sparked to life—the Triangle fire was under control on all three floors. In that brief span, the fire did more killing than any other workplace disaster in New York City history up to that time, or for ninety years afterward.

It was the job of the hook-and-ladder men to find and remove the bodies. Jacob Woll, who raised the tragically inadequate ladder outside, helped take nineteen bodies from the top of Joseph Zito's elevator car. Woll reached the ninth floor at 6:10 P.M. as the last pockets of fire were being extinguished. It was getting dark outside; harsh lights were put up inside the lofts to illuminate the destruction. From the street below, where thousands were now gathered, the lights in the ruined windows were spectral, and what they showed was even worse, because the firefighters quickly rigged block-and-tackle sets on each side of the building and began lowering corpses. As the sad bundles dropped slowly to earth, a searchlight tracked their progress. Policemen stationed on each floor under the davits reached through the windows to guide the cargo down, so that the bodies would not bang against the side of the building. The first victims started down sometime after 8 P.M., and the ghastly chore continued past midnight.

Woll later said he lowered fourteen victims before Lt. Charles Lauth relieved him. They were the workers that died by the Washington Place door. Not far from them, in the ruins of the smaller of two dressing rooms, Lauth found eleven more corpses. Down they went. He also discovered the burned remains of two young women huddled together in a tiny space behind the toilets. Across the room, by the Greene Street door, Capt. Ruch estimated that about twenty bodies were found. (Lauth did not think it was so many; he said "several.") Ruch also found "five or six" additional victims "here or there" around the room.

Contrary to lurid reports, no workers died while seated at their sewing machines. Nor did any workers die trapped in the aisles between the machine tables, according to Lt. Lauth. Every victim made it somewhere—to the windows, to hide in the dressing rooms, or to try the doors.

But the truth was awful enough. One hundred forty-six people— all but twenty-three of them women—died that day or during the days immediately afterward from the injuries they sustained in the Triangle fire. This was well over half the workers on the ninth floor that day. Strangely, there was never a complete accounting published of how the victims died. There was never even a reliable list of the dead.* But William Gunn Shepherd, the reporter, wrote that he counted fifty-four victims who had leaped or fallen to the sidewalks—thirty-three of them on the Greene Street side. Judging from their various testimonies, the firemen appear to have taken approximately fifty bodies from the loft—perhaps as many as fifty-three. Nineteen dead and fatally injured people were found in the elevator shaft. That would mean about two dozen victims died after falling from the fire escape.

Among the dead were Samuel Bernstein's brother, Jacob, who plunged into the elevator shaft, and Joseph Brenman's two sisters, Rosie and Surka, asphyxiated and burned where they fell. The Goldstein sisters, Mary and Lena, both died: Lena jumped and was quickly identified; Mary's body on the floor of the loft was so badly burned that five days passed before her family remembered a distinctive repair to one of her shoes.

Rosie Bassino jumped; her sister Irene Grameatassio burned. The Lehrers, Max and his younger brother Sam, the boy with the halo of

*See Appendix.

blond curls, died of "multiple injuries"—which probably meant that they landed feet first and unburned on Washington Place. The Miale sisters, Bettina and Frances; the Saracino sisters, Tessie and Serafina— all died, some in the building, some down below.

Those two women in their death embrace in the narrow space behind the toilets—were they sisters? Were they, perhaps, Lucia and Rosaria Maltese? Lucy and Sara, they liked to be called. Lucy was the big sister, twenty years old, and no doubt she kept an eye out for Sara, who was only fourteen, the youngest of the fire victims. Both of them were burned, but neither one as badly as their mother, Catherine, whose body could not be identified. One Saturday morning Salvatore Maltese was patriarch of a big and perfect family: a wife, two girls and two boys. That night his home no longer had any women in it.

Becky Reivers went up the elevator in the chill morning and her badly burned body came down by block-and-tackle in the damp night. Her fourteen-year-old sister now had no one to pay off her steamship ticket. Rose Manofsky was forced to leap from the burning room and so there was no one to help her sister survive the incompetence of their dissolute father. Esther Harris, the star seamstress, broke her back falling nine stories down the elevator shaft and now her family was poor again. Gussie Bierman, matronly in her pince-nez; Jennie Rosenberg with the secret joke; pretty Jennie Stern—suffocated, smashed, incinerated.

They left behind mysteries: Was Ben Sklaver the "dark, young man" with the short temper and the cool head who helped Yetta Lubitz keep her wits? Sklaver remained in the room to the bitter end, and was among those who fell from the Greene Street windows. When his body was identified, it was both broken and badly burned. Or was it Jake Kline, whose temper once inspired him to storm out of the Triangle and take the whole shop with him? He, too, died that day. Kline was last seen struggling with the Washington Place door, alongside Abraham Binevitz, another inside contractor, and Meyer Utal, the young man who tried, a few minutes earlier, to help Samuel Bernstein get the fire hoses going one floor below. Apparently Utal survived the eighth floor and—rather than running down to safety—ran up the stairs in time to enter the ninth-floor loft before the flames sealed the exits. This bold, brave act cost him his life.

Rebecca Feibisch, with the oval face and Gibson-girl throat: was she the first to die—as survivor Sylvia Riegler suggested to Leon Stein in an interview years after the fire? Riegler reported that her friend "Rose Feibush" panicked on the eighth floor and threw herself from a window before the other workers started to jump. But no person by that name died in the fire. Rebecca Feibisch was the victim with the name most closely fitting Riegler's story. Suffering from burns, fractures, and internal bleeding, Feibisch was rushed to St. Vincent's Hospital, where she soon died. This seems to prove that Riegler's memory was flawed. Feibisch's burns suggest that she remained in the factory as long as possible, even as the flames caught up to her, and that her fall was broken by the bodies of earlier jumpers.

Michela Marciano, having survived the eruption of Mount Vesuvius, found herself with Sklaver and nearly forty other workers being pushed by the flames into those Greene Street windows—or maybe she was one of the flaming rockets that Joe Zito saw coming down on his elevator car. Her body was both burned and smashed.

And then there was Rosie Freedman, the girl from Bialystok. For her death, it is necessary to go once more into the ninth-floor loft.

A dozen minutes had passed since the girls were singing:

> *And ev'ry love thought that comes a-stealing o'er your being,*
> *Must be revealing all its sweetness . . .*

The fire came first through the rear windows, onto the examining tables piled with garments. Then, almost simultaneously, it arrived in the Greene Street windows, lapping up—a curtain of heat waves undulating in the windows, sending sparks and embers to float into the waists and threads and scraps and wicker scattered around the loft. Then there were little pools of fire along the floor.

Workers started screaming, running back and forth, some pausing to brace a friend, others shoving and clawing.

The smoke was wispy at first, and then blinding—even a little smoke in the face is blinding for a moment.

There was a crowd at the Washington Place door, rattling the handle one after another, pulling, hammering with fists, clawing, pleading.

A tide of women rushed the other way—*to the roof!* Some of them were leaping from sewing table to sewing table. Some were trailing shrouds of fabric like mummies, burning. A heavyset Italian woman sagged over a table, gasping for breath.

The windows over Washington Place were full of disappearing people.

Inside the dressing rooms people deluded themselves into thinking the flimsy partitions might hold back the flames. Panic drew the oxygen down from the brain and into the limbs. It was harder and harder to think clearly. Then the walls began to smolder.

Then burn.

Fire was everywhere. The pools of fire met and spread and roared up under each oil-soaked table. Ranks of fire marched forward, relentlessly, driving the doomed along toward oblivion. The dressing rooms were in flames. Women were plunging into the elevator shaft. Bodies were tumbling from the windows in tangles. This was the zero moment, when nothing survived.

Rosie Freedman saw and heard all this, muddled by the roar of the blaze and dwindling to the point of unconsciousness. She may have been among the last to dash for the Greene Street exit—too late—or among the last to give up on the Washington Place door, or one of the very last to be driven to the Greene Street windows. We know only that she died inside the loft, and was one of the last victims to succumb. The damage that the flames did to her body was so severe that there could not possibly have been later victims falling on top of her. She was fully exposed to the fire, shielded by nothing, suffocated by the smoke even as the flames chewed through her clothes and hair. If there was pain, it was brief, for the fire burned quickly past her nerve endings. Death by asphyxia and death by shock converged, though the fire continued to burn.

7

FALLOUT

"We will get an investigation," Meyer London predicted at a protest rally a week after the Triangle fire. The Great Hall of the Cooper Union was full to the bursting point, just as it had been on the night sixteen months earlier when Clara Lemlich rallied the waist makers to their historic general strike. "We will get an investigation that will result in a law being referred to a committee that will report in 1913," London sneered. "And by 1915 a law will be passed—and after that our grafting officials will not enforce it!"

The disaster at the Triangle confirmed, in the eyes of socialists like London, that no one would protect the workers but the workers themselves. Shirtwaist strikers had shivered and starved and done hard time; they marched on the mayor and lunched at the Colony Club and charmed J. P. Morgan's clerks. Their sacrifice had attracted enormous sympathy and support. Yet the strike had not even guaranteed basic safety. If that was true—if the historic uprising in the waist factories had not forced lasting change—what reason was there to believe that even something as shocking as the Triangle catastrophe would make a difference?

But the reality was more complicated. By organizing themselves and asserting their strength, the workers were beginning to make progress. In the months since Lemlich's catalyzing speech, the International Ladies' Garment Workers' Union had grown from an insignificant few members to tens of thousands—the leading edge of an unprecedented surge in overall union membership in the city. Between 1909 and 1913, the total number of unionized workers in New York City grew eightfold, from thirty thousand to a quarter of a million. The ILGWU, for which Meyer London was a stalwart and eloquent lawyer, was now battle-tested by two of the most important strikes in urban labor history—the uprising of the shirtwaist workers and the subsequent victory by the mostly male cloak makers in 1910. The cloak makers' revolt was, Samuel Gompers said afterward, "more than a strike"; it was "an industrial revolution." The strike ended in a pioneering settlement, drafted largely by Louis Brandeis, which established a system for improving conditions and resolving grievances short of strikes. The "Protocol of Peace," as it was called, was a first step toward a place at the table for labor. In less than two years, the garment workers had moved from the back row to the vanguard of the American labor movement.

New York socialists and their sympathizers, meanwhile, were growing in strength with every election. In 1910, Meyer London ran for Congress from the Lower East Side and won 33 percent of the vote in a multicandidate race. He would be elected in 1914.

Still, no one could blame London or his audience for feeling cynical about the prospects for genuine reform. Many times before, a disaster was followed by a predictable train of consequences: shock, then outrage, then resolve, all leading to lip service dwindling into forgetfulness. Certainly, the fire at the Triangle was a sensational variation on the theme of mass tragedy: the gory spectacle of flames and smoke pouring into a clear sky in plain view of the whole city . . . helpless victims dying in sight, but just out of reach . . . the awful realization that a huge and vulnerable world existed far above the street. And yet larger disasters, in terms of lives lost, had amounted to little or nothing enduring, except grief. In 1904, on a clear summer's day, in plain sight of the shore, a gaudy riverboat called the *General Slocum*—a sidewheeler with decks stacked like a wedding cake—caught fire while taking fourteen hundred passengers, mostly women and children, up the East River to a picnic. More than a thousand perished, most of them by drowning after they plunged from the burning ship. One might have expected a lasting lesson to be learned about the need for adequate, quickly available lifeboats and life preservers. But seven years later, even as the Triangle Waist Company was burning, an ocean liner was under construction in an Irish shipyard. Its capacity would be more than two thousand passengers, yet it would carry lifesaving equipment for no more than half of them. The *Titanic*'s doomed maiden voyage was only a year away.

So the fact that New Yorkers responded to the Triangle fire with an unprecedented outpouring of relief donations, with mass meetings and emotional speeches, did not necessarily mean that it would have any important legacy. Meyer London was one of a large number of skeptics who could not imagine much good coming from New York's often corrupt political system, or from the men who vied to control it.

Among the first to weigh the electoral ramifications of the Triangle disaster was Charles Seymour Whitman, a keenly political man and district attorney of New York. Whitman was openly ambitious and understood the power of publicity. News coverage, he perceived, could help him jail criminals and expose fraud. As he put it: "Publicity is one of the mightiest engines, if not the mightiest of all engines, in the fight for right and justice in this generation," adding the (slightly dubious) assertion that "New York newspapers are mighty powers in favor of the public morals." Publicity could also help him advance his career.

A parson's son from New England, Whitman moved to Manhattan in his mid-twenties after teaching at a Brooklyn prep school. He had a law degree but no connections. If he showed much early promise, there is no record of it. Whitman seemed to rise almost by accident. People who couldn't rationalize his success began to suspect that there must be something to the man. In November 1909, while William Randolph Hearst was splitting the anti-Tammany vote for mayor—

allowing the Hall to elect crotchety Mayor Gaynor—Whitman, a progressive Republican with Hearst's endorsement, unified all opposition to the machine and was elected easily to the D.A.'s job at age forty-one.

Overnight, he became the most prominent young reformer in New York electoral politics. Socially, Whitman began hobnobbing with America's wealthiest families—he even received a much-coveted invitation to Alva Belmont's Newport mansion. The D.A. understood that he owed much to the newspapers. He was anti-Tammany but he had flair, which made the perfect combination for a hero of the New York press.

Small and trim, with a stout jaw, clear eyes, and a lush head of center-parted hair that suggested the ocean split by the prow of a ship, Whitman immediately set his sights on the governor's mansion—knowing full well that if he made it, he would be touted for the White House. Whitman took a lesson from Theodore Roosevelt's early courtship of the press. The road to the top began on the front pages.

He cultivated reporters. And he was more than just accessible and ingratiating. He surrounded himself with experts in press relations. One of the first assistants he hired as district attorney was a veteran newspaperman with special expertise in state politics; he served as Whitman's private secretary. The reporter who covered Whitman for New York's biggest daily doubled as a virtual image consultant. The D.A. listened carefully to these teachers. He came to understand what makes reporters truly happy: juicy stories and plenty of them. With his bully pulpit, subpoena power, and sway over the grand jury, the district attorney could keep news flowing as regularly as commuter trains.

From his early days as a city magistrate, down on the basement rungs of the justice system, Charles Whitman always found ways to generate stories. He personally exposed the scandal of saloon owners ignoring the legal closing times—a scandal the bibulous Whitman uncovered by glancing at his watch after a nightcap. He smashed (or got headlines for promising to smash, which was nearly the same thing in politics) the corrupt alliance among police, bail bondsmen, and Tammany Hall. This particular brand of graft worked as follows: Po-

licemen would arrest innocent people on trumped-up charges late in
the day, after the magistrate's court had adjourned. Because there was
no night court, the victims had to choose between posting bail or
spending the night in a city jail. This was an easy choice, given the
dreadful condition of the jails. The bondsman's resulting windfall was
divided among the conspiring parties: arresting officer, precinct captain, Tammany ward boss, and so on. Charles Whitman, who by then
had become chief magistrate, exposed the operation and persuaded
the state legislature to create a night court.

Whitman was also progressive, for his time, on racial and gender
issues. As chief magistrate, he hired women as probation officers for
the first time. As chief prosecutor, he appointed a black assistant district attorney, and even proposed naming a woman to prosecute juve-
nile court cases—provided he could get an extra appropriation to cover
her salary. Obviously, a woman could not be allowed to replace one of
the men on the payroll, he said.

Charles Whitman was always conscious that the right "big case,"
handled in the right way, could propel him to Albany. In an interview
just before taking office in 1910, he spoke hypothetically about the
power of a high-profile triumph: "Why, if I could get a chance to prosecute John D. Rockefeller—and win—it would be the making of me."
In his first year on the job, Whitman tackled the so-called poultry trust,
for which he got approving (but not career-making) headlines. By
spring of 1911 he had gone to work on a financial scandal, the wreck-
ing and plundering of the Carnegie Trust Company. Even so, on that
late afternoon of March 25, Whitman had his eye out for something
bigger.

The D.A. was in his apartment at the Hotel Iroquois that Saturday
afternoon, surrounded by a group of reporters, briefing them on court
business and amusing them with his trademark wry asides. Into the
room charged Herbert Bayard Swope, star reporter of the *World*, New
York's number-one paper (and willing to prove it: the *World*'s motto
was "Circulation Books Open to All"). Swope was a strapping young
redhead from St. Louis with a passion for gambling and an amazing

store of friends from every social stratum and shade of reputation. In a few years he would be a world-famous Pulitzer Prize winner for his foreign reporting, editor of the *World*, and "the most charming extrovert in the Western world," according to a competitor. President Woodrow Wilson would call him "the fastest mind with which I have ever come in contact." The tale would be told that whenever a high-ranking American visited a European potentate, the first question was invariably, "How is my friend Herbert Bayard Swope?"

At this point, Swope was just making his name, a cunning bon vivant with a knack for parlaying gossip into front-page exclusives. On the sideline, Swope was the keeper and polisher of Charles Whitman's image, steering him to big stories and advising him how to handle them. He came to fancy himself a sort of political Pygmalion, carving a future presidential contender from a block of mediocrity. Whitman, in return, gave Swope his juiciest scoops. It made sense that Swope was *not* one of the reporters clustered in Whitman's suite that afternoon.

Swope's closeness to Whitman was plain from the way he barged right in. "That will be enough, boys!" Swope declared. "The Triangle building's on fire and I think the D.A. should be there!" With that, they all dashed downstairs and hailed cabs. Traffic slowed as they neared the fire, bogging down among thousands of people chasing the sound of sirens and the plume of smoke.

When Whitman reached the building, he saw crowds straining against lines of policemen holding them back with clubs drawn. The police were under the command of Capt. Dominic Henry of the Mercer Street station, the notorious antistrike precinct of the waist makers' uprising. Capt. Henry seemed stunned to find himself back at the Triangle under such shocking circumstances. At least one of the victims lying dead on the sidewalk, Beryl "Ben" Sklaver, had been hauled to jail by Capt. Henry's men—the same sidewalk on which Capt. Henry had reluctantly arrested the wealthy activist Inez Milholland. Other corpses, like Becky Kessler's, were those of workers who had walked the picket line under the disapproving gaze of Dominic Henry and his men.

This realization—that these bodies, and this factory, had played a part in the uprising a year before—was already spreading through the crowd. "I remembered their great strike of last year, in which these girls demanded more sanitary workrooms, and *more safety precautions* in the shops," wrote William Gunn Shepherd. "These dead bodies told the result." He was the first but hardly the only writer to make the connection. Interestingly, the socialist newspaper was one of the few that did not. The *Call* focused on the relative weakness of the union at the Triangle Waist Company: "Most of the dead workers were un-organized and toiled in a scab shop." But the paper added: "No one thought of that. They were slain members of the working class—that was all that counted."

District Attorney Whitman began gathering information as the last daylight ebbed and eerie evening came on. The same police force that harassed strikers on these same sidewalks was now assigned to collect the bodies of the Triangle dead. Officers examined, described, and tagged each corpse, then placed the bodies in coffins and stacked the boxes on horse-drawn wagons. Each time a wagon was loaded with five or six dead, officers cleared a narrow path through the crowd, and the docile horses headed east from Greene Street to Broadway. From there, the wagons lumbered slowly north and then farther eastward toward a pier that served as New York's emergency morgue. Capt. William Hogan of the First Precinct supervised the tagging operation on Greene Street, while police inspector Cornelius Hayes led the grim exercise on Washington Place.

They began with the jumpers. Two officers scrutinized each vic-tim and dictated a general description. A third patrolman, trained in shorthand, transcribed the information, jotting down the gender of the victim, the hair color (if they could tell), and any distinguishing marks or jewelry. Each entry was numbered. Then another officer tagged each body with the corresponding number. By about 8 P.M., they fin-ished with the jumpers and started on the victims who had come down by rope. The coroner's office ran out of coffins, so a boat was dis-patched to a city hospital on Blackwell's Island to fetch more.

When the tagging began, bodies were piled so thickly on the sidewalks that they covered the fire hoses. The pavement was strewn with mundane possessions the victims had lost as they fell: "leather handbags, broken combs, hair ribbons, some dimes and cents, parts of clothing." Officers collected all the personal effects they could find in large wicker baskets, but within a day or two vendors began hawking what they claimed were rings and watches and torn pay envelopes that had belonged to Triangle victims.

The pavement kept refilling with bodies, from the elevator shaft, from the ninth floor, even from the basement. Every one bore gruesome signs of a violent death. A veteran policeman turned to Charles Willis Thompson of the *New York Times*. "This is the worst I ever saw," the cop said.

Charles Whitman arrived shortly after 5 P.M., just as the fire department was getting the blaze under control. He was shocked by the bloodied sidewalks and the dead forms plainly outlined under sodden sheets, where sheets had been placed at all. While he was looking over the scene, police officers introduced Whitman to elevator operator Joseph Zito. The D.A. listened as one of the day's few surviving heroes told his story. Then, to his amazement, Whitman learned that the police had Zito under arrest as a material witness. Disgusted, Whitman ordered that the prisoner be freed immediately.

A few minutes later, he heard a report that firefighters had entered the ninth-floor loft and found heaps of bodies. A floor-by-floor search of the building, from the cellar to the roof, was just beginning, but estimates of the death toll ran as high as two hundred. New Yorkers, Whitman realized, would demand that someone, or some agency, be held accountable. His job was to figure out who it should be.

Some of those who witnessed the tragedy were struck by the impotence of the fire department, which seemingly did nothing to save the trapped workers. A city coroner, Dr. D. C. Winterbottom, lived around the corner from the Asch Building, and he had rushed to the scene in time to see victims plunging from the windows. Winterbottom was highly critical of the fire department. He believed that everyone might have been saved if the first wave of firefighters had carried axes to break down the doors.

But that would be a difficult theory to sell to the public. New York took great pride in its fire department, and Chief Edward Croker, the man in charge, was perhaps the most respected public official in the city and—not coincidentally—one of the most skillful handlers of the press. Whatever Croker had to say about the lessons of the fire, and the proper distribution of blame, would be highly influential with the papers.

As the nephew of Tammany's notorious boss Croker, the chief got his start via patronage and rocketed through the ranks during the years his "Uncle Richard" ran the city. He made it to the top at the tender age of thirty-five. A man less adept at public relations would have been buried under charges of nepotism, but with time, any hint of favoritism faded into ancient history, and he became the beau ideal of public service in the eyes of New Yorkers. The chief lived a dedicated life in a small suite of rooms over the Engine Co. 33 station house on Great Jones Street. It wasn't unusual to see him run into a burning building as the roof appeared ready to collapse, just so that he could see for himself whether it was safe for his men to enter.

Croker was one of the first people Charles Whitman spoke to on the sidewalk. "I have long expected just such a fire as this," said Croker, who was naturally eager to shield himself and his men. In fact, he was on record predicting this very thing, four months earlier, after the High Street fire in Newark. The problem was simple, as the chief saw it: These buildings were too tall and too many people worked in them, with scant provision for their safety. If anyone was to blame, Croker said, it was the city building department, for failing to insist on adequate safety measures.

Whitman seemed drawn toward this explanation that first evening. Obviously, the building was not safe enough. But there was another possibility as well. The blame might belong with the factory owners. From the early minutes of the blaze, as survivors spilled down the stairs and into the streets and began telling their stories to bystanders, gossip about locked doors ran rampant through the crowd. As the evening wore on, these rumors were embellished by other (untrue) allegations: that the owners locked the doors to keep out union organizers; that they had commandeered the elevators to save themselves, and so on. Charles Thompson, the *Times* man, expressed the outrage and revulsion that took hold of the crowd. "I would like to hold the rope if there [is] ever any general movement to hang Harris & Blanck," he told a friend.

Whitman faced two possible responses to the fire. He could go after the building department, which would cast the fire as a problem of the bureaucracy, or he could go after the owners, which would cast the disaster as an individual crime. In theory, of course, he could do both, but it would be difficult to emphasize two competing theories.

In that era of scant regulation, it wasn't easy to prove crimes of negligence. But Whitman could plainly see that the question of the owners' culpability would be a major issue for the public and the press. So for the time being, he elected to keep his options open. In a statement partly dictated by the reporter Herbert Bayard Swope, Whitman straddled the question of blame.

"I was appalled at what I saw when I arrived at the fire, and am loath to talk about it," he said. Then he went on for nine paragraphs, according to the *American*. Whitman praised Joseph Zito and took credit for freeing him from the bumbling police. He said his "hurried investigation" had not shown any "prima facie evidence upon which a charge of manslaughter could be based." Nevertheless, a top homicide prosecutor would take command of the case immediately. The rest of the statement was spent aligning himself closely with the fire chief— surely the safest place to be—by promising to examine the city's building codes and force changes where necessary. "It appears from what Chief Croker has said that there is danger in many of the buildings that are termed 'fireproof,'" Whitman said. "The matter will be taken up before the April Grand Jury."

He had handled the situation deftly, seeming purposeful without foreclosing any options. If the public wanted to forget about this awful event in a month or so, Whitman was well situated to let it fade away

A tide of immigrants poured into the fledgling garment industry around the turn of the twentieth century. Abundant labor drove wages down and set off a brutal competition for work. Even tiny tenement rooms became squalid little factories, known as sweatshops. (UNITE Archives, Kheel Center, Cornell University)

High-rise loft buildings allowed men like burly Max Blanck and his partner, Isaac Harris (shown with employees of the Triangle Waist Co.), to create large, efficient garment factories in New York. Blanck and Harris cashed in on the blouse-and-skirt craze sparked by artist Charles Dana Gibson and his iconic Gibson girls, becoming the Shirtwaist Kings.

In the autumn of 1909, a strike at the Triangle factory helped catalyze the largest labor uprising the garment industry had ever seen. Some forty thousand workers, mostly women, walked out of the waist shops and astonished New Yorkers with their endurance. (UNITE Archives, Kheel Center, Cornell University)

Clara Lemlich, a young Russian immigrant, survived a brutal beating by hired thugs to rally the strikers at a crucial meeting inside the Cooper Union. "I have no further patience for talk," she cried, after a speech by the labor boss, Samuel Gompers. "I move that we go on a general strike!" (UNITE Archives, Kheel Center, Cornell University).

The shirtwaist uprising drew unprecedented support from wealthy progressive women, including Anne Morgan, daughter of the most powerful capitalist in America (in fur stole) and suffrage leader Alva Smith Vanderbilt Belmont. (Library of Congress, Prints & Photographs Division)

The Shirtwaist Kings, Blanck, left, and Harris, fiercely resisted the strike. But a year later, they faced manslaughter charges after 146 employees died in a blaze that swept the Triangle factory at closing time. Elevator operator Joseph Zito braved flames to rescue workers. (UNITE Archives, Kheel Center, Cornell University)

8th FLOOR

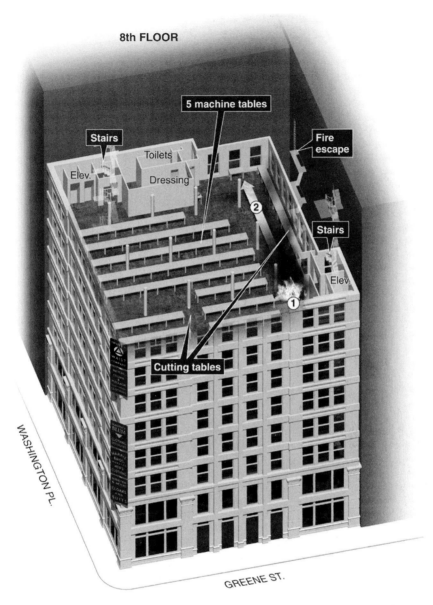

Eighth floor, Asch Building: About two hundred employees were finishing work at cutting tables and sewing machines. At 4:40 P.M., the fire starts under a table near the Greene Street stairs (1). A draft from the open door spreads the fire toward the rear airshaft (2). Workers fled, using both sets of stairs, the fire escape, and the Washington Place elevators. (Doug Stevens)

Ninth floor, Asch Building: About 250 employees worked at eight rows of sewing machines. At 4:45 P.M., fire in the airshaft entered the room (3). Flames engulfed examining tables in rear of factory and spread quickly. Other flames lapped up from eighth-floor windows. The over-crowded fire escape collapsed. At the Washington Place door (4), workers cried, "The door is locked!" Some escaped by elevators; others raced up the Greene Street stairs (5) to the roof. After those routes were cut off by the blaze about 4:51 P.M., more than 140 ninth-floor workers perish. (Doug Stevens)

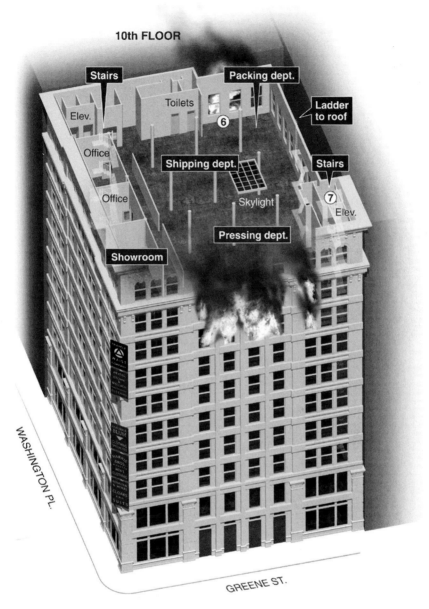

10th FLOOR

Stairs

Packing dept.

Elev.

Toilets

Ladder to roof

Office

⑥

Shipping dept.

Stairs

Office

⑦

Skylight

Elev.

Pressing dept.

Showroom

WASHINGTON PL.

GREENE ST.

Tenth floor, Asch Building: Perhaps sixty workers were employed in the pressing, packing, shipping, and administrative operations. About 4:45 P.M. owners and workers saw flames through the airshaft windows **(6).** Some escaped down Washington Place elevators, others by racing up the Greene Street stairs to the roof **(7).** (Doug Stevens)

Some two dozen workers died when the flimsy fire escape collapsed. "I hope I never hear anything like it again," a witness said.

The death trap: Flames pushed workers into this corner of the ninth floor, above the intersection of Greene Street and Washington Place, where they were among the last to die. Note the tables still standing with their sewing machines attached to a common drive shaft. The window sashes are gone from the two windows on the left, having given way as trapped workers pressed against them. (UNITE Archives, Kheel Center, Cornell University)

More than fifty workers plunged from the windows as a huge crowd watched in horror.
Afterward, coroners examined the bodies for signs of life. Then police moved in to tag the
dead. Remains were taken to the Charities Pier on Twenty-sixth Street, where thousands of
survivors, and morbid sightseers, examined the dead. Six victims were never identified.
(UNITE Archives, Kheel Center, Cornell University)

Outrage and grief swept New York in response to the fire. As rain fell, hundreds of thousands jammed the funeral route for the unidentified victims. (UNITE Archives, Kheel Center, Cornell University)

Max D. Steuer, a former garment-shop worker himself, was on his way to fame and riches as New York's greatest trial lawyer when he agreed to defend the Shirtwaist Kings. Prosecutors charged that a locked door caused some of the deaths. Steuer's cunning cross-examination of survivor Kate Alterman enhanced his reputation as a courtroom magician.

The Triangle fire was a turning point for Tammany Hall, New York's often corrupt political machine. Tammany boss Charles F. Murphy (above) embraced sweeping reforms that won a new generation of immigrants to the Democratic Party. In 1913, Tammany's old guard lined up alongside Murphy for the funeral of legendary ward boss Timothy D. Sullivan. (Murphy is far right; next to him is Tom Foley, patron of future governor Alfred E. Smith, and, far left, Thomas "The" MacManus. Reporter Herbert Bayard Swope is just behind them, with his press card in his hatband.)

Frances Perkins was having tea near the fire scene and arrived in time to see the falling bodies. Seeking reforms after the fire, she worked with the "Tammany Twins"—Robert F. Wagner, left, and Alfred E. Smith—to rewrite New York labor law, and launch the changes that would become the New Deal. In 1933, she was appointed America's first woman cabinet secretary.

under the cloak of the grand jury. If, on the other hand, the public demanded vengeance and redemption, he was positioned to try to deliver it.

The Charities Pier, located where Twenty-sixth Street met the East River, had been known as Misery Lane since the *Slocum* fire. The pier was covered by a large iron-frame enclosure painted a sickly yellow, with small windows high up on two of the four sides. It was gloomy by day and spooky by night even before the convoy of wagons came rolling up with their sad freight, and behind the wagons the desperate fathers, mothers, siblings, and cousins of the dead and missing. When the wagons arrived, they were met by a team of homeless men dragooned from the Municipal Lodging House, who were assigned to open the boxes and arrange them in two long rows. Apparently the police officers at the scene had not done a very good job of numbering the victims, because the coroner's assistants decided to do the job over again. Then the corpses were propped up in the coffins.

At midnight, the doors opened. The first in the growing line of friends and family members began shuffling up one long row and down the other. Low voices, slow footsteps, the cry of gulls, and the lapping of water punctuated the heavy silence. A faint sulfuric glow fell from lights hung high in the rafters. This did little to illuminate the coffins, however, so policemen stood every few feet holding lanterns. When a loved one paused at a box and peered close, the nearest officer dangled his lantern helpfully. The light swayed and flickered over the disfigured faces. Now and then a shock of recognition announced itself in a piercing cry or sudden sob splitting the ghastly quiet. When Clara Nussbaum found her daughter Sadie, she ran to the edge of the pier and tried to throw herself into the river.

For four days, through cold and rain, this gut-wrenching tour continued. Clara Lemlich searched the disfigured bodies for a missing cousin who later turned up alive. Misery Lane attracted ghouls and thieves along with the genuinely grieving. Forty known pickpockets were rousted from the long lines outside the morgue; police suspected that they were planning to rob the bodies. (On the Lower East Side, a prevalent rumor held that firefighters and police had already stripped the victims of most valuables.)

Eventually, a nurse from the Charities Department, Mary Gray, was stationed at the entrance, with orders to quiz everyone who tried to enter. "She had a wonderfully searching eye," said the *World*. "She turned them back by the score, but there was sweetness and tenderness in the manner in which she made way for those in whose eyes she could read genuine grief and suffering." One young woman, refused entry, pleaded with the nurse for a chance to go in. "I won't look for more than a minute!" she promised.

A teenager named Rosie Shannon joined the line at 8 A.M. on the morning after the fire. After waiting several hours, she reached the rows of coffins and began filing past the burned and battered faces in search of her boyfriend, Joseph Wilson. He had come to New York from Philadelphia not long before, intending to marry her. The previous evening, Shannon waited for Wilson to meet her after work. They were planning to pick a date for their wedding, but he never arrived. She found his badly burned body in coffin No. 34. Though his face was beyond recognition, he was wearing the ring she had given him. Shannon mentioned to a policeman that he should also have been carrying a pocket watch. When the authorities produced it, she opened the case—and there, inside the cover, was her picture staring back at her.

Another teenager, Esther Rosen, understood that her childhood was over and she was now responsible for her younger siblings when she recognized the braids she had plaited in her widowed mother's hair. The coroner had been amazed to find $852—nearly two years' wages— under a band of cheesecloth inside Julia Rosen's left stocking. Why, he asked the girl, didn't her mother use a bank? Esther had no idea what the word meant.

Many of the badly burned corpses held clues in their jewelry—rings, earrings, lockets, watches, bracelets, combs. A man identified his fiancée by an unburned scrap of her corset. A family claimed their daughter by noticing the cork inserts in her shoes. A mother recognized her child by a darn in her stocking. Joseph Flecher, the Triangle's paymaster, remembered that he once sent the ninth-floor bookkeeper, Mary Laventhal, to a dentist he knew for a gold cap on one of her teeth. Thus she was identified. After identifying her mother by her braids, Esther Rosen returned several times in search of her brother Israel. It wasn't until Friday, almost a week after the fire, that she decided the signet ring on a badly charred body must have been his.

By Wednesday night, all but sixteen of the victims had been claimed. The next day, March 30, Sarah Kupla, sixteen, died at St. Vincent's Hospital of injuries from her fall. She had never regained consciousness. The death toll was complete at 146 victims. In parts of downtown Manhattan, it seemed as though scarcely a block had been spared a death or serious injury. Celia Eisenberg was dead on East First Street; Mary and Lena Goldstein on East Second Street; Rachel Grossman, Nettie Lefkowitz, Jennie Stern, Fannie Hollander, Jennie Lederman, the Brenman sisters, and Jennie Poliny on East Third Street; Ida Pearl on East Fourth Street; Violet Schochep, Morris Bernstein, and Mary Herman on East Fifth Street; Sadie Nussbaum and Lizzie Adler on East Sixth Street.

Jennie Pildescu was dead on East Seventh Street; Rose Weiner, Yetta Fichtenhultz, Gussie Spunt, and Tessie Kaplan on East Eighth Street; Annie Starr on East Ninth Street; Kate Leone, Tina Frank, and Dora Dochman on East Eleventh Street; Mary Ullo, Josephine Carlisi, and Bertha Greb on East Twelfth Street; Annie Colletti, Nicolina Nicolosci, Antonietta Pasqualicca, Jennie Stiglitz, Anna Ardito, and Jacob Bernstein on East Thirteenth Street.

Homes lost loved ones on Attorney Street and Broome Street and Bedford Street and Bleecker Street and the Bowery; on Commerce Street and Chrystie Street and Clinton Street; on Delancey Street and Division Street and Essex Street and Henry Street and Houston Street; on Ludlow Street and Madison Street and MacDougal Street and Monroe Street; on Rivington Street and Stanton Street and Thompson Street. Four friends were gone from four apartments in a single block of Cherry Street.

By week's end, all but seven of the corpses were identified. Union leaders arranged for a funeral procession through the heart of Manhattan to honor the Triangle victims. At the same time, the Local 25 relief committee paid out small sums to cover burial expenses for members. Rosie Freedman's uncle received thirty-five dollars to bury the girl from Bialystok under a small stone in a Brooklyn cemetery. Later, after investigating the circumstances and obligations of her life, the committee granted an additional one thousand rubles—about five hundred dollars—in a lump sum to Freedman's family in Russia.

These individual poignancies, vignettes not so much of life but of death, dominated the city's newspapers for days. Indeed, there were so many tales of grief that each one could be given only a paragraph or two at most. The deeper biographies of the dead went unreported.

New York's journalists also fared poorly in figuring out what actually happened inside the factory. The *Times* ran a damning picture of a metal grate blocking an exit—a photo that the fire marshal immediately denounced as fraudulent. The *World* claimed that its reporter had found the actual lock of the death door in the debris of the fire. But it was the wrong lock and the wrong door. Other reporters relayed the disturbing news that the fire hoses in the Asch Building weren't even connected to the standpipes—unaware, apparently, that the firefighters disconnected them to attach their own hoses. An important question, never conclusively answered, was whether the hoses were in good working order before they were disconnected. Chief Croker was quoted as saying that the fire was probably caused by an explosion of gasoline-heated irons on the eighth floor—but the irons were on the tenth floor.

Thus, questions of how the victims died, who was to blame, and what was to be done all blurred with each passing day. Political leaders were vague and defensive. "I find I am powerless to take the initiative in an inquiry," said Governor John A. Dix. The mayor, William Gaynor, considered visiting the scene of the fire, but decided against it, offering no explanation. Instead, he sent his secretary, who referred all questions to Chief Croker. State labor commissioner John Williams dodged inquiries, suggesting that questions should be directed to the city building department. Building department head Rudolph Miller, meanwhile, was on vacation and unwilling to rush back to face his critics. Instead, he sent word that the blame belonged with the fire department.

The private parties also pointed fingers. Joseph Asch, owner of the building, rushed in from Norwalk, Connecticut, and went briefly into hiding at a Manhattan hotel. But then he thought better of it. He rode the elevator back down to the lobby, collared the first newsman he met, and insisted that he had done everything city officials ever asked. Isaac Harris invited reporters to his Upper West Side home, where he greeted them with his hand bandaged and his partner ashen-faced beside him. Harris and Blanck vehemently denied that the doors of the Triangle were ever locked during working hours.

BLAME SHIFTED ON ALL SIDES FOR FIRE HORROR, the *Times* declared in a lead headline. Everyone agreed that something terrible had happened, and nearly everyone at least paid lip service to the need for a significant response. But there was no consensus as to who had failed, what had gone wrong, or how to fix it. *Times* editors counseled calm deliberation. "Excited persons rarely accomplish anything," they sniffed. The best thing for New Yorkers to do, the paper advised, was to place their trust in Charles Whitman, "a man of good judgment and quick action. . . . No new laws are needed."

The *World,* in contrast, called for a raft of new laws to mandate better fire escapes, enclosed fireproof stairs, automatic sprinklers, and fire drills. The socialist *Call,* meanwhile, indicted the "bosses." HOW LONG WILL THE WORKERS PERMIT THEMSELVES TO BE BURNED AS WELL AS ENSLAVED IN THEIR SHOPS? the paper bannered. "Nothing was done to those criminal employers, Blanck & Harris," the story went on. "The only news that came from them was that they were in a 'highly nervous condition.' And no wonder, for it was these two bosses who made haste to save their own precious hides by escaping to the roof while the human beings who piled up profits for them died in burned, crushed and mutilated heaps."

That analysis was undercut by the Joint Board of Sanitary Control, a union-supported agency created by Louis Brandeis's "Protocol of Peace." Board members, chosen by the union and the manufacturers,

monitored working conditions in garment factories. Inspectors working for the Joint Board had visited more than twelve hundred New
York factories in the months after the Newark blaze, according to
board member Henry Moskowitz, a leading progressive social worker.
Virtually all those factories, he said, presented serious fire dangers.
The Triangle had been inspected, Moskowitz told reporters—and it
was among the *safer* shops on the list. While these findings strongly
indicated a need for general improvements, they seemed to undercut
the notion that Harris and Blanck were criminally negligent.

The official investigations were no less confusing. After two days of
hearings, Fire Marshal Edward Beers announced his preliminary opinion concerning the cause of the fire and why it was so deadly. The
problem was neither panic nor inadequate means of escape, he said.
"It was something else . . . [the] rush of heat that preceded the flames
themselves." This overwhelming wave killed the victims where they
stood, before they could make it through the doors, Beers said. He
added: "I do not take seriously reports that the doors were locked. . . .
The fact that workers from the eighth and ninth floors escaped by way
of the roof is evidence enough that the doors were not locked."

Undoubtedly, the fire marshal was correct in regard to the Greene
Street door. It was not locked. Dozens of people did escape through
this door, and the bodies found heaped just inside it belonged to a
crowd of unlucky workers who had waited a moment too long to make
the dash for the roof. They were asphyxiated by heat and toxic gases
"so intense that they dropped where they stood as flowers might
wither under the same influence," as Beers put it.

Beers applied his theory to *all* the doors, however, not just the Greene
Street exit. And the facts did not support his theory on the opposite
side of the ninth floor—at the Washington Place door. There was not
one survivor known to have escaped from the ninth floor by way of that
door. Charles Whitman seemed to understand this better than Beers.
The same day that the fire marshal essentially exonerated Harris and
Blanck, the district attorney's office leaked news that criminal indictments were on their way. Whitman's prosecutors, it was said, had been
overwhelmed by evidence concerning the Washington Place door.

* * *

Into this muddle of finger-pointing and confusion charged William Randolph Hearst. In the pages of the *American*, Hearst put aside investigative reporting and tearjerkers, normally strong suits for his newspapers, and instead devoted day after day to front-page headlines attacking the bureaucrats behind the building codes. As early as Monday, March 27, the second morning after the fire, when other papers were moist with the sorrow at the Charities Pier, Hearst's *American* was pushing his agenda. CITY OFFICIALS BLAMED FOR FIRE TRAGEDY, the banner headline announced, and the story revealed that it was Hearst doing the blaming. The next day, a front-page picture showed the twisted remains of the sorry fire escape, with a question directed at the Manhattan borough president: "Mr. McAneny, Who Is Responsible for This?"

Hearst even commissioned his own panel of experts in real estate, engineering, and fire prevention, including the esteemed Chief Croker, to propose new laws for safe factories. The commissioning was front-page news, "*American* Moves to Protect Shop Workers." So was the panel's first meeting, "*American*'s Experts Ready to Frame Death-Proof Fire Law." Most individual proposals were front-page news—"*American*'s Experts Draw Up Plan"—and so were the reactions of city officials. Like Charles Whitman, Hearst had large political ambitions—presidential ambitions. Through his paper, it was as if Hearst were trying to show what a good mayor he would have been in this crisis.

The *American*'s campaign greatly increased the pressure on Whitman. Though Hearst's support had been important to Whitman's election in 1909, it was inevitable that the two men would clash. They were potential rivals for the same lane of a very competitive track. The fire provided the excuse. On Friday, March 31, the *American* blasted Whitman in its lead editorial, printed in extra-large type.

"The District Attorney's Most Pressing Duty," ran the title. In a few short, crisp jabs—a cardinal virtue of Hearst journalism—Whitman was accused of paying too much attention to the Carnegie Trust scandal and not enough to "more pressing questions of culpability in the fire horror of last Saturday. The Carnegie Trust matter deals with money, which is important, of course. But this fire question deals with human life, which is infinitely more important. The people of New York are awake and in deadly earnest over the protection of those who labor in factory buildings."

Whitman was livid when he read the piece, and immediately saw that he must abandon his wait-and-see strategy. He summoned a top assistant. "What's happening in the Triangle case?" Whitman demanded.

"Well, boss," the aide answered, "we're not finished with the investigation, but very soon we'll have the case before the grand jury."

"Well, get an indictment!" Whitman ordered. He waved the editorial under the man's nose. "Here, look at it," the D.A. said. "You go and get an indictment. We can *nol pros* if we can't maintain it." That is, the case could be dropped quietly, when the pressure was off, if the evidence didn't pan out.

A disillusioned young lawyer in Whitman's office, Emory Buckner, recounted this exchange in a letter to his friend Felix Frankfurter, the future Supreme Court justice. Frankfurter was appalled. "Whitman was getting indictments because Hearst's *American* was yelling blue murder," Frankfurter later wrote. A "politically minded D.A.," he concluded, is "one of the great curses of America."

Whitman's shift was significant. New York City's ranking elected reformer was no longer focused on improving factory safety laws. His priority now was to indict Isaac Harris and Max Blanck on charges of manslaughter. He made this his personal business, frequently appearing in the grand jury room to present evidence and interrogate witnesses. One day, on the eve of the indictments, he spotted Samuel Bernstein, the Triangle manager, and machinist Louis Brown, in the courthouse hallway. Loudly enough for watching journalists to hear, he demanded to know what they were doing. Bernstein insisted that they had received subpoenas from Whitman's office to testify, but Whitman accused them of trying to intimidate witnesses. "Goddamn you," the D.A. shouted, "get out of here!"

Whitman's new emphasis took interest away from the drive for sweeping reforms. Despite ringing speeches and august committees— Hearst even sent a lobbyist to Albany to promote the proposals of his expert panel—the political will for change seemed to be flagging quickly. Scarcely a month after the fire, a special coroner's jury, composed of engineers, architects, developers, and scientists, took the unusual step of preparing recommendations for the governor and state legislature. "The disaster was of such terrible extent," the Board of Coroners explained, that it "should not be allowed to pass with the mere punishment of the men responsible."

Yet the headline in the *World* announcing the panel's conclusions said: "Public Officials Already Losing Interest in Proposed Reforms." Tellingly, it was not even a front-page headline. A month after the fire, the newspapers were losing interest, too.

Meyer London's dark prediction—that New York's political apparatus would ultimately dismiss the Triangle fire with a token gesture—appeared to be coming true. Like the Newark fire and the staggering *Slocum* disaster before it, the catastrophe at the Asch Building was fading away. Only a concerted effort in Albany could revive the idea of serious reform, and few people felt this was likely. For the first time in some forty years, the governor, John Dix, and both houses of the legislature were all under the control of the enemies of reform: Tammany Hall and Charles F. Murphy.

Murphy had his own grand, even presidential, dreams—not for himself but for the Hall. He was not content simply to run Manhattan in alliance with Big Tim Sullivan, though it was lucrative work. Murphy was a great political seer, and he could envision far more. The recent statewide elections had shown what might be possible.

But a greater future depended on Tammany's continued hold on the loyalty of working-class voters, the backbone of the Hall's power for more than half a century. New York's working-class population was growing at a phenomenal rate. If a way could be found to make the new immigrants as loyal as earlier generations, then Tammany might one day dictate policy for the entire Democratic Party and send its own men to the White House.

These were long-term issues, though, and Murphy was buried in short-term politics during March 1911. Day after day since early January, he had been suffering relentless humiliation at the hands of a freshman state senator in Albany. The boss wanted to exercise his newly won power to handpick a United States senator. In those days, senators were not chosen by direct election; state legislatures elected them. And Murphy felt that Tammany's control in Albany rightly entitled him to dump the Republican veteran Chauncey DePew and install a loyal Tiger in his place.

The young man standing in his way was named Franklin D. Roosevelt, a very distant cousin of the dazzling man who had just been president. Like his more famous relative, Franklin Roosevelt was a politician blessed with the enviable independence of the bright, brash, and wealthy. "I am pledged to no man, to no special interest, to no boss," he bragged while campaigning for the Dutchess County senate seat, in the ringing voice that would one day be famous. Murphy did not frighten him, though Roosevelt admired Murphy's political mind and would eventually make many mutually rewarding compromises with Tammany. Roosevelt had his own ambitions, and foresaw the dangers to him, an upstate aristocrat, if his party was entirely controlled by a single urban boss.

As leader of a group of nineteen Democratic insurgents from upstate, Roosevelt controlled enough votes to block the election of a new senator. By withholding their votes, they stymied the leaders of both parties. The rebels would not side with the Republicans to reelect DePew, but they blocked the Murphy loyalists as well. This stalemate dragged on through February and March as Murphy maneuvered to crush the uprising. He offered a different Tammany man in place of his original choice, giving Roosevelt a chance to declare victory and stand down. But the younger man refused the gambit. Then Murphy's men mounted a whispering campaign against Roosevelt, suggesting that he was motivated against Irish-dominated Tammany by an anti-Catholic bias. Roosevelt didn't flinch. All the while, Tammany district leaders peppered Murphy with new candidates—the headlines seemed to feature another potential senator every day. The drama continued, at a rising pitch, until the Triangle fire briefly knocked it off the front pages.

Among the district leaders loudly touting candidates was Tim
Sullivan, the "Big Feller" who controlled downtown. And Sullivan's
choice said a lot about the shifting power on the Lower East Side. Big
Tim wasn't backing a major contributor or a distinguished Tammany
judge. His man was the philanthropist and civic paragon Isidor Straus,
an owner of Macy's department store. On the surface, this was a jar-
ring, almost comical, notion. Though Sullivan was a popular despot,
he was still a despot. His money and power were wrung from what
would come to be called organized crime. From his customary table at
the Occidental Hotel on the Bowery, Big Tim skimmed the first cream
from all the vices south of Fourteenth Street. Immensely charming,
Sullivan was also extremely tough. He reigned by muscle. A major
criminal gang, the Whyos, constituted his personal army, and he was
on good business terms with all the other important hoodlums—including Monk Eastman's boys and the Paul Kelly gang. (It was an intriguing fact of downtown life that a young Italian thug named Paolo
Vacarelli would decide to do business under an Irish nom de guerre
Paul Kelly.) Big Tim owned the cops and the crooks. He was the smiling, genial face of political corruption. What possible interest could
he have in the incorruptible Straus?

Straus was Jewish, like more than half of the Lower East Side. He
was a founder and chairman of the board of the Educational Alliance,
one of the most important institutions of the Eastern European community. One of his brothers, Nathan Straus, had saved thousands of
infant lives by providing free pasteurized milk to slum families. Another brother, Oscar, was a distinguished diplomat. The Straus family
was deeply admired and trusted by the very voters drifting toward
Hearst and the socialists. Sullivan, perhaps even better than Murphy,
understood that the future of New York Democrats could rest with
these new immigrants.

The Senate battle consumed Murphy's attention in the days surrounding the Triangle fire. On March 31, he decided to go to Albany
to break the standoff. Murphy hired a railroad car and had it attached
to the overnight milk train. Arriving worn and unshaven, he checked

into Room 201 of the Ten Eyck Hotel and summoned the Tammany leaders. Things were getting out of hand: That morning, a vehement editorial denouncing Murphy as "the evil genius of democracy" had led the *World*'s opinion page. "Murphy has split the Democratic party . . . debased and degraded Democratic principles . . . discredited the first Democratic administration in sixteen years . . . [and] made the Democratic legislature an object of public derision," Pulitzer's paper declared. When Big Tim got to the boss's suite, he found Murphy sprawled on a sofa, eating eggs and drinking orange juice. Murphy finished eating in silence. At last, when everyone was gathered and the eggs were gone, Silent Charlie spoke. He had chosen a respected judge—an Irishman, James O'Gorman—for the Senate seat.

Sullivan "strenuously objected," according to the *World*, though he must have known it would do no good, except that it would make a juicy story when he recounted it to the newspaper reporters gathered in the lobby. The story would then be read and noted by every politically curious person in New York—including the leaders on the East Side. With luck, they would note that Big Tim tried to give them their first Jewish senator—which was more than Hearst or the socialists or the Republicans had done for them.

Murphy did not explain or defend his choice. He let a lieutenant do that for him. The key, Murphy's man explained, was electability. Tammany could not afford another defeat. No doubt, Straus's religion was among the reasons given as to why he could not win the seat. For about an hour, Sullivan and the lieutenant argued boisterously, but Murphy paid careful attention to Big Tim's feelings, interjecting "a word here and there" to make it clear that he concurred with much of what Sullivan said. It was absolutely true that the Hall had to capture the new immigrants—but this particular gesture was the wrong way to do it. Murphy's decision stood, and after griping to reporters in the hotel lobby Sullivan loyally cast his vote for O'Gorman.

Murphy returned home with the problem of the East Side freshly stamped on his mind. The people there were now asserting themselves at every turn: at the polls, in strikes and labor rallies, even in the pleadings of men as powerful as Big Tim Sullivan. The time for token actions was past. Whatever Murphy did next had to matter. It had to be something the East Side cared about.

That night, under the sponsorship of Anne Morgan, Alva Belmont, and others, a huge crowd packed the Metropolitan Opera House to demand action on fire safety. Once again, the plight of the shirtwaist workers brought together the forces of change. The boxes were jammed with the well-to-do, while the cheap seats were filled with East Siders. "This calamity," said the Episcopal bishop of New York, David Greer, "causes racial lines to be forgotten, for a little while at least, and the whole community rises to one common brotherhood."

Four days later, some 350,000 people participated in a funeral march for the Triangle dead. About a hundred thousand of them walked solemnly through the streets of the city as a relentless, depressing rain fell. A quarter of a million more lined the route and watched in silence. The whole city was muffled in black: black bunting on hundreds of buildings; multitudes in black dresses and suits and hats and coats; black umbrellas covering them all under a lumpy quilt. It was, the *American* noted, "one of [the] most impressive spectacles of sorrow New York has ever known."

8

REFORM

Frances Perkins was having tea with Mrs. Gordon Norris that Saturday afternoon when the wail and bells of a fire engine interrupted their conversation. The Norris home was one of the redbrick town houses on the north side of Washington Square, one of the last bastions of the silk-hat, exquisitely mannered square of Edith Wharton and Henry James. All around them rose factory towers, and immigrant housing pushed toward the square from the south and west and east. But the town houses on the north side stood their ground, aloof and genteel.

The single siren multiplied. So many fire engines, from all directions. Perkins and Norris went to the front steps to see what was happening. They saw people in the square hurrying eastward and saw smoke rising from behind the New York University law school. Fire engines tore down Waverly Place, where Perkins had her apartment. They heard screams. The two women rushed after the crowd, cutting the corner of Washington Square and hurrying onto Washington Place.

"People had just begun to jump as we got there," Perkins recalled years later. "They had been holding on until that time, standing in the windowsills, being crowded by others behind them, the fire pressing closer and closer, the smoke closer and closer." She heard the cry rising from all around her: *Don't jump! Help is coming!* But Perkins knew better than most people that there was little the fire department could do. She watched with a sickened sense of familiarity, as if she had seen it all before: the inadequate exits; the useless ladders and life nets; the untrained, panicking workers. As executive secretary of the Consumers' League, an organization devoted to better working conditions, Perkins had begun a crash course on fire safety not long before, prompted by the Newark fire. She quickly mastered the details of sprinkler systems, fireproof stairways, fire drills, and more. She knew, in an intellectual way, that New York factories were extremely vulnerable. Now before her eyes, those theories were transformed into cruel facts.

Frances Perkins was just thirty years old, not much older than the young women and young men who were dying before her eyes. Yet her experiences perfectly suited her to help redeem the tragedy of the Triangle fire. That she was there to see this tragedy with her own eyes, to be able to feel it viscerally, is one of history's intriguing strokes of coincidence.

Frances Perkins embodied many of the pressures building under Tammany Hall. She was a young urban progressive—well educated, nonpartisan, fiercely committed to the idea of an active, humane government. She believed in labor unions and the vote for women. For a time, she even considered herself a socialist.

Born in Boston to a family with deep roots in Maine, Fannie Coralie Perkins grew up in nearby Worcester, Massachusetts, where her father ran a stationery shop. She was an ebullient girl, "a natural actress," according to her biographer, George Martin. At the same time, she was imprinted with the sense of obligation and the call to charity passed down from the New England Puritans through the Congregationalist Church. Both aspects of her personality, the duty and the dynamism, were shaped and tempered at Mount Holyoke College.

Her American history professor, an early progressive named Annah May Soule, stressed the importance of seeing problems firsthand. Soule took her students into the nearby mills to observe factory life

and Perkins was struck by the dangers bristling in every piece of unguarded machinery and on every slippery floor. In those days before
workers' compensation and government disability insurance, a single
accident could ruin a family. According to Martin, Perkins realized that
"avoiding poverty therefore was not a question simply of liquor or lazi-
ness," as generations of preachers had maintained, "but also of safety
devices on machines."

Perkins was training to become a science teacher. But this new science—social science—now captured her attention. She devoured *How
the Other Half Lives,* a seminal exposé of conditions in the New York
slums published in 1890 by Jacob Riis, whose journalism helped to
open the eyes of his friend Theodore Roosevelt. Then, in her senior
year, Perkins attended a speech by an electrifying and pioneering
woman named Florence Kelley, the national secretary of the Consumers' League. Kelley had been the chief factory inspector in Illinois, a
highly unlikely role for a woman of the time. The experience left her
convinced that if people had enough information about working conditions in the new industrial order, they would demand change. The
Consumers' League tried to gather and spread such information—
especially on the topics of child labor and sweatshops. The league created labels to be sewn into the garments produced in exemplary
factories. In this respect, her work foreshadowed by a century the anti-
sweatshop campaigns of today. Kelley was ahead of her time as a feminist as well: she went by her maiden name (as Perkins would later do),
divorced her first husband, married a socialist, and translated works
by Friedrich Engels.

Kelley's words and her example jolted Perkins into "the work which
became my vocation." Perkins graduated from Mount Holyoke committed to social research and large-scale change, making her way
gradually to Chicago. She changed her name to Frances and, in 1907,
began doing volunteer work at the Chicago Commons, one of the first
American settlement houses.

The idea of having college-educated men and women reform society by living in slums and working with the poor originated in London,
where Toynbee Hall was founded in 1884. America's first settlement,

Hull House in Chicago, was created by Jane Addams five years later. (Chicago Commons came five years after that.) The settlement house movement swept the nation's cities, and by 1910 there were more than four hundred in the United States. Settlement houses were a breeding ground for progressive leaders and a testing ground for their ideas. Lillian Wald's Henry Street Settlement on the Lower East Side provided medical care at a time when no one else was serving the mass of new immigrants. Wald's nurses traveled from tenement to tenement by walking across the rooftops—it was the quickest and safest way to visit the thousands of cases they handled each year. They saw "children with summer bowel complaints that sent infant mortality rates soaring; children with measles, unquarantined; children 'scarred with vermin bites' . . . a pregnant mother with a crippled child and two others living on chunks of dry bread sent in by neighbors," wrote Irving Howe. "There was no shrinking, no condescension, no idylizing, no sentimentalism, no preening, little theorizing, nothing but work, hard and endless and free from the contaminations of self."

As a volunteer on behalf of Chicago Commons, Perkins investigated garment shops, and quickly became a proponent of organized labor, having noticed that carpenters and plumbers, with their strong unions, lived better lives. Then she landed her first paid job in her chosen field. A philanthropic group in Philadelphia hired her to study the problem of young immigrant women falling into prostitution.

A century ago, the idea of tackling social problems by collecting *facts*—as opposed to scriptural passages or philosophical tenets—was groundbreaking. The Pittsburgh Survey of 1908, for example, marked the first effort to study the entire structure of life in one newly industrialized community. About that same time the U.S. Supreme Court cited data on the effects of overwork to support an Oregon law that limited the number of hours women and minors could work. This was the first time the High Court had used social science statistics to help decide a case.

If hard data could get airplanes off the ground and stretch bridges across wide rivers, surely data could drive a campaign for social reform. Frances Perkins threw herself into her survey of indecent lodging houses in Philadelphia. She applied the lessons of Annah Soule, insisting on seeing for herself, walking dutifully up to the brothel doors and knocking stoutly.

Her next job took her to Manhattan. Frances Perkins possessed a charming openness and a winning curiosity. At art galleries, she discovered a group of avant-garde painters, dubbed the Ashcan School for their devotion to the real and the grimy. She admired their renditions of ugly tenements and crowded street scenes and bloodied prizefighters—and, sweetly, loved even more a portrait of a little girl by George Bellows, one of the best Ashcan painters. She befriended the young writers Theodore Dreiser and Sinclair Lewis, and both of them were soon infatuated with her. Though she had never done much public speaking, she volunteered to give suffrage pitches on street corners. With a colleague holding a banner beside her, Perkins would climb onto a grocery crate and hold forth to the passing crowd. She learned that short, funny speeches would get a respectful hearing from almost anyone, and that the notorious streets of New York in fact held nothing to fear.

This curiosity, this openness, gave her a pragmatic sense of human nature. Her willingness to find some good in nearly everyone led her to believe even that some good could come from Tammany Hall. During her first months in New York, while studying the problem of hunger in the West Side neighborhood known as Hell's Kitchen, Perkins came upon a penniless woman and her two starving daughters. It turned out that the woman was an alcoholic and the family's sole support was her son. But the son was in jail. Perkins tried to get help for the family through an established charity, but the agency refused to assist a drunken and promiscuous woman. (One of her daughters was born out of wedlock.) So Perkins paid a visit to Tammany district headquarters.

The clubhouse was full of cigar-smoking men, who eyed the businesslike young woman with bemusement. She requested an audience with Thomas MacManus, the district leader. "Sure, lady, sure," someone answered, and she was ushered into his office. There she found a big, round, bearded man, neatly dressed, surrounded by cronies. None of them ever called him by his given name. They just called him "The."

The MacManus had knocked G. W. Plunkitt off his perch as baron of
the West Side, an act of treachery that the colorful Plunkitt compared
to Brutus slaying Caesar. Reformers assumed The MacManus to be
utterly corrupt, but Frances Perkins needed his help.

"What's troubling you?" asked The MacManus. It wasn't her trouble,
Perkins explained, but the trouble of a family she had recently met.
"Well, I'm always glad to help anybody in trouble," The MacManus re-
plied, in time-tested Tammany style.

He asked nothing about the family's morals or the mother's life-
style. He had only two questions: Did the family live in his district?
And did Perkins? Satisfied that he was dealing with constituents, The
MacManus sent her on her way. Within hours, the young man was out
of jail and back at work.

In 1910, after completing her hunger study and a master's degree at
Columbia University, Perkins went to work for the inspirational Florence Kelley as executive secretary of the Consumers' League in New
York. Her first task was to organize a large-scale study of cellar bakeries—neighborhood bread shops scattered every few blocks through
the New York slums. The *World* had been crusading against these
places for years: "a tale of filthy floors and walls, of stifling, noxious
atmosphere, of baking materials unfit for use, of consumptive men
and women working over the dough which is to go into the bread for
thousands." Consumers' League investigators visited more than 250
below-ground bakeries; Perkins personally went to more than a hundred. They saw dirt floors, rats, cats giving birth on the breadboards,
bakers dripping sweat into their dough, sick children coughing beside the ovens. As she was pursuing that project, the factory burned
on High Street in Newark and Perkins added fire safety to her list of
issues.

The league also sent her to Albany as a lobbyist, to push a bill that
would limit the workweek for women and minors to fifty-four hours—
nine hours a day, six days a week. The bill had been stuck in the legislature for two years, going nowhere. Perkins knew nothing about
lobbying, or the state legislature, but as always she was eager to learn.

On her first day in Albany, she was given a tour of the capitol by a lobbyist for the Citizens' Union, a prominent reform organization known scornfully around Tammany as "The Cits." When Perkins and her guide reached the state Assembly chamber, they found it nearly empty. The few members present were talking and laughing idly.

Except for one: a chicken-necked man with a huge nose was seated at his desk, poring over papers. "Who's that?" Perkins asked, impressed. She later recalled being surprised by the answer. His name was Alfred E. Smith—of Tammany Hall.

The election of 1910 arrived amid sour scandal and disintegration in New York's Republican Party. The Republican reform governor, Charles Evans Hughes, had become a bit too successful, pushing legislation over conservative objections to regulate banking, utilities, insurance, and other industries. The Republican machine wanted him out. At the same time, the ranking Republican state senator was found to be taking bribes from bridge builders to support construction bills. In turn, that discovery pointed to a ring of Republican leaders using government funds to play the stock market. When Election Day came, the voters threw out the latest batch of scoundrels and suddenly Tammany Hall controlled state government. The *Times* foresaw bad things. Dominance of New York would surely revert to "the mercenary Old Guard" who cared nothing for progress except as it could be measured in their bank accounts and those of their friends.

But Murphy startled everyone by skipping over the old guard and putting the day-to-day business of the legislature in the hands of two relatively young men. Robert F. Wagner, at thirty-three, was installed as the youngest Senate leader in New York history, while in the Assembly Alfred E. Smith—known to everyone simply as "Al"—became majority leader a few days after turning thirty-eight. Mr. Murphy, the saying went in Albany, had promoted the "kindergarten class."

At first, Wagner and Smith looked like younger versions of the same old thing—brighter than the average machine hack, to be sure, and more diligent, but still mere instruments of the boss. "The Democratic caucus is Charles F. Murphy at one end of a telephone wire and the Democratic leader at the other end," the *World* complained. Running their first legislative session, per Murphy's orders, Smith and Wagner put most of their considerable energy into wresting key appointed positions—the ones that wrote the regulations and granted the contracts—away from the Republicans, and padding government payrolls with jobs for Tammany to dispense. "Using the powers of his office ruthlessly," historian Robert Caro has written, Smith "rammed through the Assembly, as Bob Wagner was ramming it through the Senate, the notorious 'Murphy Charter,' which weakened New York City's civil service system and added thousands of patronage jobs to its payroll." The Citizens' Union gave both young leaders poor marks, and branded Smith "one of the most dangerous men in Albany."

But a generation later, it would be clear that spotting these two men and elevating them together was Murphy's greatest achievement, and also an important moment in American political history. Wagner was destined to become the legislative ramrod of the New Deal, pushing bills through the United States Senate to create Social Security, to guarantee unemployment insurance and workers' compensation, to build public housing, and to protect trade unions. Smith would become one of the country's greatest governors, revolutionizing New York and serving as a sort of prototype for twentieth-century liberalism. Since the Tweed era in the 1860s and 1870s, the words "Tammany Hall" had been synonymous with graft, corruption, and the election of puppets to do the work of dishonest bosses. That ignominy was largely deserved, but with the installation of Smith and Wagner in the first days of 1911, Charles Murphy promoted the leadership that would move Tammany into an era of change, an era of reform.

Like the boss they served, they were classic Tammany material—Wagner a German immigrant, Smith mostly Irish; Wagner from the Tammany stronghold of Yorkville on the Upper East Side, Smith from the heart of the Lower East Side. Both men grew up in poverty, scrapped for what education they had, and appreciated Tammany for the fairness with which it rewarded hard work and talent.

Bob Wagner was the youngest son of a German tradesman who immigrated to America in 1886, when the boy was nine. Unable to find work in his craft, Wagner's father became a janitor, not least because the tenement he cared for gave him a free apartment for his family in the basement. Wagner supplemented the family income by selling papers and delivering groceries before and after school. But like a lot of youngest sons in immigrant families, his way was made a bit easier by the gradual rise of his older siblings. As they contributed more to the family income, Wagner was required to contribute less. He was able to accumulate enough cash to buy a flashy suit, for example—the first of many—and when he finished high school as valedictorian, his brother Gus, a cook with a steady job, offered to help him go to college.

Wagner thrived at the City College of New York. He was a star athlete, quarterback of the football team—but was even more impressive as a public speaker. This gift led him naturally to the New York Law School near the downtown courthouses. The school offered a breakneck, two-year course in legal basics; it was not the sort of place where exclusive law firms did their hiring. So after graduation Wagner started his own partnership with his friend Jeremiah Mahoney, and both men quickly threw themselves into Tammany Hall.

Service to Tammany was the best way for an unpedigreed young attorney to build a practice in turn-of-the-century New York. There was always plenty of work for Tammany lawyers, and the best of them became as rich and famous as any lawyers in the country. Wagner made himself useful as a public speaker on behalf of the Hall's candidates, addressing crowds in his slow, clear voice. His obvious skills marked him as a candidate, and soon he was elected to the state Assembly in 1904, at age twenty-six. From there, he moved into the state Senate.

Al Smith's life was something from the pages of Horatio Alger, an urban version of the iconic log cabin. "His rise," the *New York Times* declared at his death, "had no exact parallel in U.S. history." Born in the final days of 1873, in an apartment over a barbershop on South Street, Smith was a near-perfect Lower East Side amalgam: Among his four grandparents there were two from Ireland, one from Germany, and one from Italy. His parents were poor, but respectable. They lived in an enclave of decency surrounded by "the wickedest ward in New

York," as one historian put it. Yet Smith remembered a happy childhood, with the rigging of the schooners in port as his gymnasium and
the garbage-strewn river for a swimming pool.

Best of all, his boyhood coincided with the building of the Brooklyn Bridge directly outside his family's window. It was an incredible
marvel of engineering and audacity, the longest suspension bridge
in the world by a good 50 percent. Half a century before the Empire
State Building, a generation before the Woolworth Tower—at a time
when the tallest structure in Manhattan was a church spire—the
Brooklyn Bridge was grand and looming and showy. The gray-brown
stone towers, with their distinctive Gothic arches, rose 276 feet into
the air, visible from all parts of the city. It was "the crowning glory of
an age memorable for great industrial achievements," one observer
said at the time. Smith envied those lucky men "who swarmed like
flies stringing the cables and putting in the roadways." His father,
partly disabled by a hard life on a delivery wagon, was a night watchman at the construction site, and it was a highlight of Smith's young
life when he went with his father on a harrowing trip across the catwalk from one side of the unfinished bridge to the other. A few
months later, the span officially opened under cascades of fireworks.

Al was twelve when his father died. To take care of his mother, he
dropped out of school and soon was at work in the Fulton Fish Market, handling barrels and slinging fish from before dawn to the end of
the day. Other men might have M.A.s or Ph.D.s; his degree was FFM,
he liked to say—an education in life from the Fulton Fish Market. It
was a hard course, but it taught him dignity, common sense, and how
not to get taken. Once, someone said to Charles Murphy that Smith
"has a lot of ability—it's too bad he isn't a college man." Murphy stared
at the fellow and finally answered: "If he was a college man, he
wouldn't be Al Smith."

Among the lessons Smith gleaned from the FFM curriculum was
that he did not want to sling fish forever. But his next job was not much
better: hauling pipes in a pump station. In his off hours he began hanging around Tom Foley's saloon, home of the Downtown Tammany
Club. Foley, known as Big Tom, was district leader for the Fourth

Ward, and his saloon offered a graduate degree in grassroots politics. Now and then, after hearing the pleas of a needy constituent, Big Tom would signal to Smith or to one of the other hungry young men loitering near the bar. The lucky fellow was getting a contract.

Smith was a natural when it came to carrying out these Tammany errands—the mission of mercy to the destitute widow, the intelligence relay from precinct house to whorehouse. "When he was given one, he executed it with graciousness and tact," Caro wrote. "He displayed a gift for getting along with people that was so highly developed as to be almost genius." Al Smith was quick-witted, gregarious, humble, generous, kind to animals and to children. He had an actor's flair for the perfectly timed joke and the delicate barb. Like Bob Wagner, Smith became a stump speaker on behalf of Tammany candidates, and no one who ever heard him forgot the voice: blaring, nasal, and intense. The sound grabbed the attention of his audience, and the content of his speeches held them, because Smith could be funny and sometimes tender and always seemed to make sense. When an Assembly seat opened up in his district, he was a natural choice. At first, Smith disliked the Assembly. Then he started reading, and everything changed.

Al Smith was a big personality: exuberant, loud, cigar-chomping, but when Frances Perkins first saw him, he was hunched at his desk, reading intently. "That's what he does," her tour guide informed her. Smith read every word of every bill. Early in his Assembly career, frustrated by his ignorance and impotence in the chamber, Smith resolved to master the legislative process—by sheer willpower. Painstakingly, the grade-school dropout mastered the circular, windy language of the bill-drafting priesthood. He read the laws that determined which companies could compete for contracts, and over time figured out as well as anyone in Albany whose bread was buttered where. If a bill changed an existing law, he went to the state capitol library and read the original. Smith even read the entire appropriations bill, something no one in memory had ever attempted. Slowly, year by year, the workings of America's biggest, most complicated state came into crystalline focus for Al Smith, and he went from being a silent lump in the back row to one of the most influential men in government.

"Al!" bellowed another lobbyist, who had joined Perkins and the man from the Cits behind the brass rail that separated the public from the lawmakers. Smith looked up, smiled his wide, wet-lipped smile, and strode over to meet the new kid from the Consumers' League. He took an instant liking to Perkins, and immediately gave her some useful guidance. The fifty-four-hour bill she was lobbying for was bottled up in committee, he explained. "Better ask for a hearing." This information was not much in itself, but the fact that he gave it so quickly, to a complete novice, struck Perkins as generous.

The impression deepened as she worked through the winter on behalf of the bill. Perkins did request a hearing, and was brusquely turned down. Again, Smith explained what was happening. The cannery interests in rural New York were blocking the hours bill and demanding an exemption. Shorter hours, they argued, would mean tons of spoiled food during the brief periods when fruits and vegetables were ripe. Smith interceded for Perkins, and the hearing was scheduled. Then, when the day came, he bolstered her presentation by asking friendly questions that made her dry data come to life in stories of exhausted women, overworked children, and broken families.

The dominant theme in the newspapers was the unholy alliance of Murphy and the "moneyed interests"—with Wagner and Smith as their useful tools: "the Tammany Twins." But Frances Perkins came to feel kindly toward both men. They seemed much more interested in the problems of the working poor than, for example, the new progressive state senator from Hyde Park, Franklin D. Roosevelt. Smith was always friendly, always frank, and usually helpful. Roosevelt was distant and unavailable. Perkins concluded that Smith was a backer of the fifty-four-hour law.

And yet, in the end, Murphy and the moneyed interests killed her bill without a peep of protest from the Tammany Twins. Perkins discovered this in springtime, around the time of the Triangle fire. She had a vacation planned, and she wanted to go—but not if she might miss an important vote on the fifty-four-hour bill. She asked Smith for his advice.

Smith seemed to weigh for a moment how much he should tell her. "You can go along to Europe with perfect ease of mind," he told her. "The bill isn't going to be passed or reported this year."

Perkins was flabbergasted. "How do you know?" she asked. "How can you possibly know that?"

"I had a talk with Murphy," Smith answered. "You can never get it out of committee." Tammany, it seemed, had other interests. As Perkins later recalled the conversation, Smith asked her: "Do you know who one of the big contributors to the Democratic campaign fund is?"

She did not.

"It's the Huyler candy factory," Smith explained. "They're great friends of Mr. Murphy's, and they live right down there near him." The Huyler brothers did not like the fifty-four-hour bill. Candy factories were notoriously grim places to work. Boiling the chocolatey, sugary concoctions was steamy, suffocating work, and it was all done standing up—hour after hour hovering over simmering cauldrons. Workers were frequently scalded or cut. All the wrapping was done by hand—numbingly tedious labor. During the busy season before Christmas, the factories were kept going almost around the clock. Like cannery owners, the candy makers argued that a limit on hours would make it impossible to run their highly seasonal businesses.

Tammany agreed—thanks to the persuasive power of campaign contributions. The MacManus might get a lad out of jail to support his starving sisters. Big Tim might give away ten thousand pairs of shoes. But faced with a choice between big donors and endangered workers, Tammany's calculation was as simple as it was cold. Murphy had decided, and the hours bill was dead.

Then the Triangle Waist Company burned, and the factors in Murphy's calculation began to change.

As Frances Perkins remembered it, the mood of New York reformers immediately after the fire was a sort of guilt, "as though we had all done something wrong." But that mood soon hardened into resolve, a feeling that "we've got to turn this into some kind of victory." It was in that spirit, she said, that the cream of progressive New York and the leaders of downtown socialism gathered on April 2, 1911, for an emotional, sometimes contentious, mass meeting at the Metropolitan Opera House

Perkins recalled sitting on the crowded stage, representing the Consumers' League, and nearby sat a "little red-headed girl . . . fiery red hair, and blazing eyes and pretty, too." It was the first time Perkins had seen Rose Schneiderman, who was there on behalf of the Women's Trade Union League. In late 1909 and early 1910, Schneiderman had traveled throughout New England giving speeches and raising money on behalf of the striking waist makers. But Schneiderman had never spoken as memorably as she did that night, nor did she again in all her long career as one of America's legendary unionists. Perkins noticed that she was trembling as she waited her turn at the podium.

"I would be a traitor to those poor burned bodies," she began, in a voice that could hardly be heard in the huge opera house, "if I were to come here to talk good fellowship." The voice quickly gained strength. "We have tried you good people of the public—and we have found you wanting.

"The old Inquisition had its rack and its thumbscrews and its instruments of torture with iron teeth," Schneiderman continued. "We know what those things are today: the iron teeth are our necessities, the thumbscrews are the high-powered and swift machinery close to which we must work, and the rack is here in the firetrap structures that will destroy us the minute they catch fire.

"This is not the first time girls have been burned alive in this city. Every week I must learn of the untimely death of one of my sister workers. Every year thousands of us are maimed. The life of men and women is so cheap, and property is so sacred! There are so many of us for one job, it matters little if one hundred and forty-odd are burned to death.

"*We have tried you citizens!*" Schneiderman repeated. "We are trying you now, and you have a couple of dollars for the sorrowing mothers and brothers and sisters by way of a charity gift. But every time the workers come out [on strike], the strong arm of the law is allowed to press down heavily upon us.

"Public officials have only words of warning for us . . . and they have the workhouse just back of all their warnings. The strong hand of the law beats us back when we rise . . .

"I can't talk fellowship to you who are gathered here," the indictment concluded. "Too much blood has been spilled. I know from experience it is up to the working people to save themselves. And the only way is through a strong working-class movement."

Brief silence. The plain force of her words shocked the audience of thirty-five hundred people. Then came roars of approval from the East Siders crowding the opera house galleries. The reaction was more subdued in the front rows and in the private boxes, but it grew.

Such language had fractured the strike. But now, in the wake of the fire, the ringing final note of socialism no longer seemed quite as extreme to the capitalist progressives. Rose Schneiderman had expressed a depth of anger and identified a degree of guilt that every honest citizen had to acknowledge. What had happened at the Triangle *was* outrageous—this was undeniable and beyond politics. It was preventable, but it happened anyway because of complacency and greed.

When in doubt, reformers make committees. So, as Schneiderman's words still hung in the charged atmosphere of the opera house, the audience voted to send a distinguished Committee on Safety to Albany to demand change. The wealthy lawyer Henry L. Stimson—soon to be secretary of war under President William Howard Taft—was named chairman. Henry Morgenthau Sr.—a future secretary of the Treasury—was a member, along with Anne Morgan, Mary Dreier of the WTUL, Henry Moskowitz of the garment industry's Joint Board of Sanitation, and others. Multimillionaire Robert Fulton Cutting put up the money, while philanthropist John Kingsbury provided much of the organizing energy. Frances Perkins, thirty years old, with just two years in New York and only three months' experience in Albany, was placed on the committee as a lobbyist.

It was a very impressive group. But one of the great failings of many progressives was that they disdained practical politics. True, some

served in important appointed positions—like Stimson and Morgenthau—and a few even pursued elective office. But most of them
scorned the rough-and-tumble of city politics and Albany intrigue.
Nowhere was this more evident than in the attitude of the Committee on Safety. They wanted a commission of "the finest people in the
state" to study factory conditions and recommend new laws. They
wanted assurances that the commission could operate free from "the
hand of politics." They took this message to Governor Dix, a Tammany
man, who nodded politely and steered them to the legislature—specifically to Bob Wagner and Al Smith, who personified the precise
opposite.

Al Smith had been doing a lot of thinking about the fire. Frances
Perkins knew this. She bumped into him at a train station shortly after
the disaster. He told her of a long, miserable day spent visiting the
families of Triangle victims in his district. There were so many. Then
he had gone to the morgue to help his constituents through the ordeal of identifying the dead. "It was a human, natural, decent thing
to do," Perkins remembered, "and it was a sight he never forgot."
When they met again in Albany, a week or two later, Smith warned
Perkins that the vaunted Committee on Safety was doomed to fail.
They could not expect to get new laws without clasping "the hand of
politics." Politics, he pointed out, is how laws happen. Smith hated
the idea of another commission of "finest people." What was needed,
he said, was a commission of legislators.

Smith repeated the message after Governor Dix steered the esteemed committee members to his office. "Have you ever noticed,"
he asked the delegation, "how much these 'finest people in the state
of New York' have to do besides the thing you want them to do?
They're always very busy, and you can't get their attention.

"Besides," Smith went on, "it isn't the 'finest people in the state'
that have the most influence in the legislature. Citizens is all right,"
Perkins remembered him saying, "but they have got to be where they
belong. If you want to get anything done, you got to have this be a
legislative commission. If the legislature does it, the legislature will

be proud of it, the legislature will listen to their report and the legislature will do something about it."

He went on. "These fellows in the Assembly are good men at heart," he said. "They don't want to burn up people in factories. They just don't know anything about how to prevent it, and they don't really believe that there is any hazard until you show them. And they'll be more impressed if it is shown them by their own commission and own members."

This was an unusual performance, and the reformers weren't sure what to make of it. Smith and Wagner wanted a chance to do the job themselves. But over the years the reformers had learned not to take Tammany politicians at face value. The machine was good at empty promises, easily forgotten once a crisis was passed. From this angle, Smith's offer could be read as a seductive invitation to repeat the pattern—to give the matter to Tammany to be buried.

Frances Perkins initially thought Smith's advice "was absurd." (Later, she decided it was "the most useful piece of advice, I guess, we've ever had.") But practically, for all the celebrity and wealth concentrated in the Committee on Safety, the blue-ribbon panel had little room to bargain. Obviously, this was the way Tammany wanted it done. Tammany was in power, and the reformers had little sway with the Hall. There was no use arguing.

So they took what was offered: a nine-member commission, with five members from the legislature and four appointed by the governor. Wagner would be the chairman and Smith the vice chairman. The Tammany Twins had the votes and the gavel. The legacy of the Triangle fire was in their hands.

This was roughly the moment when the *World* concluded that all momentum had gone out of serious reform.

We can never know exactly what transpired between Charles Murphy and his young Albany leaders in those days and weeks. He was among the most invisible of powerful public men. Silent Charlie "left few concrete clues as to his aims," in the words of Nancy Joan Weiss. "He left no records and no formal speeches, and he granted no interviews of consequence. No letters survive and it is unlikely that they ever existed." For this reason, as Weiss put it, "reconstructing Charlie Murphy means building completely from the outside."

We have seen the world in which Murphy was operating. The city of his youth had changed radically—six times bigger, fully industrialized, awash in new immigrants who had little sense of debt toward Tammany and even less affection. Through sheer brains and cunning, Murphy was holding on. But signs of danger were everywhere—in the strong progressive showing at the most recent city elections, in the constant threat from Hearst, in the rising tide of East Side socialism, in the strikes by the newly muscular garment workers.

For all these reasons, Murphy was being pressed by Big Tim Sullivan and others to do something significant to appeal to the new immigrants. And the largest percentage of those immigrants worked in garment shops, or had loved ones that did. The Triangle fire struck directly at those people that Tammany needed most.

We know Murphy conferred regularly with Smith and Wagner. The two men joined him every weekend for lunch or dinner in the Scarlet Room at Delmonico's. Or if Murphy was relaxing at his Long Island estate, they sat down at the nearby Canoe Place Inn. By 1911, nearly a decade after becoming boss, Murphy had finally purged the "reactionaries"—the Old Guard—from positions of Tammany power. He had replaced them with younger, forward-looking men, like Wagner and Smith. "Murphy not only advanced the political interests of his 'young men,'" wrote Weiss, "but he listened to their ideas and liked what he heard."

The three men decided that the Triangle fire was the right vehicle, the perfect moment, to recast New York's Democratic Party. Murphy had the power now and the opportunity to do something dramatic. All the Tammany men, of course, knew how easy it would be to let the matter fade away, as so many crises had faded in the past. That might be what Tammany's financial backers, the men who owned the factories and hired the workers, would want them to do. But the status quo had become dangerous politics.

Was Murphy forced into it? His friends—and most authorities on Tammany history—have concluded that the boss *wanted* to do better by New York's working people. Murphy "had a quality rarely associated with Tammany Hall: a sense of government's responsibility to the public good," one historian has written. Certainly Al Smith and Bob Wagner had genuine sympathy for the working class. As Robert Caro wrote of Smith: "When he talked about social welfare legislation, it was in terms of 'us' against 'them,' of the 'people' against the 'interests,' of the Fourth Ward against the factory owners. . . . No one could listen to him talk about how doctors' bills could eat up a man's savings and leave his family destitute, about how penniless mothers feared that the 'charities' would take their children, about children who grew to manhood without ever having a pair of new shoes, without believing that his determination to help them was real."

This is not to say that Tammany *led* the fight for working people and for immigrants. Far from it. Even if Murphy's heart was in the right place, he was by nature cautious. He was goaded to the fight by the picketing shop workers, the union leaders, the socialist writers and lecturers, the progressive millionaires and college students and researchers and settlement house workers. Their influence showed itself in many ways—mass meetings, potent strikes, tens and hundreds of thousands marching. Most of all, they began to have influence in the one place Murphy cared about most: the ballot box. When these forces managed to unify themselves—as they did, briefly, during the shirtwaist strike and after the fire—their potential was undeniable.

But it was just that: potential. Murphy was actually in a position to make things happen—or make them not happen.

"I had a talk with Murphy. The bill is not going to pass . . ."

Murphy had the power.

Governor Dix signed a law creating the Factory Investigating Commission on June 30, 1911, three months after the fire. The commission's powers were unprecedented in New York history—the power to subpoena witnesses and documents, to elect its own members, to employ experts, and to change its own rules. Once it was created, the commission controlled its own future. It could remake its charter and replace its members. The legislature created it, but after that, Wagner and

Smith owned it entirely. As Richard Greenwald, a leading authority on the commission, astutely noted, it was set up as "a tool" of Tammany Hall, rather than of future governors and future legislatures—even if Tammany lost control of the government, the Tammany Twins would continue to direct the commission in every respect.

They took off running and never looked back. "Historians," Greenwald asserted, "have paid too little attention to the importance of the FIC in shaping, indeed, transforming the Democratic Party. . . . Smith and Wagner became 'liberal' heroes in New York. . . . Throughout the life of the FIC they constantly talked of morality, efficiency, social justice, and the 'duty' of the state. Smith, and especially Wagner, were *the* politicians of the time."

The change was shocking, from the Tammany of the shirtwaist strike to the Tammany of the Factory Commission in just two years. During the strike, Tammany-controlled police officers harassed the picket lines and Tammany-linked gangsters doled out the beatings. When ten thousand strikers marched on City Hall, all they got was a smile and a few empty platitudes from the Tammany mayor. Two years later, the Factory Commission stretched its slim budget—ten thousand dollars for the first year—by welcoming volunteers from the same groups that had been the backbone of the strike. Wagner and Smith took their lead investigator, Dr. George Price, from the Joint Board of Sanitary Control—a creation of the International Ladies' Garment Workers' Union. During two months in late 1911, Price sent his team of ten investigators into nearly two thousand factories, covering twenty industries. One of Price's investigators was Clara Lemlich, the catalyst of the shirtwaist uprising.

Henry Moskowitz, another Joint Board member, encouraged his wife, Belle, to join the effort. She became Al Smith's most trusted adviser on the commission. And when the Factory Commission lifted Smith into the governor's office, Belle Moskowitz went with him, quietly becoming one of the most influential women in America.

The commission's chief counsel, Abram Elkus, arrived courtesy of Henry Morgenthau, Republican progressive. "I can get you a first-class lawyer who will not demand any fee," Morgenthau wrote to Wagner and

Smith, "and he will be satisfactory to everyone concerned, including Tammany Hall." From the Women's Trade Union League came Mary Dreier, who was one of four commissioners appointed by Governor Dix. The Citizens' Union—Tammany's dreaded "Cits"—sent a lawyer to help draft legislation. Progressives from across the country flocked to join the work. Wisconsin's John R. Commons, America's leading authority on labor issues, sent his students to help with the investigations.

Frances Perkins arrived on loan from the Consumers' League to help Price, and she in turn brought in more investigators. One of them was Rose Schneiderman, the fiery speaker from the Metropolitan Opera House. Perkins, fresh from the defeat of the fifty-four-hour bill, dispatched some of these investigators to examine conditions in the candy factories—a subtle bit of revenge.

Wagner and Smith set a blistering pace, to the amazement of those who had expected the panel to slip quietly into oblivion. Initially, the Factory Commission's scope was limited to New York's nine largest cities. Still, the group averaged nearly one public hearing per week from July through December. More than two hundred witnesses delivered nearly thirty-five hundred pages of testimony. The commission met most Saturdays to discuss issues and strategies, and by year's end had proposed fifteen new laws covering fire safety, factory inspections, employment rules for women and children, and—in a bow to Perkins's earlier work—sanitation in bakeries. Eight of the proposed laws were enacted.

The following year, Wagner and Smith expanded their range. They rewrote their rules to apply to forty-five cities instead of nine. Public hearings were held across New York, producing new reams of testimony. But testimony was never as important as firsthand, eyewitness experience. In grand progressive style, George Price and Frances Perkins organized Factory Commission visits to plants and mills all over the state. They took commissioners to an Auburn, New York, rope factory where husbands and wives worked alternating twelve-hour shifts, never seeing each other except to kiss quickly as they passed at the gate. They saw a Buffalo candy factory where chocolate boiled over into open gas flames, where the single stairway had no handrail—terribly dangerous in case of a fire—and where two toilets served three hundred workers, and one of the two was broken. They hit a Cattaraugus County cannery at dawn, and found children as young as five, six, and seven working alongside their mothers. How long is the day? the commissioners wondered. The answer: Until the children passed out from exhaustion.

At one factory, Perkins said, "we made sure Robert Wagner personally crawled through the tiny hole in the wall that gave exit to a step ladder covered with ice and ending twelve feet from the ground, which was euphemistically labeled 'Fire Escape.'"

The work of 1912 produced a series of new laws in the 1913 legislature that was unmatched to that time in American history. The Tammany Twins pushed through twenty-five bills, entirely recasting the labor law of the nation's largest state. There were more fire safety laws—by that point, two years after the Triangle fire, nearly every deficiency in the Asch Building had been addressed. Automatic sprinklers were required in high-rise buildings. Fire drills were mandatory in large shops. Doors had to be unlocked and had to swing outward. Other new laws enhanced protections for women and children and restricted manufacturing by poor families in their tenement apartments. To enforce the laws, the Factory Commission pushed through a complete reorganization of the state Department of Labor.

Business leaders didn't quite know what had hit them. But gradually they started making their complaints known. Real estate interests, in particular, were upset by the number of fire safety modifications they were required to make. One member of the Factory Commission, Robert Dowling, was a New York real estate man, and he often found himself dissenting from the sweeping recommendations pushed by the volunteer staff. (Eventually he resigned from the commission, blaming Frances Perkins, in particular, for going too far.) He saw it as his job to remind Wagner and Smith of the costs involved in their unprecedented reforms. During one executive session, he referred to statistics on the number of people killed in factory fires. Notwith-

standing the catastrophe at the Triangle, he ventured, "It is an infini-
tesimal proportion of the population."

Mary Dreier was shocked. "But, Mr. Dowling," she cried, "they
were men and women! They were human souls. It was a hundred percent for them."

Smith jumped in on Dreier's side. "That's good Catholic doctrine,
Robert!" he declared. The commissioners laughed. The steamroller
kept going.

Even after he gave the green light for a vigorous, history-making effort
by Wagner and Smith, however, Charles Murphy continued to court
the "moneyed interests." He was attempting the age-old political
straddle of trying to attract new supporters without upsetting the old
ones. In 1912, Frances Perkins again lobbied Albany on behalf of the
fifty-four-hour bill, and found that Murphy continued to oppose it. This
time, however, she managed to drive the matter to a vote in the wan-
ing hours of the session. To her dismay, the Senate passed one version
of the bill while the Assembly—which had switched to Republican
control—passed another. Time was running out.

Her list of friends now included none other than Big Tim Sullivan,
who was serving that year in the state Senate, as he occasionally liked
to do. He explained to Perkins that the stalemate was intentional:
Murphy's orders. Wagner, Sullivan said, had been instructed to let the
session expire without reconciling the competing bills. Afterward, in
the next election, Tammany could claim to have tried to help the
workers, while blaming the Republicans for killing the bill. And in the
meantime, those good friends of Mr. Murphy's, the Huyler brothers,
would continue to get what they wanted.

"The guile of it," wrote Perkins biographer George Martin, "left her
speechless."

But apparently in the course of explaining the plan, Sullivan decided
to defy it. First, he staged a tricky and complicated bit of parliamen-
tary footwork to force Wagner to take up the Assembly's version of the
bill. Then, confident of success, Big Tim and his cousin, Sen. Christy
Sullivan, headed for the 8 P.M. boat home to Manhattan.

As soon as Big Tim was gone, however, Bob Wagner did some foot-work of his own. Two supporters of the bill were prevailed on to shift their votes. Again it looked as if the bill would die. For good measure, Wagner, as Senate president, called for the final vote to be taken be-hind locked doors so that the Sullivans could not return to turn the tide again.

Even that was not enough. As Perkins desperately tried to recall Big Tim and his cousin, another Tammany senator decided to buck the boss. Using his allotted five minutes for open debate before the doors were closed, Perkins's old friend The MacManus rose to deliver a speech that one observer called "drivel." Others joined in, each using his five minutes to stall for time until the Sullivans could arrive. "One," Martin wrote, "allegedly gave a lecture on birds."

All the stalling appeared to be in vain, as the last speech neared its end and the Sullivans were nowhere in sight. Perkins had sent a taxi for them, but they missed it. Then, as the doors were about to be locked, Big Tim barreled into the chamber, huffing for breath and smiling broadly. He and his cousin had jogged all the way up the long hill to the capitol.

"Record me in the affirmative!" the Big Feller bellowed. Then he turned to Perkins and said happily, as pandemonium broke out around them: "It's all right, me girl. We is with you. The bosses thought they was going to kill your bill, but they forgot about Tim Sullivan!"

That summer, the sometimes progressive governor of New Jersey, Woodrow Wilson, defeated Murphy's more conservative choice for the Democratic presidential nomination. It was Murphy's last major stand against change. That autumn, with his blessing, Tammany ran its first campaign as a true friend of the working class. Murphy assigned Rob-ert Wagner the job of drafting the party platform, and Wagner essen-tially grafted the Democratic Party onto the Factory Commission's agenda. The move was a complete success. The influential young rabbi Stephen Wise, a frequent Tammany critic, actually endorsed the Democrats—as did Henry Morgenthau, a lifelong Republican, and social worker Lillian Wald, a socialist. On Election Day 1913, Tammany scored its greatest statewide victories ever, winning two-thirds of the seats in both houses of the legislature. The Hall's candidate for governor, William Sulzer, won in a landslide. (He would soon defy Murphy, and Murphy would force him out of office in a crude power play. Silent Charlie later called the impeachment "the most serious mistake of my life.")

This was "a turning point in New York political history," one historian said of the 1913 election. Tammany had embraced the spirit of progress, the spirit of the age, and the voters responded. After that, Murphy showed even more enthusiasm for reform, smiling on Factory Commission proposals and a project to establish the first minimum wage.

Charles Murphy never publicly explained his thinking about this or anything else. But a year or two later, Frances Perkins paid him a visit at Tammany headquarters on Fourteenth Street. She was there to ask his support for the latest round of labor reform laws. After she gave her pitch, he sat quietly for a moment.

Then he said: "You are the young lady, aren't you, who managed to get the fifty-four-hour bill passed?"

Perkins said yes, she was.

"Well, young lady, I opposed that bill."

Perkins swallowed hard. "Yes, I so gathered, Mr. Murphy."

Sometimes, the boss paused a whole minute between sentences. The wait could be excruciating.

"It is my observation," Murphy said, "that the bill made us many votes. I will tell the boys to give you all the help they can with this new bill. Good-bye."

Perkins turned to leave. But then Murphy seemed to think of one more thing. "Are you one of these women suffragists?" he murmured.

"Yes, I am," Perkins answered.

"Well, I am not. But if anyone ever gives them the vote, I hope you will remember that you would make a good Democrat."

Within a few months, Charles Murphy endorsed women's voting rights, and that, too, soon became law.

9

TRIAL

B y the second week of April 1911, District Attorney Charles
Whitman was certain of this: The door to the Washington Place
stairway, on the ninth floor of the Asch Building, had been locked
when the Triangle fire broke out. In the sealed grand jury room,
Whitman and his assistants took the testimony of scores of survivors.
Again and again the young workers told versions of the same story: As
the flames entered the crowded loft, the workers ran to the door. They
pushed and pulled, twisted the knob this way and that. The door
would not budge.

Proof was up there in the debris, Whitman believed. So the prosecutor instructed his chief detective, Barney Flood, to go to the ninth
floor and find the lock. On April 10, Flood took several of his men to
the wasted heart of the Triangle Waist Company for one more sifting
of the ash and char, the scraps of clothing and hunks of machinery and,
according to one macabre newspaper account, bits of human flesh.
Spring sunshine washed through the big, empty windows over the
drifts of fine, light ash. In weighty contrast, cold steel axles lay cross-
wise along the floor every few feet, buried under the charcoal residue
of tabletops. Radiators, blackened on one side, were toppled away from

the walls, where firemen had pulled them down to make room for bodies to be lowered to the street. Metal fire pails had been flung here and there, spilled of their futility. It was strange; the walls, the ceiling, the floors, the ranks of stout supporting columns—everything structural was absolutely sound, ready to be scrubbed and sanded, painted, and reoccupied. The Asch Building had been advertised as fireproof, and indeed it was. If only its contents had been.

It was sixteen days after the fire. Detective Flood directed two Italian laborers, Giuseppe Saveno and Pietro Trochia, to start digging near the Washington Place exit. Within half an hour of Flood's arrival, they found it, not far from the exit—a blackened fragment of door with a shot bolt protruding. The bolt was heavy and rectangular, seemingly little damaged, but the locking apparatus was discolored. This suggested to Flood that the bolt had been protected from the fire by the door frame, while everything around it burned.

Here, it seemed, was the clincher to the whole case. Two Whitman assistants, seasoned Charles Bostwick and energetic, young J. Robert Rubin, had formulated a strategy of attack. The law said that factory doors could not be kept locked during working hours. But the bolt spoke for itself. The prosecutors further planned to show that Isaac Harris and Max Blanck intended for it to be locked. The Triangle owners wanted every employee to leave by the Greene Street door, under the watchful gaze of guards who searched handbags for stolen merchandise and materials. Failure to keep the doors unlocked was a misdemeanor. Finally, the prosecutors intended to show that people died because of that locked door. A misdemeanor that resulted in death was manslaughter, punishable by up to twenty years in prison.

The next day, Flood took the lock into the courthouse and told the grand jury about it. An indictment quickly followed. Once again, Flood rounded up his detectives. This time they went to 9 University Place, a few blocks from the Asch Building, where Flood knew he would find Harris and Blanck in a new factory, back at work. His agents had kept the two men under surveillance since the fire. The owners were not surprised to see the detectives; the impending indictment had been leaked to the press. With little ceremony, Flood arrested the Shirt-waist Kings.

They were arraigned that afternoon, Wednesday, April 12, and charged with six counts of manslaughter stemming from two of the 146 deaths in their factory. One count alleged that they violated the law against locked doors and thus caused the death of a sewing machine operator named Margaret Schwartz. A second count made the same allegation concerning the death of another operator, Rosie Grosso. Similar charges argued that the deaths of these women were caused by the owners' negligence in keeping a cluttered, dirty factory full of highly flammable materials. The prosecutors limited the indictments to these two deaths because the penalty was the same no matter how many counts were proven. They had yet to decide which case was the stronger.

Max Blanck, tall, beefy, and bald, loomed over his partner as they entered the courtroom, like Sandow the sideshow strongman in a tailored black suit. He sat with his big hands folded, clenching and unclenching them throughout the brief proceeding. Slight, dark-haired Isaac Harris, with his close-set eyes and protruding ears, "appeared indifferent," according to one reporter. Their lawyer entered a plea of not guilty on their behalf.

As they had shown during the shirtwaist strike, Blanck and Harris were fighters. When they realized that they were targets of the D.A., they sought out the best lawyer money could buy. They found him in a big office overlooking Broadway, a small man with an egg-shaped head, youngish, but with a reputation that was already becoming legend. People said that this lawyer sometimes went years without losing a case. They talked about the time he accepted a client on the eve of a trial on a dare. Of all the lawyers in New York affiliated with Tammany Hall, this man was the one that handled the machine's hardest jobs. He was Big Tim Sullivan's attorney.

His fee was huge, at least ten thousand dollars per man, enough to pay nearly forty shop girls for a year, and the sum was payable in advance. "I can't think until I have the money," the lawyer once snapped at a prospective client. But there was too much at stake to settle for anything but the best. The partners hired Max D. Steuer.

*   *   *

In a sense, he had been preparing for *People v. Harris and Blanck* all his life. Like the factory owners, and like so many of the dead and injured, Max Steuer—the name rhymed with "foyer"—was a Jewish immigrant from Eastern Europe who arrived in New York with nothing and started climbing. He had known steerage, and the Lower East Side tenements. He spoke perfect Yiddish and had toiled in the garment shops. These were his people. He had walked in their shoes. At the same time, he could treat this intimate knowledge as just data. For Steuer was not one of them. He was unique. This was clear even in 1911, which was the cusp of his extraordinary (and now strangely forgotten) career. Of all those steerage millions, among the legions of garment workers and former garment workers, only Steuer became the most feared attorney in this most litigious of cities, a million-dollar-a-year man, counsel to bankers and movie stars and gangsters and indicted judges and cabinet officials. His reputation would eventually grow so lustrous that Steuer rarely took clients of any stripe directly, and instead earned vast sums for telling other lawyers how to try their cases.

In time, this sort of thing would happen to him: A wealthy man was facing indictment, and his seven high-priced lawyers gathered to plan his defense. But they could not agree. Finally, one of them said, "We're getting nowhere. Let's go see Steuer."

When they tried to explain their problem to him, the lawyers once again began interrupting each other and pushing favorite theories. Impatient, Steuer cut them off. "What's your client charged with?" he asked.

"He's not charged with anything yet," said one of the seven. Steuer rose from his chair and gestured toward the door.

"Wait until he's charged with something. Then see me," said the oracle. The indictment never arrived, though Steuer's bill certainly did.

In time, his reputation would be such that a man would pay an enormous retainer simply to ensure that when he died, Steuer would not help his heirs challenge his will. His biographer, Richard O. Boyer, would quote a jurist saying that Max Steuer was "the greatest trial lawyer of our time," and then Boyer added: "Some disagree with this estimate. They would strike out the word 'trial.'"

In many ways, 1911 was the year that boosted him to this pinnacle, the year of his two greatest cross-examinations—one that destroyed a congressman and one that climaxed the Triangle trial. It was the year Steuer turned forty, or forty-one, or perhaps even forty-two. He was never quite sure how old he was. His birthday was September 6—of that he was fairly confident—but whether the year was 1870 or 1871 or even 1869 he could not say for sure. When he arrived in 1876 at the old Castle Garden immigration station at the southern tip of Manhattan, officials decided that he was six years old, but later Steuer had his doubts.

In any event, Max was the youngest child, and only son, of Aron and Dinah Steuer from the tiny village of Homino, east of Prague, in the Austrian empire. (Today the village, still tiny, is nearly the exact center of the Czech Republic.) Aron Steuer was a successful vintner, but somehow he lost everything and decided to start over in the United States. He settled his family in a tenement on the Lower East Side, in what was still a heavily Irish and German neighborhood, and found work in the garment industry.

Like nearly all children of the slums, Max worked hard at a very young age to help support the family. He sold newspapers as soon as the family settled, a tiny boy with keen eyes wrestling huge stacks of penny papers. At ten, still in knee pants, Max walked the crowded streets of his neighborhood ringing a bell to draw attention to the matches he was selling. Everyone needed matches—to light the gas lamps, to start the coal stoves, to get a cigar going, and for various home treatments of dying babies. But a boy had to sell a mountain of matches to earn a dime. So he graduated to a garment sweatshop, where he pulled basting threads after the final stitching was done. This was the bottom rung of the needle trades, blinding and tedious work that paid better than matches but still next to nothing.

Steuer's salvation was his awesome, chilly, antiseptic brain. He had a memory like a computer. He was equally piercing with numbers and with human nature. He looked at a chessboard—in his case, the courtroom was his chessboard—and instantly saw six moves ahead. His was a mind unencumbered by self-doubt or timidity or even, apparently, much reflection. The *New Yorker* declared that Steuer was born to be a lawyer the way Mozart was born to music, and added: "There is naught in this man of the virtue or of the justice of full knowledge. Nor is he unvirtuous or unjust. He is the lawyer: he is the spirit of partisanship, ruthless, mechanical, passionately cold. And morality is quite outside the matter."

His gifts came to the attention of Tammany Hall, perhaps in the form of Big Tim himself, who had a particular soft spot for former newsboys. Steuer was given a patronage job on the night shift at the post office. This allowed him to attend City College for three years while supporting his family. Eventually, the strain of work and studies grew too intense, and he quit school without graduating—but a year or so later, Max entered Columbia University Law School, where he was among the best students in his class.

"One night," he recalled long afterward, "one of the boys in my class came up to me and said, 'Steuer, none of us knows you. We like to listen to you in class and we see you there, but none of us knows you. Why don't you come out and have a good time with us after class tonight?'

"I only had a quarter in my pocket. I kept feeling it. We went to the Casino roof garden. There was a good show. I knew so little about the world that I almost ordered a round of drinks for the six of us and was going to pay for it on my quarter."

Even at the peak of his success, some thirty years later, Steuer brooded over that harrowing close call, and recounted the story as though it spoke volumes about him. It showed that he did have emotions, and among them was fierce pride. "If I had ordered that round of drinks I would never have gone back to school. I couldn't have faced my classmates," he explained. "Such little things affect your whole career."

After graduation, Steuer found no firm willing to hire an impoverished immigrant Jewish lawyer, not even as a law librarian. So in 1893 he hung his shingle in a little office on Park Row near the newspaper buildings and the courthouses. Those were wild times to be a New York lawyer. Without a doubt, the most famous firm in the city—in fact, "the cleverest, most picturesque, most sought-after, most highly remunerated criminal lawyers in the country"—was Howe & Hummel, a riotously unethical partnership that handled nearly every important murder case in New York from the end of the Civil War to the turn of the century. The firm's offices were in a storefront across from the Tombs, the infamous prison, and outfitted with a sign worthy of a department store. The enormous sign was illuminated throughout the night, so that prisoners fresh from jail couldn't miss it. Howe & Hummel ran "a veritable cesspool of perjury," according to one authority, and rarely lost a case.

Everyone knew them. In one random census at the Tombs, twenty-three of the twenty-five prisoners being held on capital charges were clients of the firm—as were virtually all the actors, musicians, and theater owners in New York, and a fair number of the millionaires. The famous Lower East Side fence Mother Mandelbaum kept Howe & Hummel on a $5,000-a-year retainer. Tammany boss Richard Croker relied on the firm after his adversary in a dispute over a ballot box wound up dead. Some people believed the firm not only defended the entire New York underworld, but also ran it.

Yet for all this extravagant business, the firm really was just two men, supported by a floating cast of junior attorneys, gumshoes, and actors on call to play the weeping wife or doting grandmother of a Howe & Hummel client. The senior partner was a large, florid man, glittering with diamonds, named William Howe, a master of the dramatic closing statement and the well-placed bribe. Once Howe delivered an entire summation from his knees. One jury not only acquitted Howe's client of murder, but took up a collection for him as well. Abraham Hummel, the junior partner, was a sort of Igor, a tiny, misshapen man who dressed in black and had a silver death's head on the end of his walking stick. Hummel specialized in breach-of-promise lawsuits—cases involving young women and rich men, sex and blackmail. For many years, being blackmailed by Hummel was almost a rite of passage for New York society swains. After a brief affair, perhaps as brief as a few minutes, word would come from Hummel that the young lady involved had sworn an affidavit that she was promised marriage in exchange for her virtue. The gentleman could settle up or read about the matter in the newspapers. Hummel kept a stove in his office where, after writing their checks, compromised men were invited to burn the affidavits. Several victims later praised Hummel as admirably trustworthy, in that he never held back secret copies for future use.

Max Steuer's first law office was just a few blocks from the Howe & Hummel factory, and given his drive, hunger, and pride, one can easily imagine him walking past the huge sign and feeling a mixture of envy and disgust. His reign, when it came, would be more dignified—and, he hoped, even more lucrative. To achieve this, however, Steuer first had to show his superiority over the old order by beating Howe & Hummel in open court. His chance came around the turn of the century. Howe, by then, was retired, but Hummel was at the top of his powers. A rabbi's large and emotional funeral procession had turned into a small riot on the Lower East Side. The organizer of the funeral, a bombastic neighborhood union leader named Joseph Barondess, hired Steuer to sue a city police inspector on brutality charges. The policeman hired Howe & Hummel to defend him. Steuer won. By the time he was thirty, Steuer was known as the "Attorney General of the City Court."

Like the young Robert F. Wagner and hundreds of other lawyers over the decades, Steuer built his early career on service to Tammany—jailhouse work initially, but quickly building into more serious matters. As Boyer put it: "Tammany district leaders [began] saying to him, 'Max, some of the boys got in a jam last night. They come up in Tombs court tomorrow. We'd like you to take care of them.' The boys were always so successfully defended that it was not long . . . until Tammany's bigger boys were calling on Max to defend them on bigger charges for bigger fees. Thus Tammany was as useful to Max as he was to it." Writer Andy Logan put it more succinctly: "He was famous for being Big Tim's lawyer."

Steuer's relationship with Charles Murphy was more strained. And yet Murphy knew enough to use him in the first crisis of his reign as boss. A roguish former police chief, Big Bill Devery, challenged Murphy's nascent leadership, and got himself elected sachem of the Ninth District. (Devery campaigned by standing on street corners handing out money to passersby.) Steuer's assignment from Murphy was to contrive legal means for keeping Devery off the Tammany executive committee, which he did. Although, to be on the safe side, Big Tim also sent Monk Eastman's gang into Devery's neighborhood to sow terror.

Because Steuer could project charm and good humor as well as icy brilliance, he became a favorite toastmaster at Tammany Hall banquets. At such an event in 1908, he ran into a rival, John B. Stanchfield. Stanchfield had just quit as counsel to Raymond Hitchcock, the most famous vaudeville comedian of the time. The next day, Hitchcock would go on trial for statutory rape, and the prosecution seemingly had him dead to rights. "There's no possible way of beating it," Stanchfield told Steuer. "Hitchcock won't admit he's guilty. He wouldn't accept my advice and take a plea, so naturally, I had to resign."

Steuer already knew all this, because Hitchcock had begged him, just before the banquet, to come to his rescue. Normally, he never took cases involving sexual perversity, but the challenge intrigued him. Steuer grandly—and loudly—asked Stanchfield to repeat his claim that no one could possibly save Hitchcock.

"Max, even you couldn't get him an acquittal," Stanchfield answered.

But he did.

Harris and Blanck were released on $25,000 bail. Steuer immediately challenged the indictment on technical grounds—a process that ate up most of the remaining months of 1911. During those months, the prosecutors trimmed the death of Rosie Grosso from their case to focus solely on one victim. Everything came down to Margaret Schwartz, and the locked door.

In the meantime, Steuer continued to burnish his record. During the summer of 1911, he scored his greatest victory yet, defending a former state senator turned lobbyist named Frank Gardner on bribery charges. Gardner was accused of trying to buy the deciding vote to de-

feat a ban on racetrack gambling. The vote belonged to an ailing senator named Otto Foelker. On the crucial day, Foelker was carried into
the Senate chamber on a stretcher, and cast a dramatic vote in favor of
reform. After he recovered from his illness, his virtue propelled Foelker
into Congress in 1910, and some newspapers began mentioning him
as a possible governor.

Everything went well for the prosecution until Steuer rose to cross-
examine the virtuous congressman. Seemingly out of the blue, he
asked Foelker: "*Parlez-vous Français?*"

"What did you say?" Foelker replied.

Steuer repeated the question. "*Parlez-vous Français?*"

"I don't know what you're getting at," said Foelker.

"It seems to me that you at least should be able to answer *oui*, in
view of the fact that you passed an examination in French with a grade
of one hundred percent. You recall taking the Regents examination so
as to qualify for the bar examination?"

The next question: "You made a grade of ninety-five in logarithms.
What's a logarithm?"

The congressman couldn't say.

The score was ninety-eight in syntax. Foelker could not define the
word.

Steuer hammered further at the witness. Did he remember taking
the Regents exam? Did he know any other Otto Foelker who might
have taken the exam around the same time? And did he happen to
know a man named Max Sosinsky?

During his customary meticulous preparation for the case, Steuer
had noticed that Foelker's mailing address, at the time of the Regents
exam, was 72 Henry Street. This happened to be a tenement where
Steuer grew up. It struck him as odd that the congressman had lived
there. So the lawyer paid a visit to his old home and asked around. As
he expected, he found no one who remembered Otto Foelker. But the
janitor recalled another resident, extremely smart—Max Sosinsky,
whose current address was the Tombs. Steuer paid a visit to Sosinsky,
who explained his business as a professional test-taker.

Foelker's credibility was shattered. But the trial continued to be a very close matter. Late in the proceedings, a man testified that lobbyist Gardner had bragged to him and his wife about the attempted bribe. Somehow, Steuer managed a second miracle: he persuaded the wife of this witness to rush to court and repudiate her husband's testimony. Exactly how Steuer inspired the wife to denounce her husband has never been clear. In any event, Gardner was acquitted.

And Otto Foelker? He never returned to Congress. Instead, he moved to Korea, where he spent the rest of his life in exile, selling real estate. The utter destruction of a United States congressman and potential governor of New York had taken Max Steuer less than an hour. What might he do with immigrant teenagers?

A long Indian summer ended on the day the trial began: December 4, 1911. A sharp northwest gale drove five inches of snow down onto the city. Striking horse-cart drivers threatened to obstruct municipal snow shovel brigades. The cold worked its way inside the courtroom. Isaac Harris wore his overcoat all day; Max Blanck wore his until the start of the afternoon session. When he removed it, he revealed a large diamond stickpin in the lapel of his suit jacket.

The defendants watched intently as the lawyers interviewed potential jurors. By late afternoon, half the panel was chosen. Judge Thomas C. T. Crain instructed the six men—by law, all jurors were men—to avoid the crowds in the courthouse hallways. "Do not be affected by any mourning or any weeping in the corridors," he said. But the scene outside Crain's little courtroom was hard to ignore. The next morning, a crowd began gathering at 8 A.M., even though the day's session was scheduled to begin at 11:30 A.M. Some two hundred people packed the hallway by the time the Triangle owners stepped from the elevator, accompanied by their attorney. "Oh mama, look! Here they come!" someone shouted. "Here are the murderers!"

Led by an elderly woman dressed in mourning clothes, the crowd surged toward the defendants. Many of them waved photographs of fire victims. "Murderers! Murderers!" they cried in Yiddish. "The women beat their chests [and] tore their hair," the *American* reported. The defendants blanched, but Max Steuer was unintimidated. Five and a half feet tall, 160 stout-chested pounds, he shoved his way through, breaking a path for his clients, who pulled their overcoats up over their faces to protect themselves from the reaching, screaming melee. Inside the courtroom, Steuer slammed the door behind them, but "the shrieking continued for several minutes and many of the women tried to force their way into the room." Finally, a platoon of policemen arrived from the nearby Elizabeth Street station. They calmed the crowd and cleared the hallway.

Safe in his sanctuary, Steuer enacted the little rituals that were essential to his courtroom persona. He took his seat as close to the jury box as he could get, then removed his papers from a modest little folder and spread them out where everyone could see. "Let the jury see that you are frank and open," he once advised a group of young lawyers. "Have your papers open where the jury can see them—let anyone see them. You are not afraid to let others know about your case." Steuer was known to place even his wallet on the table, then seemingly forget about it: just leave it there for anyone to pick up. After all, he had nothing to hide.

He moved his chair away from his clients. He did not want them tempted to forget his ironclad rule: never, *never* whisper in his ear. It looked suspicious. Then he sat back. Steuer did not take notes during testimony. Jurors were not allowed to take notes so neither did he. This was no great sacrifice, because his memory allowed him to file every detail neatly away, available for instant retrieval. He liked to provoke prosecutors into arguing with him over something a witness had said days or even weeks earlier, so that the jury could see and appreciate his total reliability when the transcript was read and he was proved right.

Steuer's chief foe in the Triangle case was Charles Bostwick, a formal-looking gentleman of about forty-five, with a brushy mustache and a brooding countenance. He looked like a British character actor who specialized in playing the pompous father of marriageable girls. Born just after the Civil War in Westchester County, Bostwick attended Columbia College and then Columbia Law School, where he was about four years ahead of Steuer. He taught for nine years at the New York University law school, specializing in corporate law, and served two terms in the state Assembly as a Republican. Late in 1909, Charles Whitman recruited him to join the district attorney's office. Either Bostwick was rich or he just dressed the part, because he managed, on his government salary, to go around in silk top hats and fur-trimmed overcoats.

Bostwick's second was a slender young attorney, about thirty years old, named J. Robert Rubin, a Republican from Syracuse with scant history but a bright future; Rubin would become an important figure in the early movie business, arranging the various mergers that created the studio Metro-Goldwyn-Mayer. In 1911, however, he was a rather callow-looking fellow, with a long face, sharp nose, and full lips. Rubin had arrived at the scene of the Triangle fire when the bodies were still bleeding on the sidewalks, and much of the grunt work of preparing the case had fallen to him. No one in the room wanted to beat Steuer more than Rubin.

To have even a chance against him, they had to listen intently to every word Steuer spoke. He could slip an advantage into even the simplest sentence. Once he was questioning Anthony J. Drexel Biddle as a character witness for the boxing impresario Tex Rickard. Steuer did not want Biddle to come across as an idle rich man. So he could not ask the usual question, "What is your occupation?" Instead, he asked, "What do you do for occupation?" It sounded the same, but Biddle was able to answer truthfully, "I'm president of the International Bible Society."

While choosing the Triangle jurors, the prosecutors heard Steuer ask: "Would you give the defendants the benefit of any doubt?" Bostwick sprang to his feet.

"I protest, Your Honor," he cried. "There is doubt in everything." Steuer had been caught. Of course the issue in a courtroom is *reasonable* doubt, not any doubt at all. But rather than nod and rephrase his question, Steuer fired back.

"I protest against the District Attorney's inference that I am not conducting myself in a proper manner!" he cried—as if to let the jurors know that his integrity was everything to him. Judge Crain soothingly explained the law regarding reasonable doubt. And thus the tone was set for much of the Triangle trial: prosecutors wary of Steuer's craftiness, Steuer prickly about his honor, and the judge ever eager to insert himself.

The panel of twelve jurors was completed on Wednesday morning, December 6. Then court adjourned for lunch. Relatives of the Triangle dead and injured hounded Harris and Blanck through the snowy streets to a nearby restaurant, then waited outside for them to finish. When the two men emerged, the crowd resumed shouting and poking at them as they hurried back to the courthouse. Judge Crain ordered police protection for the Triangle owners for the remainder of the trial.

The Triangle fire had been replayed as tragedy, as destiny, as horror story, and as political catalyst. Now it would be examined once more, as a question of justice: Was it right to hold anyone personally responsible? And if it was right, was it possible?

Judge Crain denied a perfunctory motion by Max Steuer to dismiss the case. Then he signaled to Charles Bostwick to deliver his opening statement. The crowded courtroom fell completely silent.

Bostwick began matter-of-factly, describing the layout of the Triangle Waist Company as it was on the afternoon of March 25. He imagined that the walls of the courtroom were the factory walls, and then gestured toward imaginary cutting tables and sewing machines and dressing rooms and doorways. "Near the north end of the first cutter's table, on the Greene Street side of the building"—Bostwick pointed to the spot—"is where the fire started."

Methodically, he described the various exits, the stairways and elevators and fire escape. Then he took the jurors to the ninth floor, asked them to envision the long parallel rows of machines at which hundreds of seamstresses bent to their work. "At the cry of 'fire,'" Bostwick said, "those on the ninth floor ran in every direction. Some ran to the Greene Street door . . . and went to the street. Some went to the roof. Some got on the freight elevators." (This last claim was never supported by testimony. Not one of the 155 witnesses would describe escaping by the freight elevators.) "Some ran to the fire escape on the north side of the building. Others ran to the Washington Place elevator, which made two or three trips, and some escaped that way.

"Others ran to the Washington Place door."

His voice—after rising, rising, rising—suddenly became silent for a moment. Then: "One of these was Margaret Schwartz, now dead. And it is for her death that these defendants are now on trial.

"Gentlemen of the jury," Bostwick declared, "*that door was locked.* Those who ran to that door cried out, 'That door is locked! My God, we are lost!'

"They *were* lost. . . .

"We will prove to you," he said, "that it was the universal custom to make the employees go out one way at night. . . . There stood on guard at the ninth floor a watchman, and as these girls and women went out, one by one, they would have to open their handbags or their satchels or their parcels to show that they had not taken some lace, some thread, or anything that did not belong to them. . . . That was the reason the Washington Place door . . . was kept locked."

In summertime, Bostwick allowed, when it was sticky and hot, all the doors of the factory were propped open for ventilation. "But at closing time," he said, "even in summer, we will show you that that door barred the exit of any employee."

Fortunately, he concluded, someone was able to get the door open on the eighth floor, and scores of lives were saved. But the ninth-floor door held fast. "After we have shown you that all those people escaped where the door was open on the eighth floor, but they were burned on the ninth floor . . . we will then ask you for your judgment upon the evidence according to your consciences."

It was a clear and concise speech, and when he had finished it, Bostwick called the first of his long list of witnesses. He made a slow, workmanlike beginning. Most of the witnesses that first afternoon served only to introduce certain dull facts—like who leased which floors of the Asch Building and for how long. A doctor testified that Margaret

Schwartz died of "asphyxia by smoke. The body was almost completely charred." Photographers took the stand to introduce pictures of the scene to be used as references. A consulting engineer, James Whiskeman, explained the layout of the factory, literally inch by inch.

Boring witnesses were a tonic to Max Steuer. He made it a policy to eat light on trial days so he would never get drowsy. But if jurors drifted off during prosecution testimony, it was fine with him. He was as gentle and soothing as a lullaby when he rose to cross-examine engineer Whiskeman. "If any question that I put is not clear, I wish you would call my attention to it," he cooed, "because I know absolutely nothing about the building, or construction. So I am simply groping my way in the dark."

But his attitude changed instantly if a witness became at all interesting. Battalion fire chief Edward Worth, taking the stand at the end of the day, jolted the courtroom awake. Worth cut a commanding figure as he sat, statue-straight, on the witness chair. He was a decorated department hero—he had recently piloted a boat to the roaring edge of a pier fire to save two men from drowning—and he looked the part, with strong jaw, piercing eyes, and military mustache. He recounted his frantic two-minute ride from the firehouse on Mercer Street to the corner of Washington Place and Greene Street. He described the awful sight that greeted him: the eighth floor consumed by flames and the ninth floor windows "full of people." Steuer knew what was coming next: the sickening vision of victims jumping. He blurted an objection. But Judge Crain allowed the chief to continue talking.

How many people jumped from the windows? Bostwick asked. "More than one?"

"Yes, sir. . . . I can't state how many," Worth answered.

"Do you think there were as many as ten?"

"Yes, there were more," answered the chief.

"Do you think there were as many as twenty?"

"Yes, sir."

"Thirty?"

"I object to this!" Steuer spat once more. This time, Crain put an end to the bidding.

Obviously the prosecution was going to try to present as many horrifying details as possible, hoping to rile the jurors to outrage. And Steuer was determined to have as little vivid testimony as possible. Crain would have to draw a line. That night, he apparently pondered just how grisly the trial should be, and when he came to court the next morning he drew the line in favor of the owners.

Crain would allow almost no mention of victims leaping from the windows, of the collapsing fire escape, of the rain of bodies falling on Joseph Zito's elevator car. As the judge explained in court: "conditions as they existed at the time of the outbreak of the fire and immediately before," on the eighth and ninth floors, would be received into evidence. But "any general description of outside conditions"—for example, the more than eighty plummeting bodies—"I shall exclude."

As much as Steuer hated Chief Worth's testimony about the falling bodies, he was delighted by something else Worth had mentioned, almost in passing. The chief testified that when he arrived at the fire, he saw a "small spurt of flame" along the west wall of the ninth floor. To him, this "proved that the fire was extending up the stairways."

This unexpected windfall fit perfectly into Steuer's defense strategy. If fire was burning in the Washington Place stairway, then the door was not a possible escape route. Even if the victims had opened the door, the stairs were impassable. Fire—not a lock—sealed their fate.

Steuer developed this theory as he cross-examined a parade of firefighters and policemen. Through the second day of testimony, the lawyer postulated that the first employees to reach the Washington Place door had actually opened it. They looked out. But they saw fire and smoke, and slammed the door shut again. Perhaps the door was locked, somehow, at that point—if so, the culprit was pure panic. The owners had nothing to do with it. "There was smoke in the hallway," Steuer noted as he led the witnesses through their stories. And: "the handrail of the stairs leading from the eighth to the ninth stories was burned away." Wasn't it true, he asked a firefighter, that "you could readily see [flames] if you were on the ninth flight of steps?"

The witnesses acknowledged that the stairwell was smoky, and that reflections of the eighth-floor blaze were probably visible on the stairway walls. But they denied that the passage was blocked by fire. Later, when the ninth- and tenth-floor workers began testifying, they described a fire that swept up through the rear airshaft—not through the stairs. Chief Worth was correct, up to a point. The basic movement of the fire on the ninth floor was from the west side of the factory to the east side, just as he said. That is why some of the last victims were the ones who spilled, in flames, through the Greene Street windows. But Worth had no way of knowing, as he stood there on the street, that the rear airshaft existed. He naturally assumed that any fire spreading up that side of the building had to be moving up the stairs.

At the end of the second day of witnesses, Louis Levy, a rag trader, testified that he had been buying fabric scraps from Harris and Blanck for three or four years, then reselling the scraps to be made into paper. Levy estimated that he cleaned out the bins under the Triangle cutting tables about six times a year—every two months or so. When he emptied the bins on January 15, 1911, he carted away more than a ton of light, sheer scraps: 2,252 pounds, to be exact. The bins were not emptied between that day and March 25, though the cutters had been very busy in that period. It was reasonable to conclude that at least another ton of scraps, maybe a ton and a quarter, had piled up by the day of the fire. As the ragman put it, a ton of scraps was "nothing unusual."

A ton or more of explosively flammable tinder, heaped in wooden bins in a factory where fires were fairly common. It certainly did not sound like a safe situation. On that note, the trial adjourned for the weekend.

Back in court the following Monday morning, Charles Bostwick moved into the heart of his case. Every day for a week, he called one survivor after another to tell the story of the fire. First the cutters testified concerning the birth of the blaze, those decisive seconds when the fire grew from a mere cigarette ember or match end, so easily snuffed, into a flame no bigger than the burner on a gas stove—and then, *whoosh!* It was out of control, and hundreds of people were running for their lives.

Next came the sewing machine operators, with their harrowing accounts of near-death. They took the jurors through the smoky loft, with flames in pursuit, right up to the fateful door. And when they reached that point in their stories, Bostwick asked each one to get up from the witness chair and go to a courtroom door and show the members of the jury precisely how she wrestled with the Washington Place door, tugged at it, wrenched it, and tried to *will* the door open. "I took hold of the handle and I turned it and pulled it," Mary Bucelli explained, grabbing and twisting and yanking as she spoke. "I pushed through the crowd which was near the door," testified Joseph Brenman. "I took hold of the handle and I was pulling it." Ida Nelson explained: "I pushed it and I couldn't open it. . . . I tried it one way and the other." Yetta Lubitz told of standing by the door when a young man rushed up to try it, and hearing him cry: "Oh, the door is locked! The door is locked!" Ethel Monick described how "I tried the door and I could not open it, so I thought I was not strong enough." She called for help, "and they all rushed over, and they tried to open it and it was locked. And they hollered out, 'The door is locked, and we can't open it!' "

Becky Rothstein told the jury that an operator named Sam Bernstein—not the factory manager, a different Sam Bernstein—"pulled the door, he knocked . . . he did everything." Then Bernstein himself testified: "I tried with both hands to open it. . . . There where the lock was—I wanted to tear it open!" Sophie Zimmerman said her coworkers "took hold of the handle and they turned it and they tore it—they tried to tear it, but they couldn't." Said Lillian Weiner: "I tried to turn the handle and it would not bend. It was locked."

Katie Weiner rattled the courtroom door furiously as she spoke: "I turned the knob this way and that. I pushed it toward myself and I couldn't open it; then I pushed it inward and it wouldn't go. . . . I knocked at the door. I seen the flames were too strong. . . . I stood at that door still till the last minute."

Steuer needed a whole bag of tricks to limit the damage. First, he resisted all requests by witnesses to be allowed to testify in Yiddish through an interpreter. Steuer understood that forcing witnesses to speak English would help his cause in several ways. The testimony

would be more confused and less compelling. Witnesses might be
easier to trip up on cross-examination. And many listeners—including,
perhaps, some jurors—equated poor English with low intelligence.
Steuer wanted the jurors to conclude that the Triangle workers brought
on their own deaths through foolish panic, that they were not smart
enough to save themselves. In some instances, Steuer succeeded in
forcing witnesses to testify in broken English. But Crain permitted a
substantial number of witnesses to use the interpreter. So Steuer
subtly undermined the jury's faith in the interpreter by repeatedly cor-
recting his translations. No doubt, Steuer's ability to out-translate the
translator added to his aura of mastery.

The defense attorney also tried to distract the jurors by tangling with
the judge. "I object to the number of questions that the Court is inter-
posing on this trial," he whined. He tangled with the prosecutor, too.
"You make a pretty good witness, Mr. Bostwick," he sneered after one
leading question. Steuer even tangled with witnesses, demanding to
know why Anna Gullo had changed her name, and later snapping at
Ethel Monick: "You sure do like to argue some, don't you, little girl?"

Steuer staged a sideshow. During one cross-examination, he asked a
witness for her handbag and ostentatiously measured its dimensions.
During a recess, he sent for an identical bag and hid four shirtwaists inside. Later, he found an opportunity to bait the young prosecutor, Robert
Rubin, into reaching inside the bag and pulling out the blouses—all to
get the jury thinking about thieving workers instead of locked doors.

Again and again, Steuer attacked the motives of the prosecution
witnesses. He grilled them about lawsuits they and their relatives had
filed against Harris and Blanck. "Your brother wants seventy-five
thousand dollars in one case, doesn't he?" Steuer growled at Joseph
Brenman. He ridiculed the notion that frightened workers, faced with
death, would rush to a door they had never used before. He scoffed at
the number of witnesses who claimed to have been the first to reach
the door. And he tried to paint a scene of utter panic on the ninth
floor—panic that killed workers who might otherwise have survived.

Perhaps most damaging, given the number of business owners on
the jury, Steuer alleged that the story of the locked door had been

cooked up and rehearsed in meetings with union lawyers. "Did you receive, on the twelfth of October 1911, a letter inviting you to a meeting at 151 Clinton Street, on the third floor, to meet the lawyer for the Ladies Waist and Dressmakers' Union?" he demanded of Sophie Zimmerman.

"No, sir."

"Didn't you go on the sixteenth of October 1911 to 151 Clinton Street, and didn't the lawyer go over the story of the fire with each one of you girls?"

"No."

"Well, now, didn't every one of the girls get a letter from Abraham Baroff"—the general manager of Local 25—"to come down to 151 Clinton Street?"

"No."

Steuer let it go. The idea had been planted.

The crude and blackened lock—the one rescued from the debris— was brought into the courtroom in a glass-covered, museum-style case. But for more than a week, the jurors were not allowed to see it. Several times, with the jurors sequestered, Crain heard arguments about whether the lock should be admitted into evidence. There were two key questions: Was it possible to prove that this was the lock from the Washington Place door? And if so, did its current condition prove anything about the fatal moments in the ninth-floor loft?

On Friday of the second week of the trial, as Charles Bostwick's list of 104 witnesses was nearing an end, Crain invited the lawyers to go over the evidence once more. Steuer spoke first, heaping scorn on the fortuitous discovery of the lock.

"On March 25 a fire occurred, and on March 26 all the conscience of the city is stirred by the terrible catastrophe," he began. "The newspapers published everything that can be published in the way of pictures, and on the twenty-seventh of March the theory of the locked door is already made public by every citizen. Hundreds upon hundreds of people go into that debris and seek the bodies, and the Fire Department makes a conclusive and minute and detailed search into that debris, and the whole question that is being agitated in the press day after day is locks, locks, locks, Your Honor.

"And nothing is found. When on the tenth of April, as from a clear sky, a detective goes to the premises and . . . within twenty-five minutes a lock is discovered."

Who could believe such a scenario? Steuer asked. And even if you believed it—so what? How could anyone possibly know, from a lock found on April 10, whether it had been open or closed more than two weeks earlier?

Bostwick's reply showed how much work the district attorney's office had done on this matter. Barney Flood and his detectives had determined which factory made the lock, and which hardware store received it, which maintenance crew bought it, and which handyman installed it. "We will trace [this lock] from the manufacturer to the jobber to the workman who put it on the door," Bostwick promised the judge. "And he will identify your lock. . . . The locks were not all alike in that building. This lock was put on later."

Crain was reluctant to admit the damning evidence. Several times during the trial he ruled it out, only to have Bostwick answer his reservations one by one. Finally, after hearing detailed presentations by Bostwick's experts, Crain admitted the lock into evidence. As pledged, Bostwick called witnesses who traced it from its maker, the Reading Hardware Company, through Woehr Brothers, a building supply house in Manhattan, and into the hands of one Charles W. Baxter. Baxter testified that he installed the lock at the Triangle Waist Company nine years earlier, in 1902. A new lock was needed, he testified, because a fire had damaged the original.

With the shot bolt in evidence, Bostwick was ready to complete his case. He called nearly a dozen survivors from the eighth floor, who testified in rapid succession that they had escaped down the Washington Place stairs—but only after machinist Louis Brown had unlocked the door. Rosalie Panno took the stand dressed all in black, mourning her mother Providenza, who died on the ninth floor. "Mr. Brown was washing his hands near the sink there," she testified. "And when we heard the cry of fire, he said, 'Wait here, girls, because I will open the door for you.'" Josie Nicolosi agreed. "With the key he twisted the lock," she testified. Minnie Wagner said that the owner's sister, Eva Harris, "rushed by me and shouted to me, 'My God! The door is locked!' After that I saw Louis Brown, who was wiping his hand, drop the towel and come to where we were standing, and . . . he reached in his pocket and took out a key and turned the lock."

(Later, when Brown appeared as a defense witness, he said there was a key already in the door when he reached it, which he tried to turn. But "the key wouldn't turn," he said—because the door wasn't locked. He simply "pulled the door open." Bostwick alleged that he had modified the story to protect his bosses.)

The eighth-floor witnesses served two important purposes. First, they bolstered the idea that *all* doors on the Washington Place side of the factory were routinely kept locked. Only Louis Brown's timely arrival prevented the same disaster on the eighth floor that befell the workers on the ninth. And second, they showed that the Washington Place stairs were a viable escape route, but for the locked door.

Now Bostwick approached the climax of his case. He summoned newlywed Kate Gartman to the stand, and she returned the story to the fatal loft. Gartman—she was Kate Rabinowitz on the day of the fire—had been gathering her things from the main dressing room on the ninth floor and chatting with two friends when the alarm went up. Coolly and calmly, she went from exit to exit searching for a way out. At the ultimate moment, she managed to push her way onto the elevator. Her story added little that was new. Steuer seemed to find her incredible and poked fun at her claim to have been "nice and cool and calm."

"I was as cool and calm as you are here," the witness retorted.

"Now," the lawyer smiled, "I am not half as cool as you think I am."

But Gartman's role was simple. She was called to introduce two important figures into the web of testimony: the friends who fled the dressing room alongside her. One was Margaret Schwartz, whose death was the crux of the entire trial. The other was Kate Alterman—the crucial witness.

*   *   *

She testified near sunset, the wan winter sky darkening outside the windows as the weak bulbs gathered strength in the crowded court-room. Kate Alterman cut a striking figure. She wore a dark hat with a sweeping brim as wide as her shoulders, and a dark coat with sharply contrasting lapels and cuffs. Underneath was a lacy blouse. She had a handsome oval face with huge dark eyes, a long nose and slender throat. She held her gloves in one hand and a handkerchief in the other, as if anticipating that her story would make her cry.

Kate Alterman is now shrouded by clouds of time. But it seems that she was one of six daughters of Morris Alterman, an upholsterer in Philadelphia, who emigrated from Russia with his family around 1903, around the time of the Kishinev pogrom. Apparently Morris was drawn to Pennsylvania by two relatives, already established. Henry and Samuel Alterman were the proprietors of the Central Upholstered Furniture Company on South Second Street in Philadelphia. For many years, Morris, his second wife, and his daughters all lived in Henry Alterman's house, with Samuel living across the street. As Morris's daughters began to get married, the next generation took root in the same spot. This close-knit community might explain why Kate testi-fied with a strong Yiddish accent, even though she had spent nearly half her life in the United States.

She was in her late teens or early twenties. A year earlier, in No-vember 1910, she had left her father, stepmother, and sisters and moved to New York, to a room in the Bronx. It is not known why she came to New York, but there she soon found herself in a world of young women much like her: underpaid and overworked, but also in-dependent, resolute, and freethinking. Like thousands of similar young women, she found work at the Triangle. Alterman operated a sewing machine in the third of eight long rows stretching across the ninth floor. Her spot was near the center of the row. Now and then, she could see, over the shoulders of the other workers, one of the owners passing through the room: hulking Mr. Blanck, perhaps with a diamond in his lapel, or the tailor, Mr. Harris. But the Shirtwaist Kings probably did not take note of her. At the trial, they testified that they had little knowledge concerning the specifics of their workforce. The Triangle proprietors claimed to have no idea how many individuals worked for them. The number changed from day to day, new faces always arriving, old faces gone without ever catching their attention.

After the fire, Alterman returned home to Philadelphia. But the prosecutors brought her back to New York at the beginning of the trial, and kept an eye on her for almost two weeks until the moment was right for her testimony. She entered the courtroom with her wide hat and striking coat and now the bosses most certainly noticed her.

Charles Bostwick wore a fatherly look and spoke gently as he guided his star witness through the preliminaries. Kate Alterman described the rising panic of the first moments after the alarm. "Margaret Schwartz was with you at this time?" the prosecutor asked.

"At this time, yes, sir."

"Then where did you go?"

"Then I went to the toilet room," she began. "Margaret disappeared from me. And I wanted to go to the Greene Street side, but the whole door was in flames. So I went and hid myself in the toilet room and bent my face over the sink. And then I ran to the Washington side elevator, but there was a big crowd and I couldn't pass through there."

Bostwick said nothing, and she continued her monologue.

"Then I noticed someone—a whole crowd around the door. And I saw Bernstein, the manager's brother, trying to open the door. And there was Margaret near him.

"Bernstein tried the door and he couldn't open it, and then Margaret began to open the door. I take her on one side, I pushed her on the side—and I said: 'Wait! I will open that door!' I tried. Pulled the handle in and out, all ways, and I couldn't open it. She pushed me on the other side, got hold of the handle, and then she tried.

"And then I saw her bending down on her knees," Alterman continued, "and her hair was loose, and the trail of her dress was a little far from her. And then a big smoke came—and I couldn't see! I just know it was Margaret. And I said: '*Margaret!*' And she didn't reply.

"I left Margaret, I turned my head on the side, and I noticed the trail of her dress and the ends of her hair begin to burn. Then I ran in—in a small dressing room that was on the Washington side. There was a big crowd, and I went out from there. Stood in the center of the room, between the machines and between the examining tables.

"I noticed afterwards on the other side, near the Washington side windows, Bernstein—the manager's brother—throwing around like a wildcat at the window, and pull himself back. He wanted to jump, I suppose, but he was afraid. And then I saw the flames cover him. I noticed on the Greene Street side someone else fell down on the floor and the flames cover him."

The courtroom was absolutely still. No other witness had taken them so close to the terminal moment. All around Kate Alterman, in a truly hellish scene, bodies were sinking under the flames as others went out the windows.

"And then I stood in the center of the room," she said, "and I just turned my coat on the left side with the fur to my face, the lining on the outside, got hold of a bunch of dresses that was lying on the examining table—not burned yet—covered my head and tried to run through the flames on the Greene Street side.

"The whole door was a red curtain of fire. But a young lady came, and she began to pull me in the back of my dress. And she wouldn't let me in! I kicked with my foot, and I don't know what became of her. I ran through the Greene Street side door, right through the flames onto the roof."

She was sobbing by now, and the jurors looked stunned. Here was the last instant of Margaret Schwartz's life, as she sagged near the locked door and her dress and hair caught fire. Here was the final glimpse anyone would live to share of the dying multitude and the hungry flames. Charles Bostwick must have been pleased—but he noticed one small detail missing.

"When you were standing toward the middle of the floor, had you a pocketbook with you?" he asked.

"Yes, sir. My pocketbook began to burn already, but I pressed it to my heart to extinguish the fire."

That was everything. Bostwick turned grandly to his opponent.

* * *

Years later, Max Steuer recalled that moment: "I cannot describe to you," he said, "the pathetic picture made by that little girl. I cannot reproduce the tears that were running down her cheeks, nor can I tell you how the eyes of the twelve jurors were riveted on her and how they sat craning forward, thrilled by the girl's story and how they wept when she told it." Steuer knew that Bostwick had dramatically closed the circle of his case. And he knew that he must find a way to drain the power from this testimony, to create doubt again in the minds of the jury.

Attacking the weeping survivor was clearly out of the question. Instead, Steuer decided to "toy with the story." All week long, as survivors marched to the witness stand and recounted their escapes, Steuer had been nourishing the notion, through his cross-examinations, that the prosecution witnesses had been coached. He insinuated that the union and the district attorney had conspired to orchestrate the testimony. Two days earlier, he had even tried the unusual technique of asking a hostile witness to repeat her most damaging testimony in great detail: he was trying to suggest that Lena Yaller had actually memorized a prepared speech.

As he listened to Kate Alterman's story, Steuer decided that he would try that risky technique once more. He thought he detected, as she testified, the telltale echoes of stagecraft. There was the careful pacing of Alterman's account, and the dramatic elements—like the way the smoke cleared just as she turned back to see Schwartz in the grip of death. Some of the specific words piqued his suspicions—"extinguish," for example, sounded more like a lawyer than a teenage immigrant— and also the literary turns: "throwing around like a wildcat," and "red curtain of fire." Then there was Bostwick's final question, prompting the witness for a vivid, but inconsequential, detail. Could that be an author's pride at work? Was the prosecutor cueing his star for a final line from the script? If Steuer could get the jurors to see these things as he saw them—without an ugly confrontation—they might be softly swayed away from Kate Alterman. But it must be attempted with great care.

Steuer began, as he later explained, by asking a rapid-fire series of dry, factual questions—concerning home, family, and so on. Then he hinted that her testimony was staged. "You are the last [witness], is that the idea?" he asked. Apparently Steuer had assigned a private eye to follow Alterman during her long days waiting to testify, or else he had a mole in the district attorney's office, because he was entirely familiar with her movements since her return to New York City. Why, he demanded to know, did she visit the Asch Building with Bostwick and Rubin the previous weekend? Was it so the prosecutors could fix the story in her mind? "They pointed out to you where the Washington Place door is," he charged.

"I had to point it out to them," Alterman answered.

Steuer peppered her with simple questions until "the tears had stopped," he later explained. Then he said, "I want you to tell me your story over again, just as you told it before." This was classic sly Steuer—*just as you told it before*. Without calling attention to what he was doing, he subtly instructed Alterman to *try* to repeat herself.

"I went out from the dressing room, went to the Waverly side windows to look for fire escapes. I didn't find any," Alterman began. "And Margaret Schwartz was with me; afterwards she disappeared. I turned away to get to the Greene Street side, but she disappeared, she disappeared from me.

"I went to the toilet rooms. I went out from the toilet rooms. I bent my face over the sink and then went to the Washington side to the elevators. But there was a big crowd," she continued.

"And I saw a crowd around the door, trying to open the door. There I saw Bernstein, the manager's brother, trying to open the door but he couldn't. He left. And Margaret was there, too, and she tried to open the door. And she could not. I pushed her on a side. I tried to open the door—and I couldn't. And then she pushed me on the side, and she said, 'I will open the door!' And she tried to open the door.

"And then a big smoke came, and Margaret Schwartz I saw bending down on her knees. Her hair was loose, and her dress was on the floor and a little far from her. And then she screamed at the top of her voice: *'Open the door! Fire! I am lost! There is fire!'* And I went away from Margaret.

"I left, stood in the middle of the room, went in the middle of the room, between the machines and the examining tables. And then I went in. I saw Bernstein, the manager's brother, throwing around the windows, putting his head from the window. He wanted to jump, I suppose, but he was afraid. He drawed himself back and then I saw the flames cover him. And some other man on the Greene Street side—the flames covered him, too.

"And then I turned my coat on the wrong side and put it on my head with the fur to my face, the lining on the outside. And then I got hold of a bunch of dresses and covered up the top of my head. I just got ready to go and somebody came and began—and began to chase me back, pulled my dress back. And I kicked her with a foot and she disappeared. I tried to make my escape. I had a pocketbook with me, and that pocketbook began to burn. I pressed it my heart to extinguish the fire, and I made my escape right through the flames. The whole door was a flame right to the roof."

"It looked like a wall of flame?" Steuer asked helpfully.

"Like a red curtain."

Ah, the red curtain. Steuer hoped she would repeat another distinctive expression, as well. "Now, there was something in that you left out, I think, Miss Alterman," he said. "When Bernstein was jumping around, do you remember what that was like? *Like a wildcat*, wasn't it?"

"Like a wildcat," the witness agreed.

"You left that out the second time."

Bostwick could see clearly what Steuer was up to, and he fired off an objection to the final remark. But there was little he could do to warn his witness away from the trap.

Alterman's second telling added certain details and left out others. She never went near the small, crowded dressing room in the second version; instead, she reported the chilling final words of Margaret Schwartz. On the other hand, a number of sentences and phrases were word-for-word repetitions. *He wanted to jump, I suppose, but he was afraid.*

The tactic had worked moderately well for Steuer. He had not gotten a perfect playback of the original testimony. But with hardly a hint of hostility, he had primed the jury to listen for echoes, and he had lodged the red curtain and the wildcat securely in Alterman's mind, and in the minds of the jury. He decided to repeat the exercise—with every hope that the witness would now deliver exactly what he wanted.

Again, Steuer circled away from the main story for a few minutes. This time he fired off a string of inconsequential questions about the layout of the factory. When enough time had elapsed, he struck once more:

"Now, could you tell us again what you did?"

"I went out to the Waverly side windows to look for fire escapes," Kate Alterman began, for the third time. "Margaret Schwartz was with me, and then Margaret disappeared. I called her to Greene Street—she disappeared. And I went into the toilet room. Went out. Bent my face over the sink. And then I wanted to go to the Washington side, to the elevator. I saw there a big crowd. I couldn't push through.

"I saw around the Washington side door a lot of people standing. I pushed through there. I saw Bernstein, the manager's brother, trying to open the door. He could not, and he left. Margaret Schwartz was there. She tried to open the door and she could not. I pushed Margaret on the side. Tried to open the door. I could not. And then Margaret pushed me on the other side, and she tried to open the door.

"But smoke came, and Margaret bent on her knees. Her trail was a little far from her, just spreading on the floor—far from her. And her hair was loose. And I saw the ends of her dress and the ends of her hair begin to burn.

"I went into a small dressing room. There was a big crowd. And I tried—I stood there and I went out right away. Pushed through and went out. And then I stood in the center of the room between the examining tables and the machines. Then I noticed the Washington side windows. Bernstein, the manager's brother, trying to jump from a window. He stuck his head out. He wanted to jump, I suppose, but he was afraid. And then he would draw himself back. Then I saw the flames cover him."

Alterman realized she had forgotten something that Steuer was interested in, so she added: "He jumped like a wildcat on the walls."

She returned to the story. "And then I stood. I got my coat, turning the fur to my head, the lining to the outside, got hold of a bunch of dresses that was lying on the table and covered it up over my head. And I just wanted to go! And some lady came, and she began to pull the back of my dress. I kicked her with the foot, and I don't know where she got to. And then—"

Now Alterman realized that she had forgotten something Bostwick wanted to hear. So she backtracked again. "I had a purse with me, and that purse began to burn. I pressed it to my heart to extinguish the fire."

She raced to the end. "The whole door was a flame—it was a red curtain of fire. And I went right on to the roof."

Steuer looked at her hard, but his voice was soft. "You never spoke to anybody about what you were going to tell us when you came here, did you?"

"No, sir."

Did she tell her family about the fire? Did they ask her about it? "They asked me and I told [them] once, and then they stopped me. They didn't want to talk about it anymore."

"And you never talked to anybody else about it?"

"No, sir."

By this point it hardly mattered whether the young woman had practiced her story out of honest or dishonest motives. Clearly, she had organized and rehearsed it in her head, or someone had organized it for her. It was too clear, too fine, to be the first telling. Kate Alterman was undone by the very sort of details that normally give credibility to a story. The long train of Margaret Schwartz's dress, "just spreading on the floor." The loose tendrils of Margaret's hair. The panicked frenzy of "Bernstein, the manager's brother." The unknown woman grabbing at her as she dashed to safety. The red curtain of flame. Alterman's harrowing story was built like a novel, full of muscular specifics—and specifics imply truth. But Steuer had turned this customary premise on its head. Now the details of Alterman's story—the red flame, the smoldering hair, the extinguished pocketbook—became signs of deceit. Steuer had successfully shifted attention away from the compelling, outrageous content of Alterman's testimony. Instead he implied, with quiet, ostensibly gentle questions, that the story was too good to be true. It was a cold, efficient piece of work.

Steuer never suggested any reason to doubt the details of Kate Alterman's story. There were none. Her story matched the known facts of the case perfectly. Margaret Schwartz's horribly burned body was found within a few feet of the place where Alterman last saw her. Bernstein, the manager's brother, did die in the loft, and it was entirely believable that he was "throwing about" at the windows before he succumbed. Alterman's escape to the roof was typical of the wild dashes by the final survivors. The testimony should have rung true because it *was* true.

On the other hand, Alterman was probably lying about never having told her story before. Anyone could see the care that had gone into fashioning such a clear, compelling account of the panicked situation.

Steuer circled once more, and took her for the fourth time through the last half of her testimony. Again Alterman mentioned the wildcat, the inside-out coat, the mystery woman clawing at her dress, the "red curtain of fire." Steuer pressed home her small deceit: "You never studied those words, did you?" he asked Kate Alterman.

"No, sir."

No more questions.

Max Steuer called fifty-one witnesses of his own—slightly more than a week of testimony—beginning with the state commissioner of labor, who reported that the Triangle had passed an inspection less than a month before the fire. Steuer's case could be distilled into several themes, none of which, by itself, was enough to ensure victory. All of them taken together, however, might suffice.

First, Steuer showed that the Triangle Waist Company had been a hive of activity from morning to evening, with workers constantly moving from floor to floor. Runners and foremen took the stand to recall how, on any ordinary day, they rushed from the ninth floor to the eighth floor and back, again and again, hauling bundles of cuffs and shirtfronts and sleeves to feed the assembly line. Shipping clerks testified about scurrying downstairs from the tenth floor and back again, over and over, trying to find enough garments to fill their orders. Salesmen and suppliers told of wandering from the offices on the tenth floor down to eight or nine in search of Harris and Blanck, who were always vanishing into the factory.

Gradually, the jurors came to see how implausible it was that the Washington Place doors could be kept locked constantly—as some prosecution witnesses had charged. A factory as large and busy as the Triangle, with different stages of the assembly process on each floor, could not possibly function without constant movement up and down. And it would have been terribly inefficient—in a factory that prized efficiency—to limit the traffic to a single set of stairs at one far corner of the room.

Steuer plainly saw this as his strongest material, because he put on witness after witness to talk about passing through the Washington Place door during working hours. Max Hirsch, an embroidery supplier, guessed that he had used the door "fifty, maybe seventy-five times." Samuel Rubin, a former cutter for Triangle, reported that he'd gone through the door "three or four times a week." Edwin Wolf, a manufacturer's agent, said he showed customers through the factory "half a dozen times" in two years, and had used the door every time. And so on.

This testimony was so effective that Charles Bostwick insisted, in his closing argument, that the prosecution had never tried to show that the door was *always* locked, only that it was locked at closing time. But this was not what a number of Bostwick's witnesses had said. They insisted that they had *never* seen anyone come or go through that door. Steuer planted a large seed of doubt about those claims.

But Steuer's witnesses might also have hurt his cause. Several of them acknowledged that employees were indeed expected to arrive each morning and leave each day through just one exit—the Greene Street door. A reasonable person might conclude that the other doors were locked at closing time to enforce this rule. More important, a number of defense witnesses testified that Triangle management kept keys attached to the Washington Place doors. These keys dangled from strips of light fabric, and, unfortunately, the fabric frequently broke. Several witnesses recalled times when they had gone looking for a new strip of lawn to reattach a key. Charles Bostwick seemed to miss the potential significance of this fact, because he failed to drive home an obvious question: If the doors were kept unlocked, as Blanck and others testified, what was the reason for equipping them with keys?

Steuer's second goal was to humanize the Triangle owners. Max Blanck was portrayed as the sort of man who gladly arranged for a doctor to care for an employee's sick child. Harris came across as a hands-on, attentive owner, able to recall every detail of his beloved factory, down to the precise number of sewing machines in each row on the ninth floor. Steuer invited the manager, Samuel Bernstein, to describe his heroics in the face of the fire. He called the brave bookkeeper, Dinah Lipschitz, and the plucky shipping clerk, Eddie Markowitz. He even put Harris and Blanck on the stand to recount their own brushes with death. The fact that Isaac Harris's own sister nearly died on the eighth floor, and that Max Blanck's daughters had to race past the flames to the roof, surely won some sympathy from the jurors.

But the decision to put the defendants on the witness stand did not come without a price. On cross-examination, Charles Bostwick cornered Harris on the topic of theft from the factory. Why was it so important that every employee use the Greene Street exit?

Around 1908, Harris willingly explained, the problem of stolen waists became so severe that he hired detectives to find the culprits. These men "locked up about six girls," he said, and then went to the homes of these workers. "We searched in every house," Harris said, "and found from two dozen to three dozen waists that [each of] these girls had taken." Even after the crackdown, he said, the thieving continued. Not long before the fire, Triangle managers found a young woman with two blouses hidden in her swept-up hairdo.

Bostwick asked Harris to estimate how much money the Triangle lost through theft. Steuer jumped up, objecting vehemently. Forcing Harris to answer the question would make him look petty, Steuer argued. "The newspapers will come out with headlines tomorrow that will put us out of business." But Judge Crain allowed the questions.

"How much in all would you say was the value of the goods that you found had been taken by these employees?" Bostwick pressed.

". . . In one year, you mean?" Harris asked.

"In one year."

"Prior to the fire?" Harris parried.

"Yes."

"Well." The owner paused. "Ten dollars or fifteen dollars or twelve dollars or eight dollars, something like that."

"You would say it was not over twenty-five dollars, wouldn't you?"

Steuer was on his feet again. "I object to that as immaterial!"

The judge instructed Harris to answer. "No," he said quietly. "It would not exceed that much."

A third theme of Steuer's case ended in complete confusion—which is not always the worst thing for a defense attorney. He called three witnesses: a woman named May Levantini and her friends the Mittelman sisters, Ida and Anna. On the day of the fire, Levantini was in charge of sewing fancy buttons onto premium waists; her machine was near the Washington Place door. She told an amazing story about the allegedly locked exit.

Levantini testified that she heard the alarm, saw the first signs of fire, and ran to the Washington Place door. When she got there, she found the key dangling from a strip of fabric. She said she took the key and opened the door. (Here, as elsewhere, Bostwick failed to ask why she would need a key if—as Steuer claimed—the door wasn't locked.)

She said she went onto the landing and peered over the rail. "I looked out and I seen the girls running down from the eighth floor," Levantini said. "And as I looked over that way, flames and smoke came right up and they made me turn in. . . . The smoke and flames come up which prevented me" from going down the stairs, she said. Certain that the stairway was blocked, Levantini slammed the door and wound up escaping by sliding down a cable in the elevator shaft.

Initially the Mittelman sisters seemed to confirm this tale. Ida Mittelman recalled that she had followed May Levantini through the Washington Place door and stood beside her as the smoke boiled up from below. "The smoke was thick," she remembered, and so she turned back. Anna, under considerable prompting, said her sister went through the Washington Place door, but came back because the stairs were impassable. But under Bostwick's cross-examination, Anna said she had forgotten the whole episode until May Levantini refreshed her memory. Ida, too, said she only remembered it after Anna told *her* about it. That left only Levantini's word to support the idea that the door was passable but not the stairs.

Steuer's final attack was on the lock. He called his own expert, who testified that a lock, facing the heat of such an intense fire, would have melted. But the lock inside Bostwick's museum-style case was not seriously damaged at all. It was blackened in places and battered. But it worked perfectly. To prove that the lock was intact—and also to show how easily it could have been tampered with—Steuer's expert took the lock from its fancy case and, using only a screwdriver that he carried in his pocket, removed the mechanism from the charred remains of the door and opened it to reveal the innards.

"That could have been done any time between now and that fire, couldn't it?" Steuer asked. "A million times, couldn't it, by a man no more expert than you are?"

"I could by removing that one screw, yes, sir," the witness replied.

After the closing arguments, the Triangle jurors, twelve men from business and the trades, retired to deliberate the fate of Isaac Harris and Max Blanck. It was 2:50 P.M. on Wednesday, December 27, 1911—nine months and forty-six hours after Margaret Schwartz sank under the flames. As soon as the twelve reached the jury room, foreman Leo Abrahams suggested that they take a vote. H. Heusten Hiers, an importer, counted the ballots. There were eight votes for acquittal, two for conviction, and two abstentions.

One of the men who refused to vote was Victor Steinman—a shirtwaist manufacturer. "My mind was so confused," he said afterward, "that I did not dare vote on the first ballot." He knew that the public wanted someone held responsible. He shared that impulse. And he was persuaded that the door was locked.

His only doubt was whether Harris and Blanck *knew* it was locked. And that, according to Judge Crain, was the entire issue. In his instructions to the jurors, Crain began by reading the law: "All doors leading in or to any such factory . . . shall not be locked, bolted, or fastened during working hours." Over Steuer's objections, he noted that "all" doors meant "every" door. Steuer objected again when Crain said that "working hours" included "a reasonable time" for workers to exit the factory at the end of the day.

Then the judge added instructions that were entirely to Steuer's liking. It was not enough, Crain said, to find that the door was locked at the crucial moment. It had to be locked "under circumstances bringing knowledge of that fact to these defendants." In other words, Harris and Blanck had to know that the Washington Place door was locked at that specific time on that specific day—and beyond that, the jurors had to find proof that if the door had been open, Margaret Schwartz would have lived. If they weren't sure, beyond a reasonable doubt, that Harris and Blanck knew—at 4:45 P.M. on March 25—that the Washington Place door was locked, "it will be your duty to acquit the defendants," Crain told the jurors.

Crain's jury instructions amazed many of the lawyers who came to witness the final act of the trial. In the hallways outside the courtroom, courthouse regulars "gathered in groups and freely discussed Judge Crain's charge," the *Times* reported. "Many of them commented upon the fact that he had failed to make any mention of the number of lives lost." Others found it surprising that Crain made no mention to the several defense witnesses whose testimony conflicted with earlier statements they had made. The general feeling was that Crain's instructions were overwhelmingly favorable to the defense.

Inside the sealed jury room, the panel voted a second time. Again, Victor Steinman and another man abstained. Some of the other jurors began to get angry. So on the third ballot, Steinman finally voted—in favor of conviction. He was not alone. According to various newspaper interviews with the jurors, at least three, and as many as six, jurors voted to find Blanck and Harris guilty.

More than an hour of deliberations had gone by. The jurors who had voted to acquit the owners now insisted that the judge left them no choice. They "demanded I show proof in the evidence that Harris and

Blanck knew that the door was locked on the day of the fire," Steinman recalled. They quickly wore him down. "I could not do it," he reluctantly concluded.

Anton Scheuerman also wanted to convict the defendants, but due to a mouth injury he couldn't speak effectively. Frustrated, he too surrendered. On the fourth ballot, the jurors in favor of a conviction caved and the vote for acquittal was unanimous. The jurors gave Judge Crain what they thought he had demanded.

Thomas C. T. Crain, at fifty-one, was living proof that not all highborn citizens were contemptuous of the Democratic machine. He was "one of the aristocratic 'stalwarts' of Tammany Hall," said the *Times*, a member of a distinguished New York family—his father was U.S. consul to Milan—and heir to a tidy real estate fortune. His career in politics included many successes; after joining the Tammany General Committee at the age of twenty-seven, he was named city chamberlain at thirty and tenement house commissioner at thirty-four.

By 1911, Crain enjoyed a good reputation as a judge, which he maintained for nearly twenty more years until, as he neared retirement, he was caught up in a scandal involving Tammany's alleged sale of magistrates' positions to the highest bidders. Charged with "general negligence in the conduct of his office," Crain eventually was cleared after an inconclusive, though unflattering, investigation.

This end-of-career humiliation echoed a long-forgotten incident much earlier in Crain's life, in which his competence and diligence had also come into question. And rediscovering that earlier incident casts Crain's handling of the Triangle trial in a new light. In this, his most famous case, the judge may have been swayed by bias and personal experience, because he—like Blanck and Harris—was once forced to bear the blame for a deadly fire. The incident damaged his political future and he considered it a terrible injustice.

In the early hours of March 14, 1905, a tenement on the Lower East Side went up in flames. At least 150 people—perhaps as many as 250—were sleeping in sixty tiny, unlit rooms inside the five-story building on Allen Street. Some of the residents managed to race down the stairs before the fire closed off this escape route. Others jumped safely from the lower windows. But most of the survivors had to fight their way down a crowded fire escape jammed with old furniture, boxes of clothing, and even perishable food kept in the late winter air. Some of the fire escape balconies had been boarded over to create open-air playrooms for the tenement children, and this further slowed the evacuation.

Twenty people didn't make it out, and twenty more were badly injured. Ten of the dead were children, found huddled under a skylight leading to the roof. It was locked.

Blame for the disaster fell on the city's Tenement House Department, which was assigned to ensure the safety of New York's slum apartments. And the tenement house commissioner was Thomas C. T. Crain. Crain's inspectors, it was said, had failed to keep the fire escapes clear and the skylights unlocked. Mayor George B. McClellan Jr., girding for a tough reelection fight, instantly turned on Crain, treating him "with marked chilliness," according to the *Times*.

Crain protested the unfairness of his plight and tried to defend himself. His inspectors, he said, cleared fire escapes every day, only to have them cluttered again as soon as they turned their backs. He noted that the Allen Street building had been inspected fourteen times in the six months before the fire. But the tenants of Allen Street and thousands of other tenements, he suggested, had no discipline or common sense about safety, and their panic and carelessness brought on the tragedy.

None of his protests did any good. After a coroner's jury censured his department, Crain was forced to resign. "His inefficiency was a handicap to Mayor McClellan," the *Times* wrote in a ridiculing editorial hailing Crain's departure. "Mr. Crain was temperamentally unfitted . . . [the job] called for a very different kind of man, one who could take the pace." Crain felt he had been made a scapegoat, sacrificed to the political aims and ambitions of others.

Six years later, he found himself presiding over the trial of two men in a strikingly similar situation. Blanck and Harris also felt like scapegoats being sacrificed for the bad judgment of their workers and the political ambitions of Charles Whitman. In striving to protect them, Crain seemed to bend over backwards. He enforced rules that drained the trial of the full horrific details of the Triangle disaster and issued jury instructions that essentially made it impossible to convict the owners. Because of his own experience, the judge sympathized more with the defendants than with the victims of the Triangle fire.

On December 27 at 4:46 P.M.—after deliberating for less than two hours—the jurors returned to Crain's courtroom and their verdict was read. Isaac Harris and Max Blanck dropped limply into their chairs as their wives began sobbing quietly just behind them. Spectators inside the doors roared in disbelief, and their cries were picked up in the crowded hallway outside. The Triangle owners did not dare leave through the angry throng—and so, for the first time in the history of the courthouse, two acquitted men departed via the prisoners' pen. Harris and Blanck were smuggled through the Tombs to a little-used exit. At about 5 P.M., the Shirtwaist Kings stepped into a nearly deserted street in the cold December twilight.

Their limousine was waiting around a corner, at the main courthouse entrance. They could hear the shouting of the furious crowd awaiting them, so the partners started walking toward the nearest subway station.

A young man caught sight of them and charged up the street. "Murderers!" he cried as he drew near. "Murderers! Not guilty? *Not guilty?* Where is the justice?"

He got right up to them. "We will get you yet!" he gasped. And then he collapsed onto the cobbles. As a policeman began blowing his whistle for an ambulance, Harris and Blanck ducked into the subway.

The next day's papers reported that the young man was at a local hospital, "suffering from a disordered mind." His name was David Weiner, and his sister Rose had burned to death at the Triangle Waist Company, a hundred feet above the ground, behind a locked door.

EPILOGUE

And so Charles Murphy finally embraced progress—not with the enthusiasm of a genuine progressive, much less with even a grain of Lower East Side radicalism. He was the same old round, well-fed, silent strategist, driven to change by the ever more organized demands of voters. Murphy's decisions in favor of change testify to the power of votes.

He understood that the will of the public, if organized, ultimately decides most issues, given time. The Huyler candy factory gave Murphy money, but, as the boss noted to Frances Perkins, the fifty-four-hour bill despised by his campaign donors gave him something he needed even more. "That law made us a lot of votes." When the progressives and the garment workers of New York successfully organized, even Murphy came calling.

By blessing the Factory Investigating Commission and endorsing the vote for women, Murphy helped chart the future of American liberalism. Gradually, the New York Democrats sapped strength from the progressives and the radicals. Tammany's Al Smith, bearing the legacy of the Triangle fire, grew into the dominant political figure in New York from 1918 to 1928. Then Smith passed the mantle, a bit grudgingly, to the father of the New Deal, Franklin D. Roosevelt. In the generation after the Triangle fire, urban Democrats became America's working-class, progressive party.

Though many strands and influences flowed into this phenomenon, few if any ran more directly to its core than the Triangle legacy. The rise to power of urban liberalism, symbolized by Murphy's decisions, set an agenda that has helped to define, in support or in opposition, every presidency and every Congress since. Urban liberalism became the dominant politics of the left, absorbing progressivism and supplanting socialism.

What now looks clear in the sweep of history played out fitfully at the time. Initially, Murphy's embrace of change looked like the salvation of Tammany Hall. The old, jovially corrupt Hall passed away, and in its place rose the new Tammany of Al Smith and Robert Wagner. The Hall was still driven, in crucial ways, by patronage and "honest" graft. But for the first time in many years, New York City Democrats offered a vision greater than the machine.

Old Tammany seemed to be dying even as the new Tammany was inventing itself. In 1912, a year after the fire, District Attorney Charles Whitman finally found his big case. It looked, at first, to be a classic example of exposing Tammany's sins. A corrupt police lieutenant, Charles Becker, was accused of masterminding the murder of gambler Herman Rosenthal, a spectacular gangland slaying a few yards from Times Square. In a novel use of an automobile, the gunmen escaped by getaway car. Month after month, the Becker case dominated the front pages of New York newspapers, even in the year of the *Titanic*.

Herman Rosenthal had spilled the beans on police corruption to Herbert Bayard Swope, and Swope chased his vacationing friend Charles Whitman all the way to Marble House—Alva Belmont's Newport palace—just to get a quote for his story. New York insiders buzzed at the possibility of Lt. Becker pointing the finger at one of Tammany's sachems—especially Big Tim Sullivan, lord of downtown. Rosenthal, a former newsboy, counted Sullivan as his chief patron and protector; this gave him a swagger of invincibility, if only in his own mind. So it was hard to believe that a mere police lieutenant would have arranged to murder Herman without a green light from the Big Feller.

But all the speculation died the moment Max Steuer showed up at the courthouse. Steuer quickly arranged the first in a rapid series of plea bargains by crucial witnesses. Once again, it seemed, Tammany had turned to Steuer to handle the tough stuff. Big Tim's name was never mentioned at the trial, and Becker was dispatched to the electric chair.

Just as he had envisioned, Charles Whitman rode his big case to Albany. He was elected governor in 1914 and immediately began campaigning for president.

Big Tim was doomed in any event. Even Steuer couldn't save him from his slide toward insanity, after an amazing quarter century at the top of the New York pile. What do you do with a broken giant? First, the Sullivan clan sent Tim to Congress. Then they had him committed. Even a diminished Timothy D. Sullivan was a crafty character, however. One late summer night in 1913, he was playing cards with his keepers until, one by one, they all fell asleep. He crept away with a dollar in his pocket, and started walking. He was never again seen alive.

His body was discovered two weeks later, sliced in two, unclaimed in a local morgue. Big Tim had been run over by a train. Did he fall asleep on the tracks? Was he murdered and left there? Did he lie down quietly to wait for the rumble of the locomotive? No one could say. Nor could anyone explain why one of the best-known men in New York—his portrait smiled impishly from the walls of saloons and clubhouses from the Battery to Union Square—was not identified sooner.

Twenty thousand people passed his bier to pay their respects, and more than a hundred thousand lined the route of his funeral procession. Big Tim was buried wearing cuff links studded with diamonds, and afterward, the Sullivan clan put on "a wake such as New York has never seen before," according to the *Times*. He left an estate of $2 million—more than $30 million in current terms.

* * *

While Charles Whitman rode publicity to the governor's mansion, Al Smith had something stronger: a program. In 1918, the man from the Fulton Fish Market challenged Governor Whitman for the state's top job. His narrow victory was the death blow to Whitman's presidential hopes, and the birth of his own. Smith built his victory on a foundation of working-class voters—the sort of people whose tiny apartments he had entered when he went calling on the bereaved families of Triangle victims, and whose desolation he shared at Misery Lane. "Immigrants and city dwellers recognized that he was someone in higher politics who stood up for them, accepted them as equals, and above all, who gave them respectability," biographer Robert A. Slayton wrote. Smith governed as though the ghosts of the Triangle were looking over his shoulder.

In Albany, he surrounded himself with Factory Commission alumni—such as Frances Perkins, Belle Moskowitz, and Abram Elkus—and the spirit of the commission infused their work. New York became a hothouse of progressive liberalism. Smith grew into one of the most popular figures in New York history, serving four highly effective terms. He was still Tammany's man, but Charles Murphy gave his protégé freedom to hire the people he wanted, and shielded him from meddling patronage hacks. Murphy also gave Smith leeway to pursue dynamic policies.

It was ironic: After so many years, a diamond-pure example of Tammany loyalty finally reached the highest office in the state—and the Hall had to set him free. To taint Smith would be to ruin him. And to ruin him would mean losing the political dividends Smith represented.

All that was left was the final prize: to push Smith from Albany to the White House. But Murphy ran out of time. In spring of 1924, while masterminding Smith's first, unsuccessful, presidential bid, the boss died of a sudden heart attack. Four years later, Alfred E. Smith won the Democratic nomination for president, the first Roman Catholic ever to do so. Though Smith lost to Herbert Hoover, it was the highest a Tammany man had ever risen, or ever would.

* * *

In 1932, after Hoover served his single term and the nation plunged into the Great Depression, Franklin Roosevelt began the most important presidency of the twentieth century. It was Roosevelt who brought urban liberalism to its full powers, redefining the federal government as the protector of the people, not just abroad but at home, at work, in sickness, in poverty, and in old age. He called this the New Deal.

Clara Lemlich spent the Roosevelt years as a communist, organizing protests against the high cost of food.

Roosevelt's right-hand man in the U.S. Senate, the author of more important progressive laws than any figure in history, was Robert F. Wagner. Roosevelt's secretary of labor, the first woman ever to hold a cabinet post, was Frances Perkins. Wagner and Perkins were there from the first day of the New Deal to Roosevelt's death. And both of them knew exactly where the New Deal was rooted. Wagner once won a bet during the Roosevelt years by recalling the precise date and time of the Triangle fire, more than thirty years after it had happened.

On the fiftieth anniversary of the fire, March 25, 1961, Perkins helped dedicate a plaque at the old Asch Building, and the building still stands. New York University bought it, renamed it the Brown Building, and filled it with biology and chemistry laboratories. The marker commemorated the Triangle fire victims and the wave of reform that spread from their tragedy. Perkins sat at almost the same spot where she had stood as a young woman, half a century earlier, watching death roaring in the windows a hundred feet above her head.

And what about the Shirtwaist Kings? Max Blanck and Isaac Harris ducked down the subway stairs outside a secret entrance to the Tombs, as David Weiner wailed his sorrow, and never fully resurfaced.

For a while, the newspapers kept track of them. "Triangle Partner Ruined," the *Times* reported, two months after the trial. The occasion of the story was a lawsuit against Blanck and Harris, brought by the Rapid Safety Filter Co., which had supplied the Triangle's water coolers. The company wanted $206—the amount of an unpaid bill. But under oath Isaac Harris claimed that he didn't have enough money to settle even that smallish debt. Harris's home and all his possessions were in his wife's name, he said, and she was supporting the family. His service as secretary of the newly reorganized Triangle Waist Company, he added, was unpaid. And his last ten thousand dollars had gone to Max D. Steuer. (More than a year later, the Illinois Surety Company charged that the Triangle owners had used corporation laws to hide their assets.)

In the aftermath of the fire, the Triangle partners filed insurance claims approaching their maximum coverage—an amount far exceeding their documented losses. One of the firms backing the policies, the Royal Insurance Company, was suspicious enough to order an investigation. But Steuer, it turned out, was every bit as good at financial squabbles as he was at cross-examinations. Having cleared the partners of criminal charges, he quickly bullied the insurers into line. Blanck and Harris collected more than sixty thousand dollars above any losses they could prove—about a million dollars in current terms. This was, in a sense, pure profit: more than four hundred dollars per dead worker.

Steuer also handled the many civil lawsuits filed against Harris and Blanck by relatives of the fire victims. In these matters, too, the lawyer seemed unstoppable. Nothing was ever collected from the owners. "The claimants have been tired out," the *World* wrote three years after the fire, reporting that the last twenty-three litigants had settled with an insurance company for seventy-five dollars per claim.

Blanck made the papers in 1912—fourteen months after the fire. His limousine hit two children, in two separate incidents, in the same day. The first accident was on the morning of May 23: Blanck's chauffeur, Chauncey Whalen, was driving, with Bertha Blanck in the rear seat. Whalen turned onto Beverley Road in Brooklyn just as a six-year-old girl, Jeffie Levy, dashed into the street. After the impact, Mrs. Blanck jumped out, scooped up the badly injured child, and ordered her driver to "make all speed for the Coney Island Hospital." There, she deposited the girl—and went on with her business.

Max Blanck went riding later in the day. This time, the chauffeur struck a seventeen-year-old boy, Max Moscovitz, who was only slightly injured. Blanck gave him a ride home.

Reporters turned up at the Blanck mansion on Ocean Parkway that night with questions about the little girl, but as soon as they mentioned a car accident, Max Blanck began telling them about the boy. For a moment, everyone was confused.

From behind a door his wife began shouting, "I did it! I did it!"

"Did what?" Blanck asked. "You mean to say you had an accident and didn't tell me about it?"

"Well, you didn't tell me about your accident, either!"

The most illuminating news item came late in the summer of 1913. Max Blanck was arrested again. The charge: locking a door during working hours at his Fifth Avenue factory.

Once again, Blanck turned to Steuer, whose ceaseless service is proof that the partners were never really broke. This time, Steuer made no pretense of arguing that the door wasn't locked. Instead, he maintained that the sort of chain lock Blanck had used was approved by the state labor department. Blanck's explanation was identical to the one he gave at the manslaughter trial: his employees would rob him blind if he didn't lock them in.

Here, at last, was the answer to the question posed in the trial. Did the Triangle owners, knowingly and purposefully, lock their doors? It seems they did. Locked doors were so important to them that Blanck *kept* locking the doors even after his close brush with prison, even after a locked door contributed to the gruesome deaths of 146 young women and men.

The judge in the second case did not accept Steuer's argument that the new lock was legal. He found Blanck guilty—and fined him twenty dollars. It was the minimum punishment possible, and the judge apologized for having to fine him at all.

The Shirtwaist Kings struggled to keep the Triangle alive. After the fire, to limit their liability, they reconstituted the original partnership as a corporation, with Blanck as president and Harris as secretary. For several years, they did business on lower Fifth Avenue, not far from the old factory. Then they followed the shirtwaist trade uptown, to West Thirty-third Street. But things never got back to normal for the once-mighty Triangle Waist Company. In 1914, the company was caught sewing counterfeit Consumers' League labels into its garments—faking the official seal of decent workplace conditions. In his defense, Blanck explained that the Triangle's reputation had been unfairly ruined.

The firm vanished from public records around the end of World War I, making a final appearance in the New York City directory of 1918. The fire had been a slow death for the company. Apparently Blanck and Harris continued in business together for at least another year or two, with Blanck as the dominant figure. Harris's role steadily diminished. Blanck's brothers—Harry, Isaac, and Louis—became central figures in his various companies, all bearing French-themed names: the Normandy Waist Co., the Normandy Shirt Co., the Riviera Waist Co., the Calais Waist Co., the Trouville Waist Co.

Finally, around 1920, the longtime partners split up. Blanck soldiered on with Normandy Waist (later Normandie Waist) as his flagship. Harris returned to his roots as an independent tailor. The 1925 city directory was the last to list the Harris Waist Shop. By then, Blanck's name did not appear at all.

After the fire, many leaders from many walks of life promised that no important detail of the tragedy would ever be forgotten. But much was forgotten, and soon. The facts of the disaster blurred into legend. Barely more than a decade after the disaster, the garment workers' union—the group most intimately tied to the story—commissioned a writer to record its history. Louis Levine's minutely detailed book tracked each twist and turn of internal politics and labor negotiations. But what happened at the Triangle received only a brief mention. By the 1950s, when Moses Rischin wrote the first sweeping history of the Jewish migration to the Lower East Side, facts about the fire were so scarce that his single paragraph on the topic contained nearly as many errors as details.

Fortunately, Leon Stein, a man of the union and a man of letters, wrenched key parts of the Triangle story free from history's tar pit. Working doggedly through the 1950s, Stein tracked down survivors and pored over the trial transcript. He saved much that would otherwise now be beyond recovery, and wrote what was until now the only full-length account of the tragedy, titled simply, *The Triangle Fire.*

Yet it is only at this distance, more than forty years after Stein, that we can see what the strike of the shirtwaist workers, and the deaths at the Triangle, truly represent in American history. We see now where the feminism of the strike was headed—toward a complete rethinking of the place of women in society. We know what the New York Factory Investigating Commission ultimately produced—a new model for worker safety in American mills and workshops. We know that Charles Murphy's intuitions were correct—the nation's politics were primed for a shift to the left. And we know that the response of Murphy and the New York Democrats, as it echoed and reverberated, would play a large part in dooming socialism to failure. In the time-honored style of American politics, an established party smothered a rising third party by adapting some of its core issues.

We also know the limits of those trends. Though the risk of death in the American workplace has been cut to one-thirtieth of what it was in 1911, there are still some shops and factories that would be instantly recognizable to Rosie Freedman and the rest of the Triangle dead. In 1991, in Hamlet, North Carolina, twenty-five workers died behind locked doors in a flash fire at a poultry plant. Conditions in poorer countries are far worse. A fire at a toy factory in Bangkok in 1993 left nearly two hundred workers dead. Factory owners had locked the doors to prevent theft of toys by their employees.

Charles Murphy, Tim Sullivan, Clara Lemlich, Alva Belmont, Edward Croker, Charles Whitman, Max Steuer, Meyer London . . . a New Yorker ninety years ago would have imagined that these names would last for generations. Instead, they are nearly forgotten, known only to historians, and not always well known to them.

Even Tammany Hall faded away, despite Murphy's best efforts. A new genius of New York politics arrived, named Fiorello La Guardia—

the perfect answer to many of the questions that beset the Hall. La Guardia was a socialist turned Republican, a garment union organizer, half Italian, half Jewish, and 100 percent New Yorker. He could start a speech in Italian and end it in English with a long burst of Yiddish in between. La Guardia did not need Tammany's help to galvanize the working classes. His reign as mayor during the New Deal years left the Hall a mere shell. In August 1943, the machine reluctantly sold its headquarters—a moment symbolic of utter defeat.

The buyer: The International Ladies' Garment Workers' Union.

As for the mostly nameless young women and men who went on strike in 1909 and bravely walked those relentless picket lines through a freezing winter—and especially those remarkable young people who later died at the Triangle—their memory grows. Their individual lives are mostly lost to us, but their monument and legacy are stitched into our world.

APPENDIX

What follows is the first complete list of Triangle fire victims ever compiled. None of the contemporary newspapers attempted more than daily lists of the identified dead—a system that produced wide variation and substantial discrepancies. The coroner apparently had no uniform method for compiling the names. Within a few days after the fire, most papers stopped carrying lists and simply incorporated the names of newly identified dead into their main stories about the fire, making it even more difficult to keep track of the total. As a general rule, Joseph Pulitzer's *World* did the best job of listing the victims, although near the end of the identification process the paper gave up the effort, and in other cases the *World* listed the same victim under multiple misspellings of the name.

I used the following method to arrive at this list. I knew, going in, that it should consist of 140 names. When the huge funeral parade of April 5, 1911, wound through the streets of Manhattan and Brooklyn, there were 139 identified victims and seven unidentified ones, for a total of 146. Seven months later, one of the unknown victims was identified—Catherine Maltese, the mother of fire victims Lucy and Sara Maltese—and the number of named dead rose to 140.

With that in mind I crunched the list. I began with a roster of possible victims available at *www.ilr.cornell.edu/trianglefire*, drawn mainly from the *New York Times* and from Leon Stein's book *The Triangle Fire*. In many cases this list consists of surnames only, of names with no further information, and of multiple spellings or versions of the same name. Next, I added additional names found in the *World, Call*, and *American*. The *World* was chosen because it was probably the best newspaper in New York in 1911, and certainly the largest and most aggressive. The *Call* was consulted because it had the best sources in the shirtwaist workers' union, and therefore a special access, potentially, to the families of dead union members. And I used the *American* because the Hearst paper was also aggressive and ambitious—although it very quickly abandoned any attempt to keep track of the dead.

The combined list from these five sources—Stein and the *Times, World, Call*, and *American*—ran to around 200 names. In studying the list, however, it quickly became clear that the earliest identifications, from the March 26 newspapers, were totally unreliable. The morgue did not begin making official identifications until after those stories were written. So any name that appeared *only* in a March 26 edition, unconfirmed by later papers, was scratched.

This greatly narrowed the gap between the number of names and the actual number of victims. The second step was to clean up misspellings. For example: Julia Aberstein, 19, at 53 Avenue A, in one newspaper is certainly the same person as Julia Oberstein, 19, at 53 Avenue A, in another newspaper.

Finally, it was necessary to make some judgments: for example, that "Benny Kuritz" and "Benjamin Kuritz" are both the same person as "B. Kurt." Or that "Louis Rosen," "Moe Rosen," and "Mrs. Loeb Rosen," all at the same address, had to be the same person. Perhaps twenty-five years of experience as a newspaper reporter, badgering harried bureaucrats and hastily jotting down barely heard utterances, made it easier to spot the likeliest human errors.

The reported cause of death provides clues to where and how the victim died. "Multiple injuries" describes a victim who jumped or was pushed from the windows or down the elevator shaft, or who fell from the collapsing fire escape. When multiple injuries or fractures were accompanied by burns, it probably meant that the victim died in the last moments at the elevator shaft or the Greene Street windows. In many cases, the newspapers gave the cause of death as "incineration," but I have changed that to "asphyxiation/burns" to better reflect the reality. Most of these victims died inside the loft. However, it is possible that some of those badly burned victims were found in the shaft or on Greene Street.

I have also included, in every known instance, the name of the person who identified the body. There is some chance, perhaps remote, that such information could be useful to families trying to trace possible connections to Triangle victims.

Ultimately, when I finished scouring all the sources and tripping over stray names deep in this newspaper story or that one—and after eliminating all the names that seemed wrong or duplicative—I was left, to my amazement, with exactly 140. In other words, all the likely names are here and none of the unlikely ones, and it comes out to the right number. But confidence is not the same as certainty. This stands, then, as one man's best effort to recover the names of the Triangle dead.

List of Victims

ADLER, Lizzie, 24, multiple injuries. 324 E. 6 St. Identified by her brother Jacob. Source: Multiple newspapers, March 27.

ALTMAN, Anna or Annie, 16, fractured skull. 33 Pike St. Identified by her brother Morris. Multiple newspapers, March 27.

ARDITO, Anna, 25, burns. 509 E. 13 St. *Times,* April 2.

BASSINO, Rosie, 31, multiple injuries. 57 W. Houston St. Identified by her husband, Joseph. Sister of Irene Grameatassio. Multiple newspapers, March 28.

BELLOTA, Vincenza, 16, asphyxiation/burns. 625 Washington St., Hoboken, N.J. Identified by her uncle, Ignazio Ratzo. Name also given as Ignazia Bellata. Multiple newspapers, March 28.

BENENTI, Vincenza/Vincenzo, 22, multiple injuries. 17 Marion St. Identified by Fideli Babenti (relationship unknown). Multiple newspapers, March 27.

BERNSTEIN, Essie, 19, asphyxiation/burns. 77 Essex St. Identified by her father, Morris. Multiple newspapers, March 28.

BERNSTEIN, Jacob, 22 (28?), multiple injuries. 224 E. 13 St. Identified by Jacob Lehman (relationship unknown). Multiple newspapers, March 27.

BERNSTEIN, Morris, 19, multiple injuries. 309 E. 5 St. Identified by his brother, Herman. Multiple newspapers, March 27.

BIERMAN, Gussie, 22, burns. 8 Rivington St. Identified by Annie Brotsky (relationship unknown). Name also given as Gertie. Multiple newspapers, March 27.

BINEVITZ, Abraham, 20 (30?), fractured skull. 474 Powell St., Brooklyn. Identified by Isaac Weisman (relationship unknown). Name also given in various sources as Benowitz/Benowich/Robinowitz. Multiple newspapers, March 27.

BRENMAN, Rosie, age unknown, asphyxiation/burns. 257 E. 3 St. Identified by her brother Joseph, accompanied by the family dentist. Sister of Sarah. Multiple newspapers, March 31.

BRENMAN, Sarah "Surka," age unknown, asphyxiation/burns. 257 E. 3 St. Sister of Rosie. *Times*, April 2.

BRODSKY, Ida, 16. 306 102 St. Identified by her cousin, Minnie. Multiple newspapers, March 28.

BRODSKY, Sarah, 21, burns. 205 E. 99 St. Identified by her cousin, Morris, and her "sweetheart," Isidor Brozolsky, who recognized a gold ring he had given her. Multiple newspapers, March 28.

BROOKS, Ida or Ada, 18, burns. 126 Graham Ave., Brooklyn. Identified by the cork soles on her shoes by a brother-in-law (name unknown). Multiple newspapers, March 28.

BRUNETTE, Laura, 17, multiple injuries. 160 Columbia St., Brooklyn. Identified by Libero Morello (relationship unknown). Name also given as Brunetta. Multiple newspapers, March 27.

CAPUTTO, Frances, 17, multiple injuries. 81 DeGraw St., Brooklyn. Identified by Salvatore Natone (relationship unknown). Name also given as Capotto/Cabutto/Capatta/Capatto. Multiple newspapers, March 27.

CARLISI, Josephine, 31, multiple injuries/burns. 502 E. 12 St. Identified by her brother, Vincent Buccemi. Multiple newspapers, March 27.

CARUSO, Albina, 20, multiple injuries. 21 Bowery St. (Also given as 21 New Bowery St.) Identified by Annie DeLucca (relationship unknown). Multiple newspapers, March 27.

CASTELLO, Josie, 21, burns. 155 Cherry St. Identified from the style of her shoe by her brother, Benny. Name also given as Crastello. Multiple newspapers, March 29.

CIRRITO, Rose or Rosie, 18, multiple injuries. 135 Cherry St. Identified by her brother (name unknown). Multiple newspapers, March 27.

COHEN, Anna, 25, burns. 104 Melrose St., Brooklyn. Identified by Louis Gabbe (relationship unknown). Multiple newspapers, March 27.

COLLETTI, Antonia or Antonina, "Annie," 30, burns. 410 E. 13 St. Identified by her mother, Rose, and by a cousin, Dominic Leone. The original identification was in multiple newspapers, March 27. That body turned out to be that of Rosie Freedman. The corrected identification was in the *World*, March 28.

DOCHMAN, Dora, 19, burns. 524 E. 11 St. Identified by two false teeth by her cousin, Louis Shulowitz. Name also given as Clara and Dockman. Multiple newspapers, March 29.

DOWNIC, Kalman, 24, severe injuries from jumping. 214 Monroe St. Identified by his brother-in-law, Harry Kurack. Name also given as Dovnik and as "Dominick Kalman." Multiple newspapers, March 27.

EISENBERG, Celia, 17, fractured skull. 14 E. 1 St. Identified by her brother, Isidor. Name also given as Isenberg. Multiple newspapers, March 28.

FEIBISCH, Rebecca, 17/18, multiple injuries/burns. 10 Attorney St. Identified by her brother-in-law, Jacob Gottfried. Name also given as Feibush/Feibusch/Ferbisch/Feicisch. Multiple newspapers, March 27.

FICHTENHULTZ, Yetta, 18, burns. 299 E. 8 St. Identified by her sister, Fannie. Name also given as Dichtenhultz. Multiple newspapers, March 29.

FITZE, Daisy Lopez, 24, multiple injuries after jumping into net; died at New York Hospital. 11 Charlton St. Name also given as Dosie L. Fitzie. Multiple newspapers, March 28.

FRANK, Tina, 17, burns. 342 E. 11 St. Identified by a friend, Patrick ??rito. Name also given as Frank Tina and Jennie Franco. Multiple newspapers, March 27.

FREEDMAN, Rosie, 18, asphyxiation/burns. 77 E. 4 St. Identified by her uncle, Isaac Hine. Originally identified as Annie Colletti. Multiple newspapers, March 28.

GERSTEIN, Molly, 17, fractured skull. 325 E. 101 St. Identified by her brother, Michael. Name also given as Gernstein. Multiple newspapers, March 28.

GETTLIN, Celia, 17, fractured skull. 174 Clinton St. Name also given as Celina Gittlin. Identified by brother, Morris. Multiple newspapers, March 27.

GOLDSTEIN, Esther, 20, multiple injuries. 143 Madison St. (Address also given as 33 Broome St. and 248 Broome St.) Identified by her brother Israel. Multiple newspapers, March 26–27.

GOLDSTEIN, Lena, 23, fractured skull. 161 E. 2 St. Identified by brother Jacob. Multiple newspapers, March 27.

GOLDSTEIN, Mary, 18, asphyxiation/burns. 161 E. 2 St. Identified by the buttons on her shoe by her brother, Jacob. *World*, March 31.

GOLDSTEIN, Yetta, 20, asphyxiation/burns. 282 Madison St. Identified through her signet ring and cuff buttons by her cousin, Abraham Levine. Multiple newspapers, March 28.

GRAMEATASSIO, Irene, 24, asphyxiation/burns. 6 Bedford St. Identified by her husband, Attore. Sister of Rosie Bassino. Multiple newspapers, March 28.

GREB, Bertha, 25, multiple injuries. 161 Nassau Ave., Brooklyn. Identified by her brother (name unknown). Name also given as Geib. Multiple newspapers, March 27.

GREENBERG, Dinah, 18, asphyxiation/burns. 273 Watkins St., Brooklyn. Identified by her brother-in-law, Abraham Mendelson. *World,* March 27.

GROSSMAN, Rachel, 17, asphyxiation/burns. 98 E. 7 St. (98 E. 3 St. ?). Identified by her cousin, Samuel Greenberg. *World,* March 27.

GROSSO, Rosie, 16, asphyxiation/burns.174 Thompson St. Identified by the style of her slippers by her cousin, John Zingalo. *World,* March 27.

HARRIS, Esther, 21, multiple injuries. 131 Chester St., Brooklyn. Died after plunging down the elevator shaft. *Times,* March 28.

HERMAN, Mary, 40, asphyxiation/burns. 511 E. 5 St. Identified by her brother, Dr. M. Herman. Her death was the specific subject of the coroner's jury, which found responsibility on the part of Blanck and Harris. Multiple newspapers, March 28 and April 17.

HOCHFIELD, Esther, 22, asphyxiation/burns. 292 Monroe St. Identified through her jewelry by "a man who said he was [her] sweetheart" and by her father, Benjamin. Name also given as Hochfeld/Goldfield/Gochfeld/Gorfeld. Multiple newspapers, March 29–30.

HOLLANDER, Fannie, 18, asphyxiation/burns. 257 E. 3 St. Idenitified by her cousin, Joseph Wieselthiel. Multiple newspapers, March 27.

HOROWITZ, Pauline, 19, multiple injuries and burns. 58 St. Mark's Place, Brooklyn. Identified by her brother, Samuel Horowitz. Multiple newspapers, March 27.

JAKOFSKY, Ida, 18, asphyxiation/burns, 294 Monroe St. Identified by her cousin, Samuel Saffre. Name also given as Jakobowski. Multiple newspapers, March 27.

KAPLAN, Augusta "Tessie," 18, multiple injuries and fractures. 326 E. 8 St. Identifed by her brother, Harry. Name also given as Caplan/Kepple. Multiple newspapers, March 27.

KAPPELMAN, Becky, 18, badly burned. 191 Madison St. Identified by Yondel Johnston (relationship unknown). Name also given as Koppelman/Kabbleman. Multiple newspapers, March 27.

KENOWITZ, Ida, 18, asphyxiation and body charred; died at St. Vincent's Hospital. 238 Clinton St. Identified by by her cousin, Minnie Zubtkin. Name also given as Kenovitz/Konowitz/Kenowitch. Multiple newspapers, March 27–28.

KESSLER, Becky, 19, multiple injuries. 276 Madison St. Identified by Morris Kessler (relationship unknown). Multiple newspapers, March 27.

KLINE, Jacob, 28, asphyxiation/burns. 1301 Washington Ave., Brooklyn. Identified through his watch by his cousin, Herman Kline. Name also given as Klein. *Times,* March 28.

KUHLER, Bertha, 20, asphyxiation/burns. 99 E. 4 St. Identified by Yeppa Titter (relationship unknown). Multiple newspapers, March 27.

KUPFERSMITH, Tillie, 16, multiple injuries and burns. 750 E. Second Street. Identified by her uncle, Morris Schwartz. Name also given as Cupersmith/Kupersmith. Multiple newspapers, March 27.

KUPLA, Sarah, 16, multiple injuries; died at St. Vincent's Hospital, March 30. The last victim to die, she never regained consciousness. 1503 Webster St., Brooklyn. Multiple newspapers, March 31.

KURITZ, Benjamin "Benny," 19, multiple fractures and badly burned. 406 E. 10 St. Identified by his father (name unknown). Name also given as Kurt. Multiple newspapers, March 26–28.

L'ABBATO, Annie, 16, multiple injuries. 509 E. 13 St. Identified by brother Frank. Name also given as L'Abotte, L'Abbate. Multiple newspapers, March 27.

LANSNER, Fannie, 21, fractured skull. 23 Forsythe St. Identified by her brother-in-law, Charles Brass. Name also given as Launsner/Lanser. Multiple newspapers, March 27.

LAVENTHAL, Mary, 22, asphyxiation/burns. 604 Sutter Place, Brooklyn. Identified by her brother, Benjamin, and by her dentist. Name also given as Loventhal/Laventhol/Leventhal/Lowenthol. Multiple newspapers, March 27–30.

LEDERMAN, Jennie, 20, asphyxiation/burns. 152 E. 3 St. Identified by her ring by her brother, Morris. Multiple newspapers. March 27.

LEFKOWITZ, Nettie, 23, asphyxiation/burns. 27 E. 3 St. Identified by her brother, Archer. Multiple newspapers, March 28.

LEHRER, Max, 22, multiple injuries. 114 Essex St. Identified by Harry Melzer (relationship unknown). Brother of Sam. Multiple newspapers, March 27.

LEHRER, Sam, 19, multiple fractures. 114 Essex St. Identified by Harry Melzer (relationship unknown). Brother of Max. Multiple newspapers, March 27.

LEONE, Kate, 14, asphyxiation/burns. 515 E. 11 St. Identified by a lock of hair by her uncle, Dominic Leone. *Times*, March 28.

LERMARCK, Rosie, 19, asphyxiation/burns. 177 E. 100 St. Identified by Nathan Lermarck (relationship unknown). Name also given as Lermack/Lermark. Multiple newspapers, March 27.

LEVIN, Jennie, 19, asphyxiation/burns. Address unknown. *Times*, April 1.

LEVINE, Pauline, 19, multiple injuries. 380 South 4 St., Brooklyn. Identified by her cousin, Louis Mart. Multiple newspapers, March 27.

MALTESE, Catherine, asphyxiation/burns. 35 Second Ave. Identified on December 18, 1911, when her husband, Serafino, finally recognized one of her possessions. Mother of Lucy and Sara. Leon Stein, *The Triangle Fire*, p. 204.

MALTESE, Lucia "Lucy," 20, asphyxiation/burns. 35 Second Ave. Identified by her father Serafino. Sister of Sara, daughter of Catherine. Multiple newspapers, March 27.

MALTESE, Rosaria "Sara," 14, asphyxiation/burns. 35 Second Ave. Identified by her father Serafino. Sister of Lucy, daughter of Catherine. Multiple newspapers, March 27.

MANARA, Maria, 27, multiple injuries, 227 E. 28 St. Identified by her husband (name unknown). Name also given as Manabel. Multiple newspapers, March 27.

MANDERS, Bertha, 22, multiple injuries and burns; died at St. Vincent's Hospital. Address unknown. Identified by papers in her pocket. *World*, March 27.

MANOFSKY, Rose, 22, multiple injuries; died at Bellevue Hospital. 412 E. 74 St. Identified by her mother (name unknown). Multiple newspapers, March 27.

MARCIANO, Michela "Mechi," 20 (25?), skull fractured and body badly burned. 272 Bleecker St., identified by Charles Curarbina (relationship unknown). Multiple newspapers, March 27.

MEYERS, Yetta, 19, asphyxiation/burns. 11 Rivington St. Identified by her brother, Abraham. Multiple newspapers, March 30.

MIALE, Bettina, 18, multiple injuries. 135 Sullivan St. Identified by her brother, Joseph. Sister of Frances. Multiple newspapers, March 27.

MIALE, Frances, 21, asphyxiation/burns. 135 Sullivan St. Identified by her uncle, Pietro Dalio. Name also given as Maiale. Sister of Bettina. Multiple newspapers, March 28.

MIDOLO, Gaetana, 16, asphyxiation/burns. 8 Commerce St. Identified by her brother, James. Multiple newspapers, March 28.

NEBRERER, Becky, 19, multiple injuries and burns; died at New York Hospital. 19 Clinton St. Name also given as Nersberger/Nerberer. Multiple newspapers, March 26 and 27.

NICHOLAS, Annie, 18, multiple injuries; died at New York Hospital. 126 E. 110 St. Identified by her mother (name unknown). Multiple newspapers, March 27.

NICOLOSCI, Nicolina, 21 (22?), multiple injuries and burns. 440 E. 13 St. Identified by her cousin Dominic Leone. Name also given as Michelina, Nicolosi/Nicolosei. Multiple newspapers, March 27.

NOVOBRITSKY, Annie, 20, fractured skull and badly burned. 143 Madison St. Identified by her brother, Israel. Name also given as Vovobrisky. Multiple newspapers, March 27.

NUSSBAUM, Sadie, 18, asphyxiation/burns. 641 E. 6 St. Identified by "a peculiar stitch used in darning her stockings" by her mother, Clara. Name also given as Nausbaum. Multiple newspapers, March 27–28.

OBERSTEIN, Julia, 19, fractured skull. 53 Avenue A. Identified by her brother-in-law, Isaac Kaplan. Name also given as Aberstein. Multiple newspapers, March 27.

ORINGER, Rose, 20, multiple injuries; died at St. Vincent's Hospital. Address unknown. Multiple newspapers, March 27.

OSTROWSKY, Becky, 20, multiple injuries and burns. 108 Delancey St. Identified by her brother, Simon. Name also given as Astrowsky. Multiple newspapers, March 27.

OZZO, Carrie, 22 (19?), multiple injuries and burns; died at Bellevue Hospital. 1990 (1919?) Second Ave. Identified by her brother-in-law, John Scalia. Name also given as Uzzo/Nuzzo. Multiple newspapers, March 27.

PACK, Annie, 18, asphyxiation/burns. 747 E. 5 Street. Identified by her clothing by her brother Louis Ashkenazy. Multiple newspapers, March 27.

PANNO, Providenza, 43, asphyxiation/burns. 49 Stanton St. Identified by her husband, Frank. *World*, March 29.

PASQUALICCA, Antonietta, 16, multiple injuries. 509 E. 13 St. Identified by her brother, Nicholas. Name also given as Pasqualiato. Multiple newspapers, March 27.

PEARL, Ida, 20, asphyxiation/burns. 355 E. 4 St. Identified by her brother, Jacob. *World*, March 29.

PILDESCU, Jennie, 18, asphyxiation/burns. 515 E. 7 (11?) St. Identified by her sister, Yetta. *World*, March 29.

PINELLO, Vincenza, 22, asphyxiation/burns.136 Chrystie St. Identified by her brother, Louis, and by her dentist. Name also given as Vencenza. Multiple newspapers, March 29.

POLINY, Jennie, 20, asphyxiation/burns. 152 E. 3 St. Identified through the ring she was wearing, by her brother, Morris. Multiple newspapers, March 27.

PRATO, Millie, 21, asphyxiation/burns. 93 MacDougal St. Identified by her brother, Anthony. Multiple newspapers, March 27.

REIVERS, Becky, 19, asphyxiation/burns. 215 Madison St. Identified through earrings she wore, by her cousin, Annie Marcus. Name also given as Reivvers/Reiners. Multiple newspapers, March 27.

ROOTSTEIN, Emma. Address unknown. *Times*, April 1, 1911.

ROSEN, Israel, 17, asphyxiation/burns. 78 Clinton Street. Identified through his signet ring by his sister, Esther. Son of Julia. *Times*, April 1.

ROSEN, Julia, 35, multiple injuries. 78 Clinton St. Identified by the braids in her hair by her daughter, Esther. Mother of Israel. Multiple newspapers, March 28.

ROSEN, Louis or Loeb, 38, asphyxiation/burns. 174 Attorney St. Identified by his sister and by his cousin, Mark Smelski. Multiple newspapers, March 28.

ROSENBAUM, Yetta, 22, asphyxiation/burns. 302 (802?) E. Houston St. Identified by a scar on her left knee, by her father and her brother, Samuel. Multiple newspapers, March 28.

ROSENBERG , Jennie, 21, asphyxiation/burns. 242 Broome St. Identified through rings she wore, by her uncle, Morris Grossman. Multiple newspapers, March 27.

ROSENFELD, Gussie, 22, asphyxiation/burns. 414 E. 16 St. Multiple newspapers, April 2.

ROSENTHAL, Nettie, 21, asphyxiation. 104 Monroe St. Identified by her cousin, Herman Rosenthal. Multiple newspapers, March 28.

ROTHNER, Theodore "Teddy," 22, multiple injuries. 1991 Washington Ave., Bronx. Identified by his brother, Max. Name also given as Rottner/Rotha/Rothen. Multiple newspapers, March 27.

SABASOWITZ, Sarah, 17, asphyxiation/burns. 202 Avenue B. Identified by her father, Meyer. Multiple newspapers, March 28.

SALEMI, Sophie, 20 (24?), asphyxiation/burns. 174 Cherry St. Identified by her brother, Antonio. Name also given as Frances. Multiple newspapers, March 27–28.

SARACINO, Serephina "Sara," 25 (19?), asphyxiation/burns. 118 E. 119 St. Identified by her father, Vincenzo. Sister of Tessie. Name also given as Saretsky. Multiple newspapers, March 27.

SARACINO, Teraphen "Tessie," 20, asphyxiation/burns. 118 E. 119 St. Identified by her father, Vincenzo. Sister of Sara. Name also given as Saretsky. Multiple newspapers, March 27.

SCHIFFMAN, Gussie, 18, fractured neck and skull. 535 E. 5 St. Identified by her sister Bertha. Multiple newspapers, March 27.

SCHMIDT, Theresa "Rose," 32, asphyxiation/burns. 141 First Ave. Identified through jewelry by her husband, Oscar. Multiple newspapers, March 27.

SCHNEIDER , Ethel, 30, asphyxiation/burns. 95 Monroe St. Identified by her shoes by her uncle, Jacob Golding. Name also given as Snyder. Multiple newspapers, March 27.

SCHOCHEP, Violet, 21, asphyxiation/burns. 740 E. 5 St. Identified through jewelry, by her mother (name unknown). Multiple newspapers, March 27.

SCHWARTZ, Margaret, 24, asphyxiation/burns. 745 Brook Avenue, Bronx. Identified by her dentist. Name also given as Swartz. Her death was the specific subject of the trial of Blanck and Harris, December 4–29, 1911.

SELZER, Jacob, 33 (30?), multiple injuries. 510 E. 136 St. Identified by David Grossman (relationship unknown). Name also given as Feltzer/ Seltzer/ Zeltner. Multiple newspapers, March 27.

SEMMILIO, Annie, 30, skull fractured and badly burned. 471 Ralph Ave., Brooklyn. Identified by her brother, Thomas Balsano. Multiple newspapers, March 27.

SHAPIRO, Rosie,17, asphyxiation/burns. 149 Henry St. Identified by clothing, by Max Segalowitz. Multiple newspapers, March 27.

SKLAVER, Beryl "Ben," 25, fractured skull and burns. 169 Monroe St. Identified by Josef Redsky (relationship unknown). Name also given as Sklawer/Sklazer. Multiple newspapers, March 27.

SORKIN, Rosie, 18, multiple injuries. 382 Georgia Ave. Identified by her uncle, Louis Sorkin. Multiple newspapers, March 27.

SPUNT, Gussie, 19, asphyxiation/burns. 823 E. 8 St. Name also given as Spant/Sprint/Sprunt. Multiple newspapers, March 26 and 28.

STARR, Annie, 30 (32?), asphyxiation/burns. 734 E. 9 St. Identified by her cousin, Ida Dubaw. Multiple newspapers, March 28.

STELLINO, Jennie, 16, multiple injuries. 315 Bowery. Identified by her brother, Joseph. Multiple newspapers, March 28.

STERN, Jennie, 18, multiple injuries. 120 E. 3 St. Identified by Fannie Pheffer (relationship unknown). Name also given as Stein. Multiple newspapers, March 27.

STIGLITZ, Jennie, 22, asphyxiation/burns. 231 E. 13 St. Identified by her fillings by her cousin, David Witzling, and by her dentist. Multiple newspapers, March 29.

TABICK, Samuel, 18, asphyxiation/burns. 513 E. 148 St. Identified by his cousin, U. Mansky. Multiple newspapers, March 27.

TERDANOVA, Clotilde, 22, multiple injuries. 104 President St., Brooklyn. Identified by her sister, Rose. Name also given as Terranova/Gerranova. Multiple newspapers, March 27.

TORTORELLA, Isabella, 17, fractured skull and burns. 116 Thompson St. Identified by her brother, Nicholas. Name also given as Torpalella. Multiple newspapers, March 27.

ULLO, Mary, 26 (23?), multiple injuries. 437 E. 12 St. Identified by Ernest Meule (relationship unknown). Name also given as Gullo. Multiple newspapers, March 27.

UTAL, Meyer, 23, asphyxiation/burns. 163 Chrystie St. Identified by his uncle, I. Robinson. Multiple newspapers, March 27.

VELAKOWSKY, Freda, 20, multiple injuries; died at New York Hospital. 639 E. 12 (123?) St. Name also given as Freida and Vilakowsky. Multiple newspapers, March 27–28.

VIVIANIO, Bessie, 15, asphyxiation/burns. 352 E. 54 St. Identified by her brother, Rosario. Name also given as Viziano, Vivianis, Viviana. Multiple newspapers, March 27.

WEINER, Rose, 23, multiple injuries and burns. 119 E. 8 St. Identified by her sister Mrs. Minnie Rashke. Multiple newspapers, March 27.

WEINTRAUB, Celia "Sally," 17, multiple injuries. 187 (186?) Ludlow St. Identified by her brother, Max. Name also given as Weinduff. Multiple newspapers, March 27.

WELFOWITZ, Dora, 21, asphyxiation/burns.116 Division St. Identified by her uncle, Ephram Zabinsky. Multiple newspapers, March 28.

WILSON, Joseph, 21, asphyxiation/burns. 528 Green St., Philadelphia. Identified by his fiancée, Rosie Solomon. Multiple newspapers, March 27.

WISNER, Tessie, 21 (27?), multiple injuries and burns. 129 Second Ave. Identified by Samuel Weiss (relationship unknown). Name also given as Weisner. Multiple newspapers, March 27.

WISOTSKY, Sonia, 17, asphyxiation/burns. 303 E. 8 St. Identified by Paul Judytz (relationship unknown). Multiple newspapers, March 27.

WONDROSS, Bertha, 18, multiple injuries; died at St. Vincent's Hospital. 205 Henry St. Identified by her mother (name unknown). Name also given as Wandrus. Multiple newspapers, March 27.

UNIDENTIFIED

UNIDENTIFIED

UNIDENTIFIED

UNIDENTIFIED

UNIDENTIFIED

UNIDENTIFIED

NOTES

Prologue

. . . . was for ninety years the deadliest . . . The echoes of the Triangle fire in the World Trade Center disaster of Sept. 11, 2001, were unmistakable, as scores of victims threw themselves from skyscraper windows while thousands of witnesses watched in horror.

Death was an almost routine workplace hazard . . . Los Angeles *Times*, Nov. 21, 1999: "35,000 U.S. workers were killed on the job in 1914, and another 700,000 were injured." Two weeks after the Triangle fire, the *American*, Apr. 9, 1911, carried this double-barreled headline that didn't even make the front page: "73 Dead in Pennsylvania Mine Disaster /115 Alabama Convicts Perish Underground."

Chapter One

Burglary was the usual occupation . . . The beating of Clara Lemlich was fully reported in *Call*, Sept. 16, 1909.

Some of Clara's comrades . . . Photographs of Lemlich and her colleagues can be found in Orleck: *Common Sense.*

. . . leering, pinching foremen . . . cf. Tyler, *Look for the Union Label*, p. 81: "We are now fighting to purify the factory . . . [of] those foremen . . . who have been continuously insulting the girl employees." Also, Metzker, ed.: *A Bintel Brief*, p. 72.

"I read the book" . . . Orleck: *Common Sense.*

She found the routine humiliations . . . Mary Brown Sumner, "The Spirit of the Strikers," *The Survey* 23, Jan. 23, 1910, p. 554.

"The hissing of the machines" . . . Orleck: *Common Sense.*

With a handful of other . . . ibid. There are good accounts of the early years of the ILGWU in Levine: *The Women's Garment Workers,* p. 148; Howe: *World,* pp. 287–324; McCreesh: *Women in the Campaign.*

Some men even . . . McCreesh: *Women in the Campaign.*

Using her gifts . . . Orleck: *Common Sense,* p. 48.

Leiserson was widely known . . . *Call,* Sept. 3, 1909.

Clara Lemlich attended . . . Orleck: *Common Sense.*

"Ah—then I had fire . . ." "Clara Lemlich Shavelson," *Jewish Life,* November 1954.

She was born with it. . . . The biography of Clara Lemlich is drawn from several sources, especially Orleck: *Common Sense.* Also: *Jewish Life,* November 1954; Sumner: "The Spirit"; and *Women in World History: A Biographical Encyclopedia,* vol. 9, Anne Commire, ed. Waterford, CT: Yorkin, 2001.

It was the job of his wife . . . This attitude, broadly drawn, is reflected in many works, including Howe: *World,* p. 8. A useful tempering note comes from Sorin: *A Time,* p. 17: "This picture of the scholarly husband spending all his time in the *bet hamidrash* (house of study) and the *shul* while his wife slaved away . . . has been overdrawn . . . few families . . . could afford so unproductive an economic arrangement."

A memoirist . . . Gannes: *Childhood in a Shtetl.*

Lemlich's childhood corresponded . . . Sorin: *A Time;* Howe: *World.*

This was one of the largest . . . Howe: *World,* p. 26.

It was not just the poor . . . Howe: *World,* pp. 24–25, 57–63; Gannes: *A Childhood.*

So-called detective agencies . . . cf. *Call,* Oct. 5, 1909.

One man who grew up . . . This is Alfred E. Smith, in an incident reported in multiple biographies, including Slayton: *Empire Statesman.*

Eighteen thousand immigrants per month . . . cf. Connable: *Tigers:* ". . . the City's darkest age . . . it is remarkable that a revolution did not occur."

Late summer in those days . . . from many sources, especially Robert Alton Stevenson, "The Poor in Summer," *Scribner's Magazine,* Sept. 1901, pp. 259–277.

So many people in so little space . . . 12 of the 17 most crowded census tracts in New York were on the Lower East Side. All contained more than 500 people per acre. (*Thirteenth Census of the United States: 1910.*) The density and smells are reported in Howe: *World,* pp. 148–154.

Inside a sweltering . . . The description of an East Side tenement was influenced by the author's tour of the Lower East Side Tenement Museum, 97 Orchard Street, New York. Also by Howe: *World,* pp. 150–159.

William Dean Howells sounded . . . Howells: *Impressions and Experiences,* New York: Harper & Bros. 1896.

In 1909, there were more . . . *Times,* Sept. 26, 1909.

. . . a season of strikes . . . cf: *Call,* July to Sept. 1909.

. . . More people worked . . . Howe: *World.* A huge percentage of these, a quarter of all New York City workers and up to 70 percent of Jewish workers, were in the needle trades, according to Henderson: *Tammany and the New Immigrants.*

. . . factory owners were slow . . . An excellent discussion of wages in the garment industry can be found in Howe: *World*, pp. 144–146. The author concluded that the average wage in the industry was a little over $10 per week in 1910. At the same time, estimates of the minimum living wage ranged from about $8 to $14 per week. (The high number came from the progressive Russell Sage Foundation.)

. . . Women's Trade Union League . . . Good histories of the WTUL can be found in Dye: *As Equals and As Sisters;* McCreesh: *Women in the Campaign;* Orleck: *Common Sense.*

. . . A subcurrent of sexual . . . An extensive discussion of progressive worry over the problem of prostitution is in Friedman-Kasaba: *Memories.*

. . . hailed the neckwear workers . . . Call, Oct. 7, 1909.

. . . rally at which Frank Morrison . . . There are a number of good histories of the shirtwaist workers' strike, including Dye: *As Equals;* McCreesh: *Women in the Campaign;* Orleck: *Common Sense;* and the official ILGWU histories—Levine: *Women's Garment Workers;* Tyler: *Look.*

. . . one of the grandest . . . Accounts of the Hudson-Fulton festival appeared in all New York newspapers Sept. 20–Oct. 1, 1909. Specific details are taken from the *Times* coverage.

. . . an estimated ten thousand . . . The Antique Automobile Club of America offers a good overview of automotive history at *www.acca.org/history/cars.*

The commercial towers . . . a history of the record tallest buildings in the world can be found at *skyscraper.org.*

Within a few blocks . . . A good description of seedy downtown is in Slayton: *Empire Statesman.*

Progress had its own . . . The literature on the progressive movement can be daunting. Martin: *Madame Secretary* contains as good an introduction as I found, and there is a vigorous essay on the subject in Tyler: *Look*, pp. 48–52. But the spirit and tone of the movement is perhaps best experienced by scrolling through *Survey* and *McClure's.*

. . . newspapers competed desperately . . . cf: *World*, Oct. 21, 1909.

Tammany Hall . . . In my history and discussions of Tammany, I drew extensively from Weiss: *Charles Francis Murphy;* Greenwald: *Bargaining;* Henderson: *Tammany and the New Immigrants;* Connable and Silberfarb: *Tigers.*

"A reformer can't last" . . . Riordan: *Plunkitt*, p. 17 ff.

Big Tim Sullivan agreed . . . quoted in most Tammany histories.

". . . the curse of the nation." . . . Riordan: *Plunkitt*, p. 11 ff.

"Tammany preaches contentment." . . . Quoted in Connable: *Tigers.*

The machine protected . . . cf: Huthmacher: "Charles Evans Hughes and Charles F. Murphy: The Metamorphosis of Progressivism," *New York History* 46. Also Weiss: *Murphy*, pp. 14–18, 39.

. . . "thorough political organization . . ." Murphy, in "A Tribute," Riordan: *Plunkitt.* The East Side district described was Murphy's own, Weiss: *Murphy.*

. . . "get a followin' . . ." Riordan: *Plunkitt*, p. 10.

Although Tammany soldiers . . . Henderson: *Tammany and the New Immigrants.*

Young men who wanted... Good discussions of the "contract" system are in Caro: *Power Broker;* Slayton: *Empire Statesman.* Tammany's approach to charity in general is well explained in Weiss: *Murphy,* pp. 33–35 and colorfully throughout Riordan: *Plunkitt.*

"... anti-liberal patriarch..." Connable: *Tigers.*

Downtown, in the most populous... *Times,* Sept. 13, 1913. "[T]he man who for a generation ruled supreme in politics south of 14th Street."

"... I'll find the feller"... quoted in multiple histories, including Connable: *Tigers.*

Sullivan's operation grossed... Connable: *Tigers.*

The key to the corruption... The findings of the famous Lexow Commission investigation into New York graft can be found in most histories of New York City.

But now nearly half... *Thirteenth Census of the United States: 1910.*

... directing traffic and collecting tolls... *Times,* Sept. 13, 1913. "[Sullivan was] beloved of the Bowery and dreaded by men toiling for the uplift of the state."

"It is the fate"... quoted in Weiss: *Murphy.*

But the mood of ordinary voters... *Times,* April 26, 1924, quoted Fiorello La Guardia: "[Murphy] was a great leader because he always kept his hand on the pulse of the people. He gauged the popular will and when the demand for change was high, he granted the reforms that he could afford."

At age fifty-one... By far the best Murphy biography is Weiss: *Murphy.* Biographical information was also culled from the newspaper obituaries of April 26, 1924, and from Connable: *Tigers.* Weiss had this to say about Murphy as a transitional figure: "[He was] capable of bridging the gap between old and new." See also Greenwald: *Bargaining.* "[Murphy] anticipated, long before his contemporaries in professional politics, that social welfare programs would be more important to the people that Tammany Hall."

When he died... Roosevelt, quoted in Connable: *Tigers.* "The New York Democratic organization has lost probably the strongest and wisest leader it has had in generations.... He was a genius who kept harmony, and at the same time recognized that the world moves on."

"... most perceptive and intelligent..." Connable: *Tigers.*

"He fully understands..." New York City Mayor William Gaynor, quoted in Connable: *Tigers.*

According to George Washington Plunkitt... Riordan: *Plunkitt,* pp. 3–6.

... Murphy apparently took his share... Weiss: *Murphy,* pp. 23, 59–63.

When he took control... Weiss: *Murphy,* pp. 18–24. Also *Times,* Apr. 26, 1924: "It has always been said in favor of Mr. Murphy that he ran his saloons as orderly resorts.... His influence and frequently his direct action was always against commercialized vice in any form." The *Times* quotes Rev. William S. Rainsford, an Episcopal rector in New York: "If all Tammany leaders were like [Murphy], it would be a respectable organization."

... consolidating the dirty business ... Henderson: *Tammany and the New Immigrants:* "[Murphy] was opposed to the involvement of machine members in gambling or prostitution, although his reliance on Big Tim . . . necessitated his tolerance of both in the Sullivan domain."

The East Side of Murphy's youth ... Henderson: *Tammany and the New Immigrants.* Henderson's analysis of the 1910 Census found that the East Side was only 1 percent Irish and 3 percent German.

Italians were, for many years ... This sweeping generalization is dealt with in more detail in many sources, including Foerster: *Italian Emigration;* Rose: *The Italians.*

"It is hard to understand ..." Howells: *Impressions.*

... they rarely voted ... Henderson: *Tammany and the New Immigrants* found that 7,687 out of 260,000 eligible Italian-born voters were registered in 1910—less than 3 percent. *Call,* Feb. 28, 1910, quoted the Italian-American Civic League saying, "There are 500,000 Italians eligible and fewer than 20,000 of them vote"—less than 4 percent.

On the other hand ... This contrast between the Italian and Jewish communities and their relationship to Tammany is the core of Henderson: *Tammany and the New Immigrants.*

... "as popular with one race" ... Riordan: *Plunkitt,* p. 48.

Big Tim Sullivan went ... Henderson: *Tammany and the New Immigrants:* "[Sullivan] took them as fast as they came [and] flung them into his melting pot."

... William Randolph Hearst ... Nasaw: *Chief;* Swanberg: *Citizen Hearst.* The 1905 election is summarized, at least, in any comprehensive history of New York City. Henderson: *Tammany and the New Immigrants* is especially pertinent in this context. His analysis of returns shows the strength of Hearst among Jews, and the ability of only Murphy and the Sullivans to deliver their own wards for McClellan. *Times,* Apr. 26, 1924, reported that cartoons that appeared in the Hearst newspapers during the 1905 campaign, showing Murphy in prison stripes, created a lasting hatred in the boss.

East Side radicalism ... The vitality of the Jewish political scene is central to Howe: *World,* for example pp. 101–115, 310–321. He describes the nature of East Side socialism, as does Tyler: *Look,* emphasizing the Hebrew concept of *tzedaka,* embodying both justice and charity. Howe also details the role of the *Forward,* which is also discussed in Henderson: *Tammany and the New Immigrants* and Cahan: *The Education.*

Every morning, the boss ... Weiss: *Murphy.* Her account of the Scarlet Room is at pp. 31–32.

He was a listener and a watcher ... Weiss: *Murphy,* p. 30; Connable: *Tigers:* "His only answers were 'yes,' 'no' or 'I'll look into it.'" "Most of the troubles . . ." was advice recalled by Mayor Jimmy Walker in several Murphy obituaries.

On September 17 ... Trager: *The People's Chronology.* The text of the play can be found at *www.vdare.com/fulford/melting_pot_play.htm.* I do not, however, endorse the rest of the website's anti-immigration philosophy.

Chapter Two

...a worker named Jacob Kline... This story, originally reported without names in *The Survey,* December 1909, was more fully reported in Stein: *The Triangle Fire,* p. 162.

...anonymous cogs ... cf: trial testimony of Harris: "I never asked them their age; to me they looked, some of them perhaps would be as, oh, something like 18, some 17, some 16 ... I heard them speak Italian or Jewish or English ... I didn't investigate it carefully."

They lived in splendor... Details of the Blanck and Harris households come from the 1910 Census.

It was the largest... This testimony at the trial was disputed by defense attorney Steuer.

...two thousand garments per day... from testimony of Max Blanck.

Their salesmen ... A number of Triangle salesmen and department store buyers testified for the defense in the trial.

Besides the Triangle ... The partners' ownership of Diamond is documented by McFarlane: "The Triangle Fire," *Collier's,* May 14, 1913, and in Levine: *Women's Garment Workers,* p. 153. Their ownership of International is reported in *Call,* Sept. 30, 1909. Their ownership of Imperial is disclosed in the trial testimony of Louis Levy. Blanck's participation in firms with his brothers is clear from New York City directories between 1900 and 1920.

Even veteran employees ... The formality of address is evident throughout the testimony of defense witnesses.

People came and went ... cf. Harris testimony: "Q. And you had no method of keeping a record of those who actually came [to work]? A. No, sir. Didn't come today—come tomorrow. Didn't come tomorrow—come next day, or something like that."

...both men were born ... *Twelfth Census of the United States, 1900.*

By the early 1890s ... ibid.

For the first time ... Howe: *World.*

Sweatshops were generally ... Good discussions of the difference between sweatshops and factories at the dawn of the twentieth century can be found in Howe: *World,* pp. 154–159; Levine: *Women's Garment Workers;* Tyler: *Look.*

The growth of the garment industry ... Levine: *Women's Garment Workers.*

The Jews of Hungary ... Howe: *World,* pp. 80–84.

The link might be nothing... Howe: *World,* pp. 183–190, has a good account of the workings of the *landsman* connections. He also dicusses the Pig Market, p. 63. On that subject, see also "The Pig Market," by William M. Leiserson in Stein, ed.: *Sweatshop,* pp. 41–42.

"The contractor in the clothing trade ..." quoted ibid. cf: Levine: *Women's Garment Workers:* "Fifty dollars was sufficient ..."

"The boss of the shop ..." quoted ibid.

According to one survey ... ibid.

Some, like Max Blanck ... The financial status of Blanck and Harris when they arrived in the United States is unknown. However, only a very small percentage of Eastern European immigrants arrived with as much as $50.

When Max Blanck was ... *Twelfth Census* ... *1900.*

... his brother Isaac joined ... ibid.

Other brothers ... cf. New York City Directories.

In 1898 ... *Twelfth Census* ... *1900.*

... difficult to reconcile ... The 1900 census has no perfect match for the Triangle's Isaac Harris. There is, however, a listing for a tailor named Isaac Harris at the East Tenth Street address. His wife and family are also listed. They do not match the wife and family that Harris had when he was interviewed by the census taker in 1910. This presents three possibilities: (1) Harris had two families, and was on the verge of leaving the first family to start the second one when the census taker came in 1900; (2) There were two different Isaac Harrises living at the same address on East Tenth Street in 1900, and the census taker met only the second one; (3) The 1900 census taker made an error, or invented a family for Harris in order to save work for himself.

... the business partnership came first ... The earliest solid evidence of a partnership is in the 1900 City Directory, when the Triangle Waist Co. appears on Wooster Street. However, at the trial Samuel Bernstein testified that he had worked for Blanck and Harris, together, for "about fifteen" years, which would date their partnership to 1896 or 1897.

... between them they had all the skills ... Stein: *Triangle Fire*, pp. 158–159; various trial testimony.

"I laid out ... Isaac Harris testimony, trial transcript.

... first truly class-shattering ... Milbank: *New York Fashion*, p. 48: The importance of the shirtwaist "cannot be underestimated."

... more than five million women ... *American Businesswoman*, November 1911.

Nearly a third ... *Thirteenth Census* ... *1910* as cited in *Report of the Factory Investigating Commission, Vol. I*, p. 272. Of 1,003,981 factory workers in New York, 293,525 were women.

"The outfit of ..." Milbank: *New York Fashion*, pp. 44–45.

Charles Dana Gibson thought so ... Downey: *Portrait*. "The American girl, crystallized and typified by Charles Dana Gibson."

... "the Helen of Troy ..." quoted ibid, p. 186.

Another writer, Robert Bridges ... quoted ibid, p. 196.

... "most famous art creation ..." *Times*, Nov. 11, 1910.

... the Gibson man ... Downey: *Portrait*, p. 173.

Harris and Blanck had taken a lease ... The dimensions and appearance of the Triangle factory are drawn from various trial testimony, especially from the consulting engineer James Whiskeman, and from the author's tour of the former Asch Building, since renamed the Brown Building of New York University.

The "loft" skyscrapers ... McFarlane: "Fire and the Skyscraper," *McClure's*, Sept. 1911, p. 467. Here, as elsewhere, McFarlane's work was invaluable.

. . . an average of three . . . ibid.

Some writers have suggested . . . cf. Stein: *Triangle Fire.*

. . . the Triangle expanded twice . . . from various trial testimony.

. . . half the workers . . . Thirteenth Census . . . 1910.

A fire in the daytime . . . quoted in multiple newspapers after the Newark High Street fire of Nov. 26, 1910.

Owners of large factories . . . Tyler: *Look.*

One was the "inside contractor" . . . The issue of the inside contracting system is one of the most difficult to pin down in this story. On one hand, the inside contractors were leaders in the garment strikes of 1909–1910. Cf. Greenwald: *Bargaining,* p. 22, in which the role of contractors in the seminal Rosen Bros. strike is discussed. On the other hand, the system did frequently exploit young workers. Cf. Levine: *Women's Garment Workers,* pp. 147–148.

Locked out . . . Call, Sept. 28, 1909.

. . . a garish battalion . . . Details of the melee with the prostitutes, *Call,* Oct. 4–5, 1909.

. . . Beryl "Ben" Sklaver . . . Call, Oct. 14, 1909. This is the first time that a victim of the fire has been shown to have been beaten and arrested on the picket line. The identification, however, is not perfect. In the *Call* story, the arrested worker's name is given as "Sklavin." An examination of Ellis Island arrival records, and an Internet search of current U.S. telephone directories, indicate that "Sklavin" is virtually unheard of as a surname, while "Sklaver" is rare, but known. The chance that a factory of 500 people would have two workers with such similar, but unusual, names—"Ben Sklavin" and "Ben Sklaver"—is very near zero. It is far more likely that the *Call* reporter, in a great hurry, misread the handwritten records of the court clerk, and saw the "-er" ending as "-in."

. . . hired thugs went after . . . Call, Oct. 27, 1909, and Nov. 6, 1909.

Union leaders had come . . . McCreesh: *Women in the Campaign,* p. 136.

. . . hit on the idea . . . The arrests of the WTUL leaders are in *Call,* Nov. 2–5, 1909. The Mary Dreier arrest made all the New York newspapers, cf: *Times,* Nov. 5, 1909.

Meanwhile, momentum built . . . cf. *Call,* Oct. 23, 1909.

Blanck welcomed a reporter . . . Times, Nov. 6, 1909.

. . . a private letter . . . Call, Nov. 6, 1909.

Chapter Three

The story of the uprising of the shirtwaist workers has been told in a number of places; for example: Dye: *As Equals,* esp. pp. 88–103; McCreesh: *Women in the Campaign:* esp. pp. 128–171; Levine: *Women's Garment Workers,* esp. pp. 144–167; Tyler: *Look,* esp. pp. 46–62; Greenwald: *Bargaining,* esp. pp. 13–65. Given my emphasis on the feminist quality of the strike, it is worth noting Greenwald's caveat: "Emphasis on gender, however, misses the substantial role of male workers in the strike."

Clara Lemlich's moment . . . The Cooper Union meeting is central to nearly every telling of the uprising story. Contemporaneous accounts can be found in most New York newspapers, Nov. 23–24, 1909.

. . . after a month of postponements . . . *World*, Nov. 24, 1909, reported that the union had raised a strike fund of $60,000, which may have reflected bluffing by Local 25 leaders. Benefits were set at $2.50 to $3 per week for workers with dependents and $1.50 per week for single workers (Levine: *Women's Garment Workers*)—or enough to support a strike of 6,000 to 8,000 workers for a little more than three weeks (cf: *Call*, Jan. 6, 1910, putting the cost of supporting that number of strikers at "2,500 per day").

Samuel Gompers . . . A good sampling of the views of Gompers on a range of subjects, including socialism, can be found at *www.inform.umd.edu/EdRes/Colleges/ARHU/ Depts/History/Gompers/webl.html*, a project of the University of Maryland library, home of the Gompers papers.

. . . counseled caution . . . Greenwald: *Bargaining*, p. 26.

. . . Feigenbaum . . . Panken . . . Sketches based on Howe: *World*, pp. 241–244, 311.

. . . "talk, talk" . . . *World*, Nov. 24, 1909.

One authority . . . McClymer: *Triangle Strike*, p. 31. "Her speech, the vote, and the taking of the oath were almost certainly planned carefully beforehand."

But in interviews . . . *World*, op. cit. "To tell the truth, I hardly remember leaving my seat," Lemlich said.

According to the Forward . . . A translation of the article can be found at *www.womenhist.binghamton.edu/shirt/doc16*.

A committee of fifteen . . . *Call*, Nov. 23, 1909.

. . . Rose Perr sat down . . . Perr's story is detailed by Sue Ainslee Clark and Edith Wyatt, "The Shirt-Waist Makers Strike," from *Making Both Ends Meet: The Income and Outlay of New York Working Girls*, New York: Macmillan, 1911, reprinted in McClymer: *Triangle Strike*, pp. 58–67.

. . . more and more meeting rooms . . . *Call*, Nov. 26, 1909.

. . . published its demands . . . *Call*, Nov. 23, 1909.

Elizabeth Dutcher . . . *Call*, Nov. 24, 1909.

. . . Italian priests . . . *Call*, Dec. 2, 1909, and Jan. 21, 1910 (reporting a visit by a priest to the Triangle factory).

"In general, Italian girls . . ." Glanz: *Jew and Italian*. Glanz discusses this issue in depth in pp. 38–53. Other good examinations are in Greenwald: *Bargaining*, pp. 31–35; Levine: *Women's Garment Workers*, esp. p. 156; Friedman-Kasaba: *Memories*, esp. p. 165.

. . . the leading Italian official . . . *Call*, Nov. 25, 1909.

Euphoria swept . . . multiple newspapers, inc. *Times*, Nov. 24, 1909.

. . . Lemlich . . . walked the circuit . . . *Call*, Nov. 25, 1909.

A union official . . . *Call*, Nov. 26, 1909, quoting Bernard Weinstein: "The strike is a great success. It is much better, much more enthusiastic, than we expected." See also Dye: *As Equals*, p. 90: ". . . stunned by the turnout . . ."

Even more important . . . *World*, Nov. 24, 1909. Later in the strike there were allegations that the cutters' union was secretly supplying labor to keep the shops going.

More than seventy . . . *Call*, Nov. 25, 1909.

Factory owner David Hurwitz . . . *Times*, Nov. 26, 1909: "It is a foolish, hysterical strike, and not five percent know what they are striking for."

Twenty leading factory owners . . . *Call*, Nov. 25, 1909; *World*, Nov. 25, 1909.

The Triangle owners fought . . . The stories of dances at the Triangle come from various trial testimony by employees.

. . . *Hoffman House hotel* . . . *World*, Nov. 28, 1909.

. . . *violence returned* . . . *Times*, Nov. 27, 1909.

"Dainty little Violet" . . . McCreesh: *Women in the Campaign*, p. 141.

Their fates would depend . . . cf. *World*, Nov. 26, 1909.

. . . *Magistrate Willard Olmsted* . . . His exact quote, contained in most histories of the strike: "You are on strike against God and Nature, whose firm law is that man should earn his bread in the sweat of his brow." The WTUL solicited a response from George Bernard Shaw, who cabled: "Delightful medieval America always in the intimate personal confidence of the Almighty."

". . . Lexington and Bunker Hill . . ." *World*, Dec. 6, 1909.

. . . *sensation was Alva* . . . cf. *Times*, Jan. 26, 1933; also Commire, ed.: *Women in World History*.

. . . *storming the closed doors* . . . *World*, Dec. 10, 1909.

. . . *Gibson, for one* . . . Downey: *Portrait*.

. . . *Rose Pastor Stokes* . . . *Times*, Dec. 1, 1909; June 21, 1933.

. . . *appearing at crowded meeting halls* . . . *World*, Nov. 29, 1909, Dec. 1, 1909.

Some union leaders . . . *Times*, Dec. 3, 1909.

Suffrage was not high . . . For example, Mother Jones, the legendary labor leader, did not support suffrage (*Times*, Dec. 1, 1930). Jones was the keynote speaker at a socialist rally for the shirtwaist strikers. *Call*, Dec. 10, 1909: "We are fighting for a time when there will be no master and no slaves."

. . . *just hours after staging* . . . *World*, Dec. 1, 1909.

The sidewalks were jammed . . . multiple newspapers, Dec. 6, 1909. The Maoris appeared in the *World*.

"Throng Cheers On . . ." *Times*, Dec. 6, 1909.

Suffragists and socialists . . . cf. Ida Tarbell, in *American Federationist*, March 1910: "[The shirtwaist strike] seems to me the clearest example of the growing sense there is on all sides of the relationship between classes, of the interdependence, consequently of their mutual responsibility."

"We want something now . . ." *World*, Dec. 6, 1909.

. . . *manufacturers had dramatically* . . . The number of settlements was reported each day in the *Call*.

Some frustrated strikers . . . *World*, Dec. 9, 1909; *Times*, Dec. 17, 1909: ". . . aged and strong eggs."

"You girls . . ." *Times*, ibid.

"With the beginning . . ." *Times*, Dec. 15, 1909.

. . . Anne Morgan . . . The portrait of Morgan is drawn from Strouse: *Morgan*, pp. 520–31, and *Times*, Jan. 30, 1952.

"Greatest Financial Power . . ." *World*, Dec. 3, 1909.

An editorial cartoon . . . ibid.

"They are grand . . ." quoted in Strouse: *Morgan*.

"Anne began . . ." ibid.

"We can't live . . ." *Times*, Dec. 14, 1909.

. . . lunch at the Colony . . . multiple newspapers, Dec. 16, 1909.

"In halting . . ." *World*, ibid.

One newspaper asserted . . . *American*, Dec. 29, 1909: "a princely check of at least five figures."

Lists of donors . . . cf. *Times* and *World*, Dec. 14, 1909.

. . . inviting Morgan and Marbury . . . multiple newspapers, Dec. 15, 1909.

Society women lent . . . multiple newspapers, Dec. 21, 1909.

Rose Perr and several . . . *World*, Dec. 23, 1909.

. . . Inez Milholland . . . *Times*, Nov. 27, 1916.

"The college girls" . . . *American*, Dec. 13, 1909.

. . . Fannie Horowitz . . . *Call*, Dec. 31, 1909.

When plans were hatched . . . *American*, Jan. 12, 1910.

Even Helen Taft . . . *Times* and *American*, Jan. 16, 1910.

. . . cross racial lines. . . . *Call*, Dec. 22, 1909.

. . . police had reverted . . . A fair sense of the reputation the police had in the labor community can be found in *Call*, Aug. 6, 1909, and in the *Call*'s frequent reference to the police as "cossacks."

In fact, a study . . . *American*, Dec. 24, 1909.

With that goal . . . Belmont's trip to night court was covered by all the papers in their Dec. 19 and 20, 1909, editions. Her quotes come from the *American*, Dec. 20, 1909, which offered one of the fullest accounts. Her appearance is derived from sketches by court artists for the *American*, ibid., and *World*, Dec. 20, 1909.

"For almost the first time . . ." *World*, Dec. 22, 1909.

In Philadelphia . . . The Philadelphia strike is a stirring story, unfortunately overshadowed in history. Just as the wealthy progressives backed the strike in New York, such Philadelphia elites as the Biddle and Drexel families offered support in that city. The story is told in *Call*, Dec. 21, 1909, through Feb. 2, 1910.

. . . fifty replacement workers . . . *Call*, Dec. 23, 1909.

Theresa Serber Malkiel . . . *Times*, Nov. 18, 1942; Malkiel: *Diary*, esp. introduction by Basch.

Clara Lemlich was her protégée . . . Orleck: *Common Sense*, p. 55.

Early in the uprising . . . multiple newspapers, Dec. 4, 1909. Lena Barsky was arraigned Dec. 6, 1909 (*Call*, Dec. 7, 1909).

"A remarkable meeting . . ." *Call*, Dec. 16, 1909.

"It was amusing" . . . *Call*, Dec. 22, 1909.

"A belief is prevalent..." Call, Dec. 28, 1909.

Inside the WTUL ... cf. Mary Dreier letter to Margaret Dreier Robins, dated Feb. 17, 1910, from the Robins papers at the University of Florida. Quoted at *www.womhist.binghamton.edu/shirt/doc15.htm.*

Christmas Day 1909... World, Dec. 26, 1909.

... editorial justifying the uprising... Times, Dec. 6, 1909.

Their next move ... More complete accounts of the strike negotiations are in Greenwald: *Bargaining,* pp. 47–53, and Levine: *Women's Garment Workers.*

A chastened Robert Cornell... American, Dec. 25, 1909.

... Cornell quietly resumed... Call, Feb. 5, 1910, reported that Cornell sentenced Sophie Gabrilovitz to five days in the workhouse for shouting "scab."

A special "strike extra" ... *Call,* Dec. 29, 1909. The eight-page paper included stories explaining the strike in Italian and Yiddish.

... "how intelligent, well-dressed..." Call, Dec. 28, 1909.

Several bold... American, Dec. 30, 1909.

This extravagance... Call, Dec. 30, 1909.

... what the rank-and-file wanted... multiple newspapers, Dec. 27–28, 1909; cf: *American,* Dec. 28: "'Union or Nothing' Cry/9,000 Striking Shirtwaist Girls."

A committee... Times, Jan. 6, 1910.

Carnegie Hall... multiple newspapers, Jan. 3, 1910. *Call* was the one best-attuned to the tensions just breaking the surface. See also Greenwald: *Bargaining,* pp. 42–43: "[T]he event was an effort by the strikers and the union to take back the strike from their wealthy allies by redefining the issues."

Only one city magistrate... World, ibid. The same paper, on Dec. 19, 1909, described Kernochan as a "dashing young afianced clubman."

... Anne Morgan issued... Call, Jan. 4, 1910.

O'Reilly responded... American, Jan. 5, 1910.

At least one board member... World, Jan. 6, 1910.

... Eva McDonald Valesh... Times, Nov. 9, 1956. Dye: *As Equals* documents long-standing tensions between the AFL and WTUL over the issue of socialism in the labor movement, quoting Valesh: The WTUL was "full of socialism, masked by its perfunctory interest in the strikers."

He was lukewarm... Greenwald: *Bargaining,* p. 15: "Gompers believed that women's current advance out of the home and into industry was unnatural and unhealthy."

"A Disgraceful Spectacle"... Call, Feb. 1, 1910.

The last few thousand... The grim endurance of the last six thousand or so hold-outs through the second half of the strike is evident in the pages of *Call;* cf. Jan. 5, 1910: "Union Is Handicapped by Lack of Money."

... twenty-five hundred pennies... Call, Jan. 6, 1910. Their names were Rebecca Gerson, Fannie Brass, Rose Koplet, and Anna Cermack.

... "the labor bailer"... Call, Jan. 12, 1910.

... William "Big Bill" Haywood... Call, Jan. 31, 1910; *Times,* May 19, 1928.

The Lower East Side busied... Call and *Forward,* Jan. 10–Feb. 5, 1910.

... whose shops had already ... Call, Jan. 23, 1910.

Alva Belmont called ... multiple newspapers, Jan. 8, 1910.

Inez Milholland ... multiple newspapers, Jan. 18–19, 1910. Her father's work is in *Times*, July 1, 1925. Arresting Capt. Dominic Henry, who later responded to the Triangle fire, is quoted in *Call*, Jan. 28, 1910: "I thought she was a superior person so I merely asked her to go away."

... Max Schlansky's private detective agency ... Call, Jan. 8, 1910.

... slow season was ending ... Call, Jan. 26, 1910. "The season is here, or nearly so, and the orders must be filled."

... Leiserson's ... Clara Lemlich's shop settled Jan. 23, 1910 (*Call*, Jan. 24, 1910).

"Triangle Co. Yields ..." Call, Feb. 8, 1910.

"With blood this name ..." Forward, Jan. 10, 1910. An English translation is avilable at *www.womhist.binghamton.edu/shirt/doc16.htm*.

Chapter Four

Workers weren't welcome ... From various trial testimony.

... neatly knotted tie ... multiple newspapers, Mar. 27, 1911, contain pictures of Zito in his tie.

Sam Lehrer was there ... Descriptions based on photographs of victims in *Call*, Mar. 27, 1911. Biographical information on the victims comes from "Report of the Joint Relief Committee," which is available at *www.ilr.cornell.edu/trianglefire/texts/ reports*. Relevant passages from the report:

Anna Cohen ... "A.C., 25 years old, dead, union member, lived with sister M., 19, and E., 16, who earned $5.00 and $4.00 respectively. A main support; two brothers, one very prosperous who did not live with the girls, and one married, did not contribute to the support of any of the girls. Tried to persuade E. Younger sister, to go into Clara de Hirsch Home; refused. $250.00 were given girls, who were all satisfied. Total, $250.00."

Dinah Greenberg ... "D.G., 18 years old, dead, earned $10.00 a week, eight months in this country, union member, lived with brother, A., also waistmaker, union member, married, with brother sent money to very needy dependents in Russia. Brother anxious for lump sum to send himself, to Russia; also, $25.00 for tombstone. $300.00 paid brother in April, receipt taken. Total, $300.00."

Ida Pearl ... "I.P., 18 years old, killed, union member, earned $17.00 a week, boarded; brother J., earned $7.00 a week, only member of the family in this country; buried by the union, and tombstone also erected by the same organization. Matter of Russian dependents referred to Red Cross, July 27, 1911: Red Cross reports that family in Russia are very needy and I. contributed regularly. They have sent their father 600 roubles. Total, plus 600 roubles."

Esther Harris ... "E.H., 21 years old, earned $22.00 a week, union member killed. Lived with father, peddler, earns very little, mother, M., also in Triangle disaster, escaped, earns $5.00 a week; L., 19, earns $5.00 a week, R., 13, and J., 8. E. was the main support of the family, whose income does not average $15.00 a week. $35.00

given in emergent relief and $50.00 given in lump sum by Committee to father who will start a small business. Total, $535.00."

Rose Manofsky . . . "R.M., 22 years old, dead, earned from $10.00 to $12.00 a week, lived with rheumatic father in room back of small tailor shop, with little sister, M., 14 years old. Step-mother divorced and step-sister lived near by; two brothers, H., painter, earns $5.00 a week and S., a baker, out of work, did not live home. Father hardly a proper guardian for M.R. was the homemaker, as well as the support of the family. $22.50 paid for new clothing for M., $10.00 for immediate relief, and $200.00 paid to Clara de Hirsch Home for entrance fee for M; $77.50 reserved for M. when she comes out of the Clara de Hirsch Home; and $150.00 paid to father in lump sum.Total, $460.00.

"Note: M. refused to stay in Clara de Hirsch Home; is now boarding and supporting herself. Money supplied as needed."

Sadie Nussbaum . . . *Times*, March 28, 1911.

Becky Reivers . . . B.R. orphan, 18 years old, killed . . . earned $7.00 a week, union member, lived with and supported only remaining member of family, M.R., 14 years old, in this country four months. M. operated on for adenoids, sent to German Home for Recreation for Women and Children, for a week. Balance on Steamship ticket here settled, $11.50; M., entered at Clara de Hirsch Home, $200.00. Total paid on case up to date $277.75 . . . $263.25 held for M. who is now under the care of Miss Dutcher, Women's Trade Union League. Has no relative in this country except aunt, Mrs. L. M. is doing well in Clara de Hirsch Home. Total, $541.00.

Rosie Freedman was born . . . Her story was stitched together from the following sources: "Report of the Joint Relief Committee;" *Thirteenth Census . . . 1910;* fire insurance maps and ships' arrival records, interwoven with the lives and experiences of the million-plus immigrants that shared her experience and whose history is recorded in the sources cited above. She should not be confused with the last known survivor of the Triangle fire, Rose Freedman, née Rosenfeld, who escaped the fire by dashing to the roof. *Times*, Feb. 17, 2001; Dec. 30, 2001.

Bialystok was a thriving . . . Dubnov: *History; Encyclopaedia Judaica.*

. . . Russian revolutionaries detonated . . . cf: Aronson, *Troubled Waters.*

. . . Russian mobs burned . . . Klier, ed.: *Pogroms*, esp. pp. 195–243.

. . . "ferment and enlightenment . . ." Howe: *World*, pp. 15–20.

"The generation gap . . ." Gannes: *Childhood.*

"There is no revolutionary . . ." Klier, ed.: *Pogroms.*

A leading historian . . . The best overview I found of the pogroms was Klier, ibid., and especially the essay by Lambroza. This is the basic source for material on pogroms.

. . . Kishinev . . . ibid., pp. 196–207; Singer, ed.: *Russia at the Bar;* Wolf, ed.: *Legal Suffering; Times*, April 7–15, 1903.

For nearly two days . . . ibid.; Singer, ed.: *Russia at the Bar:* in which the mob asked the chief of police, "Is it permitted to kill Jews?" And the "chief rode off without answering."

. . . Gomel endured . . . Klier, ed.: *Pogroms*, 207–220.

. . . rampage through Odessa . . . ibid.

...June 14, 1906... ibid., pp. 237–238; *Times,* June 15–20, 1906; *Encyclopedia Judaica* pp. 886–887; Gilbert: *Encyclopedia of the Twentieth Century;* Aronson: *Troubled Waters.*

... Black Hundreds ... Klier, ed: *Pogroms,* p. 225.

"The greatest destroyer..." ibid., p. 231.

... Isaac Hine ... *Thirteeth Census... 1910.*

... the most common route ... Howe: *World,* p. 28, discusses the main routes from Eastern Europe, with important material following on the experience of emigrants making their way along this path.

... bowels of a steamship ... ibid., pp. 39–42.

A female investigator ... *American* and *World,* Dec. 14, 1909.

At Ellis Island ... This essential immigrant experience is told in many places, including Howe: *World,* pp. 42–50.

A writer to the ... Metzker, ed.: *A Bintel Brief,* pp. 103–104.

... 77 East Fourth Street ... Details concerning Freedman's home and neighborhood derive from *Thirteenth Census... 1910,* New York City Directories and *Insurance Maps of the City of New York,* New York: Sanborn Map Co., 1905.

... "a completely Jewish world..." Zalem Yoffeh, quoted in Henderson: *Tammany and the New Immigrants.*

... bustling community ... cf. Sohn: *Activities.*

...former Willett Street ... Mendelson: *The Lower East Side,* pp. 71–72.

... open on the Sabbath ... cf. Howe: *World,* p. 128: "By 1905–1906 it was no longer rare for stores in the East Side, 'even on Hester Street,' to be open on the Sabbath."

... mothers toiled long ... Elizabeth Watson, "Home Work in Tenements," *The Survey* 25 (Feb. 4, 1911), pp. 772–781; Annie S. Daniel, "The Wreck of the Home: How Wearing Apparel Is Fashioned in Tenements," *Charities* 14, No. 1 (Apr. 1, 1905), p. 624; Mary Sherman, "Manufacturing of Food in the Tenements," *Charities and the Commons* 15, 1906, p. 669; Mary Van Kleeck, "Child Labor in New York City Tenements," *Charities and the Commons* 18, Jan. 1908; "Toilers in the Tenements," *McClure's,* July 1910; *Preliminary Report of the Factory Investigating Committee* (1911), p. 573.

... so-called dumbbell design ... Lewis F. Palmer, *Charities and the Commons* 17, pp. 80–90. "For a breeder of ill-health and immorality and as a menace to life the 'dumbbell' type cannot be surpassed." Also: *Report of the Factory Investigating Commission Vol. XV,* pp. 465–492. For tenement life generally, Howe: *World,* pp. 87–90.

... "the most dangerous..." Arthur E. McFarlane, "The Inflammable Tenement," *McClure's,* Oct. 1911, p. 690.

... perpetually choked ... cf. *Times,* Mar. 16, 1905: "It is the habit of tenement dwellers ... to obstruct fire-escapes. They are under the necessity of utilizing every available inch of room"—as cold storage for food in winter and as a playroom for children in summer.

...cramped conditions... Howe: *World,* pp. 171–183.

"Neighbors began to whisper..." Metzker, ed.: *A Bintel Brief,* pp. 49–50.

Room and board ... Clark: *Working Girls.*

. . . plenty to do . . . Howe: *World,* pp. 208–215.

. . . the Educational Alliance . . . ibid. pp. 229–235.

"I ask you" . . . Metzker, ed.: *A Bintel Brief,* pp. 109–110.

. . . lectures . . . cafés . . . Howe: *World,* pp. 238–244.

On oppressive summer days . . . Robert Alston Stevenson, "The Poor in Summer," *Scribner's Magazine,* Sept. 1901, pp. 259–277.

. . . dance halls . . . World, Feb. 13, 1910.

One of the biggest shows . . . Bordman: *American Musical Theater,* pp. 301–302. "Ev'ry Little Movement" by Otto Harbach and Karl Hoschna, New York: M. Witmart & Sons, 1910.

No more than a handful . . . several witnesses, trial transcript.

There were eighteen . . . Isaac Harris recited the number of machines at each table during his testimony in the trial transcript. These numbers differ from the standard assertion that the Triangle had eight rows of machines on the ninth floor with thirty machines per row (cf. Stein: *Triangle Fire,* p. 53). Harris's numbers are persuasive for several reasons. First, Harris was certain: "I remember exactly the tables. . . . I laid them all out on the floor from my office . . . I laid out the factory and I put in the machines and everything that was done about putting up the factory was done by me." Second, this is what is called by trial lawyers "an admission against interest," which is considered especially credible. Saying there were 278 machines on the ninth floor made the factory seem even more crowded and dangerous than saying there were 240 machines. Third, these numbers account for the reality of the structural columns scattered throughout the room. Obviously, the columns would get in the way of a certain number of machines on certain tables.

. . . the work was minutely differentiated . . . A good summary of task division in a waist shop: "U.S. Bureau of Labor *Bulletin,* No. 183," Washington, 1916, pp. 18–20.

Fashion editors in Paris . . . McFarlane, "The Triangle Fire," op. cit.; Milbank: *New York Fashion,* p. 56.

Keeping the shirtwaist fresh . . . Milbank: *New York Fashion,* p. 51.

The range of possibilities . . . cf. *Times,* Nov. 27, 1910: advertisement for the Forsythe Waist House on 34th Street near Herald Square. Prices advertised ranged from $2.50 for plain white lawn to $150 for Irish lace (a $2,500 blouse in current terms). See also *Times,* Nov. 6, 1909.

. . . no-smoking policy . . . This fact was stipulated to as the truth by both sides in the trial transcript. The technique of exhaling through the lapel is described in Stein: *Triangle Fire.*

. . . migration even larger . . . cf: Foerster: *Italian Emigration:* a net migration of 3.8 million Italians to the United States between 1882 and 1911, "well-nigh expulsion."

. . . an environmental disaster . . . multiple sources, esp. Foerster, ibid.: "within sight of the blue sea . . ."

. . . eight hundred thousand returned . . . Italian immigration was extremely sensitive to the economic situation in the United States. During the 1908 depression, there was actually a net loss of Italians in America; return migration exceeded arrivals by 105,000 (Henderson: *Tammany and the New Immigrants*).

... *Michela Marciano* ... This identification of victim Michela Marciano with "M. M." of the relief committee report is extremely sketchy. It rests mainly on the fact that Marciano lived very near Our Lady of Pompeii church in Greenwich Village, which would have been the most hospitable neighborhood for a young woman from the Vesuvius region. None of the victims that might match "M. M." in the report appears in the 1910 Census, so there is little to go on beyond matching initials.

Striano lay among ... *Dizionario Enciclopedico Italiano; Encyclopaedia Britannica; www.multimap.com.*

... *Frank Perret, living on Vesuvius* ... Perret: *Vesuvius Eruption.* Additional details of the eruption come from *Times,* Apr. 6–June 15, 1906.

... *"chocolate colored mud"* ... *Ottaviano* ... *San Giuseppe* ... ibid.

... *"a Vast Desert"* ... *Times,* Apr. 12, 1906: "... indescribably wretched."

... *impossibly far off* ... cf. *Times,* Apr. 12, 1906: "For these people, whose homes and crops have been destroyed, there is little consolation in the statement of scientists that ultimately the valley and hillsides will become as fertile as ever." And: "It is believed that ... it will take ten years to bring the land under cultivation again" (*Times,* Apr. 14, 1906).

As late as May 30 ... *Times,* May 31, 1906.

... *Michela found much that was familiar* ... The early Italian experience in the United States is detailed in Williams: *South Italian Folkways;* Fenton: *Immigrants and Unions;* Rose: *The Italians;* Foerster: *Italian Emigration.*

... *supposed to defer* ... Williams: *South Italian,* p. 97: "On the whole, young Italian men prefer old-fashioned wives."

... *Evil Eye.* ... ibid.

... *"a lot of fun"* ... A tape of Leon Stein's interview with Pauline Pepe is available at the Kheel Center of Cornell University. Cf. Friedman-Kasaba: *Memories of Migration,* p. 155.

Thousands of women ... Clark/Hyatt: *Working Girls' Budgets,* Oct. 1910.

... *"inadequately guarded machinery"* ... Sue Ainslee Clark and Edith Wyatt, "Women Laundry Workers in New York," *Survey.* p. 401.

Rose Glantz ... Stein: *Triangle Fire,* p. 54.

Chapter Five

This account of the Triangle fire is drawn primarily from the trial transcript at the New York County Lawyers' Association ("trial transcript") supplemented by Leon Stein's notes and photocopies from the transcript, on deposit at the Kheel Center of Cornell University's School for Industrial and Labor Relations ("Stein transcript"). William Gunn Shepherd's eyewitness account of the fire was invaluable, which can be found in Stein: *Sweatshop;* McClymer: *Triangle Strike;* and at *www.ilr.cornell.edu/trianglefire/texts/stein_ootss/ootss_wgs.html.* Certain statements in Shepherd's account seem to me that they must be mistakes—especially his report of seeing a man walking on the roof, then jumping. This doesn't seem to match any other accounts. In fact, it would be impossible to see someone walking on the roof of the Asch Building from the street, because the cornice rises about five feet above the rooftop (author's own observations). I can imagine that perhaps someone told Shepherd this story and he accepted it as true, or even that an editor took this invented detail from another dispatch and added it to Shepherd's piece. The material I have taken from the Shepherd report is all supported by other witnesses. Finally, I have drawn from McFarlane, "Fire in the Skyscraper," *McClure's*, Sept. 1911, and, sparingly, from the contemporary newspaper reporting. Students of the fire should be very careful about accepting everything in the newspapers, especially in the coverage from the first day or two after the fire. With the exception of Shepherd, all the reporters on the scene were trying to reconstruct events from interviews in the chaos immediately following the tragedy— many wild stories were spun, and many true stories were garbled. For example: One newspaper reported that three cutters formed a human bridge across the airshaft from an Asch Building window to a window in the next tower a dozen or more feet away. It is doubtful that such a thing is even physically possible, and it certainly did not happen in this case.

    ... she tracked every cog ... Lipschitz, trial transcript.

    ... tallied the credits ... Approximately 400 of the roughly 500 Triangle workers were paid by the piece, rather than on a straight weekly wage, according to Harris, trial transcript.

    ... ten thousand to twelve thousand ... Blanck, Stein transcript.

    ... one of the earliest employees ... S. Bernstein, trial transcript.

    ... Louis Alter, an older cousin ... L. Alter, trial transcript.

    ... Mary, typed the bills ... M. Alter, trial transcript.

    ... "made a price" ... S. Bernstein, op. cit.

The Asch Building occupied ... Whiskeman, trial transcript; Moore, Stein transcript; author's observations.

The cutting table closest ... Abramowitz, trial transcript.

    ... hundreds of pounds of scraps ... L. Levy, trial transcript.

Dangling from a wire ... Max Rothen, quoted in *American*, March 26, 1911.

As Bernstein ran ... S. Bernstein, trial transcript.

Workers were required ... multiple testimony, trial transcript.

Just beyond the partition ... S. Bernstein, op. cit.

    ... Lipschitz worked feverishly ... Lipschitz, op. cit.

Two floors up ... M. Alter, op. cit.

    ... into the burning room ... Senderman, trial transcript.

"Is it open wide?" ... S. Bernstein, trial transcript.

    ... both tyranny and tenderness ... There were conflicting testimonies concerning the character of Samuel Bernstein. Many employees saw him as a fierce and even violent surveyor. Consider, for example, his role in throwing Jacob Kline out of the factory. But others recalled moments of kindness. Pauline Pepe, interviewed nearly fifty years later, vividly remembered Bernstein as "a lovely man" (Stein tapes, Kheel Center, Cornell University).

"The line of hanging patterns ..." quoted in *American*, Mar. 26, 1911.

... *"the boy was burning"* ... S. Bernstein, op. cit. However, see Chapter Six, re: Utal.

... *Brown was the machinist* ... Brown, trial transcript.

Ida Cohen, a sewing machine operator ... I. Cohen, trial transcript.

"I can't get anyone!" ... Lipschitz, trial transcript.

... *lovely and springlike* ... multiple newspapers, Mar. 26, 1911.

... *United Press news agency* ... A number of Internet sites mistakenly attribute the *World*'s Mar. 26, 1911, story to Shepherd, because soon after the fire, he joined the *World* staff, where he enjoyed success as a foreign correspondent.

... *Glass rained* ... Stein: *Triangle Fire*, pp. 12–14.

... *John Mooney, ran* ... D. Donahue, trial transcript; Stein: *Triangle Fire*, op. cit.

... *beast named Yale* ... Stein: ibid.

Officer Meehan ... Stein, *Triangle Fire*, pp. 14–16.

... *met Louis Brown* ... Brown, op. cit.

... *scarcely wide enough* ... J. Moore, op. cit.

After Mary Alter ... M. Alter, trial transcript.

... *salesmen loitered* ... Silk, Teschner, trial transcript.

... *ordering some embroidery* ... Silk, ibid.

Like Samuel Bernstein ... Harris, trial transcript.

... *little Mildred Blanck* ... Blanck, Stein transcript.

Harris turned to Emile Teschner ... Teschner, op. cit.

The chief shipping clerk ... Markowitz, trial transcript.

... *two stairways* ... Whiskeman, trial transcript.

... *Bernstein arrived, bursting* ... S. Bernstein, trial transcript.

... *hauled Wesselofsky up* ... ibid.

... *the chief dispatcher* ... Donahue, trial transcript.

... *"all the windows..."* Mahoney, trial transcript.

... *the chief saw* ... Worth, trial transcript.

... *Engine Co. 18 rolled* ... Ruch, trial transcript.

Frank Sommer ... multiple newspapers, March 26–27, 1911.

... *Professor Francis Aymar* ... *Times*, ibid.

... *the boss was met* ... Harris, trial transcript.

... *cutting himself badly* ... *Times*, op. cit.

Silk offered to carry ... Silk, trial transcript.

... *Senderman noticed Teschner* ... Senderman, trial transcript.

... *NYU law library* ... multiple newspapers, March 26, 1911.

... *"the most perfect"* ... S. Bernstein, trial transcript.

Chapter Six

There was never a day ... Harris, trial testimony.

... *about three dozen* ... ibid.

... *angling and jockeying* ... This fact emerges clearly from the testimonies of scores of sewing machine operators at the trial.

Yetta Lubitz ... Lubitz, trial transcript.

. . . layout of the ninth floor . . . Whiskeman, trial transcript; Moore, Stein transcript.

. . . one early Triangle employee . . . Pauline Newman, "Letter to Michael and Hugh" at *www.ilr.cornell.edu/trianglefire/texts/letters/newman_letter.html.*

. . . the ninth floor was emptied . . . These alterations were discussed at length in various trial testimony. This would suggest that previous accounts of the fire were wrong in counting oil-soaked floorboards as a contributing cause of the blaze. The amount of oil around the shop in general has been exaggerated; remember that the Triangle made white cotton blouses. The factory had to be fairly clean or blouses would have been routinely stained.

Ethel Monick . . . Monick, trial transcript.

Anna Gullo . . . Gullo, trial transcript.

Consider Max Hochfield . . . A tape of Leon Stein's interview with Max Hochfield is available at the Kheel Center of Cornell University.

. . . "screaming and crying. . ." Bucelli, trial transcript.

Lena Yaller remembered . . . Yaller, Stein transcript.

. . . Abe Gordon . . . Stein: *Triangle Fire,* pp. 57, 79.

. . . badly conceived, badly designed . . . Moore, Stein transcript.

. . . "pile of rubbish" . . . Sun, March 26, 1911.

. . . "indications on the west wall . . ." Worth, trial transcript.

. . . the elevator operators . . . Zito, trial transcript; multiple newspapers, March 26, 1911.

Nelson was standing . . . Nelson, trial transcript.

. . . Weiner had been cutting . . . K. Weiner, trial transcript.

Joseph Brenman . . . Brenman, trial transcript.

"The flames were too strong" . . . K. Weiner, op. cit.

First they tried to scramble . . . Gartman, trial transcript. (Between the day of the fire and the day she testified, Kate Rabinowitz married and became Kate Gartman.)

Kate Alterman chose . . . Alterman, trial transcript. Her complete testimony can be found at *www.law.umkc.edu/faculty/projects/ftrials/triangle/triangletest1.html.*

Sarah Cammerstein watched . . . Cammerstein, trial transcript.

"I could feel them pushing. . ." Stein, *Triangle Fire,* p. 64.

Sarah Friedman . . . S. Friedman, Stein transcript.

May Levantini jumped . . . Levantini, trial transcript.

"In America . . . they don't let you burn" . . . A. Gullo, trial transcript.

The ladder rose steadily . . . Woll, trial transcript.

. . . looked up or right or left . . . Author's observations from the ninth-floor windows over Washington Place.

The first man stepped . . . Worth, trial transcript.

. . . looked, from up there . . . Author's observations.

. . . foreman rang the quitting bell . . . A. Gullo, trial transcript.

"I paused a moment on the ledge" . . . World, March 27, 1911.

"When they came down entwined . . ." cf. McFarlane, "Fire in the Skyscraper," p. 479: "the impact of those three bodies was equal to a dead weight of sixteen tons."

She flung her hat . . . Shepherd.

Sally Weintraub . . . McFarlane, "Fire," op. cit., identified this victim as Celia "Sally" Weintraub.

The two teams of firefighters . . . Ruch, Mahoney, trial transcript.

. . . *bodies were found in a heap* . . . Woll, trial transcript.

. . . *a second cluster* . . . Ruch, op. cit.

. . . *fire-safe factories* . . . McKeon, *Fire Prevention*. This pamphlet gives a clear sense of the history and state of the art in fire prevention at the time of the Triangle fire. The author had been hired to survey the Triangle factory before the fire and noted the problem of locked doors. Also: *Preliminary Report of the F.I.C.*, vol. 1, pp. 154–99: "The Fire Hazard," by H. F. J. Porter.

City officials explained . . . McFarlane, "The Business of Arson," *Collier's*, a five-part series in April and May 1913. This series included "The Triangle Fire: The Story of a 'Rotten Risk'," May 17, 1913, a detailed investigation of the incentives created by the insurance industry for factory owners like Blanck and Harris to arrange arson fires, and the history of suspicious fires at their premises.

A little after 5 A.M. . . . McFarlane, ibid.

. . . *"three feather factories . . ."* McFarlane, "The Business of Arson," part I, op. cit.

. . . *a particular obsession* . . . Blanck's habit of checking locks and jiggling doorknobs was a recurring motif in the trial transcript.

. . . *locked doors multiplied* . . . *Times*, March 26, 1911.

He never heard back . . . ibid.

. . . *They "were foreigners"* . . . Hochfield interview tape, op. cit.

. . . *got the blaze under control* . . . Ruch, trial transcript.

Firefighter Felix Reinhardt . . . Reinhardt, trial transcript.

Woll, who raised . . . Woll, trial transcript.

. . . *lights in the ruined windows* . . . multiple newspapers, March 26, 1911.

. . . *Charles Lauth relieved him* . . . Lauth, trial transcript.

Contrary to lurid reports . . . The idea of "skeletons" slumped over the machines, as poet Chris Llewellyn put it, is a riveting myth of the Triangle fire, but untrue. It got started with a bit of creative paraphrasing by the *World*, March 26, 1911, claiming that fire chief Edward Croker "had seen . . . skeletons bending over sewing machines." The anonymous author's imagination may have been building on the Newark fire four months earlier, when one older woman worker did die in her chair, either frozen by terror or killed by a heart attack.

. . . *last seen struggling* . . . *Times*, Dec. 14, 1911, reporting the testimony of Ida Schwartz.

The damage . . . Freedman's body was nearly unrecognizable, and was initially claimed by another family as the body of fire victim Annie Colletti.

Chapter Seven

"We will get . . ." *Call*, Apr. 2, 1911.

. . . *beginning to make progress* . . . Various authorities offer assorted measures to document this, but they all confirm the same advances. McCreesh: *Women in the*

Campaign, p. 128, says there were "13,000 members" of Local 25, "9,000 of whom were women." An article on Clara Lemlich in *Jewish Life*, Nov. 1954: "a treasury from next to nothing to $2,400 a week." Cf. Sorin: *A Time*, p. 131.

... *grew eightfold* ... Howe, *World.*

The cloak makers' revolt ... Until fairly recently, the cloak makers strike (known as the "revolt" in the same way the waist makers' strike is known as the uprising) was the more studied of the two because the Protocol of Peace was a landmark in the history of industrial democracy. Detailed accounts can be found in Levine: *Women's Garment Workers;* Tyler: *Look;* Greenwald: *Bargaining;* McCreesh: *Women in the Campaign.*

... **Meyer London ran** ... Henderson: *Tammany and the New Immigrants;* Howe: *World.*

... **the** General Slocum ... Ellis: *Epic. Times*, June 16, 1904. Cf. Butler, Daniel Allen, *"Unsinkable": The Full Story of RMS* Titanic. Mechanicsburg, PA: Stackpole Books, 1998.

... *power of publicity* ... *World,* Jan. 9, 1910.

A parson's son ... Whitman's biography is drawn from a variety of sources, including: Logan: *Against,* esp. pp. 140–149; *Dict. of Am. Bio.; Times,* March 30, 1947.

He was anti-Tammany ... cf. *Times*, Sept. 29, 1909, quoting Whitman: "The only way you can throw the fear of God into Tammany Hall is by nominating and electing a man for District Attorney who will do his full duty at all times."

Small and trim ... *World,* op. cit.

... *Whitman's private secretary* ... *Times,* Dec. 19, 1909.

... *image consultant* ... Logan: *Against,* pp. 45–51.

As chief prosecutor, he appointed ... *World,* Dec. 10 and Dec. 19, 1909.

... *"prosecute John D. Rockefeller* ..." *World,* Jan. 9, 1910.

... *in his apartment* ... *Times,* March 26, 1911.

Into the room charged ... Logan: *Against;* Kahn, *Swope.*

Swope was a strapping ... *Times,* Junes 21, 1958.

... **Capt. Dominic Henry** ... multiple newspapers, March 26, 1911.

... *more safety precautions* ... In fact, I did not find any example of union leaders listing workplace safety among the issues at the core of the waist makers' uprising while the strike was on. The idea that safety was a key demand seems to have begun after the strike, and gained momentum with the Triangle fire. It is possible that safety was a topic widely discussed during the strike that did not make it into the newspaper coverage.

... *scab shop* ... *Call,* March 27, 1911. It isn't clear what made the *Call* think of Triangle workers this way; similar language was not used during the uprising itself. "Report of the Joint Relief Committee" showed that many of the dead and injured fire victims were union members.

... *tagging operation* ... various witnesses, trial transcript.

"leather handbags ..." *Sun,* March 26, 1911.

... vendors began hawking... *World*, March 29, 1911.

... "worst I ever saw"... Thompson's "Letter to Wm," from the Charles Willis Thompson letters at Cornell University library is available at *www.ilr.cornell.edu/ trianglefire/texts/letters/dearwm_letter.html.*

Disgusted, Whitman ordered... multiple newspapers, March 26, 1911.

Winterbottom was highly critical... *Times*, March 30, 1911.

... most respected public official... *World*, March 28, 1911.

"I have long expected..." multiple newspapers, March 26, 1911.

... "hold the rope..." Thompson, "Letter to Wm," op. cit.

... statement partly dictated... Logan: *Against*.

"I was appalled..." *American*, March 26, 1911.

The Charities Pier... the scene at the morgue, here as in the Prologue, is drawn from the newspapers of March 26–31, 1911, and Stein: *Triangle Fire*, which deals with the process of identifying the dead in much more detail than I have done.

Clara Lemlich searched... *Call*, March 28, 1911.

... scarcely a block... See Appendix for a list of the known dead.

... a damning picture... *Times*, March 27, 1911.

... actual lock... *World*, March 27, 1911.

... weren't even connected... multiple newspapers, March 27, 1911.

Political leaders were vague... multiple newspapers, March 26–30, 1911.

Joseph Asch... *Times*, March 27, 1911.

Isaac Harris invited... *Times*, March 26, 1911.

"Blame Shifted..." *Times*, March 28, 1911.

"Excited persons..." ibid.

... raft of new laws... *World*, March 27–28, 1911.

"How Long..." *Call*, March 27, 1911.

Joint Board of Sanitary Control... multiple newspapers, March 27, 1911. A history of the Joint Board is in Tyler: *Look*, pp. 126–33.

The problem was neither panic... *World*, March 29, 1911.

The same day... multiple newspapers, March 29, 1911.

"City Officials Blamed..." *American*, March 27, 1911.

Whitman was livid... Logan: *Against*, p. 149, quoting from *Felix Frankfurter Reminisces*.

One day, ... he spotted... *World*, Apr. 11, 1911; S. Bernstein, trial transcript.

... "Officials Already Losing Interest..." *World*, Apr. 25, 1911.

Murphy had his own... *Times*, Apr. 26, 1924: "... what Mr. Murphy is said to have told friends was his ambition... the placing of a Tammany man in the White House." Also Weiss: *Murphy*.

... Murphy was buried... The story of the fight to pick a senator is detailed in the *Times* and *World*, Jan. 1–March 31, 1911. Also Weiss: *Murphy*, pp. 48–49.

Murphy did not frighten him... LaCerra: *Roosevelt and Tammany*.

... Sullivan's choice... *Times*, March 30, 1911.

... Big Tim wasn't... multiple newspapers, Sept. 13, 1913; Logan: *Against*.

Straus was Jewish... *Dict. of Am. Bio*.

... *"evil genius..."* *World*, March 31, 1911.

... *the plight of the shirtwaist workers*... cf. Greenwald: *Bargaining*, pp. 311–12.

"This calamity"... multiple newspapers, Apr. 2 , 1911.

... *a funeral march*... multiple newspapers, Apr. 6, 1911.

Chapter Eight

Frances Perkins... The biographical material on Frances Perkins comes primarily from Martin: *Madame Secretary*, a truly outstanding biography, supplemented by other biographies; *Times*, May 15, 1965; *Dict. of Am. Bio.; Nat'l Cyclo. of Bio.;* and a lecture she gave Sept. 30, 1964, and transcribed in the collection at the Kheel Center.

... *was having tea*... Martin: *Madame Secretary*, pp. 84–85; Kheel lecture.

... *crash course on fire safety*... Martin: *Madame Secretary*, p. 78.

... *settlement houses*... Martin: ibid.; see also Howe: *World*.

"There was no shrinking..." Howe, *World*, pp. 90–94.

... *paid a visit to Tammany*... Martin: *Madame Secretary*, pp. 82–83.

... *knocked G. W. Plunkitt*... Riordan: *Plunkitt*, pp. 33–36: "Caesar had his Brutus... and I've got my 'The' MacManus.'"

... *study of cellar bakeries*... Martin: *Madame Secretary*, p. 77.

... *"a tale of filthy floors..."* *World*, April 19, 1911.

When Election Day came... The legislative careers of Al Smith, especially, and of Robert F. Wagner in passing are told concisely and well in Caro: *Power Broker*, pp. 114–129. The skeptical early editorials are quoted at p. 122.

Bob Wagner... The Wagner biography is drawn from Huthmacher: *Wagner*.

Al Smith's life... The Smith biography is drawn from various sources, esp. Slayton: *Empire Statesman;* Caro: *Power Broker;* Moskowitz/Hapgood: *Up; Times*, Oct. 5, 1944.

"His rise"... *Times*, Oct. 5, 1944.

... *"the wickedest ward..."* Slayton: *Empire Statesman*.

... *"the crowning glory..."* New York Mayor Abram Hewitt, quoted at *www.lihistory. com/6/hs601a.htm*. This site was the source for most of the data on the Brooklyn Bridge.

... *"If he was a college man..."* Caro: *Power Broker*, p. 122.

"That's what he does"... Martin: *Madame Secretary*.

"I had a talk with Murphy"... ibid., p. 83–84.

... *began to change*... cf: Greenwald: *Bargaining*, pp. 127–68, esp. p. 129: "In short, the fire connected separate progressive forces and melded them into a new coherent political force." Also Weiss: *Murphy*, pp. 81–82; Caro: *Power Broker*. George Price, in *The Ladies' Garment Worker*, Sept. 1911, noted the key factor of labor votes in making things change: "The salvation of the working class depends upon the workingmen themselves.... As long as [they] leave their protection out of their legislative demands... so long will there be unsafe factories."

... *a sort of guilt*... Kheel lecture, op. cit.

... *"I would be a traitor..."* multiple newspapers, Apr. 3–4, 1911. There are some variations in the text from the newspapers. This version is taken from Stein: *Sweat-shop*, pp. 196–97.

. . . send a distinguished Committee . . . multiple newspapers, ibid.; Martin: *Madame Secretary.*

She bumped into him . . . Kheel lecture; Martin: *Madame Secretary*, pp. 88–90.

"Have you ever noticed" . . . Kheel lecture.

. . . "few concrete clues . . ." Weiss: *Murphy*, pp. 2–3.

. . . conferred regularly with Smith and Wagner . . . ibid., pp. 52–54.

. . . Canoe Place Inn . . . ibid., pp. 78–81.

. . . "his 'young men'" . . . ibid., p. 75: quoting Murphy, "I encouraged the selection of young men for public office . . ."

. . . The three men decided . . . Martin: *Madame Secretary:* "More than any others, these three [Murphy, Wagner, and Smith] brought the Democratic Party of New York into the twentieth century."

. . . status quo had become dangerous . . . Eldot: *Gov. Smith:* "Murphy embraced progressivism in self-defense."

Murphy "had a quality . . ." Connable: *Tigers.*

He was goaded . . . Weiss: *Murphy*, pp. 67–68: "His unique staying power was due in no small measure to his growing awareness of civic responsibility. . . . Charles Murphy may have been . . . oblivious—at least in the beginning—to the magnitude and meaning of the pattern he was engineering. Yet, while Murphy ruled Tammany Hall . . . New York State woke up in the midst of the Progressive Era."

. . . make things happen . . . Weiss: *Murphy*, p. 87, quoting Ed Flynn: "none of the progressive legislation in Albany could have been passed, unless . . . [Murphy] urged it and permitted it to be passed."

. . . the Factory Investigating Commission . . . An excellent overview of FIC history is in Greenwald: *Bargaining*, pp. 302–334, which includes these wise words: "It makes more sense to see reform, first, as a process with many actors, and second, as a process in which individuals themselves changed." Other sources include Martin: *Madame Secretary*, pp. 103–121; Caro: *Power Broker;* Kheel lecture.

"Historians . . . have paid . . ." ibid, p. 312.

"Smith, and especially Wagner . . ." ibid., p. 313.

. . . backbone of the strike . . . Greenwald: *Bargaining*, pp. 314–315.

Clara Lemlich . . . American, Dec. 11, 1911.

Henry Moskowitz . . . This progressive came to call the FIC legislation "the most enlightened labor code ever placed on the statute books of any state." Hapgood: *Up.*

. . . most influential women . . . The story of Belle Moskowitz is told in Caro: *Power Broker.*

. . . "a first-class lawyer" . . . quoted in Greenwald: *Bargaining*, p. 308.

. . . the group averaged . . . A good summary of the FIC's initial burst of action is in Martin: *Madame Secretary.* FIC records are available at the New York State Archives; a summary of the material is at *www.sara.nysed.gov/holding/aids/factory/history.htm.*

Eight of the proposed . . . Preliminary Report . . . vol. I. Almost 80 years later, a writer made the intriguing argument that a single workers' compensation bill mattered more than all the regulatory legislations, by creating a fiscal incentive for owners to improve safety. *Times*, Nov. 18, 1999.

    In grand progressive style . . . multiple sources, esp. Martin, *Madame Secretary.*

    Eventually, he resigned . . . *Final Report* . . . vol. I.

    "But Mr. Dowling" . . . Martin: *Madame Secretary.*

    . . . *Perkins again lobbied* . . . This story is told in greater detail in Martin: *Madame Secretary*, pp. 91–98.

    . . . *none other than Big Tim* . . . cf. Logan: *Against*, pp. 55–60, quoting Alvin Harlow: "Perhaps there was never a more perplexing admixture of good and evil in one human character than that of Timothy D. Sullivan."

    . . . *actually endorsed the Democrats* . . . Greenwald: *Bargaining*, p. 315.

    . . . *"the most serious mistake . . ."* Weiss: *Murphy*, p. 55. Also Greenwald: *Bargaining*, p. 309: "Wagner and Smith and Tammany Hall soon realized that [they] could ride the Triangle hobby horse to great political advantage. The Republican Party had disintegrated."

    . . . *Frances Perkins paid* . . . Martin: *Madame Secretary*, pp. 99–100.

Chapter Nine

    . . . *the prosecutor instructed* . . . *World*, Apr. 12, 1911.

    . . . *cold steel axles* . . . Photographs of the ruined ninth-floor loft appeared in several newspapers; the one from which I gained the most was on the front page of the *American*, March 27, 1911.

    They were arraigned . . . multiple newspapers, esp. *World* and *American*, Apr. 12, 1911.

    . . . *Sandow the sideshow strongman* . . . Eugene Sandow, 1867–1925, was the most famous bodybuilder in the world between 1900 and 1920. Among many honors, he was made Royal Professor of Physical Culture by King George V, *Times*, March 28, 1911. cf. *www.sandowmuseum.com.*

    . . . *affiliated with Tammany Hall* . . . Boyer: *Steuer;* Steuer was a delegate to the 1916 Democratic National Convention, along with Murphy, Smith, and Wagner.

    . . . *Big Tim Sullivan's attorney* . . . Logan: *Against*, p. 125.

    . . . *ten thousand dollars* . . . *Times*, Feb. 25, 1912.

    "I can't think . . ." Boyer: *Steuer*, p. 17.

    Like the factory owners . . . Steuer's biography is drawn from Boyer: *Steuer;* A. Steuer: *Steuer; Times:* Aug. 22, 1940; *New Yorker:* May 16, 1925, May 16 and May 23, 1931; *Dict. of Am. Bio.*, vol. 52, pp. 672–673.

    . . . *million-dollar-a-year man* . . . The Hearst newspapers routinely called him "Million-Dollar Steuer" until the lawyer complained personally to Hearst himself (a client), Boyer: *Steuer*. Aron Steuer put his father's fee at $1,000 per day as early as 1918 (roughly equivalent to $2,000 per hour in current terms).

    In time, his reputation . . . cf. Otto G. Obermaier and Barry A. Bohrer, "A Century of New York's Crimes, Criminals and Trial Lawyers," *The New York Law Journal*, Jan. 10, 2000: ". . . his courtroom exploits were . . . legendary."

... *"Wait until he's charged . . ."* Boyer: *Steuer*, pp. 39–40.

... *an enormous retainer* . . . A. Steuer: *Steuer*.

... *"the greatest trial lawyer . . ."* Boyer, *Steuer*, p. 11.

... *never quite sure how old* . . . A: Steuer: *Steuer*.

... *antiseptic brain* . . . ibid.: "He liked to refer to the law as an exact science—the nearest thing to mathematics."

"There is naught . . ." New Yorker, May 16, 1925.

... *"only had a quarter"* . . . Boyer: *Steuer*, pp. 26–28.

Howe & Hummel . . . Rovere: *Howe & Hummel*.

His chance came . . . A. Steuer: *Steuer*.

... *"Attorney General of the City Court"* . . . ibid.

... *relationship with Charles Murphy* . . . Boyer: *Steuer*, p. 99. Boyer tells the story of a lawsuit Steuer tried in which Murphy was a defendant.

... *Big Bill Devery* . . . ibid., pp. 90–98; Weiss: *Murphy*, p. 28.

... *a favorite toastmaster* . . . Boyer: *Steuer*, pp. 78–89.

... *Raymond Hitchcock* . . . ibid., pp. 124–144.

... *never took cases* . . . A. Steuer: *Steuer:* "Cases involving sexual abnormality were so repellent to him that he refused to appear in one under any circumstances."

... *released on $25,000 bail* . . . multiple newspapers, April 12, 1911.

... *challenged the indictment* . . . Steuer's appeal was partially successful; a number of counts were thrown out by the appeals court. 134 N.Y.S. 409.

Gardner was accused . . . Boyer: *Steuer*, pp. 44–57; A. Steuer: *Steuer; New Yorker*, May 16, 1931.

... *the trial began* . . . Trial coverage was carried in nearly all New York newspapers between Dec. 4 and Dec. 30, 1911—but it was less coverage than one might have expected. The Triangle trial rarely made the front page.

... *five inches of snow* . . . cf: *Herald*, Dec. 5, 1911.

"Do not be affected . . ." multiple newspapers, Dec. 5, 1911.

"Oh, mama, look!" . . . American, Dec. 6, 1911. cf: *Evening Post*, Dec. 5, 1911: "Women Jeer Blanck and Harris."

Five and a half feet tall . . . A. Steuer: *Steuer*.

... *shoved his way through* . . . Times, Dec. 6, 1911.

... *enacted the little rituals* . . . Boyer: *Steuer*.

"Let the jury see . . ." from a speech to the Fordham Law School (undated), quoted ibid., pp. 39–43.

... *did not take notes* . . . A. Steuer, *Steuer;* Boyer: *Steuer; New Yorker*, op. cit.: "Max has a freak memory. . . . [H]e has no more need for notes than Gertrude Ederle for water wings."

... *Charles Bostwick* . . . World, Dec. 19, 1909; *American*, March 28, 1911 (photograph).

... *J. Robert Rubin* . . . Times, Sept. 11, 1958.

. . . slip an advantage . . . Boyer: *Steuer.*

While choosing the Triangle jurors . . . Times, Dec. 5, 1911.

. . . adjourned for lunch . . . multiple newspapers, Dec. 6, 1911.

. . . opening statement . . . trial transcript.

. . . a policy to eat light . . . cf. speech to Fordham, op. cit.

"If any question . . ." Whiskeman, trial transcript.

. . . chief Edward Worth . . . Worth, trial transcript; *World,* April 8, 1911.

. . . Steuer's defense strategy . . . based on a close reading of the trial transcript.

. . . "handrail of the stairs . . ." Mahoney, trial transcript.

. . . "readily see [flames] . . ." ibid.

. . . denied that the passage was blocked . . . ibid., quoting firefighter Oliver Mahoney, who fought the blaze at the eighth-floor Washington Place door: "The flames did not reach that hallway [meaning the Washington Place stairs] through that door during my time there."

. . . buying fabric scraps . . . Levy, trial transcript.

. . . the following Monday morning . . . summarized from trial transcript.

"I took hold . . ." Bucelli, trial transcript.

"I pushed through . . ." Brenman, trial transcript.

. . . "I couldn't open it . . ." I. Nelson, trial transcript.

"Oh, the door is locked! . . ." Lubitz, trial transcript.

"I tried the door . . ." Monick, trial transcript.

. . . "he did everything" . . . Rothstein, trial transcript.

. . . "they tore it . . ." Zimmerman, trial transcript.

"I tried to turn the handle . . ." L. Weiner, trial transcript.

. . . "it wouldn't go . . ." K. Weiner, trial transcript.

. . . whole bag of tricks . . . trial transcript generally.

. . . bait the young prosecutor . . . Deitschman, Stein transcript.

"Your brother wants . . ." Brenman, trial transcript.

"Did you receive . . ." Zimmerman, trial transcript.

The crude and blackened lock . . . The colloquy over the lock is available in the Stein transcript. Stein: *The Triangle Fire,* pp. 183–187, contains a more detailed recounting of the testimony and cross-examination concerning the lock.

Rosalie Panno . . . R. Panno, Stein transcript.

. . . "he twisted the lock" . . . Nicolosi, Stein transcript.

. . . "rushed by me . . ." M. Wagner, trial transcript.

Later, when Brown appeared . . . L. Brown, trial transcript.

. . . newlywed Kate Gartman . . . Gartman, Stein transcript.

She testified near sunset . . . multiple newspapers, April 19, 1911.

. . . cut a striking figure . . . American, Dec. 19, 1911, a drawing.

. . . one of six daughters . . . Alterman's family size comes from Stein transcript. A search of Philadelphia city directories and marriage records revealed how rare the name Alterman was in that city, so it wasn't hard to track all the Alterman families. Between 1915 and 1922, five daughters of upholsterer Morris Alterman

got married, according to the license bureau records. The number and age of these young women strongly suggests that Morris Alterman was also the father of Kate Alterman. After settling on Morris Alterman as her father, I was able to add a bit of information by analyzing the city directories and marriage records of that era.

"At this time, yes, sir" . . . Alterman: Stein transcript.

. . . *Steuer recalled* . . . Speech to 43d Annual Meeting of the Missouri Bar Association, quoted in *America Speaks*, pp. 422–440, esp. pp. 432–437.

. . . *trying to suggest* . . . Yaller, Stein transcript.

. . . *he later explained* . . . *American Speaks*, op. cit.

Apparently Steuer had assigned . . . Alterman, Stein transcript; A. Steuer, *Steuer*.

. . . *primed the jury to listen for echoes* . . . cf: *Evening Mail*, Dec. 30, 1911, quoting juror Victor Steinman: "they told their stories like parrots."

. . . *for the third time* . . . Alterman, trial transcript.

. . . *Steuer called fifty-one* . . . Steuer opened his case Dec. 18, 1911 (multiple newspapers, Dec. 19, 1911). The summary of his presentation is based on reading the trial transcript.

. . . *the problem of stolen waists* . . . Harris, trial transcript.

. . . *complete confusion* . . . Levantini, trial transcript; I. Mittelman, trial transcript; A. Mittelman, trial transcript. Beyond this confusion, Steuer's case was also damaged by admissions from several of his witnesses that they recived pay raises from Blanck and Harris shortly before they testified. Multiple newspapers, Dec. 22, 1911.

. . . *"A million times, couldn't it* . . . *"* Kelly, trial transcript.

After the closing arguments . . . Attended by Alva Belmont and Inez Milholland, among others (*Herald*, Dec. 22, 1911).

. . . *foreman Leo Abrahams suggested* . . . This account of jury proceedings comes mainly from juror Victor Steinman's post-trial interviews, esp. multiple newspapers, March 28, 1911. Foreman Abrahams pronounced Steinman's version "substantially correct." *Times*, Dec. 29, 1911.

. . . *jury instructions amazed* . . . *Times*, Dec. 28, 1911; *Herald*, Dec. 29, 1911.

"I could not do it" . . . In fact, Steinman believed that "some panic-stricken girl might have turned the key in an effort to open it. And if that was so, Harris and Blanck could not have known of it," *Evening Mail*, Dec. 27, 1911.

. . . *wanted to convict* . . . *American*, Dec. 28, 1911, quoting Steuerman: "I have a growth on my tongue and for fifteen months I have been under medical treatment. I speak with difficulty and it is for this reason that I could not maintain my positions . . . I wanted to hold out . . . I believe this verdict is a miscarriage of justice."

Thomas C. T. Crain . . . his biography was drawn from *Times*, March 30, 1942; Mitgang: *Once Upon;* Northrop: *Insolence*.

. . . *inconclusive, though unflattering* . . . Mitgang, *Once Upon:* "He was never accused of dishonesty, only of incompetence. [Crain] seemed more pathetic than villainous."

. . . *early hours of March 14"* . . . multiple newspapers, March 15, 1905.

Blame for the disaster ... *Times*, March 17, 22, and 25, 1905. March 25 headline: "Verdict Unjust, Crain Says."

None of his protests ... *Times*, March 25, 1905.

... *their verdict was read* ... multiple newspapers, Dec. 28–29, 1911.

... *young man caught sight* ... *Times*, Dec. 28, 1911.

Epilogue

... *Murphy finally embraced* ... My interpretation of this sequence, in which Murphy reacts mainly to the changed will of the voters, is not the only way of seeing things. At the time of Murphy's death, the *Times* placed the emphasis on Murphy's failure to prevent the 1912 Democratic nomination from going to Woodrow Wilson, and his subsequent denunciation by Wilson and party elder William Jennings Bryan (Apr. 26, 1924). However, Murphy permitted the creation of a vigorous Factory Investigating Commission fully a year before the 1912 convention.

... *Tammany's Al Smith* ... Slayton: *Empire Statesman*; Caro: *Power Broker*.

... *a bit grudgingly* ... In fact, after Roosevelt captured the 1932 Democratic nomination that Smith thought should have been his, the Tammany man became extremely bitter. FDR's complex relationship to Tammany, and to Murphy and Smith specifically, is explained in LaCerra: *Roosevelt and Tammany*.

... *the Triangle legacy* ... Frances Perkins drew this line directly: "This is the way we started the move which became the New Deal" (Kheel lecture, op. cit.); "Not in Vain," in Stein, ed.: *Sweatshop*, pp. 200–201; Mitgang: *Once*: "[I]t can be said that Roosevelt first learned about political compromise and the need for social reform" from Smith and Wagner. But of course there were precursors to the Triangle reforms, so it is possible to trace this legacy further back in time. Cf. *Times*, May 15, 1965: "[T]here were some who said that the entire New Deal relief program was nothing more than an expanded version of the Consumer's League platform."

... *seemed to be dying* ... The story of the Becker-Rosenthal case is best told in Logan: *Against*. Steuer's role: pp. 123–128.

Big Tim was doomed ... multiple newspapers, Sept. 13–18, 1913.

... *best-known men* ... *Times*: Sept. 15, 1913: "[his] face was better known to more thousands of New Yorkers, probably, than that of any other person within the limits of the Greater City."

Twenty thousand people ... multiple newspapers, Sept. 18, 1913.

... *"someone in higher politics"* ... Slayton: *Empire Statesman*; Smith biographies generally.

... *freedom to hire* ... Caro: *Power Broker*; *Slayton*, ibid.; Weiss: *Murphy*.

... *Lemlich spent* ... Orleck: *Common Sense*; *Jewish Life*, Nov. 1954. For an extremely detailed discussion of the struggle sparked within the ILGWU, and especially Local 25, when socialists like Lemlich further radicalized into communism in the late 1910s, see Levine: *Women's Garment Workers*.

... *author of more important progressive* ... Huthmacher: *Wagner*.

... *"Ruined"* ... *Times*, Feb. 25, 1912.

... *hide their assets* ... McFarlane: *"The Triangle Fire,"* op. cit.

... *"claimants have been tired out"* ... Stein: *Triangle Fire*, p. 207.

His limousine ... *Times*, May 25, 1912.

... *locking a door* ... *Times*, Aug. 21, Sept. 20, Sept. 27, 1912.

... *struggled to keep* ... New York City Directories, 1912–1925.

... *faking the official seal* ... *National Consumer's League and Others v. Triangle Waist Co.*, Sup. Ct., County of New York, July 1914.

Louis Levine's ... *book* ... Levine: *Women's Garment Workers*. The author's actual name was Louis Levitski Lorwin.

... *first sweeping history* ... Rischin: *Promised City*.

... *Hamlet, North Carolina* ... multiple newspapers, Sept. 4, 1991; *Washington Post*, Nov. 8, 2002.

... *toy factory in Bangkok* ... multiple newspapers, May 11, 1993.

Fiorello La Guardia ... Mitgang: *Once;* Weiss: *Murphy*, p. 92–100: "[S]uch men as Al Smith and Fiorello LaGuardia, while serving as bridges between reformers and bosses, actually carried reform into the New Deal and left the machines behind."

... *symbolic of utter defeat* ... *Times*, Aug. 27, 1943.

NOTES ON SOURCES

N one of the figures in this book is alive today. Many of the central figures—from powerful Charles F. Murphy to Blanck and Harris, the Shirtwaist Kings, to spectral Rosie Freedman and Michela Marciano to Kate Alterman, the crucial witness—left little, if any, record behind. I have pieced this story together from many sources, some of which require special citation.

My most important source, underpinning the whole book and crucial to the writing of chapters two, five, six, and nine, was the transcribed testimony from the trial of *People of the State of New York v. Isaac Harris and Max Blanck.* For more than thirty years, historians have believed this document to be lost, and indeed, they were partly right. The only known copy was scheduled to be transferred to microfilm in the late 1960s as part of a preservation project at the New York City Municipal Archives. But somewhere along the way, the transcript was lost. (One imagines it moldering away in a mislabeled box in a Bronx warehouse, but more likely it was thrown out.) Furthermore, no living person is known to have read the transcript. Author Leon Stein may have been the last person to do so, in the late 1950s, while researching his excellent book, *The Triangle Fire.* Stein dictated notes as he went, and photocopied about 170 of the nearly 2,300 pages. Afterward, Stein, too, noted the central importance of that transcript to any effort to tell this story. In thanking the ghost of court reporter Steward Liddell, Stein wrote: "It is from that record that many who were trapped in the Asch building but somehow managed to escape speak directly in the pages of this book with sworn veracity."

Arguably, a municipal archive that fails to preserve the one document essential to understanding a pivotal event in the city's history is not much of an archive at all. And the trial transcript is only one of a long list of records that New York City didn't bother to keep. The proceedings of the coroner's jury in the Triangle fire cannot be found. The records of the fire marshal's investigation, ditto. Then, after a year of vain searching for the transcript, I came across a cryptic endnote to a biographical dictionary entry on Max D. Steuer, suggesting that certain "trial records" were stored at the New York County Lawyers' Association. I determined that this was a downtown, working-class lawyers' alternative to the blue-blooded Association of the Bar of the City of New York in midtown. Dutifully, though with little real hope, I contacted the NYCLA and asked if they had the transcript. Initially, the staff there turned up nothing on the Triangle fire. But the extremely helpful librarian, Ralph Monaco, didn't stop there. After several days of research, Monaco determined that Max D. Steuer, upon his death in 1940, bequeathed his personal, leather-bound copies of the testimony from his greatest cases to the NYCLA. *People v. Harris and Blanck* had been resting quietly, and apparently untouched, in the association's library for sixty years when Monaco rediscovered it. He graciously invited me into the association—a private library—to read it.

For some of those sixty years, the three fat volumes of the transcript enjoyed a place of honor in the President's Room. Then, as the memory of the great lawyer faded to nothing, Steuer's books were relegated to a dismal corner in a basement storage room. *Sic transit gloria mundi.* Along the way—perhaps by theft, perhaps after the basement flooded in the late 1990s—volume two disappeared completely.

For a week in the spring of 2001, Monaco and the NYCLA staff hosted me at a long oak table by the window in the twin shadows of the World Trade Center towers. Each day at lunchtime, I got a sand-wich and ate on the Trade Center Plaza. Every evening I worked until closing time, always slightly worried that Monaco would soon decide to kick me out, because no matter how carefully I turned the ancient pages, my trip through the transcript was doing it no good. After ninety years, the cheap typewriter paper—just under 1,400 pages of it, repre-senting roughly 100 of the 155 witnesses—literally crumbled between my fingertips. Photocopying the books was out of the question, but I was allowed to take extensive notes. In those fragile pages, the trial came to life. And not just the trial: the fire itself, and the survivors, and the Triangle factory.

To this foundation I added Leon Stein's undated notes from his reading of the complete transcript sometime in the 1950s. These notes are in the collection of the Kheel Center at the Cornell Univer-sity School of Industrial and Labor Relations. The Stein papers include a verbatim copy of Kate Alterman's testimony and complete copies of the (rather dull) closing arguments by Steuer and prosecutor Charles F. Bostwick. I have donated my own notes from the Steuer transcript to the Kheel Center. And with the support of Cornell and NYCLA, a project is underway to create digital images of the battered document. In the preceding source notes, I have referred to my reading of the Steuer transcript as "trial transcript." Material from Stein's notes is cited as "Stein transcript."

(In mentioning the Kheel Center, I note the excellent website main-tained by the center on the subject of the Triangle Fire. It is a model of what can be done by a research library to make information widely available to the general public. The home page is at *www.ilr.cornell.edu/ trianglefire.*)

The second invaluable resource was Leon Stein's book, *The Triangle Fire.* His clear and factual account of the fire, originally published in 1962, put the story back on firm historical ground after fifty years of neglect, and enriched the record with his interviews of twenty-five survivors, all now dead. Some of the most haunting details of this story—the image of Rose Glantz singing "Ev'ry Little Movement," for example—survive thanks to Stein's gentle but effective interviews.

A third source requiring special mention was Irving Howe's masterpiece, *World of Our Fathers*. This meticulously detailed, wonderfully organized, brilliantly written history of the community and culture of the Eastern European Jews in New York informed nearly every page of my book. I read it awestruck.

Two extraordinary, but little-read, works of scholarship were extremely valuable. In 1968, Smith College published its prize-winning undergraduate thesis, *Charles Francis Murphy, 1858–1924: Respectability and Responsibility in Tammany Politics*, by Nancy Joan Weiss. This small book completely altered my understanding of just how wise a very young person can be. It shows a more acute understanding of politics and of human nature than most people attain in a lifetime. Richard A. Greenwald's unpublished 1998 dissertation, "Bargaining for Industrial Democracy?: Labor, the State, and the New Industrial Relations in Progressive Era New York," is, likewise, marked by enormous sophistication, deep research, and crystal-clear thinking.

Last, this book rests on the work of two long-dead journalists: William Gunn Shepherd, author of the only professional eyewitness report of the fire, and Arthur E. McFarlane, whose muckraking talents were fortuitously focused on the problem of fire at the very moment that this shocking blaze struck New York. The work of both men was crucial to understanding what happened on March 25, 1911—and why.

SELECTED BIBLIOGRAPHY

Newspapers

New York *Times*, New York *World*, New York *American*. New York *Call*, New York *Tribune*, New York *Evening Post*, New York *Herald*, New York *Evening Mail*, New York *Sun*, *Jewish Daily Forward*, Newark *Evening News*, Newark *Star*, Washington *Post*, Philadelphia *Exponent*.

Periodicals

McClure's, *Collier's*, *The Survey*, *Charities and the Commons*, *American Businesswoman*, *New Yorker*, *Jewish Life*.

Books

(Titles marked with * were especially useful and are recommended for readers with a deeper interest in the subjects of this book.)

Aronson, I. Michael. *Troubled Waters: The Origins of the 1881 Anti-Jewish Pogroms in Russia*. Pittsburgh: University of Pittsburgh Press, 1990.

Baker, Kevin. *Dreamland*. New York: HarperCollins, 1999.

Banks, Eugene and Read, Opie. *The History of the San Francisco Disaster and Mount Vesuvius Horror*. [Publisher unknown.] 1906.

Bordman, Gerald. *American Musical Theatre: A Chronicle*. London: Oxford University Press, 2001.

*Boyer, Richard O. *Max Steuer: Magician of the Law*. New York: Greenberg, 1932.

Briggs, Vernon M. Jr. *Immigration and American Unionism*. Ithaca: Cornell University Press, 2001.

America Speaks: A Library of the Best Spoken Thought in Business and the Professions. Basil Gordon Byron and Frederic Rene Coudert, eds. New York: Modern Eloquence Corp., 1928.

Cahan, Abraham. *The Education of Abraham Cahan*. Trans. by Leon Stein, Abraham P. Conan, and Lynn Davison. Philadelphia: The Jewish Publication Society of America, 1969.

*Caro, Robert. *The Power Broker: Robert Moses and the Fall of New York*. New York: Random House, 1974.

*Clark, Sue Ainslee and Wyatt, Edith. *Making Both Ends Meet: The Income and Outlay of New York Working Girls*. New York: Macmillan, 1911.

Women in World History: A Biographical Encyclopedia. Anne Commire, ed. Waterford, CT: Yorkin, 1999.

Connable, Alfred and Silberfarb, Edward. *Tigers of Tammary: Nine Men Who Ran New York*. New York: Holt, Rinehart and Winston, 1967.

Downey, Fairfax. *Portrait of an Era, as Drawn by C. D. Gibson*. New York: Charles Scribner's Sons, 1936.

Dubnov, Simon. *History of the Jews: From the Congress of Vienna to the Emergence of Hitler* (*Vol. 5*). New York: South Brunswick, 1973.

Dubofsky, Melvyn: *Industrialism and the American Worker, 1865–1920*. Arlington Heights, IL.: Harlan Davidson, 1975.

*Dye, Nancy Schrom. *As Equals and Sisters: Feminism, the Labor Movement and the Women's Trade Union League of New York*. Columbia: University of Missouri Press, 1981.

Eldot, Paula. *Governor Alfred E. Smith: The Politician as Reformer*. New York: Garland, 1985.

Ellis, Edward Robb. *The Epic of New York City: A Narrative History*. New York: Old Town Books, 1966.

Faith, Nicholas. *Blaze: The Forensics of Fire*. New York: St. Martin's Press, 2000.

Fenton, Edwin. *Immigrants and Unions, A Case Study: Italians and American Labor, 1870–1920*. New York: Arno Press, 1975.

*Foerster, Robert F. *Italian Emigration of Our Times*. New York: Russell & Russell, 1919.

Friedman-Kasaba, Kathie. *Memories of Migration: Gender, Ethnicity and Work in the Lives of Jewish and Italian Women in New York, 1870–1924*. Albany: State University of New York Press, 1996.

Gannes, Abraham P. *Childhood in a Shtetl*. Cupertino, CA: Ganton Books, 1993.

Gilbert, Martin. *A History of the Twentieth Century* (*Vol. 1, 1900–1933*). New York: William Morrow & Co., 1997.

Glanz, Rudolf. *Jew and Italian: Historic Group Relations and the New Immigration* (*1881–1924*). New York: Shulsinger Bros., 1970.

Gould, Milton S. *The Witness Who Spoke with God and Other Tales from the Courthouse*. New York: Viking, 1979.

Green, James R. *The World of the Worker: Labor in Twentieth-Century America*. Urbana: University of Illinois, 1998.

Hapgood, Norman and Moskowitz, Henry. *Up From the City Streets: A Life of Alfred E. Smith*. New York: Grosset & Dunlap, 1927.

*Henderson, Thomas M. *Tammany Hall and the New Immigrants: The Progressive Years.* New York: Arno Books, 1976.

*Howe, Irving. *World of Our Fathers: The Journey of the Eastern European Jews to America and the Life They Found and Made.* New York: Touchstone (Simon & Schuster), 1976.

*Huthmacher, Joseph J. *Senator Robert F. Wagner and the Rise of Urban Liberalism.* New York: Athaneum, 1968.

Kisselhoff, Jeff. *You Must Remember This: An Oral History of Manhattan from the 1890s to World War II.* New York: Schocken, 1990.

Kahn, E. J. Jr. *The World of Swope.* New York: Simon and Schuster, 1965.

Pogroms: Anti-Jewish Violence in Modern Russian History. John D. Klier and Shlomo Lambroza, eds. Cambridge: Cambridge University Press, 1992.

LaCerra, Charles. *Franklin Delano Roosevelt and Tammany Hall of New York.* Lanham, MD: University Press of America, 1997.

Levine, Louis (Lewis Revitzki Lorwin). *The Women's Garment Workers.* New York: Arno & The New York Times, 1969 (originally published 1924).

Lipset, Seymour Martin and Marks, Gary. *It Didn't Happen Here: Why Socialism Failed in the United States.* New York: W. W. Norton, 2000.

Llewellyn, Chris. *Fragments from the Fire: The Triangle Shirtwaist Company Fire of March 25, 1911: Poems.* New York: Viking, 1987.

Logan, Andy. *Against the Evidence: The Becker-Rosenthal Affair.* New York: McCall Pub. Co., 1970.

Lukas, J. Anthony. *Big Trouble: A Murder in a Small Western Town Sets Off a Struggle for the Soul of America.* New York: Simon & Schuster, 1997.

Maclean, Norman. *Young Men and Fire: A True Story of the Mann Gulch Fire.* Chicago: University of Chicago, 1992.

*Martin, George. *Madam Secretary: Frances Perkins.* Boston: Houghton Mifflin Co., 1976.

McCreesh, Carolyn. *Women in the Campaign to Organize Garment Workers, 1880–1917.* New York: Garland, 1985

McKeon, Peter Joseph. *Fire Prevention: A Treatise and Textbook.* New York: The Chief Pub. Co., 1912.

Mendelsohn, Joyce. *The Lower East Side Remembered & Revisited: History and Guide to a Legendary New York Neighborhood.* New York: The Lower East Side Press, 2001.

A Bintel Brief: Sixty Years of Letters from the Lower East Side to the Jewish Daily Forward. Isaac Metzker, ed. Garden City, NY: Doubleday, 1971.

Milbank, Caroline Rennolds. *New York Fashion: The Evolution of American Style.* New York: Harry N. Abrams, Inc., 1989.

Mitgang, Herbert. *Once Upon a Time in New York: Jimmy Walker, Franklin Roosevelt and the Last Great Battle of the Jazz Age.* New York: The Free Press, 2000.

Nasaw, David. *The Chief: The Life of William Randolph Hearst.* New York: Houghton Mifflin, 2000.

Northrop, William B. and John B. *The Insolence of Office: The Inside Story of the Seabury Investigation.* New York: G. P. Putnam's Sons, 1932.

O'Nan, Stewart. *The Circus Fire: A True Story of an American Tragedy.* New York: Anchor Books, 2001.

Orleck, Annelise. *Common Sense & A Little Fire: Women and Working Class Politics in the United States 1900–1965.* Chapel Hill: University of North Carolina, 1995.

Pasachoff, Naomi. *Frances Perkins: Champion of the New Deal.* New York: Oxford University Press, 1999.

Perret, Frank. *The Vesuvius Eruption of 1906: Study of a Volcanic Cycle.* Washington, DC: The Carnegie Institute of Washington, 1924.

Rickard, Maxine Elliott. *Everything Happened to Him.* New York: Frederick A. Stokes Co., 1936.

Riis, Jacob. *How the Other Half Lives: Studies Among the Tenements of New York.* Intro. by Donald N. Bigelow. New York: Hill and Wang, 1957.

*Riordan, William L. *Plunkitt of Tammany Hall: A Series of Very Plain Talks on Very Practical Politics.* Intro. by Arthur Mann. New York: Meridian, 1991.

Rischin, Moses. *The Promised City: New York's Jews, 1870–1914.* New York: Harper Torchbooks, 1970.

Root, Jonathan. *One Night in July: The True Story of the Rosenthal-Becker Murder Case.* New York: Coward-McCann, 1961.

Rose, Philip. *The Italians in America.* New York: George H. Doran Co., 1922.

Rovere, Richard H. *Howe & Hummel: Their True and Scandalous History.* Intro. by Calvin Trillin. New York: Farrar, Straus Giroux, 1985.

Severn, Bill. *Frances Perkins: A Member of the Cabinet.* New York: Hawthorn Books, 1976.

Simonhoff, Harry. *Saga of American Jewry 1865–1914: Links of an Endless Chain.* New York: Arco Publishing Co., 1959.

Russia at the Bar of the American People: A Memorial of Kishinef. Isidor Singer, ed. New York: Funk & Wagnall's, 1904.

*Slayton, Robert A. *Empire Statesman: The Rise and Redemption of Al Smith.* New York: The Free Press, 2001 (read in typescript).

Sohn, David. *The Activities of the Bialystoker Community in America.* New York: The Bialystoker Center, 1934.

Sorin, Gerald. *A Time for Building: The Third Migration, 1880–1920. The Jewish People in America.* Baltimore: Johns Hopkins, 1992.

*Stein, Leon. *The Triangle Fire.* Philadelphia: Lippincott, 1962; and in a new edition with intro. by William Greider, Ithaca, NY: Cornell University Press, 2001.

Out of the Sweatshop: The Struggle for Industrial Democracy. Leon Stein, ed. New York: Quadrangle/The New York Times Book Co., 1977.

Stella, Antonio. *Some Aspects of Italian Immigration to the United States.* New York: G. P. Putnam's Sons, 1924.

Steuer, Aron. *Max D. Steuer: Trial Lawyer.* New York: Random House, 1950.

Swanberg. W. A. *Citizen Hearst: A Biography of William Randolph Hearst.* New York: Macmillan, 1961.

Trager, James. *The People's Chronology: A Year-by-Year Record of Human Events from Prehistory to the Present.* New York: Henry Holt, 1992.

Tyler, Gus. *Look for the Union Label: A History of the International Ladies Garment Workers Union.* Armonk, NY: M. E. Sharpe, 1995.

Preliminary Report of the Factory Investigating Commission, (3 volumes). Robert F. Wagner, chairman. Albany, NY: The Argus Co., 1912.

Second Report of the Factory Investigating Commission, (3 volumes). Albany, NY: J. B. Lyon Co., 1913.

Third Report . . . (2 volumes). Albany, NY: J. B. Lyon Co., 1914.

Fourth Report . . . (2 volumes). Albany, NY: J. B. Lyon Co., 1915.

Final Report of the Factory Investigating Commission. Albany, NY: J. B. Lyon Co., 1916.

Weinberg, Sydney Stahl. *The World of Our Mothers: The Lives of Immigrant Jewish Women.* Chapel Hill: University of North Carolina Press, 1989.

*Weiss, Nancy Joan. *Charles Francis Murphy, 1858–1924: Respectability and Responsibility in Tammany Politics.* Northampton, MA: Smith College, 1968.

Wellman, Francis L. *The Art of Cross-Examination (4th ed.)* New York: Dorset Press, 1986.

Williams, Phyllis A. *South Italian Folkways in Europe and America: A Handbook for Social Workers, Visiting Nurses, School Teachers and Physicians.* New Haven, CT: Yale University Press, 1938.

The Legal Sufferings of the Jews in Russia. Lucien Wolf, ed. London: T. Fisher Unwin, 1912.

Unpublished Dissertations

*Greenwald, Richard A. "Bargaining for Industrial Democracy?: Labor, the State, and the New Industrial Relations in Progressive Era New York," New York University, 1998.

Jensen, Frances Brewer. "The Triangle Fire and the Limits of Progressivism," University of Massachusetts, 1996.

Schmoll, Brett Jordan. "Gendered Death in Public Life," University of California at Santa Barbara, 1998.

Waisala, Wendy Ellen. "To Bring Forth a Note of One's Own: Contested Memory and the Labor Literature of the Haymarket Tragedy, the Triangle Fire and Joe Hill," New York University, 1997.

ACKNOWLEDGMENTS

On March 25, 1990, I was covering New York for the *Miami Herald*. A deranged man firebombed a nightclub in the Bronx, killing eighty-seven people. Someone mentioned that day that it was the deadliest fire in New York in precisely seventy-nine years. And that was how a man from the suburbs in Colorado first learned of the Triangle fire. A year later, after moving to an apartment near Washington Square, I discovered that I lived just a block from the scene, and that the building still stood. I used to pause on Washington Place as I walked past the former Asch Building and look up, and wonder what, precisely, had happened. Enough wondering eventually produced this book.

In my Notes on Sources, I explain at length my debt to Ralph Monaco and the library staff of the New York County Lawyers' Association; also to the ghost of Leon Stein and the keepers of his papers at the Kheel Center of the School of Industrial and Labor Relations at Cornell University. I also received help from libraries at Columbia University, New York University, the Municipal Archives of the City of New York, the New York State Archives, the National Archives, the Department of Vital Records for the City of Philadelphia, and the Lower East Side Tenement Museum.

Christopher James and the public affairs staff of New York University generously allowed me to visit the eighth, ninth, and tenth floors, and the roof, of what is now the Brown Building of NYU. It was extremely humbling and helpful to stand where the Triangle workers stood—to look into the pit of the airshaft, to hurry down the winding stairs, to stand in a ninth-floor window over Washing-ton Place. Prof. Stephen Small allowed me to climb up on his office heater to the window from which the first man jumped. Prof. Richard L. Borowsky greeted me in his laboratory by pointing under an expensive machine and saying, with uncanny accuracy: "That's where the fire started." It turned out that his grandmother was one of the thousands of young immigrants who worked for a time in the Triangle.

The resource in which I spent the most time—genuinely exhilarating hours—was the Library of Congress. The range and scope of that collection is mind-boggling, and yet the place is so well run that you can take a notion at 11:30 A.M. that you want to know more about "Ev'ry Little Movement," for example, and by 1 P.M. you will have seen the sheet music, read a history of the song, and listened to a 1912 recording. Photographs, recorded speeches, unpublished dissertations, obscure journals, antique maps, old city directories, forgotten pamphlets . . . everything. I am grateful to William Price and the welcoming, helpful staff of research librarians.

The Urban Institute gave me the use of a quiet little office in which to write, asking only that I make clear that this excellent center of research in no way vouches for this book. Laudy Aron and Bob Planansky made this possible.

The *Washington Post*, where I have proudly worked for the past eleven years, was abundantly supportive of this project in every possible way: with time, resources, understanding, and encouragement. For this, I thank Leonard Downie, Steve Coll, Liz Spayd, Maralee Schwartz, and Don Graham.

Friends and family buoyed me in many ways: love and thanks to Joel Achenbach, Melanie Ball, Henry Ferris, Kyle Gibson, Michael Grunwald, Lucy Shackelford, Tom Shroder, Mit Spears, Doug Stevens, Clara, Adeline, Ella, Henry, and my main *mensch* on this project, Gene Weingarten. Esther Newberg was more than an agent; she was a friend. And no writer could want a harder-working or more committed editor than Joan Bingham.

The dedication reflects my greatest debt.

INDEX